Audrey O'Donohue

A LIFE of Enlightenment

Volume I

The Journey of an
Extraordinary Woman

First Edition: Published by Inspired Publishing Ltd. 2019

Second Edition: Published by Enlightenment Publishing in partnership with Influence Publishing Inc. June 2022
ISBN: 978-0-6454636-0-6

Copyright © 2019, 2022 by Audrey O'Donohue.
All rights reserved. No part of this publication may be reproduced, stored in or introduced into a retrieval system, or transmitted, in any form, or by any means (electronic, mechanical, photocopying, recording or otherwise) without the prior written permission of the publisher. This book is sold subject to the condition that it shall not, by way of trade or otherwise, be lent, resold, hired out, or otherwise circulated without the publisher's prior consent in any form of binding or cover other than that in which it is published and without a similar condition including this condition being imposed on the subsequent purchaser.

Editor: Natalie Brown
Cover Design: Audrey O'Donohue
Typesetting: Tara Eymundson

DISCLAIMER: Readers of this publication agree that neither Audrey O'Donohue, nor her agent, nor her publisher will be held responsible or liable for damages that may be alleged as resulting directly or indirectly from the use of this publication. Neither the publisher, nor the agent, nor the author can be held accountable for the information provided by, or actions resulting from, accessing these resources.

Acknowledgements

To Suzy and Natalie my agents.
My friends.
Thank you for all you have done.
Thank you for what you are about to do!
But most of all,
Thank you for being you!

A Note From The Author

Writing this book felt like a revelation to me. I sat at the computer and had only to focus on a time and the whole event opened. I could see the people involved, hear their conversations and often knew their thoughts. It was like a motion picture in replay.

It is my life story written in the third person. Perhaps this has been an unusual way of writing a book but it has pleasured me well. I trust the reading gives you just as much pleasure.

Once I finished and submitted Volume 1 to the publishing house, the owner stated in an email to me: "The writing is excellent, the story absolutely captivating and engrossing and I couldn't put it down. I think this book has the potential to become a movie in due course." These encouraging words have been very inspiring to me as a new author and confirm my decision to continue and write Volume 2.

It is my wish that this book is of great value to you and trust you will enjoy reading it and perhaps learn from my life anything you need to better yours.

Warm regards,
Audrey

Contents

ACKNOWLEDGEMENTS iii

A NOTE FROM THE AUTHOR v

1 England, November 1935. 1

2 1939—The Stand Off 7

3 The Beginning of Audrey's Education 15

4 Magic and Shenanigans 21

5 The Engagement 29

6 The Lessons 37

7 Audrey's New Rule: Don't Do Anything Unless It Makes You Smile. . . 45

8 Taking a High Dive. 53

9 Handling the Class Bully 57

10 A Nightmare Event. 63

11 Marriage and Reactions 69

12 Exploits and Education 73

13 Interesting Viewpoints. 81

14 Getting to Know Each Other. 93

15 The Jilting of Audrey's Fiancé 101

16 Doctor Gordon Gets Married. 107

17 The Heart Doesn't Break, It Stretches With Exercise. 113

18 Audrey Creates a Blowout. 121

19 Keeping Abreast of Life 127

20 Finding the Least Possible Effort to Succeed. 133

A LIFE of Enlightenment

21	Audrey Decides To Be The Very Best Girl She Can Be	137
22	One's Inner Intuition Is The Best Schooling	145
23	Audrey's First Kiss	155
24	Audrey's First Taste of Independence	165
25	Teaching Mr Eichorn a Lesson	169
26	Learning, Training and Romance	177
27	Fred Decides To Emigrate The Family	189
28	June 1951—The Voyage to Australia	195
29	Awakening to Real Romance?	201
30	The Arrival in Western Australia	215
31	Life Begins in a New Country	219
32	Lollies at the Cinema	225
33	Out on the Town	233
34	Mr Griffiths Gets Audrey a Job	239
35	The Beginning and End of a Career	249
36	Lectures at The American College of Personal Efficiency	253
37	April 1954—Dwayne is Born	257
38	Mason and the Ultimatum	263
39	The Disappearance of Dwayne	271
40	A New Job, a New Romance	275
41	The Divorce Plea	283
42	Audrey Joins a Real Estate Firm	291
43	The Marriage Proposal	297

Contents

44	Audrey Learns a Rescue Remedy	305
45	A New Opportunity	313
46	Entertaining Guests and the Tomato Sauce Cake	317
47	The Unexpected Affair	323
48	Meeting Brian	331
49	Zurich and Gabriel	339
50	A Meeting of Souls	349
51	Meeting Gabriel's Family	363
52	Do All The Golden Places Have Short Leases?	369
53	Clyde and Tiffany's Visit	373
54	Michael's Proposition	379
55	Audrey To The Rescue	397
56	"Darling It's Alright to Let it Go"	405
57	America	411
58	Disillusionment with the Org and Return to Australia	419
59	Audrey's New Job at Overmans	425
60	Walter	435
61	Brian's Visit to Australia	441
62	An Unexpected Event	451
63	Audrey's Wedding and Honeymoon in Africa	457
64	Audrey's New Business	463
65	Only Time Gets In The Way	471
	APPENDIX	475

CHAPTER 1

England, November 1935

Dorothy set up the ironing board and laid the iron on top of the wood burning stove to heat. The birthing pains for the baby's arrival had started more than an hour ago. She wanted to iron the new matinée jacket she had finished sewing the night before. There were plenty of clothes that her daughter Margaret had grown out of, but she wanted this baby to have something new.

She was worried that the attempts to abort this child may have deformed it. There had been punching in the stomach, and then the business with the knitting needle that Fred, her husband had inserted, but all to no avail. Margaret was only nine months old when Dorothy suspected she was pregnant again. They couldn't afford another child so soon. She had drunk almost a whole bottle of gin, soaking in a hot tub, but although she had been quite ill from the experience the baby remained stubbornly inside her body. She hoped for her husband's sake that this time it would be a boy.

Dorothy placed the tiny jacket on the ironing board. She turned to pick up the iron. Another contraction started. She grasped the edge of the ironing board. An earwig ran across it. Dorothy screamed, knocked the ironing board over and fell backwards, into a chair. She couldn't stand anything that crawled! She lay gasping in the chair, glad that it had been there to break her fall and happy that her husband was away getting the midwife. Fred couldn't understand how a woman could go through childbirth without too much complaining and yet fall apart if she saw a mere spider. Dorothy tried to explain that the rewards were different but he just shook his head with irritation and called her a silly woman. Nevertheless, it felt too difficult to bend down to stand the ironing board on its legs again; she decided Fred would have to take care of it. She didn't have to tell him about the earwig; although she knew he loved her in his own way, she didn't want to give him an opportunity to disparage her fear.

Dorothy struggled out of the chair. She felt exhausted. She made her way to the bed that for convenience sake had been brought down from upstairs and been placed in a corner of the large kitchen. From here she could supervise her other child, and the cooking which her husband or her mother-in-law would have to do.

She rested on the bed, pleased that Jane, her mother-in-law, had taken Margaret. She was happy to be alone for a while. She wondered what this baby would look like. She was hoping it would have dark hair and brown eyes like Fred and that it would be a boy. Fred had said that if they were stuck with having this child, the least it could do was to be a boy. She suddenly realised that all babies were born with blue eyes and that they changed at a later date. Dorothy shied away from her thoughts taking her any further; she didn't want to think about Alan with his green eyes, especially at a time like this when her baby was due.

The front door opened. She heard voices and steps crossing the living room and then her husband and the midwife were standing at the bottom of the bed.

Fred picked up the ironing board while Dorothy talked to the midwife about her current state. She realised that it had been a while since the last contraction; in fact, they seemed to have stopped. Fred gave a little snort as the midwife explained that the shock and noise when the board collapsed and falling into the chair may stop progress for a little while, but no doubt

England, November 1935

it would resume again shortly.

The midwife asked Fred to make a cup of tea and under the clatter of the teacups and running water Dorothy told her in a low voice what had really happened. The midwife nodded sympathetically. She thanked Fred for the tea, helped Dorothy to sit up to drink hers and filled the next hour with friendly chatter. When the contractions did not start again, she left, instructing Fred to come and get her when they recommenced.

It was the fifth of November 1935; bonfires were lit, fireworks exploded; potatoes were placed in the fire and eaten despite being hard one side and charred the other. The women brought out treacle tart and sticky toffee and the children ran around the bonfires, squealing and ooh-oohing as jumping jacks made little explosions around their feet and rockets raced towards the sky before exploding into a multitude of colours.

Leaning heavily on Fred's arm, Dorothy wandered out to watch the fireworks. Even Fred was wishing that the contractions would start again so that this baby business would be over and done with and everyday things would return to normal.

They went to bed that evening expecting to be woken in the early hours of the next morning when it seemed most babies chose to come into the world. However the event failed to eventuate and for that day and the next it seemed as though this baby had changed its mind about arriving at all. Doctor Thomas, sent by the midwife, looked concerned and said that if nothing happened in the next forty-eight hours Dorothy must be hospitalised.

On the 8th of November at two o'clock in the morning Fred set off to get the midwife and at three forty-five another baby girl was born into the Southgate family. Fred was a bricklayer but yearned to be a doctor. He was vexed at being bullied out of the room at a crucial time. When he was finally given the baby to hold, he was the one who noticed that it didn't have any eyebrows and its fingernails had yet to grow. The baby had a faint fuzz of golden blonde hair and green eyes that had a faint blue ring around each iris.

A LIFE of Enlightenment

When Fred commented on this the midwife shrugged and said "well Fred, you take them as they come and there's naught you can do about it. The nails and the eyebrows will grow and I can't say much about the eyes. It's true most are born with blue but they change to brown, hazel, and green or whatever later; maybe hers changed in the womb. After all she is three days late!"

The baby lay in Fred's arms looking straight into his eyes. He knew that babies couldn't see anything until they were six weeks old or more; nevertheless this look made him feel uncomfortable. As though the baby wanted to put him at ease, it smiled. Dimples appeared in its cheeks. Fred was stunned. "Hey, he said, you're not supposed to do that until you've got wind or something, or until you're old enough! Did you see that?" he appealed to Dorothy. She smiled and said "Here, let me have a good look at her."

Fred handed the baby over and Dorothy gazed at it with rapture.

"What shall we call her?" Dorothy looked enquiringly at Fred.

"How about Jane after my mother?" he said.

Dorothy shook her head "No. not plain Jane, how about Brenda?"

Fred grunted, "It's too common"

"Well then," Dorothy said, "what about Audrey?"

"What sort of a fancy name is that?" Fred sniffed.

Dorothy said, "Well I like it, the next one may be a boy and you can name that one, now let me have my way with this one. How about a middle name?

"No!" Fred said, "One name's enough for anyone, why do you want two? Margaret's only got one; it's confusing and too much to write when you fill out forms. One's good enough for me and by God, it'll be good enough for the rest of the family." "So, Audrey, what do you think of your name?" Dorothy gazed into the green eyes of her baby.

The baby smiled and the dimples were once again apparent. "Fred," she called, "Look, she's smiling, and she likes it. She likes her name!"

Fred looked impatient and was already onto other matters. "What are we going to do about breakfast? Me stomach thinks me throat's been cut,

England, November 1935

it's that empty."

Into this interesting little world, Audrey started her first day on planet Earth.

CHAPTER 2

1939—The Stand Off

When Audrey's sister Margaret was four-and-a-half she went to school. Her birthday was in June. She was allowed to go in the year she was five and it was now the first week of January and the start of a school year. As her mother was helping her to get ready, Audrey, who had just turned three in the previous November, also got ready. Her mother gave Margaret a brown paper bag with her lunch in it and explained what was in it and when to eat it. She told her to be mindful of the teacher; to say "Yes Miss" or "No Miss"; not to speak unless spoken to, and to answer politely. Her mother explained that if she wanted to go to the lavatory, she must put up her hand and ask nicely.

Audrey said, "where's my lunch?"

Dorothy smiled and gave her a hug. "You can come with me to see Margaret settled, but you can't stay; you're too young to go to school!"

"Why is she going to school?"

"To learn her letters and her sums, and to learn to read and write," her mother said. "You can go when you're five, but now you're only three and a bit, so you've got to wait 'til you've grown some more."

Audrey, looking puzzled, stared at her mother. "But I can count to 100 and I know all my letters, so why can't I go? I want to know how to read."

Her mother answered, "Because it's the law!"

"What's that?"

Dorothy sighed, "It's the rule. You can come with me but you can't stay, and that's that!"

Audrey looked outraged. She went to a drawer got out a paper bag, went to a cupboard, got out the bread and butter, stood on a chair at the table and appealed to her mother, "Can I have a jam sandwich?" Her mother, happy to change the subject, said "I'll make you one."

"No," Audrey said. "You just cut the bread, please, I'll make it." "You always put too much jam on and get it in a mess." Her mother walked over to the table and cut her one slice of bread from the large white loaf.

Audrey spread some butter, then a large portion of strawberry jam and folded the slice in half. Jam began to ooze from the sides. She picked her sandwich up and ran her tongue around the edges to get rid of the excess, laid it on the table, pushed down with two hands, licked off the jam again and then put the sandwich in the brown paper bag.

She jumped off her chair and said, "I'm ready to go!"

Her mother smiled, and told Audrey she could carry her bag to school and back, and eat her sandwich later. Dorothy urged both children toward the door, took a hand of each one and walked up the street to the local primary school. She found the classroom, introduced herself and the children to the teacher, saw Margaret to a desk, and looked around for Audrey. She found her seated at a desk in the back. She was so small that only a few strawberry blonde curls identified her whereabouts.

Her mother held out her hand. "Come," she said, "it's time to go home."

Audrey shook her head, "No, I'm not coming. I want to stay." Her mother said again, more firmly, "Come on!"

Audrey said "No."

Dorothy was shocked; "Don't you dare defy me that way!" She picked Audrey up and carried her protesting child out of the room, looking apologetic and ashamed as she passed the teacher.

1939 – The Stand Off

Once outside, she set Audrey on the ground, lectured her about her behaviour, and again said, "You're too young, you have to wait. Do you understand me?"

"I want to go back!"

Dorothy sighed. "You'll do as you're told and I'll have no more backchat from you!" She took Audrey's hand and said "We are going home!" as she pulled the reluctant child along until she started to walk properly.

Audrey was quiet.

Once home Dorothy gave her a large piece of wood, a bag of lead nails, and a hammer. Audrey took them, sat on the floor and began to hammer the nails into the wood. This was her favourite play. Her aim was deadly. Only once had she hurt her thumb from holding the nail too long. Fred said she should have been a boy. She'd make a good carpenter.

Now she seemed happy; school was not mentioned, but when lunchtime came, she refused to eat her jam sandwich. Her "not hungry plea" was constant all day. When she refused to eat at tea time, Dorothy became concerned. Fred said, "Leave her alone, she's probably coming down with something. Her temperature is normal. See how she is tomorrow."

Audrey continued to be polite but consistently refused food of any kind. She continued to play with her nails and obeyed all her mothers' wishes except her orders to eat something.

Margaret was brought home by a neighbour who had a daughter the same age, and she offered to take and return Margaret each day for the first week. After that, the children would be allowed to go by themselves. Margaret was happy to walk with her friend, so Dorothy agreed to the arrangement and thanked her neighbour.

The whole of the next day Audrey refused to eat. When she refused her milk as well and would only accept water, Dorothy became very concerned.

Her mother told her that if she didn't eat she would get sick and that she might die.

Audrey said, "That's alright." and continued to hammer her nails.

A LIFE of Enlightenment

When he came home after work, Fred took her temperature and poked her all over, saying "Tell me what hurts!" Audrey smiled but said nothing. Fred said that if she didn't eat breakfast the next day the doctor had better be sent for.

Later the next morning, Dorothy sent for Dr. Thomas, but when she opened the door it was a young, tall, dark, good looking man who stood in the doorway.

"Good morning Mrs Southgate, my name is Dr. Gordon. I understand you sent for Dr. Thomas, but he has recently retired. I'm looking after some of his patients and Doctor Hillside is taking care of the rest."

Dorothy stood aside and he stepped into the living room. Audrey stared at him from the other side of the room, as though transfixed. She suddenly ran across the room and wrapped her arms around one of his legs, and cuddled it as though it was her Teddy Bear.

Dr. Gordon said, "Well, this is a lovely welcome!" He raised a hand to stop her mother pulling her off; placed his bag on the floor, and picked up Audrey, holding her away from him so that he could see her face. The green eyes stared penetratingly into his; she said "Hello" with the dimples flashing as she smiled. He was entranced. He felt somehow that he had held her before, although he knew that this could not be correct. He pulled her into his chest and she promptly threw her arms around his neck and kissed his cheek. He returned her kiss as she pulled back and gazed into his eyes. The look was familiar and disconcerting. For some reason he felt happy but at the same time he became aware that he was in this house for a reason. He set her down on the floor. She moved to his side and took his hand. He smiled at the mother and enquired, "Well now, who is my patient?"

"She is!" Dorothy pointed at Audrey.

He smiled at the little girl holding his hand. "What is your name?" he asked softly.

"Audrey."

"What a pretty name! Come, Audrey, let me have a look at you."

The Doctor led her to the couch; he picked her up and sat her down

1939 – The Stand Off

beside him.

"Has she got a rash anywhere?" he asked.

"No," her mother replied. "It's just that she won't eat. Hasn't eaten for two and a half days and now she's refusing her milk as well; all she drinks is water."

Dr. Gordon gazed at the little girl beside him. She looked back with a happy smile.

"Let's see if we can get to the bottom of this, Audrey, shall we?"

She nodded, still smiling.

"Could you remove your dress?"

Audrey nodded. She climbed off the couch and stood in front of him with her back turned.

"Buttons, please!" she said, over her shoulder. He smiled and undid the top two buttons before Dorothy could come forward to assist.

Audrey pulled the dress over her head dropped it on the floor pointed to her vest and said "This, too?"

He nodded, and she removed her vest, dropping it onto her dress.

Her mother immediately sprang forward and picked them up, shaking them out before putting them neatly on the arm of the couch. She made a small tut-tut sound as she did this. Audrey, who still had her eyes fixed on the doctor, said "Sorry" without looking at her.

Doctor Gordon picked her up and laid her on the couch next to him. He checked her temperature, her pulse, and her blood pressure. He checked her ears, her eyes, her nose and her throat. He got out his stethoscope and even though she obligingly took deep breaths and coughed when asked, he could find nothing wrong. He asked her to get dressed. She did so, again turning to him to fasten her buttons.

"Alright, Audrey," he said, "Tell me why you don't want to eat?"

She was silent; she glanced towards her mother and then back to the doctor with an appealing look.

"Mrs. Southgate," he asked, "would you mind leaving us for a moment? I feel we have a secret here we need to talk about." Dorothy nodded. "I'll put the kettle on, come in the kitchen, Doctor, when you're ready."

Doctor Gordon picked Audrey up and placed her on his knee. It seemed she couldn't look at him without smiling. He was amused at his urge to reciprocate.

"Now," he said, "what is going on?"

"Help me; I want to go to school and they won't let me in!" Audrey said.

"Who won't let you in?"

"I don't know. It's 'the rule', mum says."

"Don't you have to be five years old to go to school?"

"Yes, but I know my letters! Listen!" She recited her A to Z at great speed. "And my numbers too! I can count to 100. Margaret can't do that and they let her in, so why can't I go? I want to be able to read now! I can't wait 'til I'm five!"

"Is this why you are refusing to eat?"

"Yes, I'm never going to eat again until they let me in, even if I get sick and die!"

Audrey looked calm and determined. Doctor Gordon was aware that this was not a statement he could ignore. He felt that somehow he knew and understood this child, and that he had a responsibility that he was yet to understand, to take care of her.

He was amazed at her assessment of the situation and the statements she made that belonged more to a six or seven-year-old. Her manner and confidence matched an older child; yet she was tiny and looked younger than her age.

"Audrey", he said, "the people who make these rules are in the Education Department. I don't have anything to do with these people. I'm a Doctor. If it was a hospital or something similar, I may be able to help, but I don't come into contact with the Education Department. Do you understand?"

She nodded, "But you're *my* doctor; if you tell them I will die if I can't go to school, they will listen to you!"

"You're very assertive for your size, aren't you!" he said in amazement.

"What does that mean? Is it good?"

1939 – The Stand Off

She beamed at him, reached for his hand, and held it between hers. "Please," she said, "I don't know any grown-ups that will help me…only you!"

He felt helpless. The green eyes looked steadily into his and he felt that this was a matter where he had no choice.

"Alright, Audrey," he said. "I will write a letter to the Education Department. I will do my best. But you have to do something for me!"

"Yes, yes!" She was excited. She climbed on the couch, threw her arms around his neck, and kissed him on the cheek. "Oh, thank you!" she said, her face glowing.

"Audrey, I will write the letter for you right away, but I may not get an answer for a little while. If the Education Department say yes and you have not eaten there will not be a little girl called Audrey still alive and able to go to school. Now, I promise to write the letter. Do you promise me that you will eat?"

She nodded. He stood her on the floor facing him.

"Audrey, say *'I promise to eat my food!'*"

She repeated his words, looking at him mischievously. "Your smile is full of mischief!"

The Doctor found himself smiling back at the dimpled face. She replied, "Yours is too!" and laughed, burying her head in his knee.

He patted her head and said that he must go to the kitchen to talk to her mother and get some details of her school. As he left the room, she danced around with happiness, her face full of certainty, knowing she had an ally.

Doctor Gordon, musing on the conversation, felt he had been superbly handled by a small but very aware child, and that he had little idea of how it had happened. He only knew that despite the newness of the situation, somehow he loved this little bundle of mischief. He was aware that he had pledged his help and that it seemed correct to do so. There was something in this situation that intrigued him; something familiar about this child who provoked feelings that he didn't understand. He felt that somewhere he knew an older version of this child but the details escaped his knowledge. He also had an idea that on some level she knew all about it even though he did not.

Dorothy looked up as he entered the kitchen and pointed to the cup. "Milk and sugar?"

As he sipped his tea, he summarized his conversation with Audrey, and explained the promises they had both made.

Dorothy was aghast, "You would do that for her? But don't you think it's a risk? Don't you think she'll have difficulties at her age? I don't know what her father is going to say. He'll hit the roof, I'm sure!"

Doctor Gordon reassured her. "If the letter I intend to write works, I will be happy to talk to your husband. And don't worry about difficulties if she does go to school. My feeling is that it won't be Audrey who will be having them."

Two months later, on a Monday morning, armed with a consenting letter from the Education Department, her mother accompanied Audrey to school.

Later that year in September, England declared war on Germany.

CHAPTER 3

The Beginning of Audrey's Education

Audrey was ecstatic about going to school. All the children in her class were one to two years older and a great deal taller.

During the first morning recess, the tallest girl came up to her and said, "What are you doing here? You're just a little squirt!" Audrey was not sure what a squirt was, but she could tell from the girl's manner that it was not intended to be complimentary. Not sure how to handle this, she planted her feet apart, put both hands on her hips and stared up without blinking into the other girl's eyes. The steady gaze although devoid of anger was intimidating. The girl shrugged, then walked away and Audrey learned her first lesson in handling the class bully.

Holding her sister's hand she went to school and returned home the same way. Although as sisters they had some similar features, their colouring was very different. Margaret had her mother's auburn hair and blue eyes, and she was a good head taller than Audrey. She was a very feminine, pretty little girl who loved her dolls. She played quietly and nicely with other little girls, stayed away from the boys and their rough games, and was very obedient. Her mother proudly said that you could take Margaret anywhere and she would always be a credit to her parents. She always looked bandbox fresh, neat and tidy. She was happy and an excellent reflection of what good little girls were supposed to be.

The most outrageous action Audrey ever saw her sister do was with a pair of scissors. Dorothy had a clothes airer that in winter often stood in front of the fire. Damp clothes were draped upon it almost forming a tent. Margaret liked to sit under this and one of her favourite pastimes was to be given an old clock which she painstakingly took apart with a screwdriver. She was not interested in putting it together again, but being a neat and tidy little person, she placed all its parts in a box before presenting it to her father. One particular day however, she crawled under her tent with a pair of scissors and proceeded to cut off fabric from any garment that hung in her vicinity. Long sleeved shirts become short sleeved, sometimes on only one side. Knickers were left without any crotch, and hankies were shredded. Her mother caught her before she had gone too far at demolishing the family wardrobe. Margaret was very contrite and never again of her own volition stepped beyond the boundaries her parents had set.

Audrey however was a different matter. Despite the similarity of some of her features, she looked like a stranger in her family. Her skin was very white, her eyes green, her hair was a strawberry blonde, and she had dimples that no-one in the family ancestry had ever sported before.

Audrey did not recognise limitations and seemed devoid of fear. She made up her own rules for living and behaviour, and followed them faithfully. When confronted with something that did not match what she expected or wanted Audrey was apt to plant her feet apart, put her hands on her hips and say, "What is this?"

She preferred boys with their rough games to girls with their tea parties; had a wild sense of adventure, and towards the end of the day always tended to look as though she had been in a war. The hem of her dress was often down in more than one place, and her socks seemed to have shrunk into her shoes. Her hair was a tangled mess. Leaves and bits of twigs made a home there after her tree-climbing exploits, and although she was made to wash so much that she thought her skin would surely scrub off, she would

The Beginning of Audrey's Education

be dirty from some escapade within the hour. If anyone commented on her white skin, she would say that it got dirty very quickly and had to be washed often. Margaret often made her show her hands before holding one of them to go to school.

Audrey's second week at school was one of the most joyous in her young life. She learned the sounds of the letters that she knew. Finding out that A says "ay" or "ah" and B says "buh" and so on, was a major enlightening moment and with it came the realization that now she knew how to read!

Within a week she was picking up anything that had letters on it and practising the sound of all the words. By the end of a month she could read almost everything except very long difficult words and she was far ahead of her classmates. Made aware of a dictionary by her teacher, who found her demands for the meaning of words valuable but interruptive during class, Audrey found a dictionary at home and made it her own. She developed a passion for books that placed their value far above any of her other possessions. Audrey took her toys and dolls, keeping only her loved blue teddy bear, and irrespective of their value, exchanged those for any book that the recipients were willing to give. Her vocabulary improved enormously and she chatted away like a grown-up.

Her mother was astounded at the disappearance of the dolls that she had spent evenings sewing for and dressing.

She confronted Audrey who put her head on one side and said, "I'm sorry. I thought they were mine!"

Her mother was silent.

"Please don't buy any more dolls for me; I just want books now and forever and ever."

Audrey hugged her mother's legs and wandered off.

Dorothy felt that although she couldn't dispute her daughter's argument, she had lost the opportunity of teaching her relevant values.

She talked to her daughter the next day. Audrey was reading one of the books she had exchanged for a doll that was very lovely with a pretty face and eyes that blinked. It had a celluloid body with arms and legs that could be moved in its sockets Dorothy had made a pretty dress with matching knickers for Audrey's Christmas present.

Her mother explained to her that the doll had cost a great deal of money and that the book in her hand was only worth a few pennies. "You must see" she said, "that the doll was very valuable compared to the book."

"It isn't if you don't really want it," Audrey replied.

Her mother was cross. She found the honesty offensive. She got up to walk away, saying as she went, "Money doesn't grow on trees you know!"

She had only gone a few steps when she found Audrey besides her, tugging at her skirt. Dorothy stopped. "I'm sorry if I upset you," Audrey said.

The little face looked worried. Her mother bent down and hugged her, saying, "It's alright; you keep saying you don't want dolls, but we keep buying them, because you are a little girl and little girls are supposed to like dolls; tell me why you don't."

"They are not alive!" Audrey answered.

"But you love your Teddy Bear and he's not alive. At least he wasn't the last time I saw him!"

Audrey smiled. "Yes, but he is soft and nice to cuddle. The dolls are hard and cold."

"Oooh"! Her mother said. "Would you like a rag doll?"

"No thank you, I only need one thing to cuddle and that's Teddy."

"Your books are not alive either, you know."

Audrey was pensive, "But the people and animals in them are…they do things."

Her mother gave up. "Just remember what your father is always saying, 'Money doesn't grow on trees.'"

"Oh, but it does!"

"What gave you that idea?" Her mother asked.

Audrey said, "Money is made from paper and paper is made from trees, so you see…" she trailed off into silence.

"And who told you that, may I ask."

"A tree surgeon."

The Beginning of Audrey's Education

"You don't know a tree surgeon!"

"Yes I do. He makes sick trees well again. Sometimes he has to cut off a branch that is sick so that the rest of the tree can get better."

"And where did you meet this tree surgeon", Dorothy asked. Audrey was pensive. "In my dreams" she said at last. "I talk to him there."

Dorothy told Fred about the conversation, saying that she didn't know where Audrey got the ideas she came out with. Even if they were right, it didn't seem proper, somehow.

Fred, who didn't know what to make of it and who was frustrated at trying to understand his youngest daughter's shenanigans, fell back on his standard retort. "She's *your* daughter; you're supposed to understand her. I could do it better if she was a boy, but she's not, although she behaves like one most of the time. She's not a bit like our Margaret." Audrey's tomboyishness was a source of worry to her mother. Audrey seldom played with her sister, who liked to play tea parties and mothers and fathers with her dolls. Audrey tolerated Doctors and Nurses, providing she was never the patient, but most of the time she was out with the neighbourhood boys, persuading them that she could play cricket, football, and climb walls and trees and catch tadpoles with the best of them. The boys gave her tasks to do that many of them would have barely considered before allowing her into their circle; she uncomplainingly did all of them and gained their respect. If her mother had seen her climbing up high walls and walking along a narrow-curved top before the boys could count to a hundred, she would have wondered if Audrey was ever going to survive childhood.

When Dorothy told her she should spend more time playing with girls, Audrey asked why.

Her mother told her that girls were like her and boys were different. Audrey said with finality "That's why I like them better, they are much more fun. Girls are too frightened to play properly."

CHAPTER 4

Magic and Shenanigans

Audrey had three uncles. Franklin was her father's brother. Franklin fancied himself as a conjurer and a magician. Audrey was fascinated by all the tricks he showed her with cards and his sleight of hand. He was kind and let her know many of his secrets, provided that she promised faithfully never to reveal them to anyone. Audrey took her promises very seriously, and with her hand "crossed her heart and hoped to die" if she shared the secrets with anyone.

Her uncle bought her a box of tricks that boasted a whoopee cushion that made a rude noise when sat upon, and which the whole family and all visitors became subject to; various card games; feathers and flowers and scarves that appeared from sleeves and coats, which Audrey had to grow into mastering; and invisible string that was very strong and one of her favourites.

She took the string to school. The blackboard stood on an easel supported with two pegs that went through holes in the front legs. Rope stretched between the front and back supports and when taut kept the blackboard firmly in place while the teacher wrote on it with chalk.

Audrey had been placed in the front of her class because of her small stature and also her dimpled smiles made her look the picture of mischief. Her father without cause would often gruffly ask, "What have you been up to?" When she said "Nothing," he would snort and say "Well, you look as though you're about to be up to something, so mind you watch yourself." She felt that her teacher shared a similar belief.

Arriving at school early one day, she tied her invisible string to one of the front pegs. Her teacher wrote on the board and turned to talk to the class. Audrey pulled on the string, the peg came out, and the board collapsed behind the teacher. Audrey rushed forward to help, picking up the peg and putting back in its hole while the teacher picked up the blackboard. Audrey was hysterical with suppressed laughter, which merged with the merriment of the class who welcomed any diversion.

She managed to do this three times before slipping the string off, under the beady eye of the teacher who didn't see the cause but correctly suspected Audrey's helpful participation. She loved her box of tricks and often on coming home from school, tormented the family with them until bedtime.

Audrey always went to bed earlier than her older sister. Finding her was tricky as she often disappeared around this time. She would hide behind the couch, or go down to the cellar and sit on the steps, reading a book. In summer, because it was light until nine pm, she would be found playing in the nearby field or talking to the milkman's horse, oblivious of the time.

One evening her father tucked her into bed and offered to show her a magic trick. She was delighted. He sat on the edge of her bed, unbuttoned his trousers and took out his penis. This was something new for her.

She thought it looked like a funny sausage. Her father said, "I will show you a trick with this but you must first cross your heart and hope to die."

Audrey nodded and said the familiar words.

"Now," her father said, "if you stroke this and at the same time say abracadabra each time, it will grow right before your very eyes!"

Audrey did as her father asked and watched with fascination the rapid growth of his penis.

"How does it do that?" She wanted to know.

Magic and Shenanigans

Her father told her that she would only find that out when she was grown up. He said, "This is our secret. You must not tell anyone, and we can only practise this when you and I are by ourselves. I will let you practise this as often as I can. Do you understand?"

She nodded and gave him a hug and a kiss goodnight.

After this he came often. She learned how to make his penis big and then smaller by tugging and rubbing it, but she thought this was very messy and sticky. Her father gave her a hanky to wipe her hands, but when he had gone she often went quietly to the bathroom to wash them. Without knowing why, Audrey began to have misgivings about this secret. It often worried her before she fell asleep. She wanted to talk to her mother about it but her promise held her back. She felt she needed another listening friend apart from Dr. Gordon.

She had at this time a realization. Audrey slowly became aware of another part of her that seemed separate but attached. This was a part of her that was a spectator, a silent witness to the events in her life; that passed no judgement, made no comments but simply observed with a kind of attached detachment. It was a part of her that was completely unemotional about any happening, but seemed to care for her, if not the event. There was something comforting about this which she found difficult to even put into words, even for herself; an unseen loyal friend that was and would always be there; who watched with interest but with no different viewpoint her handling of any situation she experienced.

Audrey knew that whatever event happened in her life, it would always be alright for this part of her, and if only all of herself could view her entire life this way, she could handle anything.

Just before her fifth birthday her father told her she could have whatever she wanted. To his amusement she ordered a cricket set and a football, knowing that if she had the equipment the boys would always let her play. Despite her mother's protests, who thought she ought to have something girlish or even a book, Audrey got what she desired.

Shortly after Audrey's birthday, her sister got the measles. Doctor

Gordon who came to visit the sick child was greeted with great enthusiasm from Audrey. She sat on his knee and told him about school and showed him how well she could read. He was amused and touched by her obvious affection. She hugged him enthusiastically but always with warmth and tenderness. She had a habit of putting one hand on the side of his face and gazing into his eyes with rapture. She made him feel like a long-lost friend who had come home. He said this to her when she was sitting on his knee. She smiled and said, "You *are* a long-lost friend!"

He was surprised, but before he could question her further she was pulling at his hand and saying, "Come to see Margaret and make her better."

Margaret had a severe case of measles and it was only after three visits that Doctor Gordon would allow her to attend school again the following week. Talking to Dorothy he said, "I am amazed that Audrey has not caught the measles, considering that they share the same room and often the same bed. Her mother said, "Well, she's one on her own, I don't profess to understand her. My mother says she's been on this earth before; and maybe she has. I can't fathom her, but she seems to be doing alright."

Doctor Gordon smiled and said, "Well, she seems to have escaped measles. Let me know if Margaret doesn't continue to improve."

On the same day that Margaret went back to school, Audrey awoke covered with spots.

Audrey was not content with just having measles. In rapid succession she contracted whooping cough, German measles, mumps, yellow jaundice and chicken pox. She barely got out of bed before she was ordered back into it. She grew listless and thin, lost her appetite and then stopped eating. Her mother could not tempt her to eat and the different flavoured tonics Doctor Gordon brought were drunk but made no difference to her desire for food. Her main interest was his visits. She brightened and always managed a smile and a hug for him, but her passion for her books diminished.

The family's and Doctor Gordon's strong concerns took on an aspect of urgency. This was highlighted by Doctor Gordon stating with firm inten-

Magic and Shenanigans

tion, "Audrey, if you don't eat, you may die!"

Audrey laid her hand on his cheek, smiled and said, "That's alright!"

He sat on the side of the bed, considering her and thinking that something else was happening aside from her many illnesses.

"Audrey," he said, "Is there something that you would like to talk to me about?" She hesitated, and then shook her head. "Audrey, I feel there is something that you need to tell me that may help you to get better…"

Again, she shook her head and looked at him pleadingly, before saying an emphatic "No."

He recognised all the firm intention behind the 'No' and decided to respect it. If she had something to say, it would have to be when she was ready.

She held his hand, looking at him with a small smile, and suddenly she said, "I love you."

For some reason he felt his eyes fill with tears. He held her close to his chest for comfort and to hide his tears. Over her shoulder he brushed them away and fought to regain his composure.

"Audrey," he said, "you must eat. I do not want to lose you. I love you too!"

She gave a small smile and shook her head.

"Audrey, if you will eat something, anything at all, your mother will cook or get whatever you want. If you will do this, when you grow up I will marry you!"

She was quiet, gazing at his face as though she needed to know it by heart.

"When will I be grown up?" she asked.

He smiled as he answered, "When you are twenty-one."

"That's a long time away…"

"Yes, but in the meantime, we can be engaged."

"What is 'engaged'?"

Doctor Gordon patted her hand. "I am going to send your mother in to explain that." He smiled as he left the room.

Her mother entered immediately. She said, "Doctor Gordon says you want to know something, what is it?

Audrey asked, "What is 'engaged'?"

"What a strange thing to ask at your age. Well, when you decide to get married but don't do it right away, you get engaged. You have a ring so that everyone knows you are engaged, and the person you are going to marry is called your fiancé. You go out together, to pictures and for walks or whatever you want, and you buy each other presents for birthdays and Christmas. Does that answer your question?" Audrey nodded her thanks and said, "I need to talk to Doctor Gordon now."

Her mother, aware that she was being dismissed left, and a few moments later Doctor Gordon came and resumed his seat on the bed.

"Well, Audrey, what have you decided?"

She said "Alright, we can be engaged, do you know all about it or do you need to ask my Mum?"

"No, Audrey, I *do* know all about it. Now if you become my fiancée, do you promise to eat so that you will grow up to be a big girl so that I can marry you when you are twenty-one?" She nodded.

"What would you like to eat?"

She thought for a moment and then said "Tomato soup, please!"

His voice was filled with pleasure as he said, "That's my girl!" He kissed her forehead and, not wanting to leave her in case she changed her mind, called out to her mother. "Your beautiful daughter would like some tomato soup, Mrs Southgate!"

Dorothy was filled with happiness. She got a tin of soup from the larder, opened it, added some milk, and warmed it over the gas stove that had recently been installed. She placed it on a tray and took it in to Audrey. She found with amusement the newly engaged couple discussing the colour of stone desired for the ring. Doctor Gordon said, "Red it shall be. Whatever my little girl desires!"

He propped Audrey against her pillows, laid the tray on her knees and gave her the spoon.

Magic and Shenanigans

There was silence and then sighs of relief as she took her first mouthful and swallowed it. The Doctor grasped Dorothy's hand and gave it a gentle squeeze. He was aware of Dorothy's whole body relaxing as Audrey swallowed one spoonful after another, and he was overwhelmed with gladness and pleasure at watching this little girl eat after such a long time.

Audrey only managed half the soup. She was concerned that she was letting them down and looked a little guilty as she asked, "Can I finish it later? My tummy is full." Her mother hugged her and said, "Of course. Thank you for eating at last. Now we can get you better."

Doctor Gordon stroked Audrey's hair and said, as he left, "I will see you very soon, and perhaps I will have a surprise for you."

CHAPTER 5

The Engagement

Doctor Gordon returned three days later to give to Audrey a small box wrapped in pretty gold paper and tied with a silky white bow.

She opened it carefully, not wanting to spoil the paper or its trimmings, to reveal a white box. Inside, resting on a black velvet cushion was a gold ring with a red garnet glistening and sparkling in the light.

Audrey was speechless.

Dorothy was completely taken aback. She moved away from the bed muttering "Ooh, you shouldn't have; I don't know what her father's going to say. That's real gold, isn't it? Oh, my goodness!"

Audrey stood up on the bed and threw her arms around Doctor Gordon. "Thank you! It is beautiful. Can I put it on now?"

Doctor Gordon took her left hand and, taking the ring from the box, placed it on her engagement finger. It was too big, so he removed it and placed it on her second finger which although not perfect, was a better fit.

He explained to her that she had lost weight, but that now she was eating again the ring would soon be the right size. He said that as she grew he would get it enlarged for her, so that she could always wear it.

Dorothy went to put the kettle on, still shaking her head and having little conversations with herself. After a few moments Doctor Gordon joined her in the kitchen.

"Dorothy, please do not be upset. Our little girl is already looking so much better and I am very happy to do this for her. She's a lovable little rascal and I will be pleased to spend time with her. When she is ready she will realise that this engagement is not suitable. She will understand that I am twenty years her senior, and old enough to be her father. In the meantime, it is serving a purpose, with wonderful results." "Doctor Gordon, I am more than grateful to you and for all that you have done, but you know Audrey; she will expect you to behave like the fiancé I told her about."

She went on to tell him what she had said to Audrey about being engaged.

"Well," he said, "we shall just have to live up to that, won't we? With your permission, I will pick Audrey up after school on Wednesdays, when she is better of course, and she may accompany me to the hospital while I do my rounds. On most Saturday afternoons I could take her to a matinée at the cinema. I could use some time off and she is a most entertaining companion; very wise, beyond her years. Some of the things she comes out with are quite startling but enlightening at the same time."

"Yes, I know that very well. I've been subject to a lot of it myself. Do you know what she said to my mother the other day? Audrey had said something that my mother did not consider she could possibly know about. So my mother said, 'You've been here before, haven't you?' Audrey just smiled and said, 'yes, and so have you!' Quite took her Grandma aback, I can tell you! Trouble is that when she says something like that, it sounds real, as though she means it."

Doctor Gordon smiled. "Yes, I have experienced something similar. I think we might find out that it is real and she is speaking from some knowing conviction that is not available to all of us."

Dorothy nodded, hesitantly. "Don't let her father hear you say that. He thinks it is just a phase she's going through and that she will settle down and be like everybody else. He thinks he will understand her when that

The Engagement

happens. At this stage she has him quite bamboozled."

Doctor Gordon laughed. "I can understand that, but do we really want her to be different to what she is? In her own way she is wise, intelligent, very caring, loving, and not afraid to be herself. She does not hide behind a false front. Some people would say that 'what you see is what you get'. With Audrey, your experience of her is what you get!"

Her mother laughed. "Well, what you see is someone who looks every inch a girl and behaves more like a boy, so I guess what you just said is right."

Fred, when told of the latest developments, resigned himself to what he considered "a lot of bloody nonsense, if you ask me; still, if she's eating again, it will have to do; but I want it known that I'm not in favour of it."

It took three more weeks before Audrey regained sufficient strength to enable her return to school. She had been away for almost five months and had to catch up with her lessons. Her teacher and schoolmates were kind and friendly with the exception of Edna Robertson, the class bully. She walked past Audrey making scornful remarks about her size and her pale appearance. Audrey ignored her, but she knew in her heart that one day there would be a confrontation.

The war had now started in earnest. Gas masks had been issued. Audrey had one with Pluto on the front and her sister Margaret had Mickey Mouse. Chamber pots could be bought in the shops with a picture of Hitler on the bottom complete with a caption "Do it on him." Her father built bunks in the cellar and told the family that when the sirens sounded they were to live and sleep there until the "All clear" sounded. There were many practice runs for everyone to get used to the different sounds and routines. The children were shown where the local shelters had been dug, so that if they were caught between destinations they knew where to go. Windows were leaded over or taped to stop flying glass, and climbing of walls was forbidden to all the children, because the tops of them were covered with broken glass.

"Dig for Victory" signs appeared everywhere and there was talk of ration books being issued. People began to stock up on tinned food and non-perishable goods, creating shortages which would precipitate even earlier rationing. Soldiers in khaki, and Air Force and Navy personnel in different shades of blue, were seen walking around the streets or marching down the roads. Many of the men Audrey was used to seeing in the shops around her home had gone overseas or to training camps, and their wives took their place behind the counters.

The local cotton mill had stopped producing cotton and now was a munitions factory. Women who had never been anything but housewives had a job there and there was talk of double shifts. There was training for nurse's aides, and most of the women not working were rolling bandages at home or knitting warm garments for the coming winter to send to their men.

Fred tried to join the Army, but a tricky knee and a loose jaw, the result of his amateur boxing days, made him unsuitable. He joined the Air Raid Patrol and was often away in the evenings at practice.

The war did not seem to affect Audrey's outings with her Doctor. It was decided to call him Uncle Bill. His full name was William Thomas Gordon. Uncle Bill was his suggestion and Audrey conceded, although she very seldom called him by any name.

Each Wednesday he would place his stethoscope around her neck, while she held the other part up in the air, so that it didn't drag on the floor. Holding his hand she walked around the hospital with him. When he came to a patient he would lift her on to the bed and formally introduce her as his new assistant. She would say hello and shake hands, and as she got to know each one, the patients would let her sound their chest with the stethoscope and always coughed when asked to do so. Taking her role as his assistant very seriously, she mimicked all his actions and his questions, with the same inflection and caring in her voice that he displayed. His patients were entranced and amused. Doctor Gordon told her mother that Audrey did more for his patients than any medicine he gave them.

They became fond of her and looked forward to her visits. They show-

The Engagement

ered her with what few sweets and chocolates they had and the longer term patients knitted scarves and mittens to keep her warm in winter. She wore each of them, sometimes all at the same time, if she could not remember which lady or from which ward the gift had arrived.

Most Saturday afternoons Doctor Gordon would call for her and she would climb in his car and they would go to the cinema matinée. She was always allowed to choose the film from two or three that he thought were suitable. Her tastes varied from comedy to science fiction. After the film, they would go to a tea shop in town and have high tea. Audrey always had tea without sugar and baked beans on toast, while Doctor Gordon had raisin toast and tea. Audrey sat on three telephone books so that she could reach the table with ease. The waitresses saw them coming and always had their special place ready with the books arranged. She was lifted up, placed on the books, and she always remembered to "mind her manners" as her mother had instructed.

This was one of Audrey's favourite times. They talked of anything and everything; they discussed the film or dismissed it if it wasn't worthy of their attention.

Doctor Gordon always asked, "What has been happening with you since Wednesday?"

On Wednesdays he always wanted to know what had been happening since Saturday.

Audrey discovered early on that she could make him laugh and it became a pleasure to save up funny little items of happenings that she knew would amuse him. Sometimes he was amused simply because of the way she said something.

Sometimes it was because of what she said. She didn't always know why he found it amusing when she was being so serious about an item she was discussing.

Her mother took Audrey and Margaret aside one day and said that soon there would be another baby in the family. Audrey was overjoyed. "It will be a boy, won't it?"

Dorothy smiled and said, "We will have to wait and see." Margaret was looking forwarding to playing with it. Being alive, it would be more fun than her dolls.

The midwife came every week to check on her mother and Audrey was told that she would be bringing the baby. Each time she arrived, Audrey would race to the door asking if she had brought her baby brother. No matter how many times she was told that it could be a girl, she stubbornly refused to believe even in the possibility. "No, it will be a boy," she declared with certainty.

She was impatient for this baby to arrive. Audrey's constant question, always starting with 'when?' became an irritant to her parents and a torment to the midwife, who was held to be the most responsible in Audrey's eyes. She got upset and finally totally frustrated when each visit from the midwife resulted in no baby and only excuses that got more and more lame. After the seventh visit, Audrey tackled the midwife by blocking her exit at the front door.

"You have to tell me the real reason you haven't brought the baby," she said with a lot of intention, as she locked eyes with the midwife who found it difficult to look away. The midwife tried to think of an excuse that would stand up to Audrey's scrutiny. Most of her others had been shot down without mercy. Saying the baby wasn't ready had been dismissed with scorn. This time she said, "Audrey, babies cost a lot of money and your mother and father don't have enough pennies yet." Audrey stared at her. This was a reason she could understand. Even better, this was a reason she could deal with almost immediately.

"Stay here," she commanded the midwife. "Don't go away."

Audrey dashed upstairs to her bedroom. She had a Christmas tree money box. Coins went in at the top and landed in the planter. There was a lock underneath the planter, but she knew where the key was kept. Finding it, opening the box, she was pleased to see so many pennies, half-pennies and farthings inside. She gathered up the coins in her two small hands, carefully negotiated the stairs, and presenting them to the midwife, she

The Engagement

announced. "Here is the money for the baby. I will buy him!"

Her mother appeared and heard this announcement. The midwife at Dorothy's nod took the money and counted it. It amounted to two shillings and seven pence. Dorothy put her arm around Audrey saying, "This is very sweet of you but I'm afraid it isn't quite enough, we still have to save for a little while."

The midwife went to return the money to Audrey, but Dorothy shook her head.

"Audrey, this will help and Daddy and I thank you, but it will take just a little longer to have the right amount."

Audrey sat on the bottom step of the staircase with tears in her eyes. She gave a big sigh then stood and brightened as an idea flashed across her mind. "I will get some more, I will do jobs and people can pay me. How much more do we need?" Her question was directed at the midwife who stared helplessly at Dorothy.

Her mother put her arm around Audrey and said, "We will have to work that out exactly but we may have enough in about two weeks. Now that's not too long to wait, and your two and seven pence will help a lot."

Audrey went to her neighbours and asked them for work. She explained why she wanted to be paid a penny for each job, so that it would have to be a big one. The neighbours, sympathetic to her story, let her stand on a chair and wash dishes or sweep the back yard. In the next ten days she earned five more pennies which she gave to her mother.

Four days later her baby brother was born. He was given the name of Charles which her mother said was a Royal name.

When she was allowed into the room, Audrey marvelled at his perfection. She examined and counted all his fingers and toes. Although he had weighed almost ten pounds, she thought he was tiny but beautiful. After gazing at him with rapture she asked her mother, "What part did I buy?

"At least one of his big toes" "Which one"?

Her mother smiled "You choose!"

Audrey looked very carefully at each one. "This one," she said, pointing to the right one. "I will have this one and I will look after it all by myself."

"Well, you can wash and dry it and powder it," her mother said, "and when you are older you can cut the toe nail when it grows too long." Audrey was thrilled. She was looking forward to Doctor Gordon's next visit. There was much to tell him. She had not seen him for over a month.

CHAPTER 6

The Lessons

Doctor Gordon had been away on holidays, so she had much to tell him when next they met. She described the baby in detail, including her part in his bath time. She said, "He only has a little sausage now, but I know how it can grow." Realizing what she had said, she put her hand over her mouth and blushed, feeling as though she had almost revealed a secret. Doctor Gordon started to say that it was alright and that there was no need to be ashamed of any part of the body, but went into silence when he saw that his discourse was not easing Audrey's embarrassment.

"Audrey, is there something you would like to tell me about this?"

She gave him a resounding "No."

"Audrey, why did you say that you know his little sausage can grow? How do you know this?" She was silent, struggling to regain her composure. She wanted someone who counted to tell her father that they couldn't do the secret anymore, and she was torn between keeping the secret and asking for help. Her father had been busy with his night patrol practice and had not come to her when she was sick, or after she had gone back to school. She did not know if it was over and lived with anxiety wondering if it would happen again. She felt it would be so good to give this problem to someone else to solve, and she knew she could trust this dear man sitting opposite her, because he cared. Her mind wandered among the possibilities and then she suddenly realized that she was being quite cowardly by not facing up to her own issues. She realized she had choices and that she was never trapped in any situation except by her own thoughts.

She gave a sigh, and then took a deep breath. Her mind cleared. She saw this as a situation that was hers to handle and suddenly she knew that this one she could handle. The realization made her feel happy.

Doctor Gordon watched the play of emotions across her face. He saw the shame, the confusion and her eyes moving from one side to another as she looked at different decisions, then the head came up, she straightened in her seat, he saw her mentally meet a challenge and throw it down. She sighed, but it was a sigh of relief.

She looked up, smiling at Doctor Gordon who was waiting for a reply.

"Sometimes," she said quietly but with conviction, "I just know things." He accepted her answer graciously, knowing there was a great deal more to the situation, which one day she may or perhaps never tell.

In many ways he became her mentor. He questioned her about decisions or actions she had taken and in sorting them out or explaining them to him, she learned much about herself and also about his thinking. Their conversations were full of revelations. He challenged her and she challenged him. He became careful to censor outmoded but traditional phrases before he spoke. She dissected them and reduced them to illogical silliness in the twinkling of an eye. When she told him that a neighbour's son was missing in the Air force and that there was no news, he used the well-worn phrase "Perhaps, no news is good news." She stared at him. "How can you possibly believe that? Would you be comfortable sitting on a question mark for a long time? Wouldn't you rather have a full stop so that you could deal with whatever the truth may be?"

He laughed, "Audrey, you are quite right. Please cancel my trite remark. You should be a writer when you grow up. You have a unique way of summarizing situations that defy anyone's logic to challenge."

The Lessons

She smiled. "You challenge everything!"

Doctor Gordon nodded, "More so since I met you. You keep a man on his toes!"

Because Dr. Gordon felt that a philosophical book would be a good choice, he bought Audrey Pollyanna for her birthday. She loved the book and immediately adopted Pollyanna's attitude of 'Always finding something to be glad about'. During her growing years this philosophy saw her through many rough times.

Each birthday, Christmas and sometimes for no reason at all he bought her books. She soon had all the Pollyanna books, and then started on *Anne of Green Gables*.

She learned to read fast, devising her own method of speed reading. Once she realized that her eyes were travelling over some of the margins of each page and that there were no words there to read, she got some ribbon from her mother's sewing box; cut and glued it in two places inside the back and front cover, and covered the margins with it in an attempt to block them out. She had blue and red ribbons. Her Uncle Frank, who saw her using these, asked her what she was doing. After she had explained, he gave her sixpence saying, "its black ribbon you'll be needing; go and get some from the haberdashery shop near your school."

Audrey found the black ribbon made a great improvement, because you didn't look at it at all, and your eyes started on the second or third word in and stopped the second or third word before the end of the line. Her reading speed was now very fast and yet she never missed a single word. What was even better, her eyes got used to doing this, so that after reading half a book this way, she didn't need the ribbons anymore.

One day, as Audrey was returning home from school, she passed the field where the milkman kept his horse. The horse always came when she whistled to it. She would sit on top of the fence and stroke it and talk to it. This particular day Audrey saw the owner of the field beating the horse with a stick and shouting at it. She climbed the fence and ran at full speed across the field. When she was a yard away she hurled herself at the assailant's back and brought him down. He lost the stick. Audrey picked up the stick and began beating him with it. He jumped up and tried to get away from it, but she was a small ball of fury flaying the stick about her with speed and some accuracy and eventually he took to his heels and ran away with Audrey furiously chasing him.

When he had gone, Audrey threw down the stick and called the horse. He came with his head lowered. She took him to the fence and lifted his head, and talked to him. "Don't be sad, you have done nothing wrong. Everything is alright now." She very gently stroked his back where the stick had landed. "Come," she said. "I am taking you home with me."

She had a struggle to open the gate, but when this was done she called the horse and with one hand on its thigh, which was all she could reach, she told it to follow her. He came willingly. Audrey lived in a terraced house which had no front garden but it did have a medium sized back yard. There was a lavatory in the back yard, now seldom used, since her father had installed indoor plumbing. There was an old table under the kitchen window and the rest of the area was paved with large flagstones.

She took the horse in through the back gate and went inside to find it something to eat. She found some sugar lumps, the family's ration for the week, and some carrots. Audrey knew this was acceptable horse fodder, because she had seen it in a film. The horse ate everything from her hand. She climbed onto the table and sat on its back close to its neck, laying her head on its mane.

She was dozing, when the back gate clanged and she heard her father call, "What the hell is that?"

She sat up. "It's a horse!"

"I can see that," Fred said impatiently, "but what the hell is it doing here?"

"It's mine. I rescued him."

"Well, you can rescue him right back where he came from. There's no way you're keeping him and that's that!"

Just then the horse lifted its tail and made a huge deposit on the flagstones.

The Lessons

Audrey stared at it with admiration. She asked, "How did it manage to do all that in one go?"

"Your mother will be pleased to see that." Fred said. "Get down and clean up that mess!"

He got a spade and bucket from the toilet and laid them against the table.

"Where will I empty the bucket?" asked Audrey, looking at the outdoor toilet.

"Oh no you don't," Fred said. "There's no way you're going to go blocking up that lavatory; take it to our allotment and spread it around."

The allotment was some distance away. It was a piece of land of about sixteen square yards. A similar area was allotted to each street resident so that they could grow their own vegetables or flowers. Fred's motto was 'if you can't eat it, don't plant it', so no flowers bloomed in his patch of garden.

Audrey struggled with the spade, which was much taller than she, and then dragged the bucket, which was very heavy, up the street. She found the manure very difficult to spread with the spade, so eventually she used her hands and because there was so much of it, she placed some on one of the neighbours' gardens. She decided that the plants would now grow better because of this new fresh manure. She felt that this was something to be glad about and that even more gladness might come out of this situation, given time.

When she came home, dirty from head to foot, the horse had gone. She left her shoes outside and went in the back door. Her mother, setting the table, looked up, wrinkled her nose and said, "Up the stairs with you, my girl, and into the bath. Wash your hair too while you're at it and when you have finished, put all your clothes in the water. When you come down we need to have a long talk."

Audrey was used to 'long talks' which were very frequent in her life. In the beginning she had not minded them, because she always had a lot to say either in defence or in pointing out errors in their dissertations. However, she had been banned from saying anything until they had finished the telling off and then only "sorry" or "I won't do it again" was acceptable.

Her father said, "I'm not having my arguments shot down by anybody, least of all you, so shut your mouth, because I'm not having any more backchat!"

She found she could talk to her mother when her father was not around, but this was limited by her mother telling her to not let her father hear it. She discovered early that most people feared her father and that underneath his jovial humour, which he often showed to people who didn't matter to him, he was really a very angry man. She asked her mother about it. Her mother told her that Fred wanted to be a doctor, but that his parents couldn't afford to send him to university, so they had him apprenticed to a bricklayer, feeling that at least he would be using his hands and that he liked being outside. He had since studied and done his exams and was now a builder, but he hated the English weather which was always messing up his work and making finance difficult when he had to pay men even though they were not working because of bad weather. Dorothy said that financially he was better off as a bricklayer, but he liked the title of 'builder'.

Audrey digested this information, looking at all the consequences of not doing what you really wanted to do. She came to the conclusion that it was a mistake to do anything unless it made you smile.

On the Saturday she told Doctor Gordon the episode of the horse. He listened carefully, smiling at all the right places. When she had finished, he asked her what lesson she had learned from this event. She thought for a while and then said, "Wait until the manure is dry before you try to spread it; it's too heavy when it is wet!"

"What else?"

"Don't take a horse that doesn't belong to you!"

"Very good! What else?"

She sighed. "Are you sure there is something else?" He nodded.

Audrey looked thoughtful, slowly shook her head and said, "No I can't get it. You will have to point my nose! Is it something to be glad about?"

Doctor Gordon smiled. "Audrey why did you beat that man?"

The Lessons

"Because he was beating the horse!"

"Did you feel he was doing a bad thing, a cruel thing?"

"Yes, of course!"

"Well then, what do you think of you doing the same to him?"

There was silence. Audrey looked away. "That makes me the same as him, doesn't it?"

"Yes, I'm afraid it does."

"Don't be afraid," she said quickly as ever to pick him up. "How can you ever be afraid of helping me see things I need to know?"

He smiled at her.

"Look… I didn't know what else to do."

"Lets us look at the alternatives, Audrey. You could have gone home and told your parents about it and perhaps they could have talked to the field owner."

Audrey considered this idea. "It would never happen," Audrey said with finality. "My parents believe in looking after their own business."

"You could have telephoned the RSPCA and reported him."

"Who are they?"

Doctor Gordon explained the organization to her.

Audrey said that they probably wouldn't listen to her, because she was too young. He acquiesced that it was a possibility.

"Audrey, you can always telephone *me* at any time. If I am busy, I will return your call. I will always help you. I will ring the RSPCA for you if required. Do you understand that I will always be here for you?"

She slid off her books, came around the table and hugged him.

"Thank you," she said and kissed his cheek.

"What is your conclusion about all this now?" he asked.

"Don't do anything bad because other people are doing it. If you do, that makes you as bad as they…" She suddenly stopped, "That isn't right, is it?" She appealed to him then went on saying, "I don't think people are bad; it's just that sometimes they behave that way. I do naughty things sometimes…actually lots of times, at least my parents think so. But I'm not a bad girl really. Anyway, I have decided that from now on I am only going to do things that make me smile!"

Doctor Gordon looked pleased. "That's a good philosophy Audrey, I'm proud of you!"

"The trouble is what makes me smile, doesn't always make my parents smile!"

Doctor Gordon laughed and patted her hand. "Perhaps if you considered that pleasing your parents might make you smile sometimes, you could compromise. What do you think?"

She reluctantly agreed. "Well, I will try. Oh I wish I was grown up now, with no one making me do things all the time!" Audrey hoped that her father would also be too busy with his night patrol work to ever come to her again. If he did, she now felt that this was a situation that she could handle. Perhaps even the war was something to be glad about!

CHAPTER 7

Audrey's New Rule: Don't Do Anything Unless It Makes You Smile

Her father came to her again when she was six and a half years old. She handled him with firmness and dignity. When he sat on the bed and unbuttoned his trousers she put her hand over his to restrict his movement and said, "No, don't!" Fred stared at her. "Why not?" His tone was belligerent.

"I have a new rule… I don't do anything unless it makes me smile. This doesn't make me smile, so I'm not doing it anymore."

Fred wanted to order her to do it, but he was afraid of the repercussions. She might tell Dorothy and he didn't want that. He had to be careful. Maybe he could frighten her just with a look.

He father glared at her. She held his gaze without blinking, saying nothing.

"I thought you were into magic?" There was irritation and a flicker of hope in Fred's voice.

"Not anymore." Audrey gazed at him for a moment then said, "I'm sleepy, goodnight!"

She leaned over, kissed her father on the cheek and slid under the bedclothes shutting her eyes. She heard her father wait for a while, then give a big sigh as he left the room; she knew that he would not be back.

Audrey lay in bed thinking it over. She finally found something to be glad about. Her schoolmates were eight years old or more and already into a curiosity game of "show me yours and I'll show you mine." She was glad she did not have to play; her curiosity about boys and men was more than satisfied.

She became curious about God instead. There was much talk and encouragement to pray to him, to ask for his help to win the war; bring loved ones home; kill the Germans and Hitler. He seemed to be mentioned a great deal on the wireless and in the newspaper, and people referred to him more than they had ever done before.

Her curiosity about God was coming up to be challenged. She asked her grandmother, "How do I find out about God?"

Her grandmother gave her a Bible, told her it was hers to keep, and said, "Although you are only seven, you're such a bookworm that you will probably make more sense of it than I ever did. But then I've never been much of a reader!"

Audrey was thrilled. She sat down immediately and began to read. She read her Bible from front to back over a period of two weeks, having constant arguments in her head about its contents. When she next had tea with Dr. Gordon, he asked the inevitable, "Well Audrey, what have you been doing or finding out since Wednesday?"

She said, "I have been reading the Bible"

"Oh, what part?" he asked.

"All of it!'

Dr. Gordon stared at her. "May I ask why?"

"I was looking for God"

"Ah… and did you find him?"

She shook her head. "No, he's not in there."

He was silent.

"Maybe you should try going to Sunday school or Church," he offered.

"What is that and where is it?"

Dr. Gordon filled in the details, and the next Sunday Audrey informed her family she was going to Church and set off alone to the local Church of England. It was an easy distance, only half a mile away.

She stayed behind after what she thought was an interesting event. She liked the novelty of getting up and down, praying and singing. A lady next to her shared her hymn book and allowed Audrey to stand on the pew so that she was at the correct height to read it. However, she did not lose sight of her goal to find God and sought out the vicar, so that she could ask her questions.

She was very disappointed in his replies and came to the conclusion that he knew very little himself. He mostly never answered her questions, which he found were rather tricky and much unexpected in one so young, but stalled by saying that, "God moves in mysterious ways," or "You must have faith." Her "Why?" to both these statements remained unanswered.

Over the next few days, Audrey asked her parents and some relatives about God.

Her father said He didn't exist, and her mother wasn't sure that he did, but felt that someone very big must have created the world.

Audrey decided that someone like the Vicar, who was supposed to know what he was doing, should be able to explain it to someone else. It seemed that questions about God created a lot of ducking and diving instead of answers. She was beginning to think that most grown-ups were either still finding answers or had forgotten the original question and that's why there was all this mystery. No one knew what they were asking or doing anymore.

She went to Church one more time. As she left the church grounds, a pale sun shone through a watery sky. A rainbow full of wonderful colours arched its way in full glory from one side of the parish to the next. Audrey was entranced. She adored rainbows. She closed her eyes and imagined she was sitting at the very top of the rainbow's arch. She stretched her feet out and held her hands and arms out in front of her and started to slide down. A mixture of all the colours stirred by her feet and hands washed over her like waves. She slid all the way to the bottom landing not in a pot of gold but in a cloud of white light. She opened her eyes feeling happy and joyful. Audrey had the urge to go to the top of the arch again and slide down the other side, but the rainbow was already fading and it was long past her time to be home.

She attended Sunday school the following week, as the Vicar had recommended. He had told her that she was too young to be worrying her head about matters that concerned theologians. Audrey was not sure what a theologian was, but looked it up in the dictionary and decided that she would like to meet one.

Sunday school had no interest for her. Miss Barnes her Sunday school teacher had flaming red hair. Audrey had irrationally decided that she really did not like red hair on women. For some reason, she didn't mind it on men. Her teacher therefore started off at a disadvantage and compounded it by talking about Jesus dying for 'Our Sins'. Audrey did not see how anyone could do something like that when the people Jesus was assisting did not even know what sin they had committed. She found the concept of 'original sin' laughable. When the teacher explained that the story of Adam & Eve with the serpent and apple was symbolic but couldn't explain the symbol, Audrey decided that this was the worst detective story ever written. She found it illogical that Jesus had died on the cross. If he could turn wine into water and feed hundreds of people from two fishes and a few loaves of bread, then surely he could make himself disappear off the cross and reappear in a safe place. How did His dying save anyone anyway; and from what? People were now busy fighting each other in a war!

We were supposed to 'love your neighbours' and 'smite your enemies'. It seemed to Audrey that everyone was somebody's neighbour and every time you took out an enemy, you were harming someone's neighbour. God or Jesus loved everyone and yet if you didn't believe and worship Him, He would send you to Hell. This was a very inappropriate action for a loving human being. Finding that the Bible was written some two thousand years ago finished Audrey's interest in the religious area forever. She decided that the Bible was written by somebody in a bad mood hoping they would scare people into being good. She put it aside, deciding not to read it again.

When Dr. Gordon asked her about her search, she told him about attending Church and Sunday school.

"And did you find God?" he asked.

"No, he wasn't there, and the Vicar doesn't know much about him either, and neither does the Sunday school teacher."

She talked to him about the questions, answers, contradictions, and the seeming illogicality of it all. When she finished, he was amazed at her reasoning. Stuck for words to help her, he finally said, "Audrey, how will you feel if I tell you that God is someone that is Omnipresent; now that means God is unseen, but everywhere."

She was silent for a moment. "I don't know if that is true or not, but it doesn't make me smile."

He smiled at the familiar rejoinder, and asked, "Why not, Audrey?"

"Because it doesn't leave me with any space to call my own!" He was stunned into silence.

Finally he said, "Audrey I don't know how to help you with this anymore. You are going to have to sort it out yourself, but I want you to promise me that when you do, you will let me know your final conclusions, and all the steps along the way." She laughed, "You make it sound complicated, but I promise." A few days after this conversation, Mr Whiteside, who lived next door, died in his sleep. Audrey had often called in to see him, particularly if she saw him sitting in his window looking sadly at the cars and the people passing in the street. He was not a talkative man, and even less so since his wife had died two years ago. Audrey would go in and drag up a chair and sit next to him. Sometimes she reached out and held his hand. Often neither of them would speak a word. They would both watch the street activities for ten minutes or so, until Audrey decided to leave. Then, Audrey would pat his hand and smile at him and he would pat her head and smile back.

Occasionally they would talk. Audrey would relate one of the happenings of her day that she would hope would make him laugh or be of interest. He would listen attentively to her story and make some small comment. One day when she had explained about the horse and why it was bad to correct other people by doing what they did, he said, "You're quite the little philosopher, aren't you!"

Audrey smiled. "Is that good?"

"Well now, you could do worse," Mr Whiteside said. "There are certainly worse things to be!"

When Audrey got home, she looked up the word 'philosopher'. She found the definitions confusing. The day after Mr Whiteside died she went next door to see his body in the open coffin. Her mother was against it. "But," Audrey said, "I used to see him when he was alive, why can't I see him now that he's dead?" While her mother was trying to sort out a reply other than 'I don't think it is quite nice', which she knew would be shot down in flames, Audrey said, "I won't be long," and was out the door before her mother had time to open her mouth.

Audrey stood on a chair and looked into the coffin. She didn't touch anything as she felt this would be irreverent. Mr Whiteside looked very white. She thought he had makeup on but the whiteness was bleeding through.

Two neighbourhood ladies came in to gaze at him. One said, "Well, he's gone for sure, now."

Audrey asked, "Where did he go?"

"To heaven we hope," said one of them.

"Where exactly is that?"

"Somewhere up there," said the other one, pointing at the sky. Audrey repeated this conversation to her father that evening. Her father snorted. "If you ask me, no-one goes anywhere except in the ground in a wooden box. Anything else is wishful thinking. You can't be in two places at once now can you?"

Her mother said, "Oh, surely there is more to it than that?"

"Anything else is false hope invented by people who are scared of dying!" her father continued.

Audrey discussed these issues with Doctor Gordon.

Eventually she asked, "If he did go to heaven, *what* exactly went there, when he seems to be right here and not moving?" Audrey was prompted by her father's comments.

"His *soul* went to heaven, Audrey" Doctor Gordon replied.

"Where was it when he was here?"

"I think it was inside him."

"How did it get out?"

"I think he decided it was time for it to leave."

"Well," said Audrey, "if he decided that his soul should leave and go to heaven, where did he go after that?"

Dr. Gordon was silent. Audrey waited.

Finally, he said, "Audrey, what do you think happened?"

"Well it would seem that his soul was really *him*. Nothing else makes sense, does it?" She looked at him hopefully.

"Audrey, I think you might have hit the nail on the head."

She laughed. "Oh, I have had a lot of practice at that," she said, telling him about her favourite pastime as a little child. Audrey told him also about Mr Whiteside saying she was a little philosopher. She told him the confusion in the dictionary. "What do you think it means?" Dr. Gordon asked.

"Well it seems that everyone is a philosopher. The old lady who said, 'A stitch in time saves nine' or 'It's no use crying over spilt milk', or Pollyanna's 'always finding something to be glad about', or my father saying 'money doesn't grow on trees', or 'This too will pass'. It seems that a philosopher gives warnings or finds something good and cheerful to say about bad situations so that people will feel better; and if you are a good philosopher then you do this all the time, so you never feel sad, or at least not for very long! Would you agree with that?"

Doctor Gordon smiled, as he said, "Audrey. I think I could live with that definition!"

CHAPTER 8

Taking a High Dive

Audrey's eighth year was a very eventful one. Her parents had friends called Leonard and Alice. They owned a Bakery about two miles away from Audrey's home and would often let her help in the workroom after school. Audrey seemed to grow in tiny little spurts and was well under height for her age. She stood on a chair in the bakery, carefully filling tarts with jam or lemon curd, stirring custard or washing the baking trays in the huge sink. She loved to watch Leonard taking bread from the oven and she was intoxicated by the smells that came from the chimney and assailed her nose long before her arrival.

Leonard was also a swimming instructor and one day a week he had swimming classes at the local indoor baths. Margaret and Audrey joined his class at the beginning of one summer.

Margaret did well. She jumped off the side holding her nose and learned to dog paddle.

Audrey dived in making a belly-flop, and swam two or three breast strokes before sinking like a stone.

One Sunday, after three lessons, the family, together with Leonard, went to the large outdoor Olympic sized swimming pool a few miles away for a picnic and a swim.

The pool had very high diving boards. Audrey said, "I am going to jump off the very top board!"

Leonard said, "You're right. When you have learned to dive efficiently from the side of the pool and swim properly you can work your way up to the top board, but that will take a long time yet."

Dorothy said, "On the day you dive off the top board I will give you ten shillings." "So will I," said her father, and "I too!" said Leonard.

Audrey smiled, and ate a sandwich.

After lunch Audrey wandered around the pool, watching the swimmers and waiting for her lunch to settle. Leonard had said that you should not go in the water until two hours had passed after a meal. There was a large clock in the grounds. When the two hours were up, she climbed up all the ladders to the very top board. She was happy. She knew she could jump off the very top board without hurting herself and then she would have lots of money.

The previous day she had gone to the pictures with Dr. Gordon. Shorts were always shown before the main feature and Audrey had just seen one of a clown jumping off a diving board and pretending to ride a bicycle all the way down to a pool. But, he had never touched the water. When he was just over half way down he had changed his mind and started to back-pedal his imaginary bicycle until he was back on the top of the diving board.

Audrey felt sure that if he could do this, she could.

She sat on the edge of the board and looked down. The pool looked very small and very far away and her family looked like small dwarfs. She decided to jump right away before she was tempted to change her mind. She knew her family needed to see her, so she put her hands around her mouth and hollered their names. She watched them look all around their space yet failing to see her, so she went on hollering until they looked up and spotted her on the high board. They began to make gestures for her to come down at once.

She called, "I'm coming!" and launched herself into space. She pedalled away and then changed her mind and pedalled backwards. She was shocked to find herself still falling and when she hit the water she was hurt and emotionally outraged.

She sank, and sank, into the deep end of the pool until she felt she would never come up. Her swimming cap had come off and lots of her body parts were stinging. She wondered if this funny floating, quiet, sinking feeling meant that she was drowning.

Strong arms suddenly held her and took her to the surface. Leonard lifted her on to the side and she found herself saying between the coughing and spluttering, and the recriminations of her family which came furiously and fast, "But, I changed my mind. You don't understand I changed my mind; I shouldn't have landed on the water. I was going back!"

It took some time before it was quiet enough for them to question her and for her to tell the story of the clown.

When her father explained that a projectionist could run a film in reverse so that everything appeared to be going backwards, she felt betrayed and stupid and outraged at the grown-up world for their deception.

However, it was easy to find something to be glad about when she collected three ten-shilling notes for her money box. This was good compensation for the ugly welts that were beginning to show on her legs and arms from hitting the water at a wrong angle. Another thing to be glad about was that she would have an interesting story to tell Dr. Gordon on when he returned. He had gone to increase his knowledge at a training hospital in Scotland and would not be back for another three weeks.

However, even more significant events were to occur before then.

CHAPTER 9

Handling the Class Bully

Edna Robertson, the class bully, had systematically beaten up almost everyone in Audrey's class.

Audrey's friend, Irene, was her latest target. She ignored Audrey, realising that beating up someone who was eighteen months younger and who barely came up to her armpit would not enhance her reputation or put fear into her enemies.

When she started hitting Irene and wouldn't stop until her victim pleaded for mercy, Audrey decided that someone needed to teach her a lesson.

She went to her father and asked him to give her boxing lessons. He was amused, questioned her request, but seemed satisfied when she said that she was the smallest girl in school and needed to know how to defend herself.

Fred had done some amateur boxing and only gave it up because Dorothy could not bear the sight or the result of grown men hitting each other for no good reason.

He knelt on the floor, constantly imploring Audrey to dance around him. "Keep moving, keep moving! Don't let those feet stand still!" Audrey was a good student. He showed her how to lead with one fist and protect with the other. He taught her rules: "No hitting below the belt or when your man is down." He made her try to land blows on him and laughed at her attempts. Eventually she got beyond his defences and made contact that actually hurt... When she was good at this, she went to school and threw down the gauntlet.

During the lunch recess she approached Edna Robertson saying, "You will meet me in the field when school is finished. I am going to beat you up. If you don't come, everyone will know you are frightened of me!"

Edna was outraged. "You stupid twerp, I'll half kill you! Who do you think you are?!"

Audrey said, "Someone who isn't scared of you! What's a twerp anyway?" but got no answer.

There was good attendance for the proposed fight. All of Audrey's class were there. They could hardly believe that she had challenged Edna and were fearful of the outcome. Audrey had not seen Edna fight to any extent before. She normally punched her victims or slapped them until they cried, whimpered or begged her to stop and the bullying was often over in a few minutes. If someone fought back, they were quickly demolished by more severe punching. Edna was the tallest and the heaviest of all the girls and boys in her class.

Audrey stood face to face with her, just out of arm's reach. She was surprised at how big Edna was and Audrey's stomach felt that it was turning somersaults; however, she felt confident in remembering all that her father had taught. She began to dance around with her fists in front of her, leading first with one and then the other, but not making contact at this point.

Edna got angry. "Keep still, you little twerp, and fight!" she said, lunging with a blow towards Audrey's head and kicking out with her foot at the same time.

Audrey avoided both. "Hey, you're not supposed to kick!" Someone in the crowd called out, "Watch out, she bites and scratches too!"

Audrey discovered two things very quickly. It was not an advantage to be tall, because it was more difficult to hit down.

Handling the Class Bully

Edna was not used to a moving target. Her victims were supposed to stand still and take it or run away.

Audrey danced around and began to move in and land blows to the solar plexus and the head area. She saw blood appear from Edna's nose, and the crowd cheered. Edna landed a blow to Audrey's cheek which hurt immensely. Audrey aimed a hard swinging undercut blow to the jaw which missed but connected with the mouth. She was shocked to see more blood appear. Edna stopped and spat out a tooth. The crowd cheered again but Audrey was full of chagrin.

She wanted to end this; she moved in and delivered another blow to the solar plexus. Edna was winded and very angry. She paused for breath and then came in swinging wildly. Audrey went on dancing and blocking or ducking the wild swings and then delivered another blow to the jaw. This was enough for Edna, she turned and was about to run, but Audrey grabbed her coat. Edna pulled away leaving two buttons from her jacket in Audrey's hand, as she ran towards the school gate. The crowd surged around Audrey congratulating her, but she moved quickly away and headed for home.

Audrey walked slowly, occasionally touching her injured face. She was confused. She remembered the farmer beating the horse, then herself beating the farmer. She recalled her conversation with Dr. Gordon. Yet Edna needed to be stopped. She was careful not to be caught by any teacher and her threats had kept the pupils too scared to tell.

Audrey couldn't be sure whether she deserved to be slapped on the back or on the bottom.

She got tired of the deliberation and decided that the difference was only a matter of about eight inches, so it didn't really matter. When she went into the hairdressing shop at the front of the house, her mother stared and said, "Audrey! Whatever happened to your face?"

"I ran into something." Seeing her mother's disbelief, she added, "At full speed."

Her mother sighed and said, "Lay the table for tea, check on baby Charles;

Margaret is supposed to be looking after him; then peel some potatoes before your father comes home. Bathe your face in cold water and rub some margarine into that bruise. You are going to have a black eye." Her mother winked at her customer as she said, "It must have been some door she ran into!"

Audrey said, "How did you know?" and went off to do her mother's bidding.

That evening as the family finished dinner, there was a knock on the door. When her father opened it, Edna Robertson and her father stood on the doorstep. The father said to Fred, "Look what your daughter has done to my girl; not just her face, but her coat too!"

Fred called Margaret to the door, but as she was halfway obeying, Edna said, "It wasn't her. It was Audrey!"

Audrey left her chair and stood in the doorway next to her father. She held out her hand with the two buttons torn from Edna's coat. Edna snatched them from her hand and turned to go. Edna's father grabbed her arm and pulled her back. He gazed at Audrey and said to Edna, "Do you mean to tell me that this little squirt did that to you and you couldn't defend yourself?"

Edna shook him off with "I want to go home."

The father glared at Fred and Audrey, then turned on his heel following his daughter.

Fred looked at Audrey. "Is *this* what those boxing lessons were about?" She nodded.

"Why?"

"Because she is a bully and she has beaten up every girl and boy in my class except me, and that's only because she thinks I'm a twerp…what is a twerp?"

Fred smiled. "I don't know, look it up in that dictionary you're so fond of."

He put his hand in his pocket and pulled out a florin and gave it to Audrey. He patted her head and said, "That door you ran into was her fist,

Handling the Class Bully

wasn't it?"

She looked down and said, "I forgot to duck."

"Well, remember next time. At least you know how to fight. Remember I taught you that!"

Audrey smiled, hugged him and thanked him. Her two shilling piece would make a wonderful contribution to her money box. The next day at school, Audrey went up to Edna saying, "I'm sorry if I hurt you and got you into trouble with your father. I will not fight you anymore unless you pick on someone else in my class. If you do I will have to show you other things my father has taught me that I haven't used yet! He was a great amateur boxer and he knows how to really fight. By the way I looked up 'Twerp' and it is a pregnant fish. I think you need a better word."

Audrey looked at her waiting for a comment. When Edna said nothing, she slowly walked away, debating the philosophical ins and outs of the whole event. She decided to talk it over with Doctor Gordon.

CHAPTER 10

A Nightmare Event

Audrey's mother had been a hairdresser since she was nineteen years old. Her parents had put her to work in the Cotton Mill when she was twelve. She was the only girl. Her two brothers loved this little sister who was almost twelve years younger. One day Dorothy said that she wanted to be a hairdresser and that she was saving the few pennies she was allowed to keep, so that she could go to the Hairdressers training school in London. Her two brothers put their heads and some of their wages together and when she was fourteen they saw Dorothy off on a train to London to start her career. Dorothy's father's sister lived in Tottenham, a short train ride from the school, so Dorothy had a home and guardian in the form of Aunt Dolly.

Since she had graduated, Dorothy had worked from a room at her parents' home. Later, Fred and Dorothy's front living room had been turned into a hairdressing salon.

Dorothy was an excellent hairdresser, happy in her work and never lacked for customers. She had given up work just before Margaret had been born and had gone back to it on a part time basis after Audrey had arrived, then full time when baby Charles was two years old. The extra money was

A LIFE of Enlightenment

handy, as it allowed her to buy a few things on the black market after the ration stamps were exhausted, and this she felt was justified when it enabled her to feed her family a little better.

Sometimes they even had a friend or two to tea. Dorothy would open a tin of salmon, an absolute luxury; mash it up with two slices of brown bread, add a dash of vinegar and serve it with salad between seven people, who thought it a treat just like Christmas.

Dorothy saw that Audrey always had money in her pocket and some ration stamps. She had instructed Audrey that wherever she spotted a queue of people, she was to join it and buy as much as she could of whatever was on the other end. She was a good spotter, taking alternate routes past different shops and seldom came home from school more than two days empty handed. Sometimes she got caught in air raid warnings, but she always seemed to get home before the bombs started falling.

One winter's day after helping at the bakery, Audrey was half way between home and the bakery. She was now eight years old. The air raid shelter was at the third point of a triangle. Audrey was in the middle of the triangle and undecided about where to go. The Germans had recently launched the "doodlebug" flying bombs. The English found them very unnerving. They were used to bombs falling straight from the sky and making a noise all the way down with a resounding crash as a finale. These bombs were launched from Germany, across the sea. They had tiny wings, no pilots, and made little sound after their engine cut out and they glided to earth, and no-one knew where they were going to land. The bombs were mostly directed towards London or ports, but the odd one became a stray. Audrey found a recessed shop doorway and sat down with her back to the door. She heard a faint little cry and in the dim light saw a small kitten. She called. It came and jumped into her lap. She opened her winter coat and popped it inside to keep it warm.

With no advance warning she heard a close explosion as somewhere a building stopped a bomb's travels. The sky lit up with a reddish glow from the fire.

A Nightmare Event

Holding the kitten safe, she went to the front of the doorway and carefully looked out.

She was amazed as a flying bomb shot past her doorway travelling almost parallel with the centre of the road. It made no sound. Audrey knew that its course would take it straight into the hotel at the T junction which was about half a mile from her home. She stood and watched it, only moving back into her doorway to avoid the flying debris resulting from its explosion. She waited, then, popped her head out again. There was fire and a partial empty space where the hotel had stood. She resigned herself to waiting in the doorway until the "All Clear" sounded.

When she finally arrived home to very worried parents, it seemed that no-one wanted to listen to her story. She was told off for worrying her parents; told that she couldn't keep the cat and was sent to knock on doors up and down the street to find an existing or new owner for the kitten.

Audrey did not want to be separated from her new pet. She felt that they had shared a common experience together and that they were safe because of it. Fred said, "If that cat hasn't got another home by lunchtime tomorrow. I will drown it. Now get on with it!"

She half hoped no one would be interested in the kitten, but the first house she knocked on claimed it as their own. Audrey was glad for the kitten's sake.

She went back empty handed and with sadness in her heart. Her parents were busy sticking brown paper over broken and cracked window panes.

Her father did not go out on patrol again that night. He was busy repairing damage to his own home and his neighbours'. The next night was a quiet one. Her mother was sewing downstairs and Fred had come up to have a bath. He came into Audrey's room perhaps expectant that the two shillings would now give him leverage. Again she rebuffed him by saying that she was not going to do anything unless it made her smile.

Her father angrily said, "You will do whatever I tell you to do. What do you have to say about that?"

"Only if Mum says I have to do it too!"

"Don't you say a word of this to your mother!"

Audrey sighed, "I won't if you leave me alone."

Her father angrily left the room.

A few nights later, Audrey began to have nightmares; she dreamed that the eiderdown covering the bed turned into a forest floor that came alive with slithering snakes. The room became filled with fierce jungle animals all threatening to attack her. She woke up screaming, standing on her bed with her back into a corner. When her father tried to pick her up, she fought him. He was unshaven and to Audrey looked like a gorilla. When she had quietened down, he took her downstairs and placed her in a chair in front of the fire. Her mother made her a cup of warm Horlicks. The nightmares continued for two weeks despite the nightlight she was given. Audrey hated to leave the warm fire. When she went back to bed the nightmare would often continue as though the break had been only an interval.

She was ashamed of her behaviour and her fear. All of her young life she had found that to conquer fear you simply did whatever you were frightened to do, and that settled it once and for all. She was unsure of how to handle this because it happened in her sleep and she felt out of control when she awoke screaming.

She gave it a lot of thought. She arrived at the conclusion that it wasn't the dark of which she was afraid; it was what she thought was *in* the dark.

She decided on a course of action.

Because it was blackout time and also late November, the nights were dark grey with heavy clouds covering the moon.

Audrey had an alarm clock with green fingers that glowed in the dark. When her parents had gone to bed and she could hear her father snoring, Audrey crept downstairs in her pyjamas and slippers, unlocked the back door, and stood in the middle of the flag stoned yard. She placed the clock on the ground and promised herself that she would stay there for twenty minutes and not a minute less.

She fought the urge to stand with her back to the wall. If she got attacked from behind then so be it. Dying was better than living with this

A Nightmare Event

fear and the nightmares that wouldn't go away.

Audrey quickly discovered that it had been a mistake not to put on her dressing gown. The winter's night was cold and she was beginning to shiver from a combination of fear and cold.

She had the urge to close her eyes and though she resolutely fought this for the first few minutes, it became more comfortable to shut out the very dim dark shapes in the yard. The nightmare began. Large python snakes wrapped around her body and started to squeeze her to death. Savage lions roared right in her face. Crocodiles came out of the ground to start eating her feet and all around her blazing eyes lighting up the darkness promised even more terror. She stood there trembling from head to foot. She felt as though her stomach had come into her throat and blocked it so that she couldn't even scream. She was wet with perspiration and terrified. She felt she was going to die. After some minutes of trying to hold her ground, she gave in, picked up the alarm clock and fled upstairs to her warm bed.

Audrey looked at the clock. Only ten minutes had gone by. She sat on the side of the bed and cried with disappointment. She was still shaking with fear and cold. She climbed under the covers, berating herself for being such a coward.

Eventually she made a new resolution. The following night she was going to do it again and this time she would stay for twenty minutes and, if necessary, die. That would be infinitely better than living with the nightmares and being frightened every time she went to bed.

During all of the next school day she thought about it during class and by the time her parents had settled for the night she was ready.

Audrey felt full of courage.

She put on her dressing gown and slippers, slipped the latch on the back door and again stood in the centre of the yard. She had a slight worry that perhaps an enemy plane may see the luminous hands of the clock, but she decided the sky was far enough away. She placed the clock on the ground where she could see the figures. It was eleven minutes past eleven.

This time she tried to keep her eyes open. She had an urge to stand with her back to the wall so that the python could not get to her, but this she resisted. Eventually she closed her eyes and the nightmare began. It followed the same pattern as before. Despite the cold her pyjamas were wet with sweat, she trembled from head to foot with fear; she felt nauseous, she got eaten by the lions and then crocodiles; a tiger took her head in its mouth; the python squeezed so that she could hardly breathe; she felt she had died many times over, but she gritted her teeth, anchoring her feet to the ground.

It seemed to go on and on, with no ending in sight. She challenged and threw down the urge to leave. If she died and never recovered from this, it was alright. At the same time, she had a feeling that somehow she would go on.

Slowly and unexpectedly, the fear began to recede and everything in the nightmare began to fade. Stillness pervaded the area and she experienced a warm feeling of peace. The shivering stopped. She felt a gentle feeling of joy and happiness flow through her and a quiet feeling of gratitude at having achieved something.

Audrey looked at the clock, the fingers said eleven twenty one. She knew it was over but her determination to stay twenty whole minutes prevailed. She sat on the ground and watched the clock. She was amused that she had decided on twenty minutes and that was the time it had exactly taken in two periods to handle the nightmares. She knew without question they were over, never to return.

She was peaceful and happy.

For many years Audrey did not equate the nightmares with her father's demands. When she did, she sent him a silent thank you for helping her bring up fears that she had not known were there, and that needed to be handled for her life to be what she wanted to create it to be.

CHAPTER 11

Marriage and Reactions

Audrey spent many happy hours with her brother Charles. She taught him to play marbles and other games, including football and cricket. He seemed to like cricket the best and soon had his own ball, wicket and bat.

Margaret and Audrey had little in common in their early years. Audrey had no intention of giving up her tomboyish nature while Margaret grew more and more into a very likeable contented young girl. She disliked playing all sports or any rough and tumble type games, preferring games that mimicked being grown up.

Audrey preferred to play with the boys. She loved all sports and adventurous activities and had no longing to be an adult. She relished the fact that she now had a baby brother who could share her liking for his type of games. Her relatives shook their heads over Audrey, often saying at various times to her mother, "You will never make a girl out of her. Just look at her, she has twigs in her hair from climbing trees, she is never without scabs on her knees; she is muddy and wet from wading in the river catching tadpoles and goodness knows what else; she tucks her dresses in her knickers, her pretty hair is tied with string and shoved down her blouse and what she eats doesn't help her grow because she uses it up so fast with all this running about she does. Does she ever sit still?" "Oh yes," her mother defended her. "When she is reading a book, you won't get a peep out of her. She's in another world." Doctor Gordon returned from Scotland with another book present for Audrey. This time it was Charles Dickens's *Great Expectations*. Audrey threw her arms round him and thanked him. She had much to tell him and wanted to know everything that he had been doing also, so on this Saturday they spent all their time at the tea shop. Audrey had graduated to only one telephone book now and was proud of the little she had grown.

The tea shop ladies were always intrigued by this familiar but strange relationship between the young Doctor and the little girl. They often heard snatches of conversation and talked between themselves.

"Chattering like blackbirds they are. You wouldn't think with the age difference that they would have much to say, but they're always going at it hammer and tongs."

Another said, "You might learn a lot if you care to listen, without being obvious of course. Do you suppose it's his niece or something? It's not his daughter, 'cos she doesn't call him Dad."

"What does she call him?" "Nothing that I ever heard."

Audrey, who had excellent hearing, conveyed their chatter to Doctor Gordon in an amused gentle whisper. He smiled. "Now you go first with all your news, you seem even happier than usual, so you have obviously been winning at something, tell me all!"

After she had recounted her battle with Edna, she explained her confusion. Relating to the farmer and the horse and matching actions, Audrey said it would seem that she had done the wrong thing again, but what else was there to do?

Doctor Gordon was silent for a moment. "Audrey, sometimes there are exceptions that prove the rule and perhaps this is one of them. There are times when one has to stand one's ground even if it means hurting another, if in the long run it is for the greater good."

"It sounds like an excuse!"

Marriage and Reactions

"Perhaps I should have said the greatest good for the greatest number! Does that make it better? The greatest number in this event is your classmates whom you have now protected." Audrey looked thoughtfully into space. "I understand what you are saying but it doesn't make me smile!"

"Why not?"

"I don't know." Suddenly she was miserable. "It's a bit like the words in the Bible that say 'Love your neighbours, smite your enemies.' Everyone you meet is someone's neighbour, so when you harm one person you harm the world, don't you? It's very confusing!"

"Audrey, I think you have summed everything up in your last sentence. It is confusing. It is a confusing world we live in; but you are making better sense of it at your young age than most of the adults I know. Perhaps it is because you are young and your thinking is fresh and vibrant and not soured by a life that is not understood. You take care to understand everything that happens to you and I hope you always will."

She brightened, and went on to tell him about jumping from the swimming pool board.

"Audrey, I know you have a rule to do anything that you fear so that you can conquer it, but why do you feel you have to do that?"

"Because I don't want to live a life that has fear as a part of it!" He smiled. "Alright, Audrey, what else have you been conquering?"

Without mentioning her father, she told him about the nightmares. He watched the play of emotions across her face; the disappointment and the tears that came to her eyes when she recounted the failed first attempt and then the joy and happiness when she had finally conquered the fear.

He said, "Audrey, how old are you now?"

"Eight and a little bit!" she grinned at him, the dimples flashing in and out.

He looked at her admiringly. "All this, and you are so young!" She laughed, "Well, I will grow out of that won't I?"

He laughed in agreement and then he told her how proud he was of her courage, her attitude to life, her method of turning liabilities into assets and her ability to stand strong and confront whatever got in the way of the life she wanted to live. He stopped when he saw she was getting embarrassed. She shrugged her shoulders and said, "It wasn't really that difficult…no, that's not right. It wasn't really so difficult. Did you know that the word 'That' is not an adverb of degree? 'So' is correct. I read it in an English book. English is my favourite subject. I think it is easy for me because I read such a lot and I learn a great deal from the books I read." She was chattering with embarrassment.

"And you have used them to change the subject." He was amused.

"Well, I have finished telling you my things, now it is your turn!"

He gave her a simplified version of the new data he had learned. She listened attentively, asking an odd question when he used a word or concept she didn't understand.

Time had flown while they talked. Doctor Gordon nodded to one of the waitresses and soon the baked beans and raisin toast appeared, along with second cups of tea.

Audrey had enjoyed a wonderful time. This was her favourite part of the relationship, the sorting out; the new viewpoints that could be examined, taken to heart or rejected; the debates on the morals of an action, and the alternatives that it would be wise to consider.

Audrey did not know if Doctor Gordon got as much from this relationship as she did and would have been astonished if it had been brought to her attention.

She did not know that he related many of her ideas and even sometimes the events of her life to his patients who needed encouragement to change their viewpoints and get better, not always from an illness, but from a trauma in their life. She felt he was the kindest man on earth to put up with her when she was just a child; to teach her so many things; to laugh with her; entertain her and bring her gifts, not just on birthdays and Christmas, but whenever he went away.

She had no idea of the joy and wisdom she brought to his life and how he looked forward to all the times they spent together. She simply loved him.

CHAPTER 12

Exploits and Education

When Audrey was nine years old, or to be precise in the year that she was to be ten, she sat with all the other members of her class for the school examination for entry either to Grammar school, High school, Technical or Commercial college, or to stay on at her present school until she was fifteen. This was not supposed to happen for Audrey until the beginning of the year when she would be eleven, however she had been in her class along with older students since her first day at school, and the fact that she was eighteen months younger than even the youngest student seemed to have been forgotten. She was much shorter but everyone had got used to this long ago. In the beginning she was told she had "duck's disease." Audrey did not know what this was. Her father enlightened her by saying, "It means your arse is too close to the floor! They are ragging you because you are short even for your age!"

The designated school was decided according to the examination results.

There was no Grammar school in Audrey's town but the Girl's high school 'Greenfields' was going to be changed into a Grammar school in the near future.

Audrey's marks took her to Greenfields. Her sister Margaret was considering following in her mother's footsteps in hairdressing, but she also thought that she might like to be a shorthand typist, so off she went to Commercial College.

The war was drawing to a close. There was hope that Germany would soon surrender. Japan looked like being stubborn, so the experts said on the wireless. However, hope about the end of the war did not mean the end of rationing.

Audrey still had money in her pocket and ration books enabling her to join any queue she spotted and buy whatever was in the shop. Despite sometimes a long wait and an often "sold out" shop call before it became her turn, she was always delighted when she managed to arrive home with a parcel for her mother. Now that she was at a different school involving two bus journeys, she had new territories to explore, often walking the first journey from school into the town trusting, that she would pass a shop that was open with some goods—any goods.

Audrey was intrigued but not totally happy about going to an "all girl's" school. The boys' equivalent was at least four miles away. Seeing her male friends during breaks was out of the question.

She had a green tunic and white blouse uniform, with a green blazer and gloves that must be worn all the time one was travelling, unless one was being worn and one carried in the same hand and only then for a very good reason; a beret that had to be worn in a certain way, knee socks, black shoes and green knickers completed her winter wardrobe. In summer, green and white striped dresses and a white straw boater with a green ribbon, white gloves and ankle socks became the changes for the warmer weather.

Prefects checking the girls seemed to be everywhere. Audrey lost many points in the first few weeks for wearing her beret at a jaunty angle. Hair had to be braided or tied in two bunches or cut to just below the ear level, Audrey begged her mother for a haircut, but Dorothy refused. She loved Audrey's waves and curls and the unusual strawberry blonde colour.

She consented to dividing Audrey's hair down the back of her head and tying in into two bunches, however, she finally consented to put elastic un-

Exploits and Education

der the ribbons that Audrey was constantly losing. Audrey had already lost points for tucking her two bunches of hair down her blouse when the ribbons went missing.

Audrey chose a space near a window in every class she had to attend. From here she could gaze across the green fields to trees in the distance; make up stories in her head or daydream the period away if she thought the lesson was boring or irrelevant.

English literature, grammar, essays, spelling, straight mathematics and any kind of sport were her favourite subjects.

Writing essays was one of her favourite assignments. Her thinking was quite different from that of her classmates. Given an assignment of *"The postman knocked three times and…*write an essay," Audrey wrote "and the door fell in" and then developed it from there. Her classmates all seemed to have deliveries occurring from the postman. Parcels, telegrams, birthday cards became the beginning of a story. Audrey's was full of creaking floorboards and the mystery of a deserted house!

Algebra was introduced in her second week. She was outraged that someone would complicate a subject by throwing parts of the alphabet into numbers. Audrey refused to comply with sorting it out. She would gaze at the final question of "therefore "X" equals?" until the "X" shimmered and became a number. The answer would invariably be right but as the subject became more complex and she had to show her "workings out" she began to lose her high marks. Audrey could find no use for Algebra. An explanation from the teacher about its purpose would have helped but this was not forthcoming.

Audrey's first history lesson was learning all the dates, places and outcomes of England's battles. When she came to the Battle of Hastings in 1066 and was told that King Harold had been shot in the eye by one of his enemies she hastened to correct the teacher.

A LIFE of Enlightenment

"It didn't happen that way; one of Harold's men who was standing at the side of the field was about to send an arrow to the enemy when he got shot in the shoulder and this made him spin round and his arrow went into Harold's eye. So he actually lost an eye by one of his own men."

There was silence. Audrey had stood up to make this announcement. The eyes of the whole class were upon her. Her gaze swept the other students. "Well *some* of you must have been there too! Don't you remember?" Her look of appeal included her teacher.

Miss Whitworth fought her look of amazement before asking in her best tone of authority, "What is your name?"

"My name is Audrey."

"Sit down, Audrey! Don't ever interrupt this class again without putting your hand up first. Is that understood?" Audrey nodded.

"You are not asked or required to correct the history textbooks. You will learn what is written in them and you will be examined on that data. We are not interested in your imagined version of the loss of King Harold's eye. Do I make myself clear?"

"Yes Miss Whitworth, but it did happen the way I said, I saw it, I really did."

"I don't want to hear another word about this or any other historical event on which you may have an opinion; do you understand me?"

Audrey nodded again.

Miss Whitworth did not realise it at the time, but she had lost the interest of one of her brightest students and the opportunity to be aware of a whole new world of remembrance.

Audrey, over a period of time, paid less and less attention as more and more events that she doubted but was expected to accept, were given to her as absolute truths.

She also questioned the value of a subject that dealt with the past either rightly or wrongly. It seemed to Audrey that the present was the most important to her and that what she did in the present determined her future.

Eventually she had to write an essay on "The Greatness of the British

Empire." She loved writing and she tackled this assignment with joy.

She agreed that the Empire was great but wrote that the "Greatness" was undeserved because of the acts that it took to deserve it.

She wrote wars, battles, and killing one's fellow man or trespassing on another's land, and then killing the owners for objecting was criminal. She also noted that most of the wars she had studied had been fought on religious grounds, which religious people tended to gloss over in blind faith.

She quoted the Bible only because it suited her, and not because she believed in a book that she felt held too many contradictions. She hoped her teacher had not read that you should smite your enemies, but only that you should love your neighbours.

She remembered her talks with Dr. Gordon about the horse and the farmer, and other talks where each had agreed that because we were all the same as our fellow man you harmed yourself when you harmed another. She commented on this in her essay.

Audrey was hopeful that Miss Whitworth may have another look at her subject, perhaps from a different viewpoint.

Her essay received an 85% mark with good comments on her neat writing, her use of the English language, and her spelling, but with a final comment that the unpatriotic content left much to be desired.

Without being completely aware of it, Audrey was at the beginning of becoming wise about sharing her thoughts. She discussed this with Doctor Gordon on their way to their restaurant. "Discretion, I am told, is the better part of valour!" She stared at him, "What does that mean"?

"Discretion is acting or talking in such a way so as not to cause embarrassment."

"Who to?"

"Audrey, it is 'To whom?' and the answer is, to anyone."

"I know that valour means courage, being brave, so are you saying that it is better to be discreet rather than brave?"

Doctor Gordon smiled, "Yes, in certain situations, that is wise, especially when you are dealing with someone who is older and considers they know more than you do. Otherwise they may consider you to be precocious."

"That means 'development more mature than normal', doesn't it? I remember having to look it up when I was reading a book last year! So, why does it matter if someone thinks this? I don't understand why they would be embarrassed! You're older than I am and I can tell you things without you being embarrassed."

"But Audrey, she is your teacher!"

"So are you."

Doctor Gordon smiled. "Yes, but I am not your official teacher, and I am wise enough to sometimes wonder who is the teacher in this relationship. Ours is a partnership of student and teacher with a changing of roles at any given moment. When you correct or try to instruct your official teacher, who considers that she should know best, you place her in an unenviable position which she has to defend, sometimes by making your position less than hers, whether it is correct or not. I am sorry to have to bring this to your attention, because it is not good for you to censor your communication. Remember Audrey, no one can take away your ideas or your thoughts; but it would be wise while you are at school to be discreet in your communication. Do you understand?"

Audrey was silent, staring into space. Finally she said, "I understand it and I will do it, but frankly the whole idea gets up my nose!"

"I didn't say it would make you smile Audrey, but getting along with your teachers for the next few years might. Why not do your glad game. Find something in this to be glad about!"

She was as always mollified by his use of her expressions, and his gentle way of indicating that she should use her own philosophy, to sort out a situation that 'got up her nose'. She grinned at him; patting his hand on the steering wheel and saying "touché", letting him know he had scored a mark.

He gave her a hug saying, "Applying your viewpoints and your philosophy of the world, there is not anything that you cannot handle, once you have had time to look it over. I don't think I will ever be worried about you, now or ever! Do you realise what a remarkable thing that is to be able to say to a child, even one with a grown-up head on its shoulders?"

Audrey stared at him, "No!"

"Well that's not unexpected. Don't you ever look at yourself, or wonder who you are? Don't you ever question *you*?"

She shook her head. "Why would I do that?'

He smiled, mostly at himself. "Never mind Audrey, forget the question. Just cancel it and don't look for any answers!"

"I find life on this planet very complex!'

"Why do you say *'this planet'*?"

"Because that's where I am."

"Should you be somewhere else?

"No, not really!"

They had arrived at their restaurant. Audrey jumped out of the car, eager for her baked beans on toast. As she watched him lock the car with his key, turning to smile at her as he walked towards the door, she thought what a dear man he was and how lucky and grateful she was to have someone like him in her life.

She had no way of knowing at the time that the golden places in life often have short leases.

CHAPTER 13

Interesting Viewpoints

Audrey had been at her new school for six weeks before she got herself into trouble. Her Arts teacher gave a one-hour class assignment of drawing a horse and a cart.

Audrey managed to sketch the horse quite well, but when it came to have it pulling a cart the nightmare began.

The cart was too big for the horse, then too small, and then it looked as though it was chasing the horse by pushing the handles of the cart up its rear. Audrey got muffled giggles about this sketch. Frustrated by the whole event, she decided to go to the toilet, hoping that by the time she came back it would be time for her next lesson.

She had found that often teachers said you did not want to go to the toilet when you did.

To counteract this she had developed a method of developing hiccups at will. This always worked very well. She began to hiccup, while continuing to look absorbed in her work.

After a while her teacher looking at Audrey's bent head and finding the hiccup sound to be most annoying, ordered her to get a glass of water and not return until she was free of them.

A LIFE of Enlightenment

Audrey would reluctantly leave the room hiccupping all the way to the door, turn them off when she was on the other side and then decide what to do with her free time.

This time she went to the toilet block. The doors of each toilet were a head's width free of the floor and way down from the high ceiling. Between the top of the doors and the ceiling was an overhead bar that went across, parallel with the door but leaving between it and the door another wide space. This space was available for what the girls called monkey swings!

One stood on the toilet seat, launched herself into space and, grabbing the overhead bar with both hands, swung back and forth until one's arms ached, before dropping to the floor.

Audrey enjoyed this immensely. On this particular day she set herself a more challenging task.

She had a monkey swing, and then landed on the floor in the same toilet. She locked the door to bar herself from an easy way out and then climbed the white glossy wall tiles using only the seat and the toilet roll holder as a foothold, until she could clamber over the dividing wall into the next unit. She slid to the floor of the second unit, repeated the action until she had locked the doors of five of the six toilets. The last one she left unlocked and walked away from it, then started on the toilets on the other side. Her aim was to see how quickly she could lock ten of the twelve units and when complete, unlock them again.

Unfortunately for Audrey, the bell sounded for the end of her Arts period, when only eight of the doors had been locked. She had to leave in a hurry for her next English class, one of her favourite lessons.

The end of this period was also the end of the school day. Audrey had forgotten about the locked doors. She went to the toilet block to find girls knocking on locked doors, shouting variations of "Hurry up in there. I'm dying to go! Why are you taking so long?" Girls were jumping up and down. Some had their legs crossed and where furiously banging on doors.

Some had taken the initiative of balancing on the sinks and using them in their urgency. Audrey was at first shocked at the consequence of her ac-

Interesting Viewpoints

tion, and then joined in the laughter with some of the girls who had been fortunate enough to use the unlocked toilets or who had come into the nearby locker room.

Some of the girls had knelt on the floor and, seeing no evidence of an inhabitant, were complaining loudly of a jammed door. Doors were shaken, then, jolted by strong shoulders, but the locks held.

Audrey thought of going into a vacant open toilet and climbing the dividing walls to unlock, but she knew she would have little chance. The next girl was in as a door even slightly opened, and the occupant was assisted out with urgency.

Watching this was a comedy for most of the spectators without urgent needs, joining Audrey who was giggling almost out of control. She left, but on the way home, little spurts of laughter threatened to burst forth as the scene re-enacted in her mind. This continued through the evening meal. When her father asked, "What's going on? What have you been up to?" She shook her head and refused to share what had happened. Before she went to sleep, her night was filled with odd bursts of merriment.

The next morning at Assembly, the headmistress Miss Keating asked the third formers to leave and attend their first lessons whilst the rest of the school stayed behind. In orderly fashion the new students filed out, curious at their non-inclusion. Audrey's first lesson was geography. She didn't mind learning maps, or the products, minerals, and farming tendencies of a country, but the data about the past of a culture or civilization was questionable. She liked Miss Milburn without being overjoyed at the subject she taught. Audrey felt that Miss Milburn liked her even though she perhaps thought her student was a little strange, because she tended to challenge the truth she was being taught about the morals and cultures of the different civilizations. Audrey had a habit of pointing out that any event was only one viewpoint and that the other fellow never got to have his say; or worse still, it was all written up from hearsay and how could this be accurate.

On this day Miss Milburn started her lesson by telling the students that someone in the Upper school had locked the doors of the third former's toilets, leaving only four available for use which created embarrassment for all the girls who couldn't use them.

She went on to say that the janitor had a great deal of extra work that evening. The Head Mistress was extremely cross and if the culprit did not own up, the whole upper school may be punished.

Audrey was astounded. She raised her hand but was ignored. Miss Milburn said, "I do not want to debate or answer questions about this, just to satisfy your curiosity!"

In desperation Audrey rose to her feet and in a loud voice said, "I did it Miss Milburn, I locked the toilets!"

There was a stunned silence. The other students stared at her, some with admiration. Miss Milburn looked amazed.

"But you have only been in school six weeks!"

Audrey looked at her silently, trying to make sense of this remark.

"May I ask what prompted you to do this?"

"It started off with a horse and cart. I could draw the horse but I couldn't get the cart in the right place or the right size; then I got hiccups and was sent to get some water and told not to come back until I got rid of them. I went to the toilet block for water and decided to have some fun, but it turned out all wrong in the end." She started off happily explaining but her voice was trailing into misery as she finished.

Miss Milburn was silent for awhile, her gaze fixed on Audrey who silently returned it.

"You had better come with me, Audrey. The rest of you copy the map of England in the beginning of your text books. There is to be no talking. I will be back very shortly!"

She left the room with Audrey following. The headmistress's office was an island in the centre of the building with only one wall attached to the outside. It was only about fifty paces from Audrey's classroom.

Miss Milburn said, "Wait here," knocked on the door, and went in closing it behind her.

She came out after only a few minutes, saying, "Miss Keating has some-

Interesting Viewpoints

one with her. When that person comes out, knock on the door, and when she tells you to come in, you may enter and give her your confession. In the meantime, wait here! Do you understand?"

Audrey nodded. She stood there for fifteen minutes or more. No one came out or went in.

After a while longer she decided to take the initiative. There was a notice on the door that stated, KNOCK. WHEN THE BELL RINGS ENTER.

Audrey knocked and listened carefully for the bell. Nothing happened. She put her ear to the door. There was no sound of talking, or papers rustling; in fact, the room was deafening in its silence. She decided there must be another exit on the other side of the island, and that the visitor and the Headmistress had left and that she was forgotten.

Tapping her fingers, she drummed a tune on the door, humming as she tapped.

The door suddenly opened. Miss Keating, a rather stern looking woman in her early fifties, asked "Who are you and what do you think you are doing?"

Audrey was taken aback. "I was waiting for the bell to ring."

"The bell does not work. I called 'Come in' some time ago. Are you deaf?"

Audrey said, "No, but why don't you get the bell fixed? It is a thick door and it is hard to hear anything through it."

Miss Keating looked outraged. "Who are you, exactly, and why are you here?"

Audrey replied, "I have come to confess about the toilets. You see, I am the one who locked them!"

"But you are only a third former! You're a new student!"

Audrey badly wanted to ask why this had anything to do with the event, but felt she had not started off well in this interchange of words.

Standing in the doorway they sized each other up.

Audrey watched her eyes and felt that perhaps they had softened a little. Miss Keating's expression went from initial outrage to crossness and then puzzlement. She gazed at this small new student who watched her with a candid steady look and found it almost impossible to believe that this little child was not only mentally but physically able to perform such an act.

"You had better come in! What did you say your name was?"

"I didn't say, but it is Audrey Southgate."

She entered the room and stood in front of the large desk. Miss Keating sat in her chair, saying, "Well, what do you have to say for yourself?"

Audrey asked, "Would you like to have all of the story or just the part that gets me into trouble?"

Miss Keating did not know quite what to make of Audrey. She seemed polite, gentle, non-defensive, confident, and completely unremorseful. There was no bowed head, no fear of repercussions; just a steady almost interested gaze.

"You are not here to ask questions but to explain yourself. Start at the beginning!"

Audrey told everything except her ability to get hiccups on demand. When she got to the part of returning to the locker and toilet room and seeing what was happening she could not keep the merriment from her voice as she described the scene. This was her undoing; Miss Keating in no uncertain terms pointed out the consequences of her act in graphic unamused detail! Although Audrey felt that a flicker of a smile that was hard to control had passed over Miss Keating's face during the discourse of the outcome, there was no glimmer of amusement now. Finally, she said, "I shall think of a suitable punishment to fit your crime. You will come back to this office ten minutes before the end of your lunch period. In the meantime, return to your class and apply yourself diligently to your lessons. Is that understood?"

Audrey said, "Yes Miss Keating. I understand!"

She turned and left the room. Her geography lesson ended as she got to her classroom and she followed the rest of her classmates to the Gym for an hour of Physical instructions. Her classmates were eager to talk to her, but the activities were not conducive to conversation.

Interesting Viewpoints

Morning recess and then Chemistry in the laboratory followed, and then it was lunchtime.

The girls ate at long tables in the school hall with a prefect at one end and a Schoolteacher at the other. Despite only minimum and necessary talking being allowed, the news of the culprit had already spread and Audrey found she was being stared at mostly with amazement by both teachers and students. She heard the words, 'She's only a third former!' here and there and was puzzled by the comment.

She went outside when lunch was over, finding a quiet corner near some bushes close to an apple orchard that adjoined the school. This was an area that the students kept away from as it was patrolled on the other side of the wire fence by Alsatian dogs.

Audrey sat on the ground with her back to the fence. One of the dogs came up and sniffed her back. She kept perfectly still. As she was not moving or trying to enter, the dog watched her for a moment and then ambled away.

Audrey had no watch. She ran indoors twice to check the time and finally at ten to one o'clock, she again knocked on the headmistress's door.

She had to wait five minutes before she heard the loud "Come in!" She was saved by only a few seconds from knocking again. Miss Keating ignored Audrey standing in front of her desk, continuing her writing as though Audrey was not there. Finally she looked up.

"I haven't found a suitable punishment for your crime as yet. You must report to me again after school! Understood?" Audrey replied, "Yes! Understood!" and left the room.

This exact same scenario was played out after school that day, before Assembly the following morning, during the morning recess, and it seemed as though the lunchtime meeting would have the same result.

In the meantime, Audrey had been subject to lots of negative comments in relation to the Headmistress; she was mean, dealt out horrible punishments, hated children and loved to see them squirm and so on. Audrey received sympathy, admiration and dire warnings of consequences from many of the older students. She decided to ignore them all but she was also aware that she was being played at the end of a fishing line until she made some move that met with approval and ended this game of being kept on tenterhooks. She wasn't sure what her response was supposed to be. Installing fear into her never entered her thoughts.

She played her glad game and wrote line after line in her copybook of all the things she had found to be glad about in this event. She had met her Headmistress face to face and talked to her (an uncommon occurrence so early in school), she had found out how physically strong she was (those walls had been slippery, hard to climb and the sliding down was not easy), she was glad she had owned up and that all the school had escaped punishment and so on and so on. Now she looked the situation over and decided that this constant going to and fro was not making her smile.

She decided to share this thought with Miss Keating. Returning during the lunch recess and being told to return after school, Audrey said, "I'm sorry but I don't want to keep coming back anymore, because it doesn't make me smile. I will come at the end of school, so please have my punishment sorted out by then; I am willing to do whatever you wish at that time!"

She smiled at Miss Keating and left the room. She returned at the end of the school day. Miss Keating motioned her to a chair, saying: "You will have to wait until all the students have left for the day and the toilet wing is empty."

She went on with her work ignoring Audrey.

After a while she told her to check the wing and report back. Audrey returned saying there was no one in the area. Miss Keating stood up. "Follow me!"

She led Audrey back to the toilet block, leaned against a wall near the basins which had a good view of all the toilets and said, "You are going to show me exactly how you did this. I want you to lock the doors, swing and so on exactly as you did on the day. I am going to stand here and watch you!"

Audrey was intrigued, but eager to comply. She stood on the seat of the first toilet, launched herself into space and had a back-and-forth monkey swing, dropped to the floor, locked the door from inside and—giving a running commentary on her actions—climbed the wall and slid down into the adjacent cubicle. Miss Keating moved to a position outside the door but standing back as far as she could, so that she could see Audrey climbing over the top of the dividing wall.

Audrey stopped, saying, "Shall I go on?"

"Yes, but continue until you have locked all of them except the last one on each side."

Audrey was happy. This wasn't a punishment. This was fun! She wondered if she had to prove that she was the culprit; maybe this is what these actions were all about. Perhaps "You're only a third former" meant she wasn't capable and now she had to prove it. She was intrigued, confused but not unhappy. She decided to be as graceful as she could and to perform efficiently for Miss Keating.

She finished locking and stood outside waiting.

Miss Keating said, "Now unlock them in the same manner you locked them."

Audrey felt this was fair as having the same locked door trauma left for the girls would not have been appropriate.

She finished and went to stand in front of Miss Keating.

The Headmistress gazed at her for a few moments before saying, "Now you will continue to lock and unlock these doors until you are tired. I shall stay here to watch you and you will not be allowed to leave until I say so. You may think this is fun, but you will sing a different tune when you have done it a few more times!"

Audrey did not reply. She turned, went into the first toilet and started the process all over again. She felt challenged. She decided she would never be tired no matter what! She was not alarmed, only determined to stay the course. She wondered how many times locking or unlocking doors up and down the toilet block Miss Keating had in mind before she would be allowed to go home. School had finished at four o'clock. The wall clock in the toilet block now stood at five thirty. Miss Keating had twice asked Audrey if she was tired and had received a resounding "No, I'm fine!"

Audrey's arms were beginning to ache and her actions were slowing down. She no longer cared for portraying the graceful or professional look as she performed; only wanting to persist in going through the motions in one cubicle and through the next despite the tiredness of her body. It somehow seemed a matter of honour and tenacity not to give in.

After more questions of "Are you tired?", statements of "You must be tired now!", "I can tell you are tired!", and "Admit you are tired!" which came every few minutes after six o'clock—to which Audrey kept replying "No, I'm fine"—Miss Keating at seven o'clock ordered her to go home.

She collected her school bag and with her head held as high as she could muster, said, "Thank you and goodnight," and left her school for home. Once outside, she walked to the main road. A park ran parallel to the road, with the playing fields of her school on the other. There was little traffic at this twilight hour.

Audrey found that her legs were trembling and she could hardly walk. She sat on the edge of the pavement with her feet in the gutter, and laid her head on her arms. She wanted to cry but she was too tired even to let the tears gush forth.

Audrey must have been there for at least ten minutes when a car screeched to a halt and a kindly voice said, "It is Audrey, isn't it?"

She looked up to see her Uncle Percy standing there with a hand outstretched. "Are you alright, you haven't been run over or hit by anything have you?"

She said "No, I'm fine!" without adding "it just feels that way!" She was overjoyed to see him. He helped her to her feet, muttering, "Oh my! We are in a bad way," as she staggered to the car.

"Too much sport and too much climbing and then I got kept in after school. Mum will be wondering where I am."

"Well then, we had better get you home, hadn't we?"

Audrey was grateful for the ride and his acceptance of the situation. He was a good uncle whom she did not see often; always friendly and cheer-

Interesting Viewpoints

ful. He owned a timber mill and had a daughter called Winnie who would probably go to the same school as Audrey in a few years.

Audrey appreciated his lack of questions. He chatted about his work and family for the next twenty minutes and then parked his car outside her parent's home.

He came in, greeted everyone, stayed in the hallway as her parents thanked him, and headed out saying, "No trouble at all; found her sitting in the gutter so to speak, quite worn out; seems she has had a rough day, too much sport and all that. Poor little blighter; still I'll bet she will be as bright as a button after a good night's sleep." He smiled at Audrey patting her head as he walked towards the open door. She wanted to hug and thank him but he was gone with a cheery wave of his hand and she was left to face her parents.

Her mother said, "It's alright, we know all about it. Miss Keating rang me and I have to go to see her at school. Are you hungry? No? Well then straight into a hot bath and then bed!" Her father looked cross and started to say something, but Dorothy laid a restraining hand on his arm and moved between him and Audrey. She ushered her upstairs, supervised her bath, and tucked her in her bed. Audrey was grateful feeling comforted and protected from her father who she knew would have much to say.

She fell asleep almost immediately.

The next morning Audrey couldn't get out of bed. All her bones ached. Dorothy told her to stay where she was, brought her some breakfast and a book to read, and left her to her own devices.

Audrey went to school the following day still sore and somewhat subdued, but able to walk as though there was nothing wrong. The students seemed ignorant of the latest happenings and she decided not to enlighten them. The teachers obviously knew. They treated her brusquely, but she felt a little more kindly.

Her father had restricted his lecture to a fierce look saying crossly "School is for learning, not for playing pranks on people. Have you got that?"

Audrey nodded.

A LIFE of Enlightenment

"Well then, this is the last time I want to hear that you've been up to no good; no more of your antics my girl; that's a warning!"

He left the kitchen. She could feel his anger and was grateful for his leaving.

Audrey did not find out what conversations had occurred between her mother and Miss Keating. She asked her mother, who volunteered that their discussions had been by telephone as the hairdressing salon was busy and it was difficult to leave clients during the day. No other information was forthcoming and Audrey did not like to ask. In this event, she felt she had experienced light repercussions from her parents and was happy to leave well enough alone!

Audrey had mixed thoughts about Miss Keating. She felt she was stern yet fair. On reflection she could see that Miss Keating had exhibited equal stamina to her own. She had stood there watching Audrey's antics for two and a half hours which must have been very trying, when all she really wanted to do was go home. Audrey also felt the mode of punishment had been not only unexpected but also quite unique.

She wondered if this would be workable for other things. If you wanted someone to stop or not to do something, and then made them do it until they were tired of it, would it be a cure?

This was something to discuss with Doctor Gordon on his next visit.

CHAPTER 14

Getting to Know Each Other

They were sitting in the restaurant drinking their second cup of tea when she told him of the latest happenings.

Doctor Gordon smiled as he said, "You are very busy working out how to handle the life you are creating, particularly at school! Tell me why it was so important to win. Did you consider Miss Keating your opponent?"

Audrey considered the matter carefully, "No, I don't think it had anything to do with winning!"

"I believe you, but only because I have not seen any evidence of you being of a competitive nature. So, Audrey, what was it about?"

"I think it was a matter of honour. Like owning up and then taking the punishment without protesting or complaining. I'm not sure but I think that had a lot to do with it."

"Do you feel Miss Keating understood that?"

Audrey shook her head, "I don't think so, but perhaps I underestimate her?"

Doctor Gordon laughed as he said, "Well, eventually she will get to know you."

Audrey sat back in her chair, "I hope not, I shall be careful to keep out of her way."

"Audrey, nothing is going to dampen your spirits for very long, I have a sense that you and Miss Keating are fated to get to know each other even if it takes some escapades to do it!"

She grinned at him saying, "I should be horrified, I don't know why I am not."

He smiled at her, "There is nothing that will ever go on in your life that you cannot handle, even if the only handling you can do is finding something to be glad about!"

She gave him a quizzical look. Their last few meetings had resulted in similar comments; all to do with her ability to handle, sort out, or be glad about something. There was something else going on here. What was it? She leaned forward, looking into his eyes, saying nothing.

For the first time in their relationship Audrey suspected there was something he was holding back from saying; she felt he was a little uneasy. This disappeared quickly as he smiled at her and said, "Come, Audrey, it is time to go!"

One week later the gamekeeper from the orchard and Audrey stood in front of Miss Keating's desk.

"Found her up a tree I did; the dogs were all barking below and she was trying to sweet talk them into being quiet. When I got her down she had three apples in her blazer pocket. Now in my book that's stealing and I want her to be taught a lesson as an example, like!"

Miss Keating gave him a severe look. "Mr Bootle, how many years have you been a gamekeeper for the apple orchard?"

"Nigh on fifteen years ma'am!" he answered proudly.

Miss Keating gave him a small smile in acknowledgement. "During that time Mr Bootle, have any of my girls stolen or even attempted to steal any of your produce?"

"No ma'am, me dogs keep 'em at bay!"

"Then the punishment this child will receive does not have to serve as an example; you seem to have the orchard protection well taken care of; I

Getting to Know Each Other

appreciate your visit Mr Bootle, and this unfortunate incident will never happen again. Allow me to show you the way out."

Miss Keating stood, led him to the door, opened it and gave him a small smile and a nod as he departed.

Now Audrey had all her attention. "Well, Audrey, we meet again, and after such a short interval. What do you have to say?"

"Well, the tree on our side overhangs the fence. I made friends with their Alsatian dog. I talked to him and eventually he let me stroke him when I poked my hand through the wire, so I didn't think he would bark at me, and he didn't. It's just that I didn't know there were three dogs and after I climbed up and over to their tree the other two arrived and made a racket, and then the gamekeeper caught me."

"Why did you do this, may I ask?" Miss Keating looked at her sternly.

Audrey sighed, "Just to see if I could. It was a challenge. The apples were proof I had been there. I suppose it is stealing but I didn't look at it that way at the time! I didn't want to eat them. They are crab apples and very sour. My Auntie Jean makes jam out of them and says that they are not fit for anything else!"

Miss Keating gave a small smile. "Audrey you have just suggested your own punishment."

Audrey, in wonder, said, "Now how did I manage that?"

Miss Keating said "For the next three lunch times you will have three crab apples to eat and nothing else. As they are liable to give you a rather bad stomach ache, you will report to the school nurse after lunch. She will dose you with some syrup of figs. Do you understand?"

Audrey nodded.

"You may leave, and Audrey…I do not want to see you again in my office."

Audrey said under her breath, as she walked towards the door, "Well I don't really want to be here!"

Two weeks later Audrey was back again.

One of her mother's hairdressing clients a Mrs Jessup, saw Audrey when she came home from school one day and smiled at her saying, "I've seen you walking past my door on your way to the swimming baths. Next time you're passing, knock and I will give you a little toffee. I make it myself from treacle. Had some tins I bought just before the war started. "Just as well; haven't been able to get it for years now." She turned to Dorothy, "Next time I come I will bring you a little, just for the family."

Dorothy was very pleased, Sweets, and toffees of any description, were very hard to get even with a ration book. Many of the shop windows were full of them, but they were really small pieces of wood in highly colourful wrappers; in reality, there was nothing for sale.

Audrey decided this knock on the door would take some organizing, but it would be worth it for some treacle toffee. She was used to walking at the back of the two-girls wide line, but Miss Rowland had moved her to the front when there had been too much merriment at the rear. Audrey decided she would have to knock on the door when she was at the front of the class and then hurry to the middle or rear in order to give Mrs Jessop time to open the door and hand her the sweets. Just before the students came to this hilly block of houses, they had to cross a main side-street. Miss Rowland stayed at the rear until all the students had crossed and then hurried to the front again. This manoeuvre left Audrey undetected for a brief time.

The following Wednesday, just after they crossed the street she knocked on the door and ran swiftly towards the rear. Mrs Jessup came to the door gave her a little bag and quickly closed it.

Audrey ran back towards the front of the student file, only to find the girls on the inside track were knocking on each door as they went down the street. Only the reappearance of Miss Rowland stopped any further knocking.

Doors began opening but the students had already passed and were well down the hill.

Miss Rowland, although aware that notice was being taken of the girls by the occupants of the houses, was not cognizant of the cause. She cau-

Getting to Know Each Other

tioned them to be quiet, and they proceeded towards the swimming baths with subdued giggles and guilty looks exchanged.

Audrey was sent for by Miss Keating the next day.

She stood in front of the desk once again, waiting for the inevitable questioning.

"Well Audrey, this is the third time you have come to see me in almost as many weeks…I doubt that I have seen any student in all the five years they spend here as much as I have seen you in less than three months. Now why do you think this is happening?"

Remembering Dr. Gordon's words, Audrey said with respect, "Perhaps we are fated to get to know each other!"

"You seem to have an answer for everything, don't you? Well, tell me what you know about knocking on all the doors in a certain block in Mill Street. Do you realise that one of the occupants was ill that day and had to leave her bed to answer the door? The school has received one telephone call after another complaining about our students. Now tell me your part in this, as I am sure you played one!"

Audrey explained it from the beginning, finishing by saying, "I didn't want anyone else to knock at any of the doors. The others must have thought it was a new game or something, so they did what I did! I'm sorry about the sick lady; would you like me to go to see her and explain?"

"Certainly not! However you are the ringleader in all this! I may add that your behaviour was not within the school rules. You do not socialise for sweets or any other reason within school hours! Do I make myself clear?"

Audrey nodded.

"You will write a personal letter of apology to all the residents in this block, whether they complained or not…You will draft a letter and bring it to me and then you will copy it in your neatest handwriting so that there is one for everyone. The letter must be most apologetic and very sincere! Have the draft ready by the end of school!"

"May I have all the names and address please?"

A LIFE of Enlightenment

"No, I will fill those in. Leave a few lines at the top of each page. Do you understand?"

"Yes, Miss Keating!'

"You may leave the room."

Audrey pondered the letter. She felt an explanation would be justified. She also felt this would probably be unacceptable as well as giving herself a great deal of writing.

In the end she wrote:

On behalf of Greenfields school and all the students who knocked at the doors in Mill St., I confess to be the ringleader in this event and do most sincerely and remorsefully apologise for any inconvenience this caused you and/or your family.

Yours truly,

Audrey Southgate

She delivered this to Miss Keating, who read it through two or three times before stating her acceptance. She commented on Audrey's neat handwriting. Audrey was pleased. It was the first validation resulting in a compliment from Miss Keating. Suddenly the Headmistress seemed more human. Audrey already respected her, but now there was even a possibility of liking her despite the apparent sternness. Audrey felt she would always be fair, if firm.

Audrey spent a long night copying fifteen letters.

Her mother, knowing the story, was sympathetic. When Miss Keating had rung the house, Dorothy did her best to defend Audrey. In desperation, she had finally said, "Well maybe she is easily led?"

Miss Keating had almost snorted. "Mrs Southgate, how can you say that? Audrey is a born leader; surely you know that by now?"

Dorothy had apologised and given up on the conversation. Fred remained ignorant of this event. He had arrived home from work and gone

Getting to Know Each Other

straight to a meeting to discuss the disbanding of the ARP.

Audrey copied her letters whilst he was away. She was grateful to her mother, who had not said that she would not tell her father, but simply told Audrey, "Get these letters finished before he comes home; he'll be tired and want to go to bed; and I don't want you staying up all hours on a school night either!"

Audrey complied, delivering the letters to Miss Keating before assembly.

There were two replies. Miss Keating sent for her and gave them to her to read. The theme of the letters was a simple "apology accepted" and "girls would be girls and sometimes mischievous, so to speak."

Audrey smiled. "I think I have been forgiven or at least my apology has been accepted."

Miss Keating nodded, but didn't return the smile. "Audrey, I have seen more of you in my office than I have seen of my head girl in the whole five years she has been in this school! You have been here only a matter of weeks. This is completely unacceptable; do you understand me? I trust that you also agree?"

Audrey nodded, but added "I feel that we are getting to know each other, although I realise you don't like the 'why' of it all!" "Audrey, that was a very poorly constructed sentence. I trust you will pay more attention to your English classes. Now go to your lessons and remember: I don't want to see you again, unless it is to congratulate you on some outstanding achievement."

Audrey left the office, wondering what would be considered an 'outstanding achievement'. She could think of quite a few but none of them would be considered academic.

CHAPTER 15

The Jilting of Audrey's Fiancé

When Audrey turned eleven, she realized one day that she had some serious thinking to do about her promised marriage to Dr. Gordon when she turned twenty-one. She was only just past the halfway mark to this special age, and already she knew she was beginning to have doubts.

Audrey loved Dr. Gordon, warmly, sincerely and with tenderness and a caring that was very mature for her age. However, when she thought about his forty-one years which would be his age when she was twenty one, her heart sank. At forty-one he would want to have his pipe and slippers; she doubted that he would want to go dancing and probably not to the picture theatre as often as before. He would probably want to stay home and have an odd friend or two around occasionally for a game of cards, just like her parents did.

Audrey found all these thoughts alarming! Where was the adventure, the challenges, the reaching for the stars and so forth? Under these circumstances, Audrey felt she could not ever marry him; she wanted him as a mentor and her very best friend; in other words, she wanted the present relationship to continue.

She hesitatingly explained this to her mother, half expecting some retribution. To her surprise her mother said, "Well you must tell him!"

"What am I going to tell him exactly?"

"That you don't want to marry him!"

Audrey knew that it was only fair to do this, but her heart sank at the thought of going through with this event.

Saturday came. The maroon car stopped outside her home and he climbed out of the driver's seat. She watched his dear familiar figure as he came to the door and knocked. Always he was courteous. Once as a child, she had run out to meet him as the car arrived.

He had explained that young ladies were always called for by a gentleman coming to the door, escorting them to the car, opening the door, and only shutting it when they were comfortably settled.

When she said that she was not a young lady, he had assured her this was not so. The size of your body has nothing to do with how you behave or how anyone should behave towards you.

"But if I don't behave like a young lady, why should anyone treat me like one?"

"Because it is a matter of honour to always be a gentleman no matter what the circumstances are or what they may become. In the same way it is a matter of honour for a young lady to behave in the same fashion."

She protested, "But everyone says I am a tomboy!"

Doctor Gordon smiled. "Perhaps you are at the moment, but that will change! You may not be aware of it, but even as a tomboy you have a dignity that comes from knowing in your heart who you are. You may not understand this now, but one day you will. A true dignity is very hard to shake and impossible to lose. It is more than just good manners. Good manners are just a demonstration and these can be learned. Dignity is knowing who you are and acting as such. Do you understand?"

Audrey felt this needed a great deal of thought and had merely nodded without comment at the time.

Today she thought back on this event; probably because she had resisted the urge to run out to greet him, only wanting to get in the car and get her

The Jilting of Audrey's Fiancé

declaration done. Now she sat quietly in the car, wondering what to tell him, how to say that she didn't want to marry in ten years' time. Doctor Gordon glanced at her and said, "You are very quiet Audrey. You are obviously pondering on something important. Do you want to tell me about it?"

"Not yet! Could we go for a walk in the Park instead of going to the pictures?"

"Of course! Broadfield Park?"

"Yes please. Do you think that courage has anything to do with dignity?"

Doctor Gordon smiled. "It may. Courage, dignity and honour may sometimes overlap or go hand in hand. What made you ask that question, Audrey?"

She sighed, "Well, I need some courage to tell you something and once you said I had dignity and I was hoping they went together."

They had arrived at the Park and he was holding her hand as he helped her from the car.

"Audrey, you know you can tell me anything. I will not be cross or judgemental, but that doesn't mean that we won't talk it over as we usually do. Now what is it you wish to tell me?" Walking, they had arrived at a park bench. Audrey tugged at his hand as he sat down beside her and then played with his fingers.

He watched her for a moment, "Audrey, you always play with my fingers when you have something of importance to tell me. This must be quite serious for you to be so anxious."

She nodded, looking him straight in the eye she said "I can't marry you!" and burst into tears.

She sobbed brokenheartedly against his chest. Above the pain in her chest she could feel his arm around her holding her close, and his murmuring "It's alright, Audrey. It is alright, really it is," and then "Oh my dear!" as her sobs got more intense.

Eventually she cried herself out. Her face swollen, her eyes red with the tears that kept coming unexpectedly, she tried to explain how she felt.

He listened attentively. "Audrey, you are quite correct. Twenty years is a big difference and I knew someday that you would think the same. It is no matter; we will always be the very best of friends and still see each other occasionally."

She was beginning to smile through her tears. She blew her nose hard into the handkerchief he had provided, wiped away the last of her tears, and handed him the hankie. He smiled putting it in his pocket, before she realized she should have got it washed before returning it. Anticipating her request for its return, he gave her a hug saying "It is no problem; it will be washed with all my other clothes that require attention. Now, isn't it time for our raisin toast and baked beans?

She smiled at him, gave him a big hug, and held his hand as they returned to the car.

In the restaurant she became her bright chatty self. She told him of the latest school exploits, saying, "You were right about Miss Keating and me getting to know each other; but she is not very keen on the idea. In her own way she says she has seen enough of me to last her for the next five years."

"I still feel that you will get to know each other better than you do now. Wait to see if that is not the case."

They ate in silence for a while; the always interested gaze of the waitress making them smile conspiringly at each other.

As Doctor Gordon poured his second cup of tea he said lightly, "Of course, now that you have jilted me, you realise I will have to find someone else to marry?"

Audrey was startled. "Why?"

"Because I would like to marry and have children!"

"Oh…when do you want to do this?"

"I might do it very soon Audrey. There is no point in wasting time!"

She was ashamed of her thought 'I don't want him to marry anyone else,' and concerned that he might pick up her thought.

He said lightly and smiling, "Audrey, how would you feel if I married another young lady. It might even be a redhead!"

The Jilting of Audrey's Fiancé

"Oh you wouldn't! Not a redhead."

He smiled at her. "I might."

Audrey decided he was teasing and changed the subject. However, the next weeks turned out to be quite enlightening.

CHAPTER 16

Doctor Gordon Gets Married

One week later Audrey came home after running an errand for her mother.

She came into the kitchen where her mother was standing at the table peeling potatoes for the evening meal. Audrey laid the shopping bag on the table and was about to turn away when her mother looking at her carefully and said, "Doctor Gordon rang up. I don't know how to tell you this, but he's getting married in three weeks and wants to know if you will be one of the bridesmaids. Do say yes!"

Audrey was stunned. The moment crystallized. Her mother was still holding a potato and the peeler; the concerned look on her face seemed etched into the moment. Nothing moved. Time froze. Audrey felt pain in her heart. Her stomach was fluttering and unshed tears were hurting her eyes. Time moved into a new now. Her mother looked at her expectantly. Audrey said in a shaking voice, "No, I can't!" hiding her face and shaking her head.

She ran upstairs to her bedroom.

Dorothy decided to leave her alone for awhile. Audrey was always better left alone when she was upset. Her mother was used to her reappearing with a philosophical insight or discussion that seemed to sort things out in her mind. This time however she decided that if Audrey did not appear when the evening meal was ready, it would be time for some motherly comfort.

Alone in her room, Audrey sat on the side of the bed, aware of the pain in her chest, and fighting the grief that was stinging her eyes and causing lumps in her throat. She made a valiant effort to be calm and collect her thoughts.

She lost.

She felt betrayed. It was illogical to be so upset. Logic demanded that she be sensible and understanding. After all he did say he would be looking for a wife; he wanted to have children. He had explained it quite well and Audrey, at least with her mind, had understood.

Now, she was amazed at her reaction. The emotion she felt was out of all proportion to what was currently happening. Some deep pain was bleeding through from some forgotten time when she was meant to suffer but had only glossed over it. Perhaps now it was time to let it all out and admit the heartache. Audrey knew there was something to discover but at this moment it seemed out of sight.

Audrey gave up and surrendered to her feelings.

Burying her head in the pillow, gulping back huge sobs that racked her chest she cried uncontrollably. Her chest ached. Her nose became blocked. She had trouble getting her breath. She felt her heart was breaking, and for the first time knew the feeling of one of the most used expressions she had previously read only in books.

It took a long time for the tears to subside. When she felt they were finished she washed her face and bathed her swollen sore eyes with a flannel.

When she returned to her room, her mother was waiting. She wrapped her arms around Audrey saying, "I thought this might happen, but you must remember you were the one who jilted him."

Her mother hesitated, undecided what next to say; she gave Audrey a hug before continuing. "You can't carry on like this; you need to wish him well. If he didn't care about you, he would never have asked you to be a bridesmaid. Only his fiancée would generally ask a girl to be a bridesmaid; the fact that he did makes it something special. You must not be selfish about this. You were a bridesmaid for your Auntie Jean so there is nothing strange in this for you. You do know all about it!"

Audrey's only response was to sniff and bury her head in her mother's chest.

Dorothy paused, gently stroking Audrey's back. "Come, this isn't like you. Now be brave and call him. Tell him you will be a maid at his wedding!"

Audrey pulled away from her mother's arms, afraid the cuddles would only want to make her cry again. She shook her head.

Her mother said, "Think about it and give him your answer tomorrow. He said he will ring again and this time he will expect to speak to you. You must talk to him!"

Audrey nodded as her mother turned to leave.

Being alone was more comfortable. She knew she needed to think this through and come to terms with it. It was difficult. Her head was unclear, her mind a muddle. She fought to rise above it, looking for a clean uncluttered space where reason could be the master of emotion.

Tears unexpectedly came from nowhere and rolled down her cheeks as though they had a mind of their own. She used another clean handkerchief, wiping her eyes and blowing her nose. Audrey was aware that the part of her that was always present but unseen was watching this event with interest, yet without comment. She was aware of this yet it didn't seem to help. She felt too tired to further sort out any of her feelings.

Audrey wisely decided to sleep on it and see how it all looked in the morning.

She undressed, put on her pyjamas, and climbed into bed. Grief, she discovered, was very exhausting.

Her mother, checking in a bit later to invite her to come downstairs for her dinner, found her asleep with swollen eyes and a red nose.

The next day Doctor Gordon phoned shortly after she had arrived home from school.

He found her sad "Hello" disconcerting. She remained silent as he talked.

"Audrey, I am so sorry that I did not tell you about Marjorie before this. It was cowardly of me. I just didn't know how to go about it without causing you too much upset. I was so grateful when you took the initiative on Saturday."

He paused but she remained silent.

"Now, I realise from what your mother has told me that the suddenness of the announcement has been a big shock. Now it is time to be honest. I have known Marjorie for almost 2 years and I love her dearly. We wish to marry and have a family. I love you also but in a different way; the same way that you love me." He paused again, continuing as Audrey did not speak.

"I so want you to be at our wedding and I would love you to be one of Marjorie's bridesmaids. Would you like to be one? Oh, one other detail Audrey, I don't want you to have any more shocks. Marjorie does have red hair…"

Doctor Gordon paused again, expecting a comment. There was silence.

He said, "Would you like to be a bridesmaid?"

Audrey said "No, thank you," and slowly put the phone down. It took Audrey another week to come to terms, not with the impending marriage, but with her reaction to it. She was used to having Doctor Gordon as her sounding board. Now her mentor seemed unavailable. Audrey felt that she was now on her own. She felt abandoned. Audrey knew this was illogical, nevertheless the feeling was there. She also knew she had to be self-sufficient and independent.

Surprisingly, the consideration was not overwhelming. It felt appropriate, sensible and even adventurous. Audrey felt this was a new phase in her life; one of growing up.

She also felt a little ashamed of her reaction to Doctor Gordon's news. She remembered a talk they had shared one day over tea. They had been discussing how most people reacted to upsets; and only a few responded.

Doctor Gordon Gets Married

He had complimented her by saying that his observation was that she usually responded rather than reacted. Now, Audrey felt she had let herself down.

They had decided that "response" came from responsibility. From realising that one's thoughts and viewpoints were one's own internal choice.

Reaction came from deciding that an external source was causing trauma and it couldn't be helped.

Most people considered this was normal and that they were at the mercy of their reaction. Audrey and Doctor Gordon had also decided that one always had a choice of which attitude to adopt at the time, and that they were only at the mercy of their own choice.

Audrey was fond of splitting up words to understand their meaning. Her conclusions were not always correct and her definitions often caused some merriment.

At that time she had suggested that the word "responsibility" meant *'to respond with ability'* and they were both happy with this new definition.

Doctor Gordon had telephoned again during her week of sorting out, asking Audrey for the last time if she would be a bridesmaid. She had said an emphatic "No." Now it was too late to change her mind. The idea still didn't make her smile, but she felt she could have at least granted his request. She wondered if she would ever see him again or had he gone from her life forever…

Audrey was not aware at the time, that—from this point on— whenever there was a trauma in her life, her method of handling it would be to come to terms with it and respond by always becoming even more self-sufficient and independent than before.

Her life indeed was changing.

CHAPTER 17

The Heart Doesn't Break, It Stretches With Exercise

Life went on.

Audrey continued with her schooling. It was uneventful for some weeks until a girl in Audrey's class reported that a special fountain pen she had been given for her birthday had been stolen.

All the girls were asked to lift the lids of their desks and two teachers devoid of pupils for that period examined each desk. The pen was found in Audrey's desk.

Audrey denied all knowledge of it. She had no idea how it had got there or who had put it there.

Her teacher's question "Well, it didn't just walk there all by itself did it?" left Audrey feeling uncomfortable.

The next remark, "You had better report to the Head. I understand you are an unconventional student and she will know how to deal with you" left nothing more troublesome to be desired.

Audrey knocked on Miss Keating's familiar door, pressing her cheek against it to hear the "Come in."

A passing teacher observing this immediately chastised Audrey and entering Miss Keating's office reported Audrey for attempting to listen to a private conversation.

Miss Keating had been discussing the Easter break with the Assistant headmistress and Audrey could tell from her overheard tone, if not the words, that she was not amused at the interruption.

Audrey felt that she was not on a winning streak this day. Eventually she was summoned into the office.

Miss Keating considered the familiar figure. "I was hoping not to see you until graduation day. Now here you are again! What is it *this* time?"

Audrey said, "Well, it's two things! Firstly, I was only listening for your 'Come In', because the bell might not be fixed yet. I was not eavesdropping. Secondly, a good fountain pen that belonged to a girl in my class was stolen and a teacher found it in my desk."

Miss Keating contemplated Audrey's face, "did you take it?'

Audrey said "No!"

"Do you know who did?

"No!'

"If you did know who took it and put it in your desk, would you tell me?"

Audrey briefly considered the question, then answered, "No!"

A glimmer of a smile passed across Miss Keating's face. "That's what I thought. You may go!"

"Do I have to come back later?"

"No, why should you?"

Audrey said "Well, I'm used to it?", looking perplexed.

Miss Keating sighed. "Sit down for a moment. We need some understanding between us! Audrey, whenever there has been some mischief in your vicinity, you have always immediately owned up when you are in the wrong. Sometimes I feel you may even delight in it, almost as though you throw down the gauntlet to see what will come out of it."

Audrey had difficulty hiding a smile.

"I can tell by your face that I am right with these words. I also know you are honest. I expect this honesty to continue throughout not only your schooling but your whole life. Do I make myself clear?"

The Heart Doesn't Break, It Stretches With Exercise

Audrey nodded.

"You may go!"

Audrey said smilingly "Thank you," with new respect and some affection in her voice.

She thought about the conversation as she walked back to her classroom. She decided she really liked Miss Keating. Audrey felt she had never been very frightened of her, but if there had been even a little fear it had now gone. She felt they had equal respect for each other and a little affection, even though that part may always remain hidden.

Audrey entered her classroom. Her teacher and the students looked enquiringly towards her, expecting her to be downcast and looking guilty. Her teacher raised her eyebrows.

Audrey said simply, "I was believed!" and bent her head over her text book.

She was looking forward to telling Doctor Gordon about this event, when she suddenly realised that she did not know if she would ever see him again.

Her mother had said that he had gone away on his honeymoon. Audrey had no idea how long 'honeymoons' were supposed to last. Did anyone really go to the moon with their honey? She felt it feasible but as unlikely as the people who might live on the moon would ever come down for a 'honeyearth'. Audrey flippantly shared these thoughts with her mother.

Dorothy said "Don't be silly," but found it impossible to answer Audrey's question regarding why is it called a honeymoon.

Five weeks after his wedding, Doctor Gordon called.

"Audrey, would you like to go to our restaurant on Saturday afternoon so that we may talk?"

"Yes please, I'm so happy to hear from you! I'm alright now and I hope you are, and I hope you are happy too!"

She could feel him smiling as he said, "I knew you would come through this and be your usual bubbling self. I look forward to seeing you."

Saturday was an eventful day.

Firstly she apologised for her behaviour. She pointed out her 'reaction' and told him she was ashamed of her inability to just 'respond'.

Doctor Gordon was quick to point out how soon she had responded thereafter. "Audrey, it doesn't matter that it took a few days for you to understand and handle this so that there was no more upset. You should be proud, not sorry. Some people go through life never handling some of their upsets. This often leaves them with bitterness or anger to a point where they don't even communicate with a person they once loved for many years; sometimes even a lifetime. You have done well."

She thanked him, considering whether to tell him all of the thoughts she had along the way to clearing her upset. She was holding his hand across the table which she had grasped in sincerity during her apology. Why not tell all of it?

She hesitated then plunged in saying, "Do you remember the story of King Harold and the arrow and the talk we had about other lifetimes?"

"Yes, I do very well." he smiled at her.

"Well, when I was upset it also seemed as though what was happening was not sufficient cause for all the upset. I thought my heart was breaking. I even thought dying might be a good idea. I felt abandoned, even though it didn't make sense. It was my awareness of a part of me that never gets involved but just looks on that stopped me, and made me look more deeply at what was happening. I feel that what I discovered, although I don't have exact details, must be correct, because when I spotted it and stopped querying what I found, the upset started to drain away just as though I had pulled the plug in the bathtub to let the water out."

She was aware she was talking very fast; indeed she was almost out of breath. Yet she knew that her thoughts had to be said.

His look of interest had not changed although she had the feeling that he knew what she was going to say.

She took a deep breath.

"We have known each other before. When I first saw you when I was just a little girl, I *knew* you. Do you remember how I clung to your leg the

The Heart Doesn't Break, It Stretches With Exercise

first day we met? I knew you were a friend. I think I loved you right away because I loved you a long time ago and I was pleased to have you back in my life; I mean, *this* lifetime! I think you knew it too, although you didn't say anything, but maybe you didn't realise all of it then, because I didn't either; but you must have felt something, because you went to so much trouble to help me. I think you thought of the engagement because we have done it before and it was a natural thing to do. I feel a lot of my upset was because it went wrong long ago, and somehow I lost you at that time. So you see, this time felt somehow like a repeat, so there were two upsets to handle. I'm not making excuses, but I think that's why it was so hard and I couldn't stop crying…Am I making sense?"

The compassionate look on his face made her want to cry. She patted his hand saying, "It's alright now; really it is. Please don't feel bad, I didn't tell you this to upset you. I just wanted to explain."

Doctor Gordon said, "Oh my dear!" Holding her two hands firmly in his own, he looked off into the distance. She could see that he was considering how to handle this, and this she did not want.

She said, "Please don't work out how to talk to me, just tell me how you feel. I know by your face that a lot is happening inside you. Just tell me about that! There is nothing that I cannot handle now. Even you denying everything I have said is alright. Really it is!"

He said, "Oh my dear Audrey, I have no wish to deny anything. While you were talking, bells were ringing in my head. I admit they sounded like alarm bells in the beginning but as you spoke, all my reactions to you right from the time we met became explained and infinitely clearer. When you said you lost me, I had the distinct impression that I had passed away. I do not know how or why I died but that is unimportant. I understand why you have always been important to me right from the time that we…shall I say resumed contact? I'm sure your terminology in this department is so much better than mine. For you it seems as natural as talking about the weather. For me it is something new and unfamiliar, and yet not as strange as I thought it might be. I am surprising myself." Audrey was delighted. She leaned over the table and kissed one of his hands. "Welcome to past lives, and I guess future ones. After all you can't have one without the other!'

Doctor Gordon laughed. In return he gently kissed both of her hands and said "Well this is the most eventful afternoon that we have had to date; don't you agree?"

Audrey smiled, "Yes, but it is also a very happy one!"

They had pushed their tea aside while they talked. It seemed like a barrier to their conversation. Now Doctor Gordon called the waitress over, apologising for ignoring the food and drink. He ordered a fresh supply.

They were quiet, waiting for their order. Looking at each other and smiling. Conversation started again as the waitress reappeared.

Audrey told him of the latest school escapades and her recent brush with Miss Keating.

He reiterated the 'constant company' he felt she would be keeping with the Headmistress, that he had predicted for the future.

Audrey frowned but didn't protest.

The wedding and honeymoon were not mentioned. This day in particular was *their* time and it seemed fitting that nothing was allowed to intrude.

As they drove to her home, they talked of future arrangements. Because he now had other commitments, they agreed to meet once a month, to skip the films, and just have tea and conversation on a Saturday.

Audrey said, "It sounds like a good title for a book, *Tea and Conversation*."

He laughed. "Then write it, Audrey. Anything you want to write will be interesting to read. Your viewpoints on life will be interesting, even to a philosopher."

"Tell me," he said, "how do you feel in your heart now? Is everything alright for you?"

"Absolutely!" she smiled at his profile. "I discovered something about hearts!"

His smile was gentle. "And what is your discovery?"

Audrey said, "They don't really break; they just stretch with exercise. I have a feeling mine is going to get plenty."

The Heart Doesn't Break, It Stretches With Exercise

Doctor Gordon gave her a hug as he handed her from his car. "I have implicit faith in your ability to 'respond' and handle anything that may come your way," he called as he climbed into the driver's seat. "I will call you in three weeks!"

Audrey watched him drive away. She felt happy and pleased with the outcome of their talk. A small part of her world had been clarified: the i's dotted the t's crossed. She still had her mentor and her best friend and although the frequency of their meetings was going to be less, it felt as though it should be. She was growing up quickly and now it was up to her to make the journey as smooth as possible. She was ready to begin the next stage!

CHAPTER 18

Audrey Creates a Blow Out

By the time Audrey was twelve she was finding school to be tiresome.

Many of her lessons she found to be irrelevant and others she regarded with disinterest. Her only interest in chemistry was in putting two solutions together that she was told must not be mixed, as they could, in the right combination, be explosive. She found the right combination and blew out one of the windows of the school laboratory.

Miss Keating gazed at her silently, before asking a resigned "Why".

Audrey said, "Well, I was told that the right combination was not easy to find. I just thought I would try it; that's all!"

"How long did it take you? How many attempts?"

"Just one!"

"How do you explain that?"

Audrey looked as perplexed as she felt. "Sometimes I just know things that *I don't know I know*…and then it just happens!"

Miss Keating blinked, and then decided to ignore the clumsy sentence structure. "Audrey, someone may have been hurt!" "But they weren't, I did it on a bench near the window, when there was no one close, just in case."

Miss Keating sighed. "What am I to do with you? Why are you like this?"

Audrey gave a small smile, "I think it is my sense of adventure. I don't mean to be wicked as such!"

Miss Keating asked, "Are you very interested in chemistry? Are you contemplating a career in this field?"

Audrey adamantly shook her head, "No, not at all!"

"Then why bother with this experiment?"

Audrey was silent, contemplating the question. "I think it was a mixture of things: it was a challenge, and I needed some interest and adventure. Chemistry has no interest for me. I like to know the purpose that something has rather than the 'how'. In other words *'How can I use this?'* I don't know what I want to do, but I don't feel a great deal of what I learn here is going to be useful, although that experiment might be useful for making fireworks!"

Miss Keating, looking slightly annoyed, asked, "What, may I ask, do you consider of no use?"

"I actually feel that way about lots of things in my life including my schoolwork. For example, learning all the dates of the Battles of the Empire; who was fighting and why; who won, (if anyone really wins a war); has no use to me unless I want to be a Historian. I couldn't wait to drop Latin after my first year and I was so happy to drop German after my second. Latin is such a dead language useful for only a few occupations, and although German is still used a great deal it is not easy on the ear; it sounds like someone who has hiccups through a mouthful of sausage."

Miss Keating, suppressing a smile and holding up her hand, said, "Enough! You are not here to disseminate your impressions of the school system of education; you are here because you have damaged school property. Now what do you have to say about that?"

Audrey looked contrite. "I will do some jobs after school and earn the money to pay for some new window glass. I have already cleaned up the mess! Will this be sufficient?"

Miss Keating said, "You will need to pay for the installation of the glass also!"

Audrey Creates a Blow Out

Audrey gave a small sigh. "Alright! I have no idea of the total cost. Do you know how much all of it will cost?"

"Not yet, I will keep you informed. You may go and perhaps you had better get started on earning those funds right away; and remember, Audrey, I don't want to see you again, unless I have occasion to congratulate you. Is that clear?"

Audrey nodded, gave a small smile of affection, and left the room.

It took her two months of doing extra chores for her mother and some of the neighbours before full restitution was made to Miss Keating's satisfaction.

After this meeting, Audrey gave some thought to what she would like to do with her life. She was fond of sports and games of all kinds. She was good at hand stand, could walk on her hands, take her body into an arch and walk on her hands and feet; turn consecutive fast somersaults, and generally would try anything that looked like a possibility. She couldn't do the splits but decided to persevere until both of the insides of her legs rested on the ground.

Perhaps she would be an acrobat entertainer. It was not long however before that thought had to be revised.

After some consideration, Audrey decided that she would like to be a Physical Training instructor and a teacher of English. Apart from her usual Sports and Gym time, her lunch hour on the grass playing field became her practise time. Irene, a friend, begged to be shown how to do hand stands. On the second day of Irene's practise, she fell awkwardly, clutching her leg and screaming with pain.

Audrey ran to get the nurse. Soon an ambulance arrived and took Irene to hospital to mend her broken leg. The following day Miss Keating and Audrey faced each other across the now familiar desk.

Miss Keating inquired, "Do you realise that when you show others potentially dangerous stunts, you may place them in jeopardy?"

Audrey looked surprised. "I didn't think it was dangerous. It is actually quite easy to do!"

A LIFE of Enlightenment

"What is easy for you may not be easy for another. You cannot go through life seeing from just your viewpoint. That attitude will get everyone concerned in trouble and you, most of all! Now, Irene will be away from school for at least four weeks. How many lessons are you going to need in life before you realise that all events have consequences?"

Audrey was silent.

Miss Keating gazed at the face that showed polite interest.

"These are your consequences! Each day after school you will go to Irene's house and summarise the lessons she has missed. You will teach her all the important points, so that she will not be too far behind when she returns. Irene will be on crutches for at least six weeks, so, on her return you will assist her as required until she is free of them. Do I make myself clear?"

Audrey was stunned. "But I'm not a teacher! I don't know how to do this!"

"You knew how to teach her hand stands; you will teach her what she needs to know for her lessons!"

Audrey protested, "But look at the results. A broken leg! I might mess up her brain!"

Miss Keating looked both amused and annoyed. "You will take notes of all the salient points of each theory lesson. You will go through them with Irene so that she has some understanding of the subject she is missing by her non-attendance. You will not damage her brain or any other part of her in the process. I will contact both your mothers to make the necessary arrangements." Miss Keating looked at her sternly. "You will perform this task well! You are quite capable and I expect good results. Take note, Audrey. I do not want to see you again for a very long time. Now you may go!"

Irene was in hospital for another week so Audrey had some time to have fun and play her own games before her spare time would be taken up with teaching. However, there were other things to contend with as well.

Audrey had always had a high energy level, but it had been diminishing for some time. Now it seemed to suddenly get worse or more noticeable. She wondered if it was because the thought of teaching Irene did not make her smile. She often felt physically tired and running for any length of time became exhausting.

She decided to mention this to Doctor Gordon in case she needed one of the tonics which she well remembered from her childhood. He immediately took various blood samples and gave her a thorough examination. The tests revealed that she had Pernicious Anaemia. This was serious.

The only solution was to eat raw liver twice a day.

Audrey had always refused to eat any animal organs. The brains, liver, kidneys, tongue, tripe and so on that her mother prepared especially during the war when little else was available, remained untouched on Audrey's plate. When it was explained to her that many of these organs removed toxins for the animal this only assisted Audrey's viewpoint. Why would you want to eat anything that in her mind resembled a vacuum cleaner?

Now she was faced with *eat raw liver or die*. This choice was familiar territory. Audrey had no fear of dying, but her intuition told her that perhaps she would be violating a trust. This was a faint idea, tantalizing, but beyond her ability to fully grasp.

She decided to eat the liver. It was a terrible chore. It was bloody and some of the fibres were hard to chew and got stuck between her teeth. It became easier when she decided to treat it like medicine. She cut small pieces and swallowed them whole as though they were pills.

She had to give up sports, gym and swimming. The chlorine in the water gave her croup, and it became inappropriate for her to attempt to get her lifesaving certificate. As Pernicious Anaemia was usually recurring, this put severe limitations on her chosen career.

In the meantime, she had to teach Irene. Audrey had to change her whole method of operation. She seldom took notes of her lessons, preferring to rely on her excellent memory or look it up in her textbook. Now, her notes were copious, although, as the days went by she found it easier to summarize the lessons. Irene was not enthusiastic about the learning process, preferring to chat or play board games; however, Audrey was too instructive to ignore and they finally settled into a routine. When Irene returned to school, she and her mother had an interview with Miss Keating.

A LIFE of Enlightenment

After this was completed, Audrey was called to account. She gave her version of the event, answering the odd question here and there.

When she had finished, Miss Keating said, "I am well pleased with you. You have performed this task well. Apparently, you have some aptitude in this area. Have you considered becoming a school teacher?"

"Not anymore! I wanted to be a Physical Educational Teacher but the pernicious anaemia has knocked that on the head. I don't mind the teaching part, but I don't want to teach schoolwork!"

"What would you like to teach?"

"I don't know. I feel I'm supposed to do something special, maybe something creative but I don't know what it is. I have an adult friend and I might discuss it with him on his next visit."

Miss Keating smiled, considering her thoughtfully. "You have written quite often for the school paper. I know you have marked your entries anonymously, but your handwriting is distinctive and all your teachers recognise the author even though the students remain in ignorance. You have style and humour. Have you considered a career in this field?"

Audrey shook her head, "It's just a hobby. Maybe one day I will get paid for it, but my family would not consider it a career or even a job. I don't think I would enjoy it anymore if it became a 'Have to'!"

Miss Keating, giving a nod of dismissal said, "Well, you are intelligent enough to be whatever you want to be. You seem to have very definite views on what you don't want. Perhaps some inspiration will come to you as you get older and wiser. You may go!"

Audrey left pondering on the shared conversation, deciding that Miss Keating wasn't a bad old stick after all, and wondering about the special part she was meant to play in the world apart from eating raw liver.

CHAPTER 19

Keeping Abreast of Life

Eventually blood tests revealed a distinct improvement and the liver became a once-a-day requirement three times a week, becoming less and less over a period of a year. Audrey was even allowed to have it quickly turned on each side in a hot pan. This improved the look of it and just a little of the taste.

Shortly after her twelfth birthday Audrey's breasts began to appear. They grew very quickly.

Dorothy bought her two brassieres and placed them in her dressing table drawer. Audrey however was still being a tomboy. She picked up the brassieres and holding them at arm's length as though they were infectious, took them downstairs to her mother, sitting at the kitchen table. Dropping them in front of Dorothy, Audrey said, "There is no way I am going to wear these!"

Dorothy answered, "There is no way in which you are not! You can't go around bouncing all over the place. It's just not nice!"

"Then I will be careful, but I am not strapping myself into these. I will feel as though I'm bandaged!"

Her mother smiled, "They are training brassieres and not as tough or restrictive as they look!"

"Well my breasts are not in training for anything so I definitely don't need them! Sorry Mum!"

With this rejoinder, Audrey left the room.

The offending articles stayed in the drawer until Audrey got tired of holding her breasts when she was running. She donned them shortly around her thirteenth birthday.

Margaret, although small in this department, had been wearing her brassieres for quite some time. She was blossoming into a very attractive young lady. She had shoes with little heels and began to paint her fingernails and toenails with red polish.

Audrey was horrified at this mutilation. She stared at Margaret's attempts to master her first walk in the new shoes, commented that her sister would probably break her neck, and when she saw the red toes and fingernails she told Margaret that she looked as though she was bleeding to death. Margaret, now just fifteen, had been interested in the opposite sex for the last two years. She had pictures of film stars cut out from magazines. Alan Ladd was her favourite. She told Audrey she was in love with him. Audrey was amazed.

"Have you met him? Do you know him? How can you love someone you don't know and have never met? That's illogical!"

Margaret frowned, "I knew you wouldn't understand. You're too young anyway and you have some weird ideas. I don't know why I bother to talk to you. One of these days you might grow up!"

Audrey and Margaret lived in two different worlds. They had different considerations and viewpoints on life and people and accordingly had little shared conversation.

Dorothy took Audrey aside and lectured her on the unkindness to her sister. Audrey was ashamed of her behaviour after her mother explained that Margaret needed all her confidence to deal with being a young lady and how to interact with boys, which for her was a new experience.

Audrey apologised to her sister and offered to give her some tips. Audrey felt that she knew all about boys, having spent her playtime with them for years, and could pass on lots of data to Margaret.

The suggestion was not well received. In Margaret's opinion Audrey's data would not include romance and accordingly was unwanted.

Boys around sixteen and seventeen began to appear to take Margaret to movies or a local dance. They were seated in the living room by Dorothy. Audrey was instructed to keep them in conversation until Margaret took the customary ten minutes to appear.

Audrey had no problem with this assignment. She chatted away about their interests and got them to talk about their planned careers, hoping something would occur to her about her own during the discussion. The boys responded well to her interest and Audrey enjoyed the interaction until her mother banned her from the living room each time one of Margaret's dates appeared. Some of the boys, when telephoning in the future, had asked Dorothy if they could speak to Audrey rather than Margaret, feeling they had found a kindred soul. Audrey, not conversant with this fact, and uninterested in dating, failed to completely understand the ban, wondering what she had done wrong.

Audrey came to terms with the impossibility of becoming a Physical Training Instructor. She could still teach English but this had been one of the choices as a compulsory second subject and she had no wish for it to become a main one.

Her parents were eager for her to become a Doctor. When she refuted the idea, the suggestions changed to becoming a Pathologist or a Radiologist. Audrey pointed out that although she was interested in people, she was not interested in bodies; sick ones in particular!

She discussed this with Doctor Gordon.

"Perhaps you would be interested in the field of Psychiatry?" Her 'No!' was emphatic.

Doctor Gordon was amused.

"Audrey, why so adamant? Have you given it any consideration; done any research; tell me why?"

"I've read a little of Freud and also some of the ways psychiatrists theorize and work. None of it makes me smile. It might be a good investment to have people coming back for years by treating symptoms and not causes so they don't really get better. I don't know much about sex as yet, but I can't see how it could be an answer to almost everything. Some of the children messed up during the war would not have had any contact, so it wouldn't apply to them. I think most people suffer from the fear of something, all sorts of various things, and I also know from experience that the only way to handle them is to face them. I learned that when I was little and I know it will always stand me in good stead. You really do need to do what you fear or to face it in some way. That really works! The trick is to get people to realise that and not blame someone or something else for their own inventions. I need to learn how to do that if I am to help them...I don't think I will learn it in the methods that are available." "Audrey, perhaps if you really looked into the subject, you may change your mind. You could qualify, and then develop your own method of dealing with your clients. Aren't you being too hasty in your judgements?"

She smiled at him, "Maybe, but I'm following my old rule which always serves me well!"

Doctor Gordon looked thoughtful, "Remind me again. Which rule is it; you have a few, you know?"

"It doesn't make me smile! So that is the end of the subject. I will find something that does and when I do I will follow my nose! In the meantime I have to remember not to follow other people's ideas, no matter how well meaning they may be!" She gave him a cheeky grin as she said this and he smiled in return. "Alright Audrey, enough said, let us change the subject and order our tea!"

They were sitting in their favourite restaurant. No longer were they the subject of speculation.

They were the regulars, accepted and liked although their less frequent schedule had been noted.

Audrey never asked him about his marriage or questioned him about

Keeping Abreast of Life

Marjorie, his wife.

It was as though she belonged to a separate part of his life and never would be included in this one. Audrey did not deliberately exclude her. She simply did not crop up in Audrey's thoughts to be considered.

This time was theirs alone; known, respected and shared by both of them and enjoyed not just by habit but by the ease and comfort that each obtained from the other's presence. Viewpoints were shared and debated, life events discussed and analysed. This was where the summing up of events took place and the future was deliberated. The warm affection and companionship between them was palpable and appreciated. Perhaps each of them knew in some deep recess of their knowingness that one day they would all meet and be together even for a short time, but that was far into the future and not to be considered now.

CHAPTER 20

Finding the Least Possible Effort to Succeed

Audrey had had enough schooling. Although Greenfield Grammar attendees almost always went on to University usually around age seventeen, the law allowed a student to leave school at fifteen. Only age counted, not the years attended.

Because Audrey was almost two years younger than her classmates this meant that when they were going to University, she could leave school.

She decided that this would be her goal. In the meantime, she had to devise a system that would get her through the next two years with the least possible effort and as little disgrace as possible. Audrey had already devised a method of dealing with the punishments that came with misdemeanours. Misdemeanours were: talking in class, obviously not paying attention, diverting another student's attention, challenging the data or the teacher, one of Audrey's earlier favourites, or making unnecessary noise or disturbance or pranks! When these occurred during class or in the corridors, the punishment was handed out by the officiating or passing teacher.

Audrey was often given a part of the Bible to learn by heart. She had to voice this to the class the next day. Although she found learning by rote and then verbalising it very easy, she had little affinity with the Bible. However, she was very happy to learn any part of Shakespeare or a verse or two from one of the famous poets that were part of her curriculum.

While the teacher was pondering what to assign her, Audrey would plead, "Please don't make me learn Shakespeare stuff or poetry. It's really quite difficult!"

She would inevitably be assigned one or the other and happily complied.

She decided to daydream or read a detective novel through every period that involved subjects that did not make her smile. Practical work required some application to show that she was making an effort, but as the majority of her lessons were based on theory she felt that the plan she was about to put into operation was a good one.

The school operated with four terms each year. There was an exam at the end of each term and a more intense one at the end of each year. The resultant marks of the end of the year exam determined whether the student went to a higher form or stayed down to repeat that year.

Audrey considered it a matter of honour to have a good if not an excellent end-of-the year report. She decided to pay little attention to subjects that had little or no interest for the whole year. A good detective novel or some imaginative daydreaming would see her through the allocated time in these periods.

At the end of the year, just before each exam she read her textbooks as though they were the best detective novels that had ever been written. Having a photographic memory served her well. She memorized text, maps, drawings, and other relevant data with ease. The data she accumulated stayed with her for some time, much of it fading after two weeks, other data lasting a little longer.

The end of each term exam saw Audrey in the bottom three of her class, a far drop from her usual middle position. However, the end of the year exam saw her in the top three. She was happy!

Her parents could not understand it; her teachers also were at a loss and said as much with comments at the end of each term and year reports. There was a suspicion of cheating, but this cleared itself when the same

Finding the Least Possible Effort to Succeed

orchestration occurred in many of her subjects.

English, literature, grammar, writing, spelling, composition and straight mathematics and all sports were her very best subjects. She loved writing essays, summaries, analysing the meaning of a verse or poem, and felt that she understood all the nuances of Shakespeare. Taking part in sports prior and after the anaemia and any athletic events made her day a happy one. Although she was a most uninterested spectator of any game or similar event, she was a very enthusiastic participant.

Her cousin Winnie became a student three years after Audrey joined Greenfield Grammar school. It took only a week for her to discover Audrey's reputation; a trouble maker, and a frequent visitor to the Headmistress. Winnie was a passionate academic and a conformist in the strictest sense of the word. She found this information most disturbing...

Winnie asked Audrey to promise that she would never divulge to anyone, particularly Miss Keating, that they were cousins or related in any way. When Audrey asked why, Winnie commented that this information would probably be detrimental and affect her own progress and reputation.

Audrey was amused but promised faithfully never to divulge any connection. She kept the promise. Winnie made it easier by avoiding her at recess and sports day and as they were always in different classes the situation was not problematic.

CHAPTER 21

Audrey Decides To Be The Very Best Girl She Can Be

Shortly after her fourteenth birthday, Audrey made a discovery that went from being a "know about" to a "know!" She had a leisurely bath. This meant that she could use some of her mother's bath salts, fill the tub so that water came up to her chin, arm herself with a good detective novel, and soak for at least half an hour unless someone else disturbed her by wanting the room.

This was a good day. Audrey climbed out, pulled the plug, wrapped a towel around her and headed for the bedroom.

There was a dressing table in the bedroom with a low drawer in the centre and high ones on each side. Over the centre drawer was a wide and tall mirror which to date had had very little of Audrey's attention. This day however, she accidently dropped the towel in front of the dressing table and her whole body was revealed in the mirror.

Audrey didn't bend down to pick up the towel; she stood very still and stared at the reflected figure. She saw the full breasts, the rounded curves and in a blinding flash of self-awareness she knew that what she was looking at was a girl; a woman, even!

The image did not seem to have anything to do with her. This was a stranger who looked to be wearing a slightly familiar face! She went on staring, slowly allowing the realization that the figure in the mirror was a body that belonged to the person she knew as Audrey, the tomboy. The realization was not anything she preferred; but she knew it had to be faced. She was a female with a female body and that was all there was to it!

Her emotions were disconcerting. She was mortified, disappointed, frustrated and then grief stricken.

Still naked, she sat on the bed and cried.

This was too much. She didn't *want* to be a girl, had *never* wanted to be a girl, she didn't even *like* girls very much. They cried over the least little thing; they were always afraid of one thing or another, usually more than one; they were illogical and behaved as though they were stupid when boys were around. They were silly gigglers and had little sense of adventure, because they always seemed to be afraid of consequences before they had ever happened.

Audrey didn't understand them, and the prospect of being one of them filled her with horror.

Now she was stuck with it!

She dried her tears, ashamed that she was giving in to a girlish trait.

Audrey had a lot of pondering to do, a great deal of sorting out. There were questions such as 'Why, were girls…girls?' And 'Why, were boys…boys?' There seemed to be no logical answer to Audrey's way of thinking. If she was now a girl, how was she to go about being a girl when she knew nothing about the area except the observable traits that she disliked? How to be a girl without being a GIRL? Questions! Questions!

She was getting cold. She wrapped her chilled body in her dressing gown and lay on the bed looking for inspiration and answers.

Finally she arrived at the conclusion that girls were girls only for the sake of boys, and boys were boys only for the sake of girls! She acknowledged that the continuation of the human race was involved but this did not have her specific attention; that came later when sex was involved.

Audrey Decides To Be The Very Best Girl She Can Be

Audrey took a long hard look at her attitude, her resistance to being a girl, and her judgement of them. She decided to change her viewpoint. Then she carried the conclusions even further. If she was stuck with being a girl then she was going to be the very best girl that she could be!

After all it was a job. Like any job, you had to find out how to do it, and then become efficient and confident in the area.

Audrey got a notepad and pencil and made some headings:

Girl Behaviour?

Girl looks?

What do Girls do?

What should girls have?

She decided to do a survey and the people to survey were the boys as this was the only reason to be a girl anyway! She was a little confused but clear in what she intended.

She sorted out some possible questions in her head, got dressed and went out looking for the boys she knew for their answers.

Audrey found two of her old playmates. She explained she was doing a survey and that the answers needed to be serious ones. She also explained that action would be taken with anyone who made fun of it. The boys knew her well enough to comply.

Audrey asked them how they considered girls should look. Did they like long or short hair, curly or straight: what about colour, what about weight and did it matter if girls were taller than themselves? How should they dress; walk; what should they talk about?

What did they like girls to do; how should they behave in restaurants; in cars; at the pictures? What sort of character and personality traits did the boys like or notice?

Audrey listened and made notes. The boys could not answer some of her questions or answered in an offhand way or deemed the answer to be unimportant. Audrey noted all this. She listened intently to anything they volunteered.

No other boys were available that day. Over the next week she interviewed a total of twenty boys ranging in ages from fourteen to nineteen years. She also interviewed four men who regarded her with amused compassion. She was surprised that the answers from any age differed little.

On completion, she reviewed the answers. Some of them were given a limited life as she went through crossing out and murmuring *"there's no way I'm doing that"* and so on down her list.

Then came acceptance. Audrey decided to put the list into practice and with her philosophy of "do it right away" almost overnight she became a girl!

Her attitude changed; she dressed differently, even in the same school clothes; walked differently; was a little quieter in her speech, and her manner softened. Audrey became very feminine in her looks and her behaviour. She took care to comb and style her hair and even became aware that it was quite nice hair and a good if unusual colour. For the first time she was really aware of the shape and softness of her body. She gave the impression that she was proud and happy to be a girl!

Her parents and her relatives were astounded at the sudden change, but her manner forbade questions, she regarded them with such friendly confidence and dignity that they were silenced before they spoke and chatted only to each other.

Doctor Gordon, aware of the change even as she opened the door, smiled and said "Oh yes! Very well done!" With him, she laughed and told him all the details. In the telling she became aware of all the fun she had derived from the exercise. He commented that perhaps she should write this up for other young ladies who may need the data, and she agreed that one day perhaps this could be done.

He was pleasantly amused and pleased at the way she showed off her new role, and amazed at her quick grasp and application of all she had learned. Suddenly she seemed an adult, and a very feminine one at that.

At their restaurant she took over the pouring of the tea. Previously the waitress had started this and Doctor Gordon continued with refills. Now Audrey thanked the waitress as she placed the tea things on the table and

Audrey Decides To Be The Very Best Girl She Can Be

said, "I will take care of the pouring from now on!"

The waitress, a little startled looked at the Doctor for confirmation. His nod and smile sent her back to her contemporaries with the news.

Audrey was sitting very upright in her chair as she talked. This was a change from her having her elbows on the table with hands on either side of her face as she leaned towards him smiling and enthusiastically talking about the latest happenings in her life.

She drank her tea with one hand and with the little finger crooked free of the cup.

He was intrigued. "Tell me," he asked, "Where did you learn so much in such a short time?"

"Emily Post, she has a book on etiquette which I borrowed from the school library."

Doctor Gordon smiled, "Of course! Did you find it agreeable?' The old Audrey grinned at him. "Not always. I decided just to apply what made me smile. Frankly, even that is not easy. I have to be aware of what I am doing all the time. I have been doing my normal things for the past fourteen years which have become a habit. Now I have to make all these new things a habit, so it is just a matter of doing them until I don't have to think about them anymore. Tell me, what do you think of the new me?"

She was aware that he was going to be careful in his answer, so she forestalled him by saying, "I know you are used to the old me and that was very acceptable to you, but you see I can't go on being a tomboy forever. I haven't told you what precipitated all this. I lost my towel in front of the big mirror in my bedroom and I saw myself completely naked. It was a shock, a huge shock. It made me cry and took me more than an hour to get over it. After that I had to come to terms with it and work out the plan and survey that I have already told you about. I decided that if I was stuck with being a girl, then I would be *the very best girl* that anyone could ever be."

His slightly raised eyebrows went with his question, "And why do you need to be this?"

Audrey was intent as she said "It isn't a need in the truest sense of the word. It is a matter of honour. If I am going to do something, it will be done well! It is an attitude that makes me smile and as you know I have always followed that rule as much as I possibly can!"

He leaned across the table and reached for her hand, "Audrey, I congratulate you, I'm sure you will continue to be what you already seem to be; a very lovely girl. I'm proud of you! No matter what role you decide to play, you will always be the 'you' that I value and love!"

She was pleased and happy. "I haven't really changed inside; this is just an acceptable facade that goes with a female body. Don't be fooled; I will still be just as strong in my questions and all my viewpoints, so don't relax your vigilance!"

He laughed, "I will not do that. I am used to being on my toes around you!"

"And I around you." Audrey smiled thoughtfully, "We get along so well, don't we? I have learned so much from you! Your questions make me think of lots of other viewpoints. I now have the habit of always going for the big picture! I'm so grateful to have you in my life. You really are the very best nose-pointer." She smiled and with sincerity softly said, "Thank you so much for being my mentor, for taking me on!" She leaned over the table and laid a hand gently on the side of his cheek.

He took the hand and kissed it.

"Audrey, I may seem like a good nose pointer but that's because you have always been willing to sniff! As for looking at the big picture, you were the one who pointed out that most people are happy looking down the wrong end of the telescope and that was never good enough for you!

I have learned much from you. You have challenged me constantly. I have given up clichés and trite remarks and standard consoling sentences. I have almost eliminated them from my vocabulary. I think well before I speak to make sure that it is worth saying. I have adopted many of your thoughts and considerations, not because they are yours but because they serve me well. Your 'for what purpose?' and 'does it make you smile?' are only two of those. So you see, the student and the teacher learn from

Audrey Decides To Be The Very Best Girl She Can Be

each other and in our case, delight in the exchange. I too, have much to be thankful for!"

Audrey was astounded! He had casually mentioned this idea before but she had dismissed it feeling he was being kind and polite. Now she knew he meant it! This was a novel idea! He was twenty years her senior and the idea of him learning something from her, was difficult to take seriously, but she knew she had to treat it with the respect it deserved.

She smiled at him as she said, "Thank you for saying all that. I know you are not just being kind, but the kindness is in saying it, so thank you!"

He leaned back in his chair, regarding her with a smiling, quizzical look, "Audrey, you are going to give the boys hell in a year or so!"

She laughed, "I have been doing that for years; now I have decided to be kind, unchallenging, and respectful towards them!"

"Then I wish them and you the very best of luck!" he said laughing. He beckoned the waitress for a refill of tea and for the rest of their time together they enjoyed each other's presence, exchanging warm smiles rather than words across the tea table.

As they were driving home, Doctor Gordon told her he would be going away and may not return for a year or so. His friend in Scotland was very ill and he was taking over his medical practice until he recovered.

He gave Audrey his new telephone number and said for her to call him at any time, and that as always he would be delighted to hear from her.

Whenever he had left on previous occasions Audrey had never called him, always waiting for his return to share all the news she had saved for their next meeting. A year seemed a very long time, but she smiled as she said, "I may not call you unless it is an emergency. I will spend the time continuing to grow up trusting that what I choose will be all the best possible ways to go about it and then surprise you with the result on your return. Even when we are not together I don't feel separate from you, so it is still alright to wait until you return to share all our news. Do you feel this is alright for you also?'

"I shall be delighted with whatever you present!" he said, smiling while taking her hand as she got out from the car, then hugged her and wished her well. It seemed that he hurried to get away and her only clue to his quick unusual departure was the hint of sadness she saw on his face.

She stood there waving long after the car had gone, until she became aware of her mother waiting by the opened front door.

Audrey knew she would miss him but she was also aware that this was appropriately her time for deciding exactly who and what she was creating herself to be. There were many roles she could try as a personality coat. It was a little like being in a play; what character would she prefer to act out and play? No roles were set; she was also writing the play. Nothing could really change who she really was; she trusted that she would never lose sight of the author!

This could be fun!

CHAPTER 22

One's Inner Intuition Is The Best Schooling

Audrey's new dignity took a tumble over the next six months. She suddenly started to grow taller. Margaret, although not a girl of medium height, was a good half head taller than Audrey. Now Audrey suddenly shot up and passed her sister by a good two inches. It seemed as though just her arms and legs grew. This made her clumsy. Audrey fell up and down steps. Her feet landed on objects before she predicted they would, and her hands were not at the end of her arms but further away. She wiped objects off tables when she meant to pick them up and had scabs on her knees from their meetings with the pavement. All her bones ached. Her mother said it was "growing pains" and would go away. Audrey's newfound dignity and her body were suffering. It was hard to be nonchalant when you were often on your hands and knees or apologising for breakages. For seven months she suffered through this, until one day she felt and realised she was co-ordinated and balanced once more. For Audrey it was a great relief.

In November she would be turning fifteen. Time to leave school. She had one month before this event to handle her parent's reaction to the idea. She was prepared for strong opposition but her only plan for handling this was to become the immovable object.

A LIFE of Enlightenment

She broached the subject after supper one evening.

"I'm going to be fifteen shortly. That is the age I need to be to leave school, and that is what intend to do!"

There was silence for a moment, and then her father stated, "That may be what you intend, but that isn't what you are going to do. Students from your school go to University and learn a profession and that's where you're going!"

"No!"

"I'm not arguing with you, I've said my piece and that's it!" Her father glared at her across the table.

"I'm not arguing. I simply said 'No'. I will stay to the end of the term at Christmas, but I will not be going back. I'm sorry if this upsets you but it is my life!"

Dorothy said, partly to calm her husband and also because she felt an ally would be required, "Let me talk to the headmistress tomorrow, and let's see what she has to say." Audrey replied "Fine, but no one is going to change my mind. I have thought about it for a long time. It's not an impulsive decision."

Fred snorted, "you're not old enough to make decisions about your future!"

"I am only doing what you say I should! You are always telling me that I should know better, but when I do you scorn at my decisions."

Her father moved towards her angrily, "Don't you give me any back chat! You're staying on until you go to University and that's that!"

Audrey said "No!" walked out of the room and then ran from the house.

She ran up the laneway to the field that backed on to her old primary school. Finding a fallen log, she sat there pondering.

She knew that now she had to handle not only her parents but also Miss Keating, and probably some immediate relatives as well. Many of the adults around her would be bending her ear with the fact that they had never had the chance that she had; that she should be grateful for the opportunity and thankful that she was a good scholar and so on and so on. Audrey

One's Inner Intuition Is The Best Schooling

could hold most of the conversation in her head. She sighed. She decided to mainly say "Yes, I understand. I realise what you are saying. Thank you for telling me how you feel!" And then move out of their space as quickly as possible.

Miss Keating was another matter. Now, how to handle this one? She decided to sleep on it.

Her father was leaving for work as she appeared for breakfast. Her mother put her finger to her lips and Audrey, recognising the cue, said nothing.

Dorothy said to Audrey as he left, "I have to ring Miss Keating and she is sure to be on our side. Don't you think you should reconsider? You will not only upset your father but the whole family. They all think that despite your pranks and trouble making that you will one day amount to something!"

Audrey smiled, "Well perhaps I will, but it won't be because I went to University. I'm sorry but I really need to do it my way, whatever that is!"

"What is your way?"

"I don't know yet. All I know is that University is not the answer. It doesn't make me smile, and I decided long ago not to do anything that doesn't make me smile!"

"What do you mean long ago? When was that and why did you decide that? It's a strange thing to say!"

Audrey was silent, thinking of her father's advances. "I decided it when I had nightmares and I couldn't stand the fear in myself. It didn't make me smile so I did something to get rid of the fear and that made me smile!"

Her mother sat opposite looking at her daughter with a quizzical expression. "I thought you had grown out of having nightmares; now you are saying you did something. What did you do?"

Audrey felt reticent. She didn't really want to get into this, but her mother's enquiring and affectionate expression could not be denied. She told her the story without any mention of her father as the source of the nightmares.

Dorothy stared at her, wondering if she would ever really know her daughter. "You did this all by yourself. But you were only about eight at the time; how could you?"

A LIFE of Enlightenment

Audrey smiled, "Well, you decide to either live a life full of fears that you never handle or you decide to face them! It was one of the best decisions I ever made. Now I feel I can face anything, Dad's bad temper or Miss Keating's opposition. I must go. I will be late for school!"

She moved around the table, kissed her mother's cheek and left the house running to catch her bus.

She moved through her morning lessons waiting for the inevitable summons. When lunch recess came and went, she wondered if her mother had a change of heart. Audrey was not looking forward to going home and facing her father's obstinate temper, but she knew it had to be done.

She rather wished Doctor Gordon was around to talk to. He may not agree but at least he would listen and understand! But, what could he understand? Audrey knew that she didn't know what she wanted to do, but she realised that almost anything she mentioned to placate them would be turned into a University course by Miss Keating, if not her parents.

She decided to promote the fact that it was "her choice" and that she needed "to be doing what makes me smile." In this, there was little with which to argue.

She concluded that when one was using what another could consider a weak argument, it was best to leave it as bare as possible.

When the summons came she felt like the immovable object ready to receive the irresistible force. She was resigned but determined.

Miss Keating gazed at Audrey across the desk. "Well what explanation do you have for wishing to leave school, or even better, for not wanting to attend University?"

Audrey said, "The first one makes me smile and the second one doesn't!"

Miss Keating looked affronted. "That is not an explanation. At the best it is an attitude."

Audrey frowned. "Surely an attitude defines explanations."

Miss Keating frowned, "I am not here to debate semantics with you! Do you realise that you could become whatever you set your mind to! You may even have had to stay on another year before you went to University; I have

One's Inner Intuition Is The Best Schooling

only recently remembered your age, but I would have made you Head Girl next year! Now, what do you have to say?"

Audrey was more than surprised. "Well, thank you very much. I appreciate your confidence in me and the honour also, but I must decline."

"There is nothing that you could do with your life that University could not improve or provide. Audrey, surely you can see that. You have intelligence, use it!"

Audrey said. "I am!"

There was silence for a moment. Miss Keating softened. Audrey could sense the coming change of attitude. She was interested but detached from what was yet to come.

Miss Keating leaned forward and in a gentler tone asked, "Audrey tell me, what it is that you want to do?"

"I don't know! All I *do* know is that it will not be learned in a school environment or at University. My intuition—that I always follow—tells me that; in the long run, one's inner tuition is always the best schooling, don't you agree?"

Miss Keating was silent. "We have known each other for quite a few years. I confess that this is the first time that I have had difficulty talking to you."

Audrey offered hopefully, "Perhaps it is because someone else asked you to do so. That has never happened before; maybe it interferes with your own thoughts!"

Again there was silence. Audrey was concerned. Miss Keating, at a loss for words, was not conveying her usual expected demeanour. Audrey was beginning to feel that perhaps she had to explain more in order for both of them to be comfortable.

Miss Keating remained silent; sitting back in her chair, gazing thoughtfully out of the window.

Audrey said, "Look, if I am going to be anything at all, it will probably be as a writer or a philosopher or both together. Neither of these things do I wish to learn from someone else. Just living on this planet can corrupt your thinking...". She stopped at the sudden surprised look on Miss Keating's face.

Miss Keating leaned forward, "What do you mean 'this planet'? Are you saying what I think you are saying?"

Audrey felt miserable. "I don't know! Sometimes, things just come out and I don't know what they mean either! Always this mystery gets me into trouble. Could we just forget I said that please? May we cancel it?"

Miss Keating again leaned back in her chair pondering Audrey. Audrey went on. "Look, I really needed to know just the basics of education... the three 'R's. I have spent eleven and a half years learning data that I really consider mostly irrelevant. After I had mastered reading, writing and arithmetic, I just felt I needed to read whatever took my interest. I realise that no- one will agree with this, but irrespective of their disagreement I cannot go on compounding this error. Even if I really needed at least fifty per cent of what I have studied, it seems it is more than enough. I will always be where I need to be to learn anything else I need. Right now it is not available at this school or at University. Please try to understand!"

Miss Keating sighed. Audrey found this a little alarming.

"Can I at least persuade you to stay for one more year and then review the matter?"

"No...Sorry, but No!"

"What am I to tell your parents?" The tone was slightly helpless; this was even more alarming!

Audrey rose, feeling warm affection for the Headmistress who for many years had really been an unacknowledged friend.

"Look, I really want to thank you for all you have been and for all you have meant to me! Underneath all the troubles we have shared I felt you were always my friend. Whatever you say to my parents will be alright with me; always you have been fair and I'm sure you will not take sides."

There was silence.

Audrey slowly stood. When Miss Keating continued to look out of the window, Audrey said, "May I go?"

One's Inner Intuition Is The Best Schooling

Miss Keating nodded. She did not look at Audrey as she left, but continued looking at the view with a thoughtful expression...

Miss Keating telephoned Dorothy the next day.

Dorothy was surprised to hear her say, "Without agreeing with your daughter's viewpoint, I feel it would be wise to let her have her way. She has the tenacity, determination and intelligence to make a success of whatever she eventually decides to do with her life. She is also using these qualities to determine her immediate future which does not include staying at school or going to University. Whatever you or I decide, if it does not have Audrey's agreement it will be a lost cause and a futile waste of time. Therefore I suggest that we let her go her own way and expect nothing less than good results. This may take some time, as she has still not determined her place in life, but this will change."

Dorothy sounded anxious. "Oh dear! I don't know what her father is going to say. He thinks she is still a child and should do as she's told!"

Miss Keating replied calmly, "If your husband wishes to estrange his daughter, then that will be the way to go! I don't advise it. No one can force a child to study or to be whatever the parents want. I'm aware that some parents may consider that Audrey has had the advantages that they were denied, and now she is throwing this advantage away. This is not so. The five years she has spent as Greenfields will be with her the rest of her life. She may even decide to go to University later. She is only just fifteen and has two years before she is of the age that is usual for her to attend. Audrey will not fall behind. It is foreign to her nature. She is a leader as you know Mrs Southgate. She will never be a follower! I must now take my leave of you and place this matter in your good hands!" Standing with a silent telephone still in her hand she tried to determine what to tell Fred. At the moment all she could think of was that there would be fireworks tonight. She decided to tell him when all the children were upstairs in bed. This to some extent would protect Audrey, unless of course he decided to drag her from her bed.

By the morning this affair may have cooled a little. Dorothy wished that

Audrey was more like Margaret, who never gave any trouble unless Audrey had got her into it when they were together. Dorothy admired Audrey's spirit but would have enjoyed it being used in a direction that did not upset Fred. She also knew that Audrey would dig in her heels no matter what Fred said, did, or threatened to do. All the fighting and shouting would be to no avail, but Dorothy did not know how to circumvent it. She went on turning the event over in her mind. It seemed there was nothing to do except prepare for an explosion.

Wait! There was one saving grace! Fred respected Miss Keating and had often applauded the punishments the Headmistress had dished out to Audrey over the years. He thought they were cunning and had manipulated Audrey in a way he wished he could have found. Perhaps Miss Keating's words would have a calming effect on him, once the initial explosion was over.

There was no calming effect. Fred exploded. How dare his daughter defy him? Didn't she know what a wonderful opportunity this was? He would have jumped at it given the chance!

What was the matter with her anyway! She had the most screwed-up thinking he had ever encountered. He felt she was an invasion from some other world, that he didn't understand and wanted nothing to do with, either!

Neither Dr. Gordon nor Miss Keating could make her see reason this time around. The nerve of it. A fifteen-year-old stamping her foot and saying what's what. He wasn't going to have it!

Yet in his heart he knew that he would... He realized he didn't have a choice.

He sat in a chair in the kitchen, pondering, but feeling calmer as he accepted the realization.

Charles, now ten years old, appeared, wanting a glass of milk. He smiled at his father as he wished him good night. Fred looked after him thinking that, well, at least he had a son who would probably do him proud one day. To hell with girls! Anyway they grew up, got married and probably just

One's Inner Intuition Is The Best Schooling

stagnated after that!

Audrey should be a bloody lawyer the way she talked everybody out of things. Fred could see her standing in a courtroom with a smoking gun in her hand denying that she had shot anyone, even saying that she had nothing to do with it; and everyone there would believe her.

Here, Fred did her an injustice. Audrey would never say 'it had nothing to do with her'! She considered everyone had 100% responsibility and no-one should ever allow anyone to take it away!

Fred sighed at the injustice of everything in his life and went to bed.

CHAPTER 23

Audrey's First Kiss

Audrey caught two buses to get from home to school and back again each day.

For some time she had regularly caught the three thirty bus from the town centre and always on that bus was the same boy from an equivalent Boys Grammar school.

Audrey had a game she played whenever she had a seat. She would choose a visible neck sitting in a seat a few forward on the same or the other side of the aisle, and by staring with fixed attention at the back of the neck, she would will the person to turn around.

Various body movements would occur before the person turned. The shoulders would shrug as though to dislodge an irritating fly; then the neck would be stroked; then rubbed, and finally the person would turn. Audrey would be looking out of the window wearing her most innocent expression and would only allow herself a slight smile after they had turned away.

One day as she saw the same boy who frequented her bus, she played this game. It took only a moment for his head to swivel. She found herself looking into his eyes with no time to turn away. He smiled. When she alighted at her stop, which she knew was also where he did, he was waiting.

He stood in front of her almost barring her way. Audrey wasn't sure what to do? Should she apologise?

He smiled, holding out his hand, "Duncan!"

"I'm Audrey", she smiled in return taking the proffered hand.

He said, "I've watched you make passengers turn their heads; today was my turn?"

She grinned at him, "Tell me, how did it feel?"

"Like a faint electrical trickle!"

She was silent, absorbing this data.

"It's a game. Something I do to make the time pass by!"

Duncan smiled, "Make time pass on Saturday. Come to the matinée show at the Rialto?"

"I will have to ask my parents."

"Alright. See you tomorrow!"

With a wave of his hand he was off!

The next day he was standing at the back of the bus, and Audrey was standing at the front.

She waited for him at the bus stop.

"Right! What's the verdict?"

She was surprised but not dismayed by his forthrightness. "I have permission, but you will have to call for me as my parents want to meet you first!"

"OK! Call for you at 1 o'clock. Gives them time to give me the third degree. The picture starts at two!"

She wanted to ask him if he minded, but instead she said, "How old are you?"

"Seventeen, the same as you."

"Why do you think I'm seventeen?"

"I found out which form you are in from one of your classmates."

Audrey gave a small sigh, "Well, I went to school very early so my age has not caught up with my school years. I'm really fifteen."

He was surprised!

Audrey's First Kiss

She said, "Does it make a difference? Does it matter?"

He was silent for a moment, "Not really! See you on Saturday!" With a wave once more he was gone!

She could sense that his forthrightness and his non lingering goodbyes were a trait of his character and one she needed to expect. His brevity with words was unexpected. Perhaps it was a lack of confidence although his demeanour did not confirm this idea. He was not sharp or abrupt in his delivery. He obviously liked to get on with things. She thought it was interesting that one could discern so much from such a brief acquaintance. She was interested to find out more.

Audrey spent the next two days looking forward to her first real date. She did not discuss it with Margaret or indeed anyone. She had no questions. Most of her life had been spent with boys. She felt she understood them and could talk to them without shyness or embarrassment. Duncan was older, but that seemed correct in a way she didn't quite understand yet. He seemed intelligent and she liked the way he called a spade a spade!

Saturday came. She put on her second best dress and took some trouble with her hair, deciding to wear it loose but with a matching ribbon to her dress. Her parents were sitting around the kitchen table. Fred, who had not been in favour of this arrangement but had been somewhat mollified by Dorothy, looked at her and grunted.

Her mother said, "You look very nice! Are you nervous?" Audrey shook her head saying "I don't think so," as there was a knock on the door.

Audrey answered the door, with a smile. "Please come in and follow me, my parents are in the kitchen."

She introduced Duncan to her parents, relieved as he said, "Duncan Taylor Sir, pleased to meet you!" as he offered his hand to her father, then her mother. Audrey realized that she had not heard his surname before.

Her father's gruff "How long have you known each other and where did you meet?" was skilfully handled by Duncan saying "We catch the same bus every day Sir. I go to the Boys' Greenfield Grammar."

When the mother asked "Where do you live?" Duncan willingly gave her his address and watched patiently as she wrote it down. He offered the telephone number, pleasing both parents.

Dorothy smiled at him, liking his politeness and his deference to Fred.

"Why, that's quite close to here. In a country town we would be neighbours."

Duncan smiled, "My parents own the grocery store up the street," knowing that would please Dorothy. Although the war had been over almost five years, rationing had still not ended in England.

Audrey admired his skill in handling the grown-ups' interrogation. He gave the impression of being polite, courteous, and with absolutely nothing to hide despite his brief replies. He was quite disarming and Audrey could feel her father's aggressiveness softening.

Eventually they left, deciding to take the twenty minute walk to the picture theatre.

Sitting next to him in the theatre, Audrey was more aware of his presence than the screen. His sleeve on occasion brushed the sleeve of her coat. The coat seemed like a barrier. When they returned after the interval she removed and folded it, placing it on her knees.

He had bought some sweets in the interval and although their hands did not touch as she held out the paper bag to him, she was aware of his warmth each time she leaned towards him.

What he was thinking was more important and claimed more of her attention than the second picture unfolding on the screen. Audrey tried to be him. She was surprised to discover that his thoughts were similar to her own. Then she realized that this is what she wanted them to be, and not necessarily what they were.

The light had almost gone as they came out into the street. England in winter was heading for darkness at this time, even on a fine day. It was cold and she was pleased as he helped her into her coat.

They gazed around and then looked at each other. Duncan asked "Walk or Bus?"

"Walk please!"

Audrey's First Kiss

He placed her on the inside, away from the kerb. She appreciated this gesture of protection, and thanked him.

He shrugged and gave her a small smile.

As they walked Audrey asked him about his career intentions. "University soon! Haven't decided the rest!"

She was amused at his brevity. "Do you always talk as though words are a scarcity? Is it a skill you have learned or natural? I would love to read one of your English compositions. It would be brief, but to the point. I would enjoy that!"

He slowed, turning to look at her, "Amazing!" Then, he continued his pace.

She wasn't sure how to take this. What part of her discourse was amazing?

She stayed silent, thinking that if she said nothing he would fill in the silence.

He did not say anything, appearing to be deep in thought.

They continued walking and soon they were at her home. She had led him around to the back lane rather than the front door which was on the street, with people passing by.

The gate was set into a brick wall. She leaned against the wall holding out her hand, thanking him for the outing and stating her enjoyment.

Duncan ignored her hand. He placed his hands on her shoulders and gazed into her eyes. "Green!" he said. Leaning forward against her chest, he placed his lips on hers and then began moving his head in small circles. With her head against the wall, Audrey had little choice but to follow him.

It was uncomfortable. She felt that the hair on a spot of the back of her head was slowly being worn away. It began to hurt. Audrey managed to get her hands between them pushing with some effort against his chest. He immediately let go. He stepped back, gave her a small smile, patted her head and said, "See you on the bus!"

Rubbing her head she watched him walk away.

Audrey evaded her parent's questions saying only what they wanted to hear. The pictures were fine, he bought her sweets, walked her home and was polite. Dorothy said he seemed like a lovely boy. Fred grunted in acquiescence.

After dinner, alone in her room Audrey considered the outing. She decided that the kiss had been what he may have considered an obligation on his behalf. Obviously, he had no idea or experience on how to go about this. Neither did she, but she had noted couples at the pictures didn't wear bald spots in their hair by winding their heads round and round when kissing. How did one really kiss?

She practised various ways on the back of her hand, realising this wasn't the same as two lips coming into contact; finally deciding that perhaps she could ask Margaret for her views on the matter.

Margaret was adamant. You didn't have to worry about kissing until you had been going out for a long time! Audrey was stunned! What was a long time? Margaret said that when you knew each other well you might feel like having a kiss.

Did Margaret know how to kiss? What should it be like?

She was not forthcoming. Audrey could not extract any more information.

Sitting on her bed, Audrey realized that according to 'Tradition' she should not have allowed Duncan to kiss her; but why not? True, she didn't want to repeat the experience, at least until he had conquered the art and made it less painful, but otherwise…?

She decided to talk to her mother when they were alone.

Her mother was just as adamant as Margaret. You didn't kiss on a first outing or even a second or a third.

Audrey's "But why not?" received a reply of "He will think you are cheap and also think he can take other liberties!"

Audrey's question "How do you know he will think that?" Dorothy's "Because he will!" was not acceptable.

She decided to ask Duncan.

On the Monday they got off the bus almost together.

She said, "Don't hurry away please, I want to ask you a question."

"What?"

Audrey's First Kiss

"Did you think I was cheap or encouraging you to take further liberties because I let you kiss me on Saturday?'

"No!"

"Why not?

"Because you didn't egg me on!"

She stared at him, considering this.

Using his brevity she asked, "More please!"

"You seemed surprised!" Duncan was smiling.

"Then or now?"

"Both" He was silent watching her face that wore a slight frown. "I'll ask you out again in about a year!"

"Why in a year? She was puzzled.

"More action, less thought!" With a wave of his hand he was gone!

Audrey found many interpretations of this conversation, particularly in regard to the last sentence.

When she saw him the next day he simply asked, "OK?"

She said "Fine thank you. Will you do me a favour?'

"Maybe!" He was wary.

"Learn how to kiss. You have a whole year to practise and I will be interested to see the result!" She grinned at him.

He laughed saying "Touché!" as he waved and disappeared.

It was almost Christmas. The time for her to leave school was fast approaching. She took care to delay her walk to a later bus leaving town or hurried to catch an earlier one.

After not seeing him for almost two weeks he appeared on the earlier bus.

He waited. "Avoiding me?"

"Yes!'

"Why?"

"I don't want to cramp your style with someone else! That's only fair!"

"Wouldn't I cramp yours?"

"I suppose it works both ways, but I'm not sure I am really interested in dating anyway. I need to sort it out more first! It seems to have rules that I'm not familiar with, and possibly don't agree with anyway!"

"Do you always think before taking action? Why not be spontaneous?"

She laughed, "That's the longest sentence I have heard you speak! I'm often spontaneous! My parents call it impulsive as it often gets me into trouble; not that I mind. I often learn a lot at those times!"

He said, "I'm leaving early with the family tomorrow for the Christmas holidays, then it's off to University. See you sometime! Merry Christmas!" And with that, he was gone.

She called out "Merry Christmas!" as he ran across the road and up the street where he lived.

Audrey examined her feelings. It was alright if she ever saw him again and alright if she didn't. Life would move on irrespective of her decision.

Irene's parents were giving her a birthday party for her seventeenth birthday. This was the first party to which Audrey had ever been invited. Parties had ceased with the advent of war and had not really started again because the rationing still existed in 1950.

Audrey and Irene had been firm friends since the broken leg affair.

Audrey wanted a new dress, a red one—one that she chose herself. Her plea of, *"Please, it can be my Christmas present!"* finally persuaded her mother.

They went shopping to a large store in Manchester. Audrey found a dress she loved and got despite her mother's protests because it had short sleeves. "I can wear my coat and take a cardigan!" She was persuasive and excited.

She polished her black patent shoes, dressed her hair with a red ribbon and a piece of holly and went to the party a few days before Christmas full of anticipation and excitement.

It was lovely. There was music; a cleared small space for dancing and lots of games. She won at musical chairs, laughed at 'spin the bottle' and 'the postman', and enjoyed the company of many of her school colleagues.

A group of boys that she didn't know stayed in a corner, eying the girls and chatting amongst themselves.

Audrey's First Kiss

Audrey was chatting to Irene and her sister Shirley, when one of the boys approached. Looking directly at Audrey he said unsmiling and politely. "Excuse me, is it alright if I touch you?"

Audrey stared at him amused and intrigued. "Where and Why?" She felt she had copied Duncan with the brevity of this question.

"Just your arm is alright."

She held out her arm. He ran his fingers down it from the elbow to the wrist.

"Thank you!" he said. "I wanted to know if you felt as soft as you look!" He smiled and wandered back to his friends.

Irene and Shirley, her sister, gazed after him. Irene said, "Let me feel too!"

"Me too!" said Shirley.

Audrey held out her arm again.

The girls "Ooohhhhed". Irene said "It's like velvet, isn't it!"

Audrey said, "I'm sure everyone's skin feels the same way!"

"No it doesn't," Irene said. "Feel mine; now feel Shirley's. Now feel yours! See…I told you!"

Audrey was intrigued. Her skin certainly felt different. It felt like a silk blouse that her mother sometimes wore on special occasions rather than velvet.

Irene said, "Why is your skin so different?"

"I don't know. I didn't know it was until now! Maybe I inherited it from my mother."

"You should ask her and feel hers too", suggested Irene. Audrey agreed and changed the subject.

She did not know how often comments about her skin would be with her for the rest of her life.

CHAPTER 24

Audrey's First Taste of Independence

On the 23rd December 1950, despite her parent's disapproval, Audrey left Greenfields Grammar School, never to return.

She felt happy and free as she boarded the bus that took her from the school into the town for the last time. She felt like smiling all the time and it was hard not to share her joy with other passengers.

Minus her beret and her gloves which she stuffed in her satchel, despite the cold weather, it was good to know that no authority telling her what to do or threatening her with misdemeanour marks could have any effect.

Even her parents' disappointed faces could not dampen her enthusiasm for the future.

Her father said, "Well, if you are not going back, you had better get a job and quick smart."

"Don't worry, I will find something that makes me smile!" Christmas came and went. As always, they went to her father's parents for Christmas dinner; they roasted chestnuts around the fire, and sang carols, oblivious of the disharmony. Fred sitting next to Audrey told her she had a good voice before tunes were invented, and that Margaret had a good voice but it had a rough passage coming out. Nevertheless, it was a happy Christmas. Despite rationing, Dorothy and Jane had managed to procure all the usual treats for the traditional Christmas dinner.

Audrey was happy. The New Year seemed symbolic with a new and different life that she was ready to begin.

She began reading the 'Wanted' advertisements looking for anything that made her smile.

An advertisement for a junior in an Architect's office, for a position requiring neat writing abilities, caught her eye.

She called for an appointment and went to their office the following day. The Assistant manager who interviewed her was surprised to see her arrive without a parent in tow. Audrey was surprised that he considered it would have been appropriate. She handed over her school reports and at his request chose to write in her best handwriting a verse from Keats and then printed the same verse.

Although he made no comment, Audrey could tell from his expression that he was impressed.

He asked if she had any questions.

She inquired about the hours of work and whether she would be writing letters and why did she need to print neatly. She was told that this would be required for plans. She mentioned that her father was a builder and felt this would somehow be an advantage because of its relation to Architecture, although she had not ever seen a plan that her father might be building. Asking a question about her wage did not occur, nor did he offer the information. Telling Audrey she would receive a letter in the next few days, he courteously closed the interview saying, "Thank you; that will be all." She noticed two other candidates in the reception area as she left.

That evening her father lectured her about finding out her wages. It should be one of the first things you ask, he told her. Her failure to find out exactly what her duties would be and her holidays led to further lecturing and instructions for the future.

"You should have told us you were going there, I would have told you what to do and how to behave and what questions to ask. It's a wonder they

Audrey's First Taste of Independence

didn't want to know why your mother wasn't with you."

Audrey was silent. She was learning something from the conversation, even though she was also aware that if she took all that was said to heart, much of it may be the wrong lesson. In her bedroom she sat on her bed and made a list of questions and answers that another or she may ask. After this, Audrey felt confident and more prepared for her next interview.

Later, as she climbed into bed, her mother came. She sat on the edge of the bed, gazing at her independent daughter.

"You know, Audrey, instead of saying 'I'm going to town', you might have been more honest and told us about this job interview…"

"I wanted to do it all by myself and surprise you. Dad said to get a job 'quick smart' so that was what I was trying to do!" Dorothy sighed, "Surely you were…uh…weren't you nervous?"

Audrey smiled, "I am so used to being put through the third degree by Miss Keating, that the interview was just a very mild version; plus, I didn't have anything to feel guilty about! That probably helped!"

Dorothy smiled back. "How do you think it went?"

Audrey considered, "I don't really know. Writing and printing seemed to be very important for their plans. I think he liked my samples!"

Dorothy continued, "You have beautiful writing, almost copperplate like your Uncle Tom's. You know he writes all the certificates for the Church. They are regarded with wonder by most people."

Audrey said, "The reception area had two other girls waiting and perhaps they have even more applicants. I went in at 4pm. Maybe they started interviewing early this morning."

Dorothy kissed her cheek. "Get some sleep. At least it has been good experience for you!"

Friday's and Saturday's paper had no wanted positions that made Audrey smile; but Monday's paper proved more interesting. A large display advertisement called for applicants to sit for an examination to attend a school for the training of telephonists for the Post Master General's (PMG) Department. Some receptionist training and minor technical repairs would also be covered and, best of all, successful applicants would be required to live in quarters away from home for a period of three months. All expenses would be covered including a weekend home leave pass once a month as required.

Audrey telephoned to get an exam date and went into town to fill in an application form. She decided to inform her parents of this endeavour only if she passed the exam and was chosen as one of the only six applicants required. Along the thirty other girls, she sat for the exam at the end of the week. Not only was it an IQ test, but also an aptitude test. She had more difficulty with this but trusted that her ability to get along with others in the personal interview test would stand her in good stead.

The next day a letter arrived from the Architect's office asking her to report for work on Monday.

She was pleased. Even her father grunting "They still haven't told you what they are paying," did not dampen her enthusiasm.

Her mother congratulated her and together they discussed her wardrobe, choosing suitable clothes for her first few working days.

Over the weekend she received intermittent advice from her father on how to behave on her first day, and of course the right questions to ask.

Audrey was very sensitive to atmosphere. It had become almost a protective device that served her well. She decided to put his advice on a shelf unless is was timely and appropriate. Dressed in clothes she trusted gave her a professional office look, Audrey set off for her first day of work on Monday morning.

CHAPTER 25

Teaching Mr Eichorn a Lesson

For the first time, Audrey felt nervous as she arrived at the office. She tried to track it down, finally deciding that it was all the unknowns involved and that all the butterflies in her stomach would come in for a landing once she knew exactly what was expected. She had brought her best fountain pen for writing and printing, but somehow felt that they would be supplying their own particular equipment.

She reported to the receptionist and then sat waiting as requested, for the Assistant manager Mr Highbury to arrive.

When he did appear, she stood offering her hand and said smiling. "Good morning, thank you for selecting me!" hoping that this sounded appreciative and grown-up.

He said as he marched ahead with Audrey following, "You were lucky, we had 50 applicants for the position!"

Audrey did not know what to say to this so remained silent. They arrived at a room which was full of a very pungent smell. "This, he said, is the plan printing room. You will be in charge of the entire plan printing, so pay attention. I will send someone to show you what to do. You are also the morning and afternoon tea and errand girl, and you must keep the small

A LIFE of Enlightenment

kitchen spotless. You will also do other requests that the office personnel may require from time to time.

If you have any questions you may come to my office only after you have used your initiative in answering them yourself. I expect you, however, to not take risks and to use your discernment. Do you have any questions?

Audrey shook her head.

Mr Highbury, showed her the kitchen and a list stating what each staff member had for tea or coffee; showed her the box for petty cash used for purchases in this area, quickly introduced her to six staff members all sitting at drawing boards, and to the accountant who sat in a separate office next to his own. There was another door that he did not take her into, saying' that's the Manager and owner of this company. His name is Mr Eichorn, you need to remember that. Always call him by name and make sure that you take him his tea promptly at ten thirty and at three in the afternoon. If you are late, your head will roll. He can be very angry when things do not go his way!" He led the way back to the plan printing room saying "Wait here, someone will come to show you what to do!"

Eventually a young man who said his name was Tom arrived. Audrey's head was reeling from the pungent smell in the room. "It's ammonia," he said when questioned. "You'll get used to it."

He showed her the intricate workings of a machine mainly comprised of rollers and liquid.

A plan went through many cycles of dips and rollers before being placed on a rack to dry.

There were three plans awaiting printing. Tom showed her how to do the first one; watched as she did the second one, and then left her saying, "You catch on quick; you don't need me anymore."

She completed the third one, tidied the room, wiped drips off the floor, and went to investigate the kitchen. She filled the urn with clean water and set it on high, meaning to time it for boiling, and set out all the coffee cups and saucers. She assumed the most elegant one was for the manager, checked the biscuit tin and finding it empty, took the small petty cash tin

Teaching Mr Eichorn a Lesson

and fled from the office looking for the nearest shop, worrying about the morning tea being late because she was not prepared.

When she returned, Mr Highbury was waiting in the passage to the kitchen. She received a lecture on leaving the office without notice or permission. Audrey apologised, running to the kitchen to check the clock. Quickly she made Mr Eichorn's tea and at 10.30 knocked on his door.

There was a bellowing "Come in!"

He sat behind his desk, a large smartly dressed man with a red angry looking face, and a head that would soon be bald.

"Who are you?" he asked in a belligerent tone. "My name is Audrey, and this is my first day."

He stared at her. "My tea is supposed to be here at 10.30, not 10.33"

"The kitchen clock said 10.30 when I knocked on your door." "Don't argue with me, synchronise the clock with my watch and make sure you are on time in the future. Now, get out of here."

Audrey left quickly, thinking that Mr Eichorn was a rather rude man.

She jumped on the counter in the kitchen, reached the clock and advanced it three minutes.

She wasn't sure if this was correct but felt it would be reasonably safe.

She made the rest of the teas and coffees and delivered them with the biscuits, listening to the comments made within earshot of 'too strong', 'too weak', 'not enough milk!'

In the kitchen she found a small writing pad and a pencil. As she collected the used cups, she asked each person again for their name, made a note of their location in the open office and wrote down their required preference.

Afternoon teatime went much better. She even got some smiles from the office staff. When she took Mr Eichorn his tea, she waited after the first knock, tried two more times and then cautiously opened the door only to find his office was empty.

Going to Mr Highbury's office, she knocked and asked him how she would know when Mr Eichorn was out or in.

He took her to a window and showed her an empty parking space behind the offices. "He has a large black car; no one else would or indeed is ever permitted to park there, so now you know!" He smiled at her, "You are showing initiative; doing well so far, now off you go."

"Do I ask the office staff for work, I'm not sure what to do apart from the plan printing, teas and running errands…"

Mr Highbury said, "They will ask you for their requirements; relax, you don't have to be a busy little bee most of the time!" At home, Audrey asked her mother what 'accountants' did.

Her mother said, "Well, I don't know everything, but mainly they look after money!"

That was all Audrey needed to know.

The next day she knocked on Mr Taylor's door and asked him for more petty cash to buy tea supplies.

"Bring me your little account book and the receipts for money you have already spent, and the petty cash tin."

"Do I have an account book?'

"In the kitchen drawer. It is a little red notebook!'

Audrey found it, but all that she could see noted, was her own details for the office staff preferences.

She found the receipts, pleased that she had thought to retain them, and returned to Mr Taylor's office.

He was kind. In just a few moments she had her first lesson in bookkeeping.

He saw her notations for the staff teas, smiled, and turning the page towards the back of the book, he tore out some other figured pages saying, "Now we shall start again with some simple bookkeeping."

He gave her a ruler asking her to rule down the page so that she had three columns, making the second and third one only one quarter the width of the first.

Audrey was then instructed to give each column a heading. The first 'Items', the second 'Money in', and the third 'Money out'. Over the top of these headings she was asked to write 'Sample'.

She followed his instructions, writing ten shillings in the 'Money In' column.

Audrey wrote various items like biscuits, tea, sugar, milk, coffee and so on with the price in the 'Money out' column. She then added each column, subtracting one from the other to show a balance and then the injection of more funds added to that balance. A line was ruled here; the balance written in the 'Money in' column and she was told to continue as she had been shown in the sample.

Audrey was ecstatic at having learned a new skill and thanked Mr Taylor profusely. Pleased by her enthusiasm, he gave her a clip on which to put her receipts, brought the balance up to ten shillings and told her to see him whenever the balance was low.

Just as she rose to leave him, he asked, "You seem interested in book-keeping; have you considered becoming a bookkeeper or even an accountant? You seem to have a good head for figures."

Audrey smiled her thanks, said she would think about it and left thinking that the kindness of Mr Taylor and the affability of Mr Highbury may perhaps make up for the angry Mr Eichorn.

However this was not to be. Audrey seldom managed to get Mr Eichorn's tea on time. If she was one minute early, he shouted rudely and sent her away. By the time she got back to the kitchen to add a little more hot water so that it wouldn't be cold, she was late when she returned to his office, bringing about more abuse. She tried standing outside his door, counting to one hundred rapidly and then re-entering, only to be cursed because the tea was not the right temperature. She began to think that he must have escaped from some lunatic asylum and that she would never ever be able to please. One day she politely asked if they could have a chat to assist getting along better. He was outraged. "Who do you think you are? Get out of my office!"

Her first week's pay mollified some of the dissatisfaction she felt. Her father told her to give half to her mother and the rest was for her fares and to spend. Although she took her lunch to the office there was little left after her bus tickets were purchased. Dorothy quietly gave her half of her contribution back, saying she might need it for emergencies. She started a savings account with Barclays Bank, putting not all but a little of her funds in each week.

When she had nothing to do, she went to Mr Taylor's office to offer her assistance. He gave her columns of figures to add up on a machine that printed out the numbers on a paper roll and added them at the end. It was very noisy and seemed to take much time. She put it aside and added them in her head writing her answers in the columns. When she had finished, she was surprised to see the answers for each column were the same.

Mr Taylor told her it was a trust account and something would be wrong if this did not happen. He pointed out that the machine printing was good for finding errors that could be made by hitting the wrong keys and insisted she use it. She complied but only after considering that if you didn't hit any keys you wouldn't make any mistakes, and that if the columns balanced then obviously you could add up correctly.

Audrey had been working for three weeks. During this time she had not been asked to do any printing or writing on plans. She disliked the plan printing room. The ammonia made her eyes water and her head fuzzy and she often spent a few hours there in the course of a day. The fan system seemed very inadequate. She got permission to occasionally go outside for a breath of fresh air and she used this to advantage.

On Friday, payday of her third week, there was a temporary power failure. The urn finally chugged its way to boiling point by eleven o'clock. She knocked on Mr Eichorn's door at ten past and entered. His torrent of abuse was unexpected. She tried to explain, but he shouted her down before she got any further than the first 'but'.

Audrey stood on the other side of the desk watching and listening to him. Suddenly she felt detached and quite unemotional about this whole event. She didn't dislike him, fear him, and nothing he said seemed to matter, but she did feel he needed a lesson.

Teaching Mr Eichorn a Lesson

Moving back a pace, waiting for him to take a breath, she took careful aim and threw the cup with its contents together with the saucer and biscuit straight at him and without saying a word she left his office, only stopping to pick up her coat and bag as she left the building for the last time.

She walked through town eventually finding her way to Broadfield Park, finding the bench where she had told Doctor Gordon she couldn't marry him, feeling comforted by his presence that still seemed to be there.

She ate her lunch before reviewing the situation.

She had no regrets. It was a relief to get away from the ammonia and Mr Eichorn. Audrey had appreciated the beginning of good relationships with the rest of the staff and would have enjoyed seeing them again, but not at the expense of what she was supposed to experience.

The immediate consideration was telling her family. Audrey could imagine the conversation, particularly her father's irritation and shouting. She decided to get another job first before telling them about this one.

Each day for the rest of the week she telephoned or went for interviews, walked through the park and even the grounds of her old primary and grammar school, went to the pictures, and generally filled in time until she was due home. Her savings disappeared. Her mother reluctantly granted her request to not pay board for two weeks because she had been told Audrey had something special to do and agreed to keep this secret.

However, half way through the following week a pay cheque for one week's wages arrived from Mr Taylor. This created questions and the truth had to be told.

Audrey was somewhat saved from her father's tirade by another letter arriving the same day granting her a place for training in the PMG Department.

This mollified the situation, until further on through the letter, details of living away from home for three months training was read by her father. He absolutely forbade it. Her mother sent Audrey on a long errand and when she returned things had quietened down.

Her father said, "It's a good job everything's found; at least we don't have

175

to shell out any more money for you, and it says here you will get some pocket money because, by gum, you won't be getting any from us! If you can't get and keep a good job like you had, where you might have got an apprenticeship as an architect and made something of yourself, then you are on your own from now on. You think you are grown-up; well I've got news for you; throwing a cup of tea at your boss isn't very grown up, I'm telling you!"

Audrey said, "In my position, you would have half killed him!" He got out of his chair with is hand raised. Audrey fled for the stairs hearing her mother saying "Don't Fred!' as her father shouted "Don't you dare give me any backchat or I'll see to you!"

For the next few days Audrey avoided her father whenever possible.

The following Monday she reported to the PMG town office, and following instructions boarded a bus that took her to a train for a training college forty-five miles from where she lived.

Audrey was excited, looking forward to a new adventure: free and happy to be relying only on her own resources.

CHAPTER 26

Learning, Training and Romance

At the designated time, Audrey boarded a train for Chorlton and was met at the station along with the five other girls by the representative from the PMG Department. His name was Bob Whitman. He introduced the girls to each other, told them they would be sharing two to a room, and that he would take them to their boarding house and inform them where to walk to the training college the next morning.

The girls were quiet and shy with each other on the short ride in the mini bus. Audrey studied them, deciding who she would prefer as a room companion. It was difficult; all that she could rely on was feeling and intuition.

As they arrived and stood in the hallway of the boarding house she quietly and slowly stood next to the person of her choice. Her moving had somehow made the girls into two to a line as they stood behind each other facing a staircase.

A lady walked slowly down the stairs surveying them with a faint smile and careful interest.

She graciously shook hands with each girl asking her name and introducing herself as the owner and manager of the boarding house. "You may call me Mrs Howard," she said, smiling, "and I am here if you feel troubled and want advice."

"In your rooms are the times for each of you to use the bathroom facilities. There are two bathrooms and lavatories that you must share, and the times will prevent collisions and arguments. All mealtimes are stipulated and these must be adhered too if you would prefer your meal to be warm and not cold. If you decide to eat elsewhere, it is necessary to inform me at least two meals in advance. The college is paying for all your meals, board and other necessary toilet facilities. Now, are there any questions?"

The girls were silent but some shook their heads.

Mrs Howard gestured to the front two girls; Betty and Norma. "Please proceed up the stairs to room 3 and unpack." Audrey and Paula were directed to Room 2 and Sarah and Barbara to Room 1.

Smiling shyly at each other as they divided the wardrobe and drawers and allocated the beds, Audrey and Paula began to converse.

In a short time they were sitting opposite each other on their beds and chatting away with gusto, until Paula said, "Perhaps we should check the meal timetable?" This led them to go rushing down the stairs looking for the dining room. It was a surprise to find four other strangers already seated, they turned out to be supervisors and teachers for the telephonist course.

They nodded in acknowledgement of the new students, but were obviously happy to keep to themselves.

The six girls shared a table and gradually began to chat and exchange personal data. The volume was somewhat subdued by their surroundings' and the presence of the four adults at another table, but they slowly warmed to each other and became friendly.

It was a Sunday evening. The girls decided to go for a short walk together around the neighbourhood and retire early to be prepared for their first day of training.

The next morning, Bob arrived at eight and escorted them to the training college. It was a huge place that trained engineers, technicians, postal workers, in fact anything at all to do with the Postmaster General's Department.

Learning, Training and Romance

Audrey was surprised to learn that her training included some technical equipment aspects, such as replacing broken plug-in cords on a switchboard, fixing minor problems with a dial and keys that functioned poorly on the front of the board. There were PBX and PABX boards to learn, and some knowledge required of even older systems that one may find in remote parts of the countryside. This was more interesting than she had imagined. Information for handling local calls, trunk calls, overseas calls, emergency calls for fire, police, ambulance and anything else that someone in the public may consider an emergency had to be learned and handled with confidence and calmness. Learning included handling suggestive, flirtatious, rude and abusive callers. These required specific, detached, firm handling and supervising control for tracing. Altogether it was quite a composite of versatile learning and Audrey could now see why it would take three months of training.

She eagerly threw herself into learning anything and everything with focused devotion. She wanted to show her family that this was an important occupation, worthy of their esteem and that she was not to be looked down on as just another "Hello girl!", often the name given to telephonists.

After a few days of assimilating most of the curriculum she rang her parents. Her mother handed the phone to her father after she excitedly began listing all the things she had to learn. Her mother felt that this would mollify her father, but Audrey barely got through a third of her listing, before her father interrupted with "I don't want to hear any more of this bloody nonsense, you should be at University learning something decent."

Audrey did not reply, asking only to speak to her mother again. Dorothy, recognising that her daughter was upset, said, "I'm sorry; I thought he had accepted this new idea but he hasn't; he still wants you to do what he never got the chance to do!"

Audrey replied, trying to hold back her tears, "Maybe Charles will want to go, but I don't. I want to live my life, not Dad's." Her mother sighed, "It's hard for anyone to understand when you refuse to use your intelligence for what it is really worth."

A LIFE of Enlightenment

"Have you considered that perhaps my intelligence is keeping me away? I don't know exactly what I want to do, but I do know in my heart that I don't need University to do it!" "Maybe not," Dorothy replied, "but it wouldn't harm either!" Audrey was quiet. She felt she had just lost her mother as an ally. She said a quiet goodbye and promised to ring the following week.

Training continued each day from Monday to Friday. Audrey did not lose her enthusiasm to learn. She found the learning fairly easy, but was baffled by the restrictions on communication. The set phrases for questions and replies were strictly enforced and were monitored by patrolling supervisors. Audrey felt that a friendly attitude and a brief enquiry here and there, particularly in response to an origination by a customer, would be more applicable. Her suggestions fell on deaf ears.

Another Friday evening came and the girls were all in favour of visiting the local dance hall. Audrey had been dancing at their own local dance hall with Margaret a few times and although lessons were not available she had learned, as most everyone else did, by observation and practise.

The most wonderful thing about going out was the lack of discipline. No-one to tell you what to wear or what time you had to be home or else! This was exquisite!

Audrey was not used to wearing much make-up; generally a little lipstick and a brush of powder on the nose sufficed.

Paula however shook her head and beckoned her to a chair in front of the mirror. She studied the reflection and then said, "Alright you have the traditional peaches and cream complexion although it's a lot paler than most, but your eyes need attention. She proceeded to apply a little green powder to Audrey's eyelids and then mascara to her lashes and more red lipstick that matched Audrey's dress.

Audrey was astounded by the result. She looked very grown up; at least eighteen. She commented on this to Paula.

"I didn't know you were only fifteen and a half!" Paula added, when she saw Audrey was about to protest. "You seem so confident and wise for your age; I thought you would be at almost eighteen like me!"

Learning, Training and Romance

Audrey was pleased. "I'm so glad we are sharing a room together, thank you for helping me!" She smiled at her companion as they left to walk down the stairs together.

The dance hall seemed crowded but as the band started up again and couples moved on to the floor, spaces opened up. It was charming to watch the couples dancing. As each dance commenced, the lights over the floor dimmed and dancing circles of light reflecting from a huge mirrored revolving ball overhead flickered over the dancers.

Audrey stood near her group entranced by the spectacle.

She did not notice the man who approached her from the side, until he touched her elbow and invited her to dance.

She accepted and smiled at him.

"Wow!" he said, "dimples too!" as he whirled her confidently around the floor.

She was busy trying to follow his steps, before she gave up and let him step out and lead her wherever he wished to go. He was an excellent dancer and as she relaxed in his arms she became aware that she was not dancing with a boy but with an adult.

He was tall. Her nose seemed to be around the middle of his tie. He was well dressed, in what Audrey called a Sunday or 'Doctor Gordon' outfit; a navy blue suit, white shirt and a red and blue tie.

She told him that she thought he looked very smart!

He moved her a little away from his chest, as she gazed at him. She noticed he had a moustache also. This was certainly grown up.

"And you are very pretty," he said. "I love those dimples!" Audrey gave him a muffled "Thank you," and let her head disappear under his chin.

The music stopped. She turned to move away, but his hand under her elbow propelled her towards the refreshment counter, and he offered her a drink.

"Just lemonade please!"

He smiled, "They don't have any strong drink here, just fruit juice, Sarsaparilla and Burdock, Ginger Beer, Vimto, that sort of thing!"

He suddenly offered his hand "My name is Lloyd Winters. I'm a sales representative and I work around this area, and you are…?"

Audrey shook the offered hand and said "Audrey Southgate, and I'm at the Post Master General training college for about three months, learning to be a telephonist and a minor technician."

They gazed at each other, each liking what they saw. Audrey only realized they were still holding hands when the drinks came. Lloyd took them to a nearby table and they talked through two more dances, before taking the floor once more. He asked her if she had a steady boyfriend or was engaged or nearly engaged.

She laughed saying, "No, I was engaged once but we ended it as he was too old for me. Now he is married to someone else!" After three more dances, Audrey excused herself to look for her friends, hoping that they would not feel deserted. However, it took a while to find them; they were all dancing with partners. They waved as they dance passed smiling and looking happy.

Another man asked her to dance. He was short and as old as her father. He gazed steadfastly over her shoulder and said not a word, dancing with careful short steps and placing much effort and manipulation onto her back, guiding her to prevent them from bumping into other couples.

When the music stopped he politely steered her back to where he had found her, said a low "Thank you!" and walked away.

She was pleased to see Lloyd coming towards her again.

They spent the rest of the evening together, dancing or talking at the table.

The girls waved when their eyes connected. Audrey relaxed, feeling comfortable with Lloyd and also with the girls.

Lloyd walked her home; the girls strolling arm in arm in front. He asked her if she would like to go to the pictures on the following Tuesday. She was delighted to accept.

Once inside the house the girls crowded in her room wanting details. How old was he? What did he do? Did he try to kiss her at any time? And the most important question of all, how old did he think she was?

Audrey answered with the answers she had learned throughout the evening. Her answer to the last question was, "I don't know; he obviously didn't think it was important because he didn't ask me!"

The girls agreed in unison that Audrey seemed much older than she was and gave many suggestions that may avoid any questions that may give away her age!

Audrey listened to the suggestions but felt that if the question really arose she would answer it. She reasoned that if Lloyd was interested in spending time with her, if would have little to do with her age.

On Saturday the girls went to see a film at the local cinema. It had a strange unhappy ending and they discussed lots of possible alternatives as they walked home. Audrey found these conversations interesting. The various viewpoints exchanged were in Audrey's eyes a reflection of the girl's individual characters.

Alone in the room with Paula she mentioned how enlightening a discovery this had been. Paula stared at her in wonder, "Do you ever stop thinking, and analysing or making two and two make four?"

Audrey laughed, "Not really, because if you really listen two and two hardly ever make four; it's usually five, six or three!" Tuesday came. Lloyd arrived to take her to a large cinema in the City. He drove quickly but with concern for other vehicles. Audrey felt confident with the assurance that seemed to emanate from his presence.

They saw a romantic comedy. It highlighted the affectionate, friendly atmosphere that already existed between them. Lloyd held her hand as they left the cinema. It felt warm, friendly and respectful; much as Dr. Gordon's had felt. Audrey found this comparison confusing. Was he another Dr. Gordon or a romantic suitor? Finding the question unanswerable, she placed it on a shelf in her mind, intending to take it down later, when perhaps there was more data to expand it.

They had a light supper at a small cafe; afterwards, he drove her home. On the way they continued their discussion of the film. He was complimentary on her insight into the characters. He said he found her very wise for one so young!

Audrey avoided comment. She asked him to talk about his work. When he told her about some of his sales techniques, how he encouraged people to buy and how he handled their rebuttals and so forth, she was very quiet. Placing herself in the shoes of the recipient she could feel some resistance to what Lloyd was saying; but felt reluctant to tell him what she had discovered.

He parked the car outside her boarding house. Turning to face her he said "You are very quiet. Did I bore you with my sales talk?"

"Not at all! It was interesting!" She smiled at him. He regarded intently.

"I have a feeling you have something to say but you are reluctant to say it. Am I right in thinking this?"

She was embarrassed; she felt she had been caught out, and now was not sure which way to go.

Suddenly he assumed Dr. Gordon's demeanour. "Come now, out with it Audrey."

She was startled, yet so used to an immediate confession that she blurted out, "Once you have told them everything about the product, why don't you sit back and simply allow them to buy?"

He stared at her, "Are you saying that I oversell my customers?"

She was contrite, "I don't know what you would call it, but I could feel a time when they were there, reaching, and then when you continued I could feel them going away!"

"Aahh!" he said. "But I always get them back!"

Audrey said, "Yes well…But if you didn't send them away, you wouldn't have to get them back or go to so much trouble and you would save time. Wouldn't that mean that you could see more people and make more sales?"

He laughed and said "Good point! I should make you my sounding board for all things important! Have you any idea of the sort of mind you have?"

Audrey shook her head, "I would not know how to answer that! How could anyone answer something so obtuse! Probably only by comparison, but to what! Everyone is so unique that I feel comparisons are irrelevant!"

"Well, if that speech wasn't a demonstration of what I was just saying, I don't know what was." Lloyd looked at her with interest.

Audrey said, "Well, I read a lot and my fiancé taught me a great deal. Perhaps I should go in now!"

He was perceptive, "You say that as though you feel you have done enough damage for one evening. Is that how you feel?" She smiled and said "Touché! A little!"

They were outside the car standing on the pavement. He took her face between his hands, gazing into her eyes. She did not know what to do about this, so she steadfastly gazed back. He smiled before gently wrapping his arms around her to hold her close against his chest. It felt comfortable and safe. She liked the warm friendly feeling. He pulled back gazing at her face as she looked up to him. Then he bent his head to kiss her. Audrey had been very wary of this happening. She did not know how to kiss or how to respond. This was a grown-up. She felt that he probably wouldn't go round and round in circles like Duncan. All of this flashed through her mind in a second.

Suddenly his mouth was on hers; she did not know whether to open it or keep it closed or something in between. She relaxed, deciding to let things take their course. The kiss was gentle. Mainly it aroused interest in itself. She was aware of soft lips and a prickling sensation under her nose and above her bottom lip. This was not pleasant. She grimaced at the moustache. He pulled away gazing at her face. Audrey smiled at him while running the sensations through her head.

So this was what it was all about. Now here he was coming back for more. She gave herself to the moment, making notes in her head of lip movements, his hands on her back; now her head as he stroked her hair. She was aware that the breathing seemed to be more obvious and perhaps quicker than before. Was that because one could only breathe through one's nose when the mouth was not available? Now he was taking deep breaths! Should she do the same? Was this part of the routine? He pulled back, staring into her eyes. "Why do I get the idea that you are conjugating irregular verbs in your head or something similar and that you are not really into this?" Audrey was mortified!

She told him about the first kiss, and also that she was a very inexperienced kisser.

"But you have been engaged" he was surprised, "please don't tell me that you were seldom kissed?"

It was time to come clean.

As she started on the Dr. Gordon story, he interrupted, commenting that it would be warmer in the car. They climbed back into their seats, twisting to face each other, and she told him about her mentor, her very lovable wise friend. He listened intently.

When she had finished he commented that it was a lovely story. That she was a born storyteller and that she should write a book!

He was studying her face. She knew the question was about to be asked.

Before he could get it out she said, "I feel I should tell you that my age is fifteen and a half!"

"Bloody hell!" came out in an extremely startled voice. He immediately apologised.

"I'm so sorry, I thought you must be at least nineteen or twenty, and you often talk as though you are at least twenty-five. Are you aware that in male circles you are regarded as jail bait?"

She shook her head. "I don't know what that means, please explain!" Lloyd explained.

Not knowing what to say, she apologised. "Well I'm sorry about this, but really we are discussing the age of my body rather than me. I understand my body is too young for you, but it will grow out of that! I felt you liked me for who I am, rather than for my body?"

He sighed. "Unfortunately they go together, and very well I may add; but I can't do this now! I wish I had met you in another three to four years. Right now this is very bad timing!"

Learning, Training and Romance

Audrey wanted to dispute this. If the timing wasn't alright then why was it happening; but she felt this wasn't going to be acceptable. She recognised a mind made up and accepted the inevitable. She leaned over, giving him a gentle slow kiss on the cheek, and said, "thank you for everything, I really enjoyed your company. You are a very nice man and I appreciate that you showed me what a kiss is really like! Good night!"

Before he could get out of the car to open her door she was gone, walking briskly up the front path, letting herself in through the front door.

Paula was fast asleep. Audrey got undressed, slipped quietly into bed, mulling over the incident, the timing, what did it all mean? Finally deciding that it was just an experience that she needed and that there was no other special significance to find, she drifted into a sound sleep, happy with all that she had learned.

CHAPTER 27

Fred Decides To Emigrate The Family

Audrey started work with Paula in the Telephone Department in her home town on the Monday following her return. She was happy to be earning some wages, and still had enough left after paying her mother board to consider buying some grown-up clothes.

In a way it was good to be home. The break seemed to have taken her a little away from parental authority, although she could feel it easing back into her life as the days went by.

Talk around the house seemed to have reverted toward immigrating to New Zealand.

Audrey wasn't sure whether or not to take this seriously. Her father constantly cursed the English weather, threatening to live elsewhere if it didn't 'buck up', but nothing had ever come of it. It seemed to be forgotten once a sunny day arrived.

This time however the discussions persisted.

When Audrey ventured an idea that she may not want to go, Fred with fierce intention said, "You're not old enough to state an opinion; for once in your life you will do as you are told!" Dorothy shook her head at her and said quietly when everyone was out of earshot, "We are just making enqui-

A LIFE of Enlightenment

ries, don't start anything now please!" Audrey complied.

One Monday, her father announced at dinner that all the family were going by train to London to make an application to emigrate.

For Audrey, this meant requesting a day off. Fred said "No! Your mother will call and tell them you are sick, but you will be well by Monday!"

Friday came and the family arrived by train and then took a taxi to New Zealand House in London.

They waited in reception for some time, before the parents were taken down a corridor to an office.

Margaret and Charles listened as Audrey shared what she remembered from school about New Zealand. There was a map on the wall and she showed them the two different islands and the capitals of each. On a world map also hanging in reception she showed them the distance between England and the Islands, and also Australia.

She talked to the receptionist, who on finding out her parents' occupations said that Builders and Hairdressers would be welcomed with open arms.

When Dorothy and Fred with a furious look on his face reappeared saying "Come on, we're leaving," and headed for the exit; the children followed.

He stood outside, his gaze darting from side to side, before he said "Right! Follow me and be damn quick about it."

He marched across the road with the family running to catch up with his strides, and stopped outside Australia House. Audrey ran to his side. "What happened in there, why are you angry?"

He turned to face her. "They want builders and hairdressers but they will only take families of four; and in case you haven't noticed we are a family of five!"

"Why don't we persuade them to take us, if we were to go in together they would see that we are a good, honest, hardworking family; did you tell them that I have a job?" "After that rejection," Fred said, "I wouldn't go there if they *paid* me, and that's that! We will see if Australia wants us.

The family marched up the steps of Australia House, waited in recep-

Fred Decides To Emigrate The Family

tion, and finally all the family were taken to an interview room.

The parents answered questions, filled in forms, and finally were welcomed as potential emigrants to Australia, subject to medicals and X-rays which were immediately arranged for them nearby.

Audrey was intrigued with the X-ray technician who measured her front ways and sideways and said "You have very fine bones." Audrey thanked him, taking this as a compliment.

The rest of the day was spent with all the family being weighed, measured, having blood tests, being medical checked in all aspects and finally having photographs taken for passports.

They arrived home late in the evening, all of them exhausted by the turn and speed of events. Two passports, which included the listing of the children and a letter accepting them for Australia arrived two weeks later, with a document asking for the parents' signature for acceptance of the offer.

When this was signed and returned, the family expected a long wait before the next ship departed for their new country. This was not to be. One week later a letter arrived informing them that they were to report for sailing from Southampton on the "SS Otranto" on the 14th June.

The sailing date was only two weeks away.

Panic reigned. The house had to be sold, Dorothy's clients informed. Audrey was not allowed to work her notice but had to leave immediately. She saw her supervisor, who was kind, and while Audrey waited arranged a reference.

Somehow it all came together. The sale of the house was left with an agency, for Uncle Tom to monitor.

The family sorted and packed. Audrey got out her school books, looking up weather for Perth and countries the ship stopped at along the way; geography, not a favourite subject, now became of interest. She was familiar with the map shape of Australia. She remembered it for exams because it looked like a Scottish Terrier's head. She remembered wheat and sheep farming and mineral deposits, and knew an 'Aboriginal Corroboree' was a sacred dance.

However, she had pictures of living in tents, defending the family from spears and boomerangs, and being pioneers in a country that needed to be tamed. This did not faze her; rather it was a new adventure and all adventures were to be savoured.

She could see Fred building houses for others from the trees that would be cut down, and her mother even in primitive conditions doing something pleasing with their wives' hair, and Margaret still doing an apprenticeship with her mother, being her assistant.

Audrey was not sure what she would be doing. Perhaps they had some sort of telephones or maybe she could teach the pioneers' children the three R's?

She decided to wait until arrival and then decide the best course of action.

The day of leaving arrived. All the relatives and a few of the children's friends had called the day before to say goodbye.

Audrey had telephoned Doctor Gordon in Scotland and was still waiting his arrival. "It is hard for me to get away Audrey, but I will see you before you leave!'

She knew he would arrive even if it was in the last few minutes.

When he did knock on their front door, one hour before the taxi arrived to take the family to the station, she flew to the front door, opened it and threw herself into his arms.

He laughed, hugging her close. It reminded Audrey of the first time she had met him when she had hugged his knee because that was all she could reach.

He gently pulled away still holding her arms, and looked at her with pleasure. "Audrey, look at you; you've grown into a lovely but very grown-up young lady. You really are going to give the boys something to handle." He was smiling as he greeted her parents then Margaret and Charles. He asked them about their decision to emigrate, commiserated with Fred about the hardship of the weather in relation to the building trade, adding that he understood Australia was a wonderful place to start a new life. He

Fred Decides To Emigrate The Family

wished them well and asked if Audrey could sit in the car with him to catch up on their special news. Fred, now mollified by all the agreements reached about his plans, consented.

Doctor Gordon and Audrey sat turned towards each other on the front bench seat smiling for a moment or so, pleased to be together again.

Audrey said, "Your news first please?"

He smiled, "Well, the most exciting news is that I will be a father before the end of this year!"

Audrey was stunned for a moment. She had not seen him for almost a year and a half; she had almost forgotten that he was married, and now here he was announcing his expected fatherhood.

She recovered very quickly, saying with honest sincerity, "Gosh, I almost forgot you were married. Many congratulations. I'm sure you will make a wonderful father, especially if you treat your children as you have treated me!" "Audrey, that is a beautiful and charming remark and I thank you for your vote of confidence. I confess that without having you in my life I would be careful and perhaps tentative in dealing with children. Much I have learned from our times together I already apply to my young patients. This has been successful and given me the confidence to learn from experience in other Doctors' consulting rooms.

Being away from you has been a continuous cognition of all we have discussed and shared together. Situations have constantly cropped up that find me falling back on some remembered remark or profundity that we have discussed, that I could apply to a current event. Knowing you has been perhaps the most treasured event of my life, and I shall never thank God enough for bringing you into my life!"

She was stunned! The lump in her throat got in the way of talking. She tried to hold back the tears, but they ran as though unhindered down her cheeks. She licked them away with her tongue and dashed them off her cheeks with her fingers until he handed her a handkerchief.

Without thinking she blew her nose and then did not know whether to give it back or keep it.

He smiled, recognising her dilemma. "Have it as a keepsake!" He pulled her close and hugged her.

When she regained her composure she said, "I could have said and meant all those words to you!"

"Yes, I do know that!" He pulled back a little, smiled at her and smoothed her hair.

"Write to me Audrey. Tell me all your life discoveries; you have such a lot of it to live especially with the adventure of going to a new country."

He gave her a piece of paper. "This is my address. I will let you know if it changes. It looks as though I will remain in Scotland for a few years. My friend is dying but I predict it will take some time. He has a son who will graduate in two years, perhaps a little longer. When he does, he can take over the practise and I will return and set up my own surgery here. Most of your relatives were my patients and perhaps they will come back to me if I return. Always, you will be able to find me. Now are you happy again!"

She nodded, leaning over to kiss his cheek.

"I love you," she said and gently squeezed his hand.

"And I love you and always will. Until we meet again, and we will! Now I must away…I can see a Taxi arriving in the rear mirror. I must quickly wish your parents Bon Voyage."

He hopped out of the car, hurrying round to open her door and help her alight. There was a quick goodbye to her parents, and then with a wave of his hand he was gone.

Audrey watched his car moving out of sight, and then turned to help with the luggage before climbing into the taxi that was to start her family's new life.

CHAPTER 28

June 1951—The Voyage to Australia

The SS Otranto, a large ship for its time, was an adventure in itself. Audrey with her sister carefully put away clothes, sharing the allocated space. The cabin trunk slid under one of the beds and acted as storage in the small cabin. The tiny adjoining bathroom could only hold one person at a time, especially if someone was sitting on the toilet. Audrey was careful to lock the door as she felt that if someone opened it she would be decapitated at the knees. The ship was slowly moving away from Southampton after a glorious send-off with a band playing; streamers were being thrown from ship to shore, and relatives waving and calling "Bon Voyage" or crying into handkerchiefs, feeling that loved ones may never be seen again. Uncle Jack and Aunt Dolly from London had come to see the Southgate family off. It was the first time Audrey or indeed any of the children had met them; they seemed pleasant and friendly. Audrey had an immediate feeling that they would meet again someday!

Once settled in the cabin she decided to explore. She asked her sister to accompany her but Margaret said, "No, we should wait here for Mum and Dad, you can't just go off on your own; you might get lost!"

Audrey said, "I need to find out where everything is, so that I *won't* get lost; you can't do that sitting here! Tell them I am learning my way around the ship so that we will all know where to go, to eat, play games, or whatever."

Margaret said, "Dad won't like it!"

Audrey grinned, "He will when I tell him where the dining room is!"

This was fun; she walked around each outside deck, going up and down stairs. Then she started on the inside of each deck. More organised now, she started at the bottom winding her way slowly to the top. She discovered two dining rooms, a large ballroom, a swimming pool, and lots of mysterious deck games. There were markings on the decks but no equipment, so it was hard to tell how to play! There was a hairdressing shop, a doctor's office, a purser's counter, a library, and a room with tables and chairs and a couple of shops. She stayed away from entries labelled crew only, no matter how tempting they looked!

She passed people finding their way to a dining room, mostly looking uncertain and a little lost. She knew it was time for dinner. Audrey hurried back to her cabin. The whole family were crowded into the tiny space. Before anyone could say anything she said "We need to go to the dining room. Come. I will show you where it is. She checked the notice behind the door to find out the name of their allocation, and opening the door said, "I know where it is, follow me!

Her father, wearing a grim look but silent, led his family behind Audrey. On entering the dining area a steward led them to their seats explaining that this is where they would always sit for each meal. Circumventing admonishments, Audrey enthusiastically began explaining the ship and her discoveries. Interest overcame disapproval and finally she had not only her family but other parents and a small child sharing the table as an audience!

The meal was excellent. Three courses came and went in rapid succession; some had strange names and had to be translated by the waiter, an affable man called Wally. Audrey managed to translate some of the French names but others had her puzzled. Vanilla pudding turned out to be ice-cream and not at all pudding as she knew it!

June 1951 – The Voyage to Australia

After dinner she took both families on a little tour of the ship. In the table and chairs room, some people without children were playing cards, waiting for the dining rooms' second sitting.

Her father said, "We've had a long day, so you are all going to bed early. We will call for you at 8am for breakfast!" To Audrey he said, "I don't want you running around the ship without so much as a by-your-leave either; you need to tell your mother or me where you are going and why. Is that understood?"

Audrey said, "Unless I fall overboard you will always know where I am. I cannot get lost and I promise to stay out of trouble! I realise the Captain can have me thrown in irons or whatever, so I promise to be good!"

Her father snorted and left the cabin.

Left by themselves, Margaret and Audrey began to undress. Margaret said, "Why do you always rub him up the wrong way and make him mad?"

Audrey said, "Is there a right way?"

Margaret said, "You are always too smart for your own good! I prefer a peaceful life!"

"That's boring!"

"No," Margaret said, "Just better!"

Audrey was silent; but she went to sleep examining this thought.

Taking it to the extreme she considered…was she really a warmonger and Margaret a pacifist? In good conscience, could she really start a war?

She had an imaginary conversation with Dr. Gordon for a few moments.

"No," he said. "You are much too loving and caring for your fellow man and too intelligent to use force to get what you want."

"What about the thrown cup of tea at my boss?" she asked the unseen presence.

"That still concerns you? Why?"

"I could understand it if I did it in anger; but I was detached and calm. It was like thinking this is the last straw so here is your tea and a lesson to boot. Maybe you will be kinder in the future to the rest of your staff so that you don't have to control them by fear. This is clearer now than it was at the time! I guess it is a little bit like the farmer beating the horse, same scenario all over again. I beat the farmer and stooped to his level! I thought I had learned a lesson from that but events don't bear it out!"

"Aren't you being too hard on yourself? How else could you have handled your Mr Eichorn?"

Audrey pondered, "I could have just left the firm; I might have said *'working for you does not make me smile therefore you need to replace me!'* That would have been without any violence on any gradient! I was calm enough at the same time to have done that, yet it seemed important to give him a lesson! Hence a cup of tea all over his shirt!"

She felt Dr. Gordon's smile as he asked, "What do you think happened after you left?"

She said, "Well, he would have jumped up in shock, and because the tea was still hot and very wet, he would have tried to hold his shirt front away from his body. He would probably have bellowed and maybe the office manager came running, or some other staff member. They would have taken in the scene and thought he had an accident, but he would have dissuaded them of that immediately by saying, *'That little so and so threw it at me. Where is she, I will have a piece of her!'* And someone will have come looking for me only to find that my coat and bag had gone. There would have been much discussion in the office. Some would have smiled and said it was a good thing, some may have said it was a brave act, and wished they had done it themselves and that it was overdue, and others would have said it won't make any difference so it was a lost cause!"

"What do you think were Mr Eichorn's thoughts after he had changed his shirt and cooled down?"

"I don't know! He might have gone on cursing me in his head. Or even decided I wasn't worth a thought and instructed the office manager to place an advertisement to replace me! I'm not sure!"

"Do you think he might have considered his own actions and perhaps modified his behaviour over a period of time?" Audrey said to the unseen but palpable presence, "Maybe! One hopes so! I just thought of something.

June 1951 – The Voyage to Australia

I still got a full week's pay and he has to sign all the cheques! So maybe he stopped being cross and did some thinking!"

"Yes. It is possible! Tell me why did this crop up; was it your discourse with Margaret or was it because of your disagreement with this former action?"

"Well, one thing led to another! I can see now that we need to immediately resolve any issue; any slight disagreement we have, mostly with ourselves otherwise we get a build-up and that muddies our thinking in the present! It is interesting, isn't it? Miss Keating said, *'Audrey you need to look at consequences before you take action!'* She was right. I need to do that a lot more! I need to look before I leap!"

She felt he was smiling and nodding as he replied, "That is a good thought! You know who you are otherwise these questions would never occur to you. All that you say and do is balanced against who you have decided to be. It is just a part of you being true to you! Nothing to judge yourself upon! You are too bright and intelligent to waste your energy on regret or taking yourself to task. Introspection is good! Are you aware that all your wisdom comes from this ability?"

Audrey was fascinated! She wondered if she was having a conversation with herself or was it that she knew Doctor Gordon so well that she could predict what he would answer; or could she really call up his presence. She wanted to telephone him but this was not possible. Why hadn't she tried this before when it was easy to pick up the telephone and say

"I have been talking to you for the last few minutes; were you aware of this?"

It was also interesting that as she began to query this, she was sure she felt his presence begin to withdraw.

Now here she was lying in the cabin with her sister asleep near her, on a ship that was taking her to a new land, and a gentle rocking motion that was sending her drifting to dreamland. Tomorrow could be even more interesting than today!

CHAPTER 29

Awakening to Real Romance?

Breakfast was a friendly affair. Everyone was rested and even Fred seemed more affable. Wally the waiter inquired about their evening and trusted they had slept well.

When Dorothy commented to Fred that he seemed like a very nice young man, Fred reverted to type. "He's just after a big tip, that's all."

Audrey hurried through breakfast, anxious to get away and explore some more. As she stood up to excuse herself, Fred demanded to know where she was going.

"To find out how to play some of the deck games!"

"Don't get too friendly with people you don't know, and make sure you are here on time for lunch!"

She nodded and moved quickly out of the dining room aware of Wally grinning at her behind her father's chair.

On the games deck, people were already signing up to take part in competitions. Audrey put her name down for everything. She didn't care about the competitiveness; she just wanted to play and needed a partner. Charles was too young at five years, and Margaret did not care for these games. Audrey was told to check the notice board in the afternoon to see who her partners were, and to be close to the table tennis board at 2.30 pm to meet her partner and play in the first round. She spent the next few hours until lunch in the library reading a book, feeling quite grown up as she was the youngest reader.

She saw her family for lunch, invited them to watch her play table tennis at 2.30pm, and set off to watch some of the deck games. They were interesting and she learned much just by watching.

At 2.20 she arrived near the table tennis area. There was a man standing near, perhaps a little older than Dr. Gordon. Their eyes met and Audrey wandered over to him saying, "Are you Mr Griffiths, my partner?"

He smiled and said, "Guilty as charged! You must be Audrey!" They smiled and shook hands.

Audrey picked up a bat and a ball saying "Shall we practice?" Audrey had not played very much 'ping-pong' as her family called it, but she had a good eye for the ball and kept her attention on it. As they warmed up, the ball stayed in play much longer. Mr Griffiths was a good player and was pleased with her as the practice went on.

Eventually other players joined them and they had a practice foursome before playing in earnest.

Mr Griffiths and Audrey easily won their first round by two out of the three games. They agreed to meet one hour before dinner for another half hour of practice, and parted already good friends.

Her family had watched the match. Her mother congratulated her; her father said, "Isn't there someone more your own age to play with?"

"I don't think so! The sports director puts everyone together. Anyway he's a good player, I don't want to lose him! You automatically play better if you play with someone who has more experience than yourself!"

"Well, I don't want you to have anything to do with his *experience*, as you put it!" Fred glared at her. Dorothy placed an arm on his saying, "Come now, he's just like another Dr. Gordon, and he's married. The blonde lady opposite watching him was his wife!"

"Well, she should be playing with him then!" Fred was not to be put off

Awakening to Real Romance?

laying down the law.

Audrey said. "If the first round is finished I am going to practice shuffle board. I'm playing it first thing in the morning and then deck tennis and deck quoits; in the afternoon another table tennis match; so I'm quite the busy bee." She grinned at her family and waved as she turned on her heel to leave.

That evening there was dancing in the ballroom. Her parents decided to take Charles to see the cartoons that preceded a later picture show.

Audrey and Margaret decided to go dancing, with Fred's *'Make sure you dance with each other'* ringing in their ears. Dorothy had smiled and given a tiny shake of her head to let them know that she would handle his requests.

After all, Margaret was 17 and Audrey just a few months off 16. They were old enough to have a dance with a male partner and had often done so.

They stood at the edge of the floor watching the very few dancers. After two more dances, some couples plucked up courage and joined the brave ones.

A young man appeared at Audrey's side, asking for the pleasure of her company. He had the straightest back that she had ever seen. He was dressed in the ship's white dress uniform. He had some decorations on his uniform, but she had no idea what they meant. He was a good head taller with black curly hair, a fair complexion, and the bluest sparkling eyes. The straight back made him seem taller than he actually was, yet he was relaxed. He guided her around the floor expertly, smiling at her from time to time. When the music stopped he led her to a small table, seated her in a chair, and offered to bring her a soft drink. She looked around quickly for Margaret, who seemed to be enjoying a similar experience.

Audrey relaxed. It was a pleasure to watch him walk. It was an unhurried, purposeful walk. It was attractive and compelling in its posture. She felt she could watch it forever!

He returned to the table, smiling. "We will talk about that interesting expression you are wearing later; in the meantime allow me to introduce myself: my name is Michael Conrad Oak, I am the third refrigeration engineer on this ship, and my home is in Glamorgan Wales. Now you are…?"

"My name is Audrey Southgate. I do not have a middle name as they were in very short supply when I was born! I lived in a place called Rochdale and also while doing some training I lived for a short time in Chorlton. With my family I am going to Perth to start a new life!" He had smiled warmly about the middle name comment. She noticed his white teeth and the dazzling smile. He was very good-looking, absolutely handsome. She was happy to be seen with him. Her face glowed!

"Now," he said, "what was that almost approving analyzing expression that you were wearing as I returned with the drinks?"

She was amazed at his perception. Her family never seemed to read her as Dr. Gordon and as Michael did. He had a beautiful voice and a faint lilting accent. She wondered if he was too good to be true! She began to wonder about the hidden horn and tails, before she realized that this type of thought belonged to her father and was really not part of who she was. Michael watched her with amusement and some intrigue. Fleeting expressions came and went across her face; the dimples which he found entrancing flickered in and out with her thoughts. She had no idea how open and vulnerable and appealing she was just to watch. Now she was looking at him with a slightly quizzical expression. He raised an eyebrow, awaiting her answer.

Audrey looked straight at him as she replied, "I loved watching you walk. You have the straightest back I have ever seen. You keep your body still and move from the hips. It presents a fascinating yet relaxed motion. I could watch it all day in admiration and not get tired. It inspires me to sit up straighter, with my shoulders back, and ask for my head to reach for the stars while looking straight ahead. Yet you do not appear to be aware of the effect you create. We have only just met, yet you already have unwittingly made this great effect! You should be proud!"

He was amazed. Her discourse was so unexpected. Intrigued, he knew she was not aware of the effect she herself created. He was reminded of a verse. *"No mortal woman was so unaware that anyone was watching her."*

Awakening to Real Romance?

He said, "Tell me, do you always answer questions with such a profound analytical discourse?" She laughed, "Yes, I guess I do! It is not deliberate! The answer arrives and I tend to just say whatever comes to mind. Do I offend you?"

"Heavens no! Promise me that you will never change, it is fascinating! Almost an education in itself. I feel I have just found a kindred soul! Do you like poetry?"

"Yes!"

"What do you like; tell me something or someone that you enjoy."

She smiled. "Well, right now I'm enjoying you! Alright, let me see... Shakespeare. Omar Khayyam. Shelley. Keats. Wordsworth, almost anyone who says the appropriate words at the appropriate time."

He beamed at her. It was a while since she had seen anyone look so happy.

He laughed, "You really *are* a kindred soul!" She had an image of him as a boy turning somersaults because he was so happy. She said, "When you were a boy did you turn somersaults when you were happy?"

"How perceptive of you! But then you *are* perceptive; actually I could turn somersaults now!"

She laughed, saying "I used to do the same! I recognise a fellow acrobat!"

"How did you get so interested in poetry? Can you quote some from memory or do you just like to browse and take it into your thoughts?" He sat down near her and placed his hand over hers. She was instantly aware of his energy that sent tiny vibrations like a trickling electrical through her skin!

"Both, I think! My quoting comes from having to learn it word for word, supposedly as a punishment for misdemeanours at grammar school. I begged not to be given it and asked for the bible which I had little time for, so of course I always got Shakespeare or similar, which I loved and found easy to memorise! Actually I enjoyed it. I also had some parts in plays that we did, mostly Shakespeare."

"You mentioned the Bible, have you read it? Why do you have little time for it?"

He was beginning to remind her of Dr. Gordon. She was not sure that this is what she wanted. She much preferred Michael to be at least the beginning of a shipboard romance. Even though she wasn't sure what that was, she had heard of it. Was sex part of a shipboard romance? Perhaps without it, it was called something else! These thoughts flew through her head like lightening. She noticed he was attentively waiting for an answer to his question.

"I read it because I was looking for God; unfortunately he wasn't in it! I read the Old and the New Testament; excellent contradictions in many places and at the end I still did not know *'Who had done it!'* I was eight or nine at the time so perhaps I wasn't the best judge; but going back to it doesn't make me smile, so I won't be reading it again!"

He was amazed. "I have never heard of someone reading both the old and new testaments at such an early age!"

"Well, the question arose and as Sunday school and the Church didn't seem to have clarifying answers, the Bible seemed to be the next best thing!"

"Yet you found no answers!"

"No, but I found more questions and that is always a good thing, don't you think?"

Michael was silent; his look was contemplative. He was reminding her more and more of Dr. Gordon! Audrey felt she had to get away from this similarity.

She changed the subject. "Tell me, what is your favourite verse of Omar Khayyam's?"

He smiled.

> *"The moving finger writes and having writ moves on!*
> *Nor all thy piety nor wit, shall lure it back to cancel half a line,*
> *Nor all thy tears wash out a word of it!"*

She said, "I recognise that! I quoted it to my mother once and she said

Awakening to Real Romance?

it's the same as *'It's no use crying over spilt milk.'* It's not the same but everyone has their own philosophy, and my mother knows most of the usual clichés."

Michael went on gazing at her with his head on one side. He wasn't sure what to say or how to handle this young lady who unexpectedly talked like a professor while she smiled and flashed dimples at him.

He decided that dancing was safe and would give him time to consider the situation.

Audrey was happy to be in his arms; she loved to dance and though she was not an expert, she was light on her feet and followed his lead with ease.

They relaxed into a companionable silence.

Now this was the romantic part she wanted to experience. Audrey liked the feel of his body as it touched hers; his hand on her back between her shoulder blades as he guided her around the floor, the feel of his shoulder under her own hand, and the hands they held together as they twirled in time to the music. Occasionally, she pulled back to look at his face, then to return his smile and was content just to be in his arms. She was happy!

The music stopped. She stood still, not wanting to leave the floor; they stood looking at each other and then their dancing continued as the band started another tune. Audrey wanted this to go on all night. She noticed her sister dancing with a young good-looking passenger. She looked pleased and content.

At 11pm the band ceased playing. Audrey knew it was time to go, preferably before her father came looking for them.

She guided Michael towards her sister, saying to Margaret, "time to go," with a knowing look.

Margaret understood the message, saying goodnight to her partner. Audrey introduced Michael, who offered to see them both to their cabin, but Audrey said, "Just to the deck if you don't mind."

Michael nodded and led the way. He shook hands with Margaret and kissed Audrey lightly on the cheek, saying "Goodnight, have a wonderful sleep, and look forward to tomorrow!"

Audrey trusted that his remark meant that tomorrow included his presence once again.

Margaret had a dreamy wistful look, with no desire to talk, which suited both the sisters.

They undressed quickly, with Audrey climbing to the top bunk at great speed.

She was more than happy! Somehow, she knew that the meetings with Michael, the talks, the debates, and the summing ups would continue each day.

She went to sleep with the vision of Michael still twirling her in his arms while she gazed at the sparkling blue eyes that held an amused but loving look.

The next day the weather was fine and cool but the sun was shining. Leaving her sister awake but drowsy Audrey was up early. Showered and dressed she joined the early morning walkers each day doing their laps around the deck. There was often a breeze that hurried one along on the port side and became a headwind on the starboard. Jackets and coats billowed in the wind. Audrey enjoyed the challenge. Most of the passengers showed relief when the breeze slowly dropped, leaving only small gusts to herald its passing presence. Watching the water, Audrey saw the sea becoming a reflection of the calmness, as the waves gentled and only the motion of the ship created any turbulence.

It was time for breakfast; another adventurous day of games and of looking forward to Michael's presence.

At breakfast her father wanted to know what everyone was doing.

Audrey said, I will be busy most of the day as I have entered all the games' tournaments.

Fred said, "You've never played shipboard games before; you haven't a hope of winning."

Awakening to Real Romance?

"I don't care about winning, I never have. I don't really like competition; I just like to play!"

"How do you explain the times you won at school then?" Fred was starting to glower.

Audrey quietly said, "Dad, perhaps I won because it was alright not to; there was no desperation there. Maybe that had something to do with it."

Her father snorted and said, "Well go tell that to all the athletes you meet, I'm sure they will agree with you." He pushed back his chair saying to Dorothy "What a lot of bloody nonsense, where the devil does she get all these weird ideas?" Audrey knowing it was time to leave gave a cheery wave and hurried from the dining room.

She checked the notice boards, found her partners, played in various games, returned for lunch and shot out of the dining room again.

Her mother found her playing deck quoits. "I've entered you and Margaret into the bathing beauty contest. You're both very pretty, and with your hour-glass figure you will do very well."

Audrey was not sure what an 'hour-glass figure' was, only knowing that her head and heart were shouting NO, NO, NO. She was stunned.

"There isn't any way that I will turn up for that. Please take me out of it!"

Margaret said, "But you have entered for all these other things, I thought you would be pleased. For heaven's sake, what is the problem?"

"It is not a skill or ability contest. I won't go in it! Please remove me!"

"Margaret doesn't want to go in it by herself!" Her mother stood with folded arms.

"Alright, I will find someone else who is going in it and introduce her and she will keep Margaret company. That's it!" Margaret went to say something else but Audrey turned her attention back to the quoits, watching her mother walk away with a little anger in her stride.

Later as she waited towards the rear of the ship for Michael to appear, she thought about her new life in Australia. She hoped that she could get a job quickly, save her money, and have her own place to live away from her family.

A LIFE of Enlightenment

She loved them, but felt that her father in particular would breathe a sigh of relief if she wasn't there. She was also tired of feeling like a fish out of water. Now, there was no Dr. Gordon to supply some light relief.

Audrey knew it was essential for her to get as independent and self-sufficient as quickly as possible. She also knew that her comments and queries to her father had to be severely curtailed if there was to be better peace in the family.

Her mother's statement, *"It was a lot quieter when you were away. Your father had no one to fight with!"* had not been lost on Audrey. But for now, there was the journey…another country to explore…and then there was Michael!

She was leaning on the rail watching the back flow of water, when he touched her shoulder as he said hello.

Audrey turned to him, again struck by the deep blueness of the eyes, the warm smile, and the black wavy hair. She appreciated the handsome look of him, but knew this interested her far less than the talk she was hoping to have. Here was a being who thought of more than the mundane items that most people considered made up their lives. Here was someone to debate with who perhaps would not consider her different or weird.

Michael was carrying a book. He gave it to her. It was a book of verses. He had a page marker inserted. She opened it as he said, "Please read me that verse and tell me what you make of it."

She read:

> "And if the Wine you drink, the Lip you press,
> End in the Nothing all Things end in – Yes –
> Then fancy while Thou art, Thou art but what
> Thou shalt be – Nothing – though shalt not be less."

—Edward FitzGerald, *Rubáiyát of Omar Khayyám*

Awakening to Real Romance?

Audrey read it again to herself, and looking at Michael asked, "What do you want to know?"

"What it means to you?

She said "It means everything is valid!"

He smiled at her. "Is that all you are going to explain?"

Audrey gave a small shrug, "Well, the 'nothing' he refers to becomes 'something' the minute it is identified, and so does everything else in the verse…which means everything is valid. I'm not sure what you want from me here! What do you think about it?"

Michael started laughing. "Scholars have been debating what this verse really means for…well I don't know how long. As far as I know, to them 'nothing is still nothing'. Now you have made it exist as 'something' and that puts a whole new concept on everything."

"Well that's true." Audrey smiled at him. "You have to have something and nothing before you can have *everything*; so all three must exist!"

Michael was looking at her with a broad and almost loving smile on his face.

Audrey wasn't sure if her answer had precipitated this, whether some of her naivety had caused amusement or was Michael just getting fond of her?

She gave a small smile, "OK Michael, please talk to me! I'm feeling confused and a little lost!?"

Thoughtfully, he went on looking at her for a few moments. She grew uncomfortable under his gaze; then he took her hand and led her to two chairs. She sat down and he tugged the other one around so that they were facing each other.

She smiled at him and waited. He took hold of both hands, holding them firmly but gently. This she liked. She gazed at him…

He said with passion, "Do you have any idea who you really are; how you appear to others; how your thought patterns go down a different road? Do you see how special you are, how fascinating you are, how enthralling it is to talk to you? Don't you ever stand back and take a good look at you?"

She was astonished; she felt almost admonished!

She said, "I don't know how to do that…take a look at oneself!" He raised his eyebrows.

Being careful to explain each step, she said, "Well, if I go over there and stand back to look at me here, then I won't be here to be looked at, will I?"

He dropped her hands, got up and walked around and then he suddenly started laughing, such an enjoyable laugh that went on and on.

He came around the back of the chair, kissed the top of her head, turned, kissed her cheek and then placed a light kiss on her lips. Audrey was so pleased; all she wanted to do was wrap her arms around him and thank him. She took the laughter and the kisses for acceptance and was thrilled that he was pleased. He said, "All this and you're lovable too!"

There was a sudden roar as Fred strode towards them, angrily asking, "What the hell do you think you are doing with my daughter? Don't you dare even talk to her again or I will report you to the Captain. She's only fifteen. Now get away from her!"

Fred was almost standing over him, shaking his fist. Michael had no option but to leave.

Audrey was mortified. She went to say something but Fred grabbed her arm and pushed her towards the steps, saying, "Go down the cabin and stay there till dinner; you are not to go near anyone of the opposite sex. You dance with your sister or not at all, and I will be keeping an eye on you. Tonight you stay in the cabin. You are not allowed anywhere. Is that clear?"

Audrey was about to respond when Fred pushed her. "Don't you give me any backchat or I'll give you what for. Now go!" Audrey went. She skipped dinner, stayed in the cabin all night, and the next day joined the early morning walkers as usual. Although she looked for Michael there was no sign of him that day or the next two days.

Despite feeling slightly sick, she played in all her games, found a pretty 16-year-old to keep her sister company, almost entered the Knobbly Knee contest out of sheer devilment, and buried her nose in the library books.

Michael found her on the top deck four days later. She greeted him with a sad smile.

Awakening to Real Romance?

Leaning on the rail next to her, he asked, looking at the ocean. "Why didn't you tell me you were fifteen?"

Audrey said, "I didn't think it was important!"

Michael slowly shook his head. "When you are under sixteen and have a father like yours, it is vastly important."

She turned and bending to look at him asked with a mischievous smile, "Why, what were you planning to do?"

He faced her with a serious very intent look that examined her face in detail, "I thought you were at least eighteen or nineteen. You are very lady-like for one so young, you talk like a professor from some advanced philosophical university. I don't want to know what your IQ is; actually I don't think you know, do you?" She shook her head. "And judging by your expression, you don't care to know either!"

She smiled in agreement. He began to walk around their space, gesturing with his hands. "And now you ask me what I was planning to do to you, with you? Well I don't know! How would anyone know? You bring up a whole heap of intentions and emotions." He was talking much faster than usual. "What is even more confusing, you seem to be oblivious to the whole thing. You have my head spinning, with admiration, with a tremendous urge to know you better, with a suspicion that you could be of great importance in my life; and an urge to make passionate love to you. At the same time I have this overall feeling that I must protect you at all costs! All this in just a few hours of knowing you. I feel as though I have been stripped bare without knowing how it happened. I want to ask you how it happened, but I already know the answer!"

Audrey blushed, as Michael continued.

"I never met anyone so oblivious and so innocent of the effect she creates; it's also part of your charm; your vulnerability…". He rubbed his head. "I don't know what I'm talking about anymore. You are just standing there looking stunned and caring and lovable!"

Audrey wrapped her arms around him. She understood all his words, but felt he must be talking about someone else. She wanted to soothe him and tell him it was alright, although she was not sure what was wrong that needed righting. At the same time, she was concerned that her father may find them, and her need to protect Michael was strong.

She pulled away, kissed his cheek and said, "Perhaps it is better that we not see each other again. I don't want to see you so distraught and I'm so sorry if I contributed to this. Being young seems to be a problem but I will grow out of this. Actually I'm sixteen in November; I'm not sure what additional license that gives me?"

Michael smiled a sad smile. He said, "It's the license it gives others that you need to be concerned about, but I'm sure you will find some optimum way of handling it!"

Audrey gazed at him, longing for him to stay but knowing he had to leave. She said, "I have loved our short friendship, I will never forget it; somehow you made me feel special and acceptable and I thank you for that! I'm not sure how I messed it up. I think I must be too young in more ways than one! I will try to look…not at myself…I can't do that…but perhaps I need to look at what I am doing to others? Is that the lesson?"

Michael smiled, "Well, it will do for now; I'm not the best teacher; but someone will come along!"

He kissed her cheek, and just like that he was gone.

CHAPTER 30

The Arrival in Western Australia

She did not see Michael for many days; instead the hours were filled with games, dancing, board games, jigsaw puzzles and reading in the library.

Audrey thought about him, missed him, his company, and the talks that to her had been precious.

She could feel his exasperation and a little anger at the discourse, without really seeing how it was warranted.

She wondered about the tirade and what had prompted it. She could only consider that her age had somehow got up his nose, cut the ground from under his intentions, and lost him a compatible partner.

Audrey was very displeased with her father. His anger was tiresome. She felt he was a complete and totally unnecessary interference in her life and the quicker she got away, the better she would be.

She felt that there had been no sexual danger from Michael. On one hand she considered that he respected her, and would put caring for her welfare more of a priority; that he was a gentleman; and secondly, she wasn't interested in a sexual relationship. For a start, she wasn't sure what that would entail. The odd kiss, more of a fleeting one, hadn't stirred any depths in her. No music played, no bells rang. It was just very pleasant and quite respectable.

Audrey knew that books didn't always depict the real thing; there never seemed to be any sex in her reading, and in the movies, everything seemed to fade out before anything really got going. Couples didn't even sleep in the same bed, and she knew that was wrong because even her parents slept together. It was an area that warranted a lot more investigation. Now, how to investigate it? As Shakespeare said, *"Ay! There's the rub!"*

With Mr Griffith's partnership they won the doubles in table tennis. Each got a trophy!

A small boy who had been watching the match, gazed at Audrey's with envy. "Gosh I wish I could have one of them".

Audrey promptly gave it to him, and then took it back with instructions for him to meet her at the same time the next day. This gave her time to show it to her parents who set great store by this type of ornament.

Audrey came second in quoits and deck tennis and nowhere in shuffleboard. She gave away all the mementos, and let her family assume that only first place got a trophy. She produced chocolates and sweets for second places and her family were content.

She took stock of the cruise and what it had meant to her. She was a much better and more polished dancer; she had learned much from all the different partners; she had skill in all shipboard games, was better at jigsaws, more alert at card games, had learned more poetry and had lots of good writings in her autograph book, and also some excellent little sketches. She had spent quality time with very handsome, intelligent gentlemen who she felt really liked and appreciated her. She had managed to get away from her family for most of each day; had met a lot of new people who came from all parts of the United Kingdom, filled with hopes and dreams

The Arrival in Western Australia

of a better life, just like her parents.

She had had fun with Wally, their table waiter, who tried to torment her and make her laugh by making 'come on' gestures and winking at her behind her father's head. He had the grace to look sad whenever she was being harassed or told off, and always gave her a warm smile as she left the table to get away, and welcomed her with the same smile at the beginning of every mealtime.

As the journey continued towards Perth, she spent some time on the top deck, watching the turbulent water flow from the stern. Sometimes she was entertained by flying fish, and once there were three dolphins that ran along the ship much to the delight of the passengers on the starboard side.

Suddenly there were seagulls screeching, diving and swooping round the boat and she knew that land—although not visible yet—would not be far away.

She collected all the families' dirty clothes and went to the ship's laundry. Her mother was pleased; her father adamant that she shouldn't talk to any crew members.

When she returned, she partially packed her cabin trunk, urging Margaret to do the same.

The journey was coming to an end.

On the last evening, she danced with Michael. It was poignant and sad. He was transferring to another ship, which meant a promotion for him. Australia would not be on his run. He said, "Perhaps it is just as well, you have some growing up to do and I need to recover from just knowing you!"

Audrey didn't know what to make of this. She decided to let it go.

She just enjoyed being in his arms, moving in unison around the floor and feeling his cheek next to hers as they twirled on the corners.

She danced three dances with him. After the last dance for the evening they held hands with others and sang Auld Lang Syne.

Michael escorted her to the outside deck where many people were intending to stay up all night to watch the ship come through the heads to the Port of Fremantle.

Michael left her there with a warm cuddle and a kiss on her cheek, saying, "I must go. I will be on duty in a few minutes."

A final hug, and he was gone. She would never see him again.

Audrey stood at the rail, gazing at the sea manifesting its usual flow past the side of the ship. She realized that everything in the world still went on its merry way irrespective of what was happening in her life. She felt even more than before that she was part of this great universe and that she had a part to play to make up the whole. The events that happened were obviously happenings that needed to be there for her journey. Audrey would have been astonished if she had glimpsed her future. There would be a marriage when she was very young; a child who would be kidnapped and not seen again for many years; another marriage that ended in divorce; a love affair with a soul mate in Switzerland; another marriage in Swaziland, Africa; various deaths to cope with; and in general a life that was full, interesting, and to put it in Audrey's future words, never boring!

But for now there was Perth ahead of her and a life to create with her family. She smiled and then shrugged her acceptance as the ship came through the heads, ready to dock at Fremantle port.

CHAPTER 31

Life Begins in a New Country

Leaning over the rail looking at the wharf and a large metal building called 'G shed', Audrey was amazed to find porters and various other workers running around doing tasks that one could have witnessed at Southampton port. She had not expected this at Fremantle.

Audrey's education of Australia had been of minerals, wheat, and sheep farming, the capital of each State, aboriginals, boomerangs, and spears.

She knew Australia was a big country; that England could fit into just Western Australia five and a half times. That the country was about three thousand five hundred miles long by approximately one thousand five hundred miles deep. It was hard to really comprehend the vast size of this continent.

She knew that they were to live in a 'Nissan Hut' to get oriented. She had no knowledge of a Nissan Hut, but assumed that it was an upgrade of a tent. She felt that the family would probably have to defend themselves from the aboriginals, which she was quite prepared to do, and that a hut was better defence than a tent. Later, it was a surprise to see buildings, shops, pavements, and people going about their daily business with no idea of the dangers they could be facing.

A LIFE of Enlightenment

She felt that her education had left out sizable gaps of data about Australia. After recovering from the surprise, she felt it was wise to put her data on a shelf and only look at whatever was immediately available and viewable.

The family slowly went through immigration. As all three children were on their parents' passports, this saved some time. Then it was customs, and afterwards, with their luggage they were taken by a bus to 'Point Walter' and assigned to a Nissan Hut, which turned out to be a large curved metal building. On the ride they could observe homes, shops, trees and streets. There were no terraced houses, no joined-together houses. Each home seemed to stand on its own large lot of land. No slate or thatched roofs could be seen. Iron or tiles seemed to be the roof order of the day, with white picket fences on some front gardens separating the home from the street. It was fascinating and interesting to see the difference. Some of the houses were built of brick, whilst others had long painted horizontal boards overlapping each other that formed the walls. All the houses seemed to lack chimneys. If they did have any, it was only one or two. Audrey assumed that sunny weather lasted a long time and people seldom required home heating.

It was July; summer in England, winter in Australia. Yet it was a warm, sunny day with a clear blue sky and hardly a cloud in sight. All of the family found the winter clothes they were wearing quite suffocating.

The Nissan hut was warm inside. They unpacked some of their clothes and changed into light dresses, with shorts for Fred and Charles.

A knock on the door heralded a vicar who introduced himself as Thomas Carstairs and offered them a ride to the beach. Observing their blank expressions, he smiled and said, "It is the same as the seaside."

The seaside! They had seldom seen the seaside in England, especially during the war years; it was too far away from their home and travelling with petrol rationing for all transportation was discouraged. Everywhere there had been signs *'Is your journey really necessary?'* Also, for many years the seaside was often cut off with barbed wire fencing to discourage enemy

Life Begins in a New Country

landings. Now, here was an opportunity to go to the seaside. Delighted, they piled into his car, three in the front, three children in the back. In no time they were at the beach. The children ran across the clean yellow sand, straight into the water, and started paddling along the shore uttering small squeals of delight. They had expected the water to be freezing cold; instead it was lovely and warm. If only they had brought or changed into their swim suits!

Even Fred and Dorothy had a paddle.

They noticed people walking along the pavement above the beach and marvelled at their ability to accept the overcoats and boots they were wearing. Perhaps they were expecting it to snow later on, although the weather told of a bright happy sunny day. It was all very mystifying.

They thanked Vicar Thomas for the ride and he promised them that in two days' time he would take them to the City.

On returning they went to the great 'Nissan Hall' for a meal. They were served a meat casserole with potatoes, cabbage and carrots, followed by jelly and ice cream. They exclaimed over the meat, such a treat to have so much when it had hardly appeared during and even after the war. Rationing in England was still applicable and had changed little after England had won the war six years before.

Listening to the staff who worked in the Hut, they were intrigued by their accent and some of the words were not understood at all.

Back in the Nissan Hut, the parents decided that everyone should have a rest. Audrey lay on her bunk and once she thought everyone was asleep, she set off to explore.

Walking through the settlement, Audrey found some benches in a quiet area flanked by trees. One of the benches was occupied by a young man dressed in white who was smoking a cigarette.

Audrey stood to the side of him saying "Hello"

He smiled, asking "Are you one of the new arrivals?'

She nodded. "Are you a cook?"

"One of 'em. I'm on all day today but after breakfast tomorrow, I have the rest of the day off. So, what's going on this arvo?"

"What is a 'this arvo'?"

He stared at her. "This arvo means this afternoon, yer know... after dinner."

Audrey smiled, "So 'arvo' means afternoon, is that an Aboriginal word?

He laughed. "Not that ah know of. So, what's going on?"

She said, "I don't know. Is there somewhere they tell you this, or is there a notice board, I should look at?"

He started laughing again. "Struth, yer are just off the boat. Are yer a perishing pomme?"

Audrey stared at him, "I'm sorry but I don't understand what you are really saying, anyway what is a 'perishing pomme'? Are you an Australian?"

"Too bloody right I em! And don't you let anyone tell yer different!"

Audrey was taken aback by this. She didn't know why he was so defensive; she wanted to ask him, but felt the question would not be welcomed, so instead she said in appeasement, "Alright, I won't allow anyone to tell me things about you except you, now, is it alright to ask you questions?"

He nodded. She sat down next to him. "How will I find out what is going on this after…arvo?"

He grinned, "What ah meant was 'what are yer doing this arvo.'"

"Oh!" She played the conversation back in her mind. "I see, you wanted to know if I had any plans."

"Right mate."

She liked the mate word. It was as though they were friends, after getting off to a bad start. She decided that it was perhaps better not to query anything but trust that it would become clear as the conversation progressed.

"My family is having a rest. I came out to explore and perhaps find someone like you to talk to, as I was intrigued by the accent I heard in the food hall. I thought all Australians spoke English, but there seems to be another language as well, and I don't understand all the words."

He stared at her and said, "Well ah hope yer not having a go at me. Ok. Yer seem honest enough. So what words did yer hear?"

Life Begins in a New Country

She said, "Well thank you for helping me... is 'having a go' the same as putting you down?"

"Too right."

"Thank you…so…someone said, *'I'm not going to believe what he says, I don't think it's dinkum.'* Now 'dinkum' in England is a liquid detergent that my mother used to wash the hairdressing salon floor. So you see I can't make head or tail of this?"

He smiled. "Dinkum means honest or honestly."

She played back the sentence in her head. "Ah, now I understand."

He was amused. "So, what else did yer overhear?"

Audrey thought for a moment. "One of the servers said, *'He's not here, he's crook!'* Now does that mean he is in jail? He has done something wrong, some criminal act?"

His roar of laughter was disconcerting, but infectious and not knowing why she began to join in.

He spluttered, "*Crook* means he is sick!"

As she quietened, she smiled and said "Well, thank you for explaining all that. I cannot think of anymore at the moment but that is probably enough for my first day in Australia. My name is Audrey, will you tell me yours?"

"Bill. It's really William, but everyone calls me Bill!"

Audrey asked, "What would like me to call you?"

"Well, ye're very proper, so ah don't mind if yer call me William…makes a change yer might say."

"Very well, William it is. Will you be here tomorrow? I might have some more questions by then."

"After breakfast."

She stood and offered her hand. "Thank you William. I will see you tomorrow."

He watched her walk away with an amused look on his face, thinking that his friends wouldn't get it if he was to talk about it. You had to be there to experience it!

CHAPTER 32

Lollies at the Cinema

Telling her family that she was going for a walk around the settlement, Audrey met William again after breakfast.

"How yer getting on?" he asked with a smile.

"Very well, although the hut gets very warm during the day!" "Leave the door open in the arvo to let in the Fremantle Doctor; that'll help."

Audrey stared at him, "Why would he even call if no one is sick?"

William grinned, "It isn't a bloke... it's a sea breeze, that comes and cools everything down. Its winter now, wait till yer experience a summer here; The Fremantle doctor is the best friend yer'll think yer've got."

Audrey said, "You have a quaint way of naming something!" He grinned. "Ah know what 'quaint' means, but it's the first time ah heard someone use it about the way ah talk."

She asked, "Were you born here?"

"No. Ah was born and raised on a farm outside Wyalkatchem. There were a drought that lasted for years; killed all the stock; ruined the wheat, so we left. Gotta job as a rouseabout for erwhile. Used to cook for a shearing team ah joined, then finally got a job here, bin here ever since."

Audrey decided not to ask too many questions. This was a part of his life that had not gone well. She felt that going into it would not assist him, so instead she asked, "Do you enjoy your work here?"

"Soright. Ow bout coming to see a film tonight? Ah've got an old bomb that will get us there; it's not far to Fremantle." Audrey hesitated. She assumed an old bomb was a vehicle of some sort and not the type of bomb she was used to hear about. She felt it would be unkind to refuse after he had shared part of his life with her; then there was her father to contend with; she decided to enlist William's help.

"I have a sister; do you have a friend so that four of us could go together. I think that is the only way my father will allow me to go. Also, you will have to dress very neatly and come to meet him before we leave, so that he can see we are in safe hands. Is this possible?"

"Christ, he said, who are yer... the Queen of Sheba?"

"No," she laughed; "Perhaps I am just one of those perishing pommes, although I confess to not knowing what that means." "Take me word fer it, it's better than being called a limey. Ah'm not goin ter explain that, so don't ask. Ah've got an assistant, he'll probably be in it; so we'll call for yer both around 6 o'clock. OK? see yer later!"

Audrey went home musing over the best way to approach her father about the coming event.

She decided to tell him some of the conversations she had been having; putting them in such a way to be amusing and make him laugh before bringing up the evening's outing. In the meantime, she took her sister aside, urging her to persuade her father to let them both go to the film.

It wasn't easy; but her father became mollified when she said the two boys would be calling to meet him, that she would look after Margaret and they would stay together all evening. The boys arrived promptly as six, looking clean, shaved, and reasonably dressed. Audrey met William

Lollies at the Cinema

outside, quickly ascertained his friend's name and then introduced them as William and David to her mother, father and sister.

Her father asked for the name of the film.

William said, "Well there are two as usual. I don't know 'bout the B one; it may be shorts, cartoons and the news, but the main one's called "The Prince who was a thief."

Fred asked what time they will finish.

David said, "You never know, but we'll bring the girls straight home, if that suits you."

"Yes, you'd better. I still think they are too young to be going out with boys, especially ones I don't even know, but their mother insists I'm being too strict, so I have said yes. Now make sure I don't regret it."

David and William both nodded and gently shepherded the sisters out of the door.

The old bomb turned out to be an old red car. It had side windows that you could take off, seats that needed more stuffing in them and a very noisy motor. Margaret and Audrey had been in very few cars, as their father had never owned one, and Audrey's trips with Dr. Gordon took place in a vehicle quite dissimilar to this one.

"In a few years, this will be a vintage car," David said as he drove. "It will need doing up eventually, but in the meantime it gets us from A to B."

"Do you both own the car?"

"Not on yer life, it's mine, but we're good mates." William patted Audrey on the knee and grinned at her. She was not sure how to object to this familiar gesture, but it was gone before she found the words.

She was aware that David spoke better English and was more understandable. Perhaps he was schooled in the City and that made a difference. She could hear Margaret telling David that she was seventeen and had been doing an apprenticeship as a hairdresser with her mother for the last two years.

She also heard her say that, "No, Audrey doesn't know what she wants to do yet, but it will probably be something reckless or even dangerous because that is what she's done for most of her life."

She heard David say, "That's amazing. She sounds so proper when she talks." Margaret answered, "She went to a grammar school, that's why. So she doesn't have an accent like we do, and so her English as my father says is often la-di-dah." Audrey went on commenting to William about some of the sights she could see. Although the night was well into dusk, street lights were abundant.

She leaned towards Margaret, "If we were in England now in the middle of winter it would have been dark by three or four o'clock in the afternoon, or the arvo as they say here. Isn't it wonderful that at six thirty here, darkness is only just beginning?"

Margaret said, "But at home, in summer you can still read a newspaper outside at nine o'clock at night. Can you do that here?"

"No, maybe until seven or seven thirty, but then it is dark." Now it was David's turn to answer and pat Margaret's knee.

They drew into a parking lot near the cinema. The boys got tickets for all and ushered them towards a door where an usherette took their tickets.

They had good seats. The girls sat together with a boy at each end. They watched the Pathé news, a road runner cartoon, and a singing animation of following a bouncing ball over the words of a song as they appeared on the screen. The audience did not join in as Audrey expected; she heard only a little humming; and could only surmise that the Australians were shy about singing in public.

Then it was interval. At the door they were given 'pass outs'. William said, "Hold on to those. Yer'll have to show em or they won't let yer in again." Turning to Audrey, he asked, "Would yer like some lollies?" Audrey was mystified, but she quickly ascertained that lollies must be short for lollipops. "No thank you!"

"How about a tub of ice cream then?"

"Thank you, yes please." She would have preferred some sweets or toffees, but these were not offered.

Margaret left to go to the lavatory. The boys were queuing at the counter

Lollies at the Cinema

and Audrey was left alone.

A small boy around three years old came and standing before her gazed at her face with an unblinking stare. She smiled at him, with no response. She was alarmed to see that he had bare feet, was wearing pyjamas and a dressing gown, and appeared to be quite alone.

She crouched down to his level, saying, "I can see you have run away from home, but please don't be frightened; don't worry, I will find a policeman who will take you back to your parents. Now, what is your name?"

"Peter."

"Peter what?

"Don't know"

She took hold of his hand and began to look around, suddenly aware that she had no idea how an Australian policeman dressed. She only knew how to find an English 'Bobby'. Did Australian police wear helmets?

A woman approached her…here was some help, she would ask her how to find a policeman.

Audrey opened her mouth to speak, but the woman, snatched the little boy from her hand saying, "What are you doing with my son?!"

Audrey said, "Oh. I'm sorry, I thought he was lost!"

"How can he be lost when I'm right here? Did he say he was lost?"

"Well no. But he's in his pyjamas and he has no shoes and he doesn't look poverty stricken…So I naturally assumed he had run away from home and I was looking for a policeman so…". She trailed off seeing the look of astonishment on the mother's face.

The woman dragged him off saying, "Really…don't you know anything?!"

Audrey thought … "Well, obviously not."

The boys arrived with the ice creams. Margaret had also missed out on the sweets and toffees.

Audrey recounted the event with the boy and his mother. Margaret was concerned but the boys thought it was very funny.

Audrey asked them to explain.

David smiled. "Aussie kids often run around barefoot, unless it's in the dead of winter when they can catch cold."

William added, "Their mum brings 'em to pictures dressed in their jamas cos they will be ready to go straight to bed when they git home. A time saver, see."

Audrey was astonished. "Alright, I will remember all this education. Now please tell me how to recognise an Australian Policeman."

"He's just a bloke in a uniform."

"Yes, but what colour? Does he wear a helmet like an English Bobby? Is there one around here that you can point to? Are they tall or over a certain height? Are some of them black, like the Aboriginals? Please, you have to remember that all this is very new, so I need details."

The boys were looking at each with little snorts here and there.

"Well, he wears a cap, no a hat, what yer call it…?" William looked at David for help.

David took up the challenge. "It's a hat, such as a high commissioned officer in one of the forces would wear. It is a hat with a peak at the front; do you know what I mean?" Audrey nodded. "His uniform is navy blue trousers and coat with a pale blue shirt and dark blue tie?"

William said, "Don't they sometimes wear a white shirt?"

David said "I don't know; now you have me confused. Tell you what Audrey, you let us know what colour the shirt is, and we will all learn something! I think you have to be a certain height; maybe five foot ten or thereabouts, not sure about that."

"Yer'll never see a black one that's fer sure!" William nodded his head wisely.

David said, "You won't even see one of those around here. They never seem to come into town."

Using their "pass outs" they were again admitted to the theatre and watched the second film. They all enjoyed it and soon they were on their way home again.

As they were driving along, Audrey asked, "Do Australians like to shorten lots of words, like arvo for afternoon, and lollies for lollipops?"

Lollies at the Cinema

There was a burst of laughter from the boys. William said leaning forward towards David, "Well we got us a couple of Sheilas here!"

"What are Sheilas?"

"Girls my dear, just girls."

"Why were you laughing?'

Because 'lollies' are just anything that isn't chocolate or chewing gum or ice cream. Nothing to do with lollipops. He turned to Margaret, "Is that why you said you didn't want any?"

"Well, I thought I was too old for lollipops. David smothered his laughter. Ok, next time say yes, and then I will ask you what sort you would like. Understand now?"

She smiled at him and nodded.

The boys offered to see them when they were off duty the next day, but Audrey remembered that Vicar Thomas was taking them to the City.

They said goodnight and went to face their father's inquisition.

CHAPTER 33

Out on the Town

Vicar Thomas drove them into town. Parking outside a large frontage of a shop in Hay Street he said, "I will pick you up at London Court, Hay Street end. You may want to wander back, about three hundred yards, and watch George fight the Dragon in the clock over London Court. It's a bit of old London; runs right through to St. George's Terrace…that's the commercial street. Enjoy yourselves. If you get lost ask a policeman or indeed anyone that can direct you to London Court. If you ask someone who doesn't know, then they must be just off the boat like you!"

He drove away leaving the five of them looking around at all the shops in the street. He had given them a map of the main city streets.

The Street map formed a rectangle. He had explained that the main shopping centre ran parallel between William and Barrack Streets, both on Hay and Murray Streets, which also ran parallel with each other. It had sounded confusing but later on it became simple to understand.

Audrey took Margaret's hand and said, "Margaret and I will explore this big shop. Would you like us to take Charles with us?"

Fred said, "No, he comes with us, I'm not sure we shouldn't all stick together."

Dorothy laid a hand on his arm. "They can't get lost here, it's not like London or Manchester, let them go."

Audrey was pleased at this support and before more could be debated, she took Margaret's arm and propelled her into the Woolworth's store.

They wondered around looking at goods they had not seen since before the war.

They came to a counter that stood like an island. It was a long rectangle about fourteen feet long by about ten feet wide. On all sides were displayed sweets, toffees, chocolates, all manner of varieties. The sisters wandered around gazing with awe at products they had not seen for a very long time.

Margaret said, "Do you think they are real or just dummies, like the ones back home?"

"I'm not sure, they look real, why don't we ask?"

"But we don't have any coupons."

"Maybe we don't need any…did the war reach as far as this?'

"I don't know."

Audrey said, "Well let's just try and buy some; let's see what happens. You go to that side of the counter and I will do this one. We will do better if we are not together in case there are some restrictions. Just ask for two ounces or a quarter of a pound, and then they won't think we are greedy. Then we can see what the reaction is and maybe get some more. Let's try it."

Armed with the money Mother had given them, they applied themselves to the task in hand.

After the first tentative start, Audrey was beginning to have fun. She moved up and down her side gathering a quarter of a pound of this and that, moving into a pound when she found nothing was being queried. She moved into the side where chocolates were being displayed. Confused at what to select, she appealed to the lady serving her, who promptly gave her a sample of anything she would like to try. Audrey would have kissed her, if the counter had not been in the way. She finally called a halt, asked for the amount she had spent, and was amazed to find she had sufficient funds to cover it. The shop assistant put all her goods into a brown paper carrier

Out on the Town

bag, and Audrey wandered around to see how Margaret had got along. Margaret also had a brown carrier bag, not quite as heavy as Audrey's because she had stuck to asking for two ounces of everything. She couldn't wait to tell Audrey that no one had asked for coupons or ration books; that she thought that it all sounded cheap and that the lady had assured her that everything she saw was real.

The girls were thrilled. They dived into the parcels, exchanging data on the different varieties and began sampling many of them.

They got thirsty and wandered into the street again. They saw a shop called a 'Milk Bar'.

Margaret said, "I wouldn't mind a glass of milk, shall we go there?"

Audrey deliberated. She did not like milk. Perhaps this was another Australian word that did not mean what it spelt; maybe they sold something else as well.

Maybe it was a bar that sold alcohol and they would not be allowed in!

"Ok, let's try, we can see if they sell anything else as well."

They wandered into the 'Milk Bar'. It had four chrome tables and a few red chairs. It was bright and cheerful. A notice board on the wall above and beyond the counter had notices of things to buy. There were pies, sandwiches, cakes and drinks and something called a milk shake, and ice creams, all listed and individually priced.

Margaret asked about a milk shake and ordered one with ice cream and malt.

Audrey ordered a warm pie and an orange drink. They sat at one of the tables. Margaret had a bite of the pie and declared it 'very good.'

They talked about some of the wonders they had seen.

Two women came in and sat down with a cup of tea. After a discussion, they did not order anything to eat but one of the ladies said, "I wouldn't have minded a bicky."

Audrey looked at Margaret and whispered, "It must mean a biscuit, but I think that's probably baby talk to a little one she has at home."

The two sisters sat there listening to the women chatter, with an accent so dissimilar to their own. They smiled at each other and Audrey made a note to find out what 'bathers' were when one of the ladies said, "The sale is still on at Foy and Gibson's, I need a new pair of bathers!"

When the ladies left, Audrey said, "Well, whatever they are they come in pairs, so we know there are two of them." Margaret said, "Well that's a start, I really thought everyone spoke English here, but there seems to be a lot of slang. I suppose we have that back home, but you get used to it and don't notice it. Here it stands out; it might take years to know all of it."

Audrey smiled, "To some extent I think it depends on who you know or mix with. I don't think professional people use much of it during the course of their work, so education plays a part in it. You can notice this by the way William and David talk. It is different. In school, I had to say, 'He hit himself over the head with a hammer', time and time again and 'Come along, now, so that we may catch the bus' instead of 'eee it imself over thee ead with an ammer' or 'cumon. We'll miss buss.' The accent and wording was knocked out of us all very quickly. Mind you, none of our family had it as bad as I'm portraying, but it could be heard all around constantly, because that was the general accent where we lived. I don't know if there is the class distinction here that we have in England, but it will always be an advantage to speak with the King's English or like the BBC announcers, wherever you go."

The sisters had had the best communication for many of their years. Audrey was aware that they were very different in their thoughts, considerations, values, and acquiescence to authority, and generally in their very different outlooks on life. They even looked dissimilar.

Margaret had lovely auburn hair, blue eyes, and a typical English complexion. She looked like Dorothy, was very attractive, with a shy smile and a desire to please; she was not a challenge to her parents. From the time she was born she had been all female in her dress and manner; she was compliant, avoided confrontations, disliked all sport and any form of violence or challenge. She never gave her parents trouble. Margaret was a born conformist. She was not intrusive, never pushed herself forward in conversation and was generally a little shy. The only time she was in trouble was when she was with Audrey and followed her lead, often while complaining about "what would Dad say?"

Audrey had strawberry blond hair, green eyes and her skin was a paler shade of white, although she had peachy dimpled cheeks which gave her colouring interest.

She loved a challenge of any description, considered that any adventure was better than no adventure; she was bold in her assessment and taking of life, very aware of others, curious about everything and was never backward in coming forward. Authority was something to be analysed and when found wanting in sense, deserved to be challenged. She was both an introvert and extrovert. She liked her own company, liked stillness, was not fond of parties or large groups, but loved a one to one conversation. She had little time for small talk although she was becoming more adept at it. She seemed like a series of contradictions. She was intelligent with more uncommon sense, way beyond her years. Audrey could have been unacceptable to others, but for her friendly, loving, generous and compassionate nature for all people and animals. She was very aware, yet unaware of herself. All her attention was 'out there'.

Their conversation had brought the sisters closer than they had been for some time. Now they asked the time of the Milk Bar lady and went in the direction of London Court to meet the family.

CHAPTER 34

Mr Griffiths Gets Audrey a Job

Six weeks later the family had news that their container of furniture was to arrive.

Soon they were transported to a house in a street called Board Avenue Belmont and the container arrived within a few hours. At first viewing, the house seemed very long. It turned out to be a 'duplex', an unfamiliar term. In England it would have been called an 'attached bungalow'.

It was strange to see the furniture from their double story brick house being fitted into what seemed to be a single storey wooden house built up on stilts. There were three steps on to a small covered porch leading to the front door.

Audrey asked her father about this. "Why is it up in the air…you can see underneath it all the way?"

Her father did not know the answer…maybe it floods in these parts?

Audrey, remembering some of her education, thought the rainfall would be insufficient.

In Australia there were many mysteries to solve.

The house had dark wooden floorboards throughout except for the kitchen/dining area which was covered with patterned linoleum.

A LIFE of Enlightenment

Margaret and Audrey shared one of the three bedrooms. There was a living room, a kitchen shared dining room, a bathroom and a toilet that lived in a little jutting outside section, along with a cement laundry trough and a space that was meant for a washing machine.

There was only one small linen cupboard built into the passage section of the bathroom.

Fred measured spaces in the bedrooms, and with Dorothy walked to the main road to catch a bus going to the city to order some wardrobes.

When they returned many hours later with a bus timetable, they complained about the lack of public transport. The family was used to having a bus pass their home every ten minutes or so; not every hour.

Audrey had been exploring. She had walked a long way up two streets as their home was set at an angle across a corner lot. She had discovered some local shops; green-grocers, a barber, a butcher, a fish and chip shop, a post office, a newsagent, and a delicatessen that seemed to be a mixture of groceries and liquor.

On her return she noticed a lady in the neighbouring front garden of the duplex and introduced herself. Katherine was a Scottish lady—the first Audrey had ever met—with a fascinating accent. She offered to visit with her husband after tea-time and talk to Audrey's parents, to offer any help and information that they may find useful. Her husband, a carpenter, was at work and not due home until the 6pm bus.

Audrey filled her parents in with all this data and then went up the street again to buy fish and chips for their evening meal. She also went to get a paper for her father and found that it could be delivered every day. The shopkeeper also told her that milk in a bottle could also be delivered.

Audrey decided to take the initiative and ordered both. Wardrobes arrived two days later, and the family unpacked and settled in. Margaret and Audrey went shopping locally with their mother and stocked the kitchen.

On the Saturday Fred and Dorothy went to buy a washing machine and a large ice box. The newsagent arranged for the ice man to call regularly.

It seemed to Audrey that order for living in their new abode was finally

Mr Griffiths Gets Audrey a Job

established.

The next item on the agenda was to find a school for Charles and jobs for the rest of the family. Their neighbours, Katherine and Simon her husband, became invaluable friends. They had emigrated six months before and knew all the pitfalls, unexpected differences and what to expect in a new life. Fred and Dorothy were grateful to have such pleasant and helpful new friends.

Fred decided to go to the Master Builders Association for information, Dorothy to the National Hairdressers Association. Margaret noticed a job in the Spode department of Caris Bros in the City and rang for an interview from a nearby call box.

Audrey saw nothing available for herself in the 'wanted ads'. However, she recalled that her table tennis doubles partner Mr Griffiths, was to be the Manager of Royal Perth Hospital. Hospitals had switchboards, so...

However, the girl on the switchboard told her she was not authorised to connect directly to Mr Griffiths and wanted Audrey to speak to his secretary.

Audrey decided 'No'; she preferred to deal directly with the lion in his den.

The next day she arrived at the main office desk at RPH as it was commonly called. She had written Mr Griffiths a note; placed it in an envelope marked personal; and now she handed it over and said she would wait to see if there was a reply. After fifteen minutes she was ushered into his office.

He was holding her note and smiling. Audrey said, "I hope you don't mind me taking the initiative but it seemed difficult to me to arrange a meeting on the phone."

He shook hands and indicated a chair.

She sat and then asked him about employment. She told him of her experiences and qualifications, adding that if there was not an immediate opening on the switchboard, that she would be happy to do anything else. She told him of her visits to the hospital with Dr. Gordon. Because of his questions she happily disseminated about the beginning and end of her engagement. He seemed amused, thoughtful, friendly and even intrigued. She concluded by saying, "You see I am quite happy to be among people and good at cheering them up, so I can do anything to help. I am quick to learn; as you know I had never played table tennis before. So I can work in the office if someone shows me what to do. I don't really want to do anything with just bodies if there is no-one attached but otherwise..." she trailed off, looking at him.

He took a deep breath and leaned back in his chair. She had the feeling he was trying not to laugh.

He excused himself and left the room.

Audrey wondered if she had said too much. After all he did ask and she had only answered his questions. She had an imaginary session with Dr. Gordon asking for his viewpoint, but Mr Griffiths returned before she had an answer.

"Audrey, I will employ you, but not on the switchboard. All switchboards personnel are seniors and you are not yet sixteen. It is a very busy board requiring excellent handling and good knowledge of the hospital administration and function. I will start you off in the general office. You will be in charge of the mail. This means that you will have a list of all the patients in all the wards as well as a list of the Doctors and other key personnel who may receive mail. You will need to divide it up into the various wards and offices and deliver it twice a day. You will also, on your second visit, pick up any outgoing mail and deliver or post it, whatever is appropriate. This will take up most of your day. The rest of the time is yours. Are you interested?"

Audrey said, "Oh Yes please!"

"Very well, my secretary will take you to 'Personnel' who normally would have been doing this interview with you. They will go through your duties once again, register you on the payroll and tell you when to start. It's been lovely to see you again Audrey. I feel I have not let my table tennis partner down. Go well!"

He got up and came around to shake hands. Audrey took his hand but then raised it and gave his fingers a kiss saying "Thank you, for being so

Mr Griffiths Gets Audrey a Job

kind. I will not let you down."

He laughed, saying "I'm sure you won't," then walked her to the door where his secretary was waiting.

She was to start her new job the following Monday.

When she arrived home the air around Fred was explosive. He had been told that he had to take an examination before he would be allowed to operate as a builder.

He had told the official who had the bad fortune to deliver this news that he knew where he could stick it and an angry Fred had walked out.

Dorothy had found the same thing at the Hairdressers association, but she had simply asked when the next examination was, booked in for it and decided that with her experience she would be able to teach them a thing or two.

Audrey found it enlightening. She thought again of her conversation with Dr. Gordon about responding with ability or reacting. Her father's angry reaction would always be his downfall.

She thought her news would ease the tension. She tried to tell it with all the details in an amused fashion, hoping to make her father smile. Dorothy was pleased and gave her a hug. Her father said, "What do you expect, she'll worm her way in or out of anything at the drop of a hat; at least there will be some money coming in."

Two days later Margaret got her job at the Crockery Spode department at Caris Bros in the City.

Her father after a few days of cursing got employment as a Supervisor at the Public Works Dept or the PWD as it was called.

Audrey was getting used to the shortening or initialling of Australian Words and places. She thought it a quaint concept and mostly amusing.

She was looking forward to joining the Australian workforce.

Audrey was delighted and happy to start work. She was good at organizing, had an orderly mind, and found her job easy and rewarding once the

A LIFE of Enlightenment

initial confusion of locating everything had settled. She delivered the mail to each ward on the various floors, leaving it as instructed at the nurse's desk. She asked for the numbers of each bed and then arranged the patients' letters in that order from the nurse's station, making it easy for the nurse to just deliver rather than sort. This alone endeared her to them, so she offered to deliver all the mail to each bed. Being quick and speedy at her job, she found she had lots of spare time and although she had asked for extra office duties, none had been forthcoming. She enjoyed the interaction with the patients, often going back to the ones who seemed to have few visitors. She chatted to them, asking about their families, pets, their plans and so on; they began to look forward to her visits. This reminded her so much of Doctor Gordon that she was often surprised to find herself not holding his hand.

She wrote to him; a long letter telling him about her first impressions of Perth, her new home, the Australians. "You will be surprised to know I am working at Royal Perth Hospital but not in any medical capacity. I am delivering and sending mail and chatting to the patients (all this without carrying your stethoscope or holding your hand.) I expect to be on the switchboard when a vacancy occurs, even though they have a rule to only have seniors in that capacity. Finding out all about the wards and different departments will stand me in good stead and with my experience and knowledge of boards there really isn't a reason not to have me as the first candidate for a vacancy. Being young seems to get in my way too much. I know I will grow out of this but trying to convince someone else that ability and not numbers should count is not an easy task. This is a strange planet and everything in it seems to go in slow motion! I sometimes wonder what I am doing here." There was more; some to inform him, some to amuse. She asked him questions about his life and work and Scotland.

He replied that his friend had passed away, that he was returning to join a colleague in his home town, that he enjoyed being married and that his wife was enjoying her role as a mother. He was delighted to hear all her news. He asked her about the 'planet' remark. "This is not the first time you have commented about this planet. Is there more to this that you would like to tell me?"

Audrey could not answer this. She wrote "Sometimes I say or write things because they feel like a truth, but that doesn't mean I can explain them, not even to myself. One day I will know whatever I need to know to answer this. Treat it like a day dream for now."

She discovered her mother was also corresponding to Dr. Gordon. This was fine, except that she felt that any news would be duplicated.

Because she was not in his presence, it seemed inappropriate to have their usual philosophical discussions. The mail and answers took too long. After a short time she stopped writing, leaving the news to her mother. She asked only that her love be sent with each letter. Occasionally she sent him a postcard with 'Thinking of you, Love Audrey' as its sole text.

Margaret had heard of a dancehall in the City called the Embassy. They asked Fred if they could go on the Saturday evening. Permission was granted provided they caught the last bus home at 11.30pm.

As they were both working and contributing to the family income, this seemed to give them some added leeway with Fred.

Going to the Embassy sometimes on a Friday evening, sometimes Saturday and occasionally both became a large part of their lives.

They were popular with the boys, never lacked for partners, and handled offers of a ride home from the men with aplomb. Audrey had a maxim of *'refuse the offer but never the man'*. This worked well for her.

As usual, everyone thought she was older than her age although Margaret seemed to have little trouble in this area.

Eventually, with some persuasion, after a year a dancing partner was allowed to drive them home. Sometimes there were two males who had come to the dance together. Audrey and Margaret would have danced with them for most of the evening. Good night kisses were allowed but no touching. Life continued.

They spent little time in the City centre. The Embassy was far away from the shopping centre and weekends were also filled with household chores allocated by their mother. Long ago Dorothy had taken her exam, passed with flying colours and indeed had spent the majority of the practical time in showing them lots of new methods, as England was far ahead in this area. She had a job as a hairdresser at a large department store and was happy there.

Charles was doing well at school. It had taken some time for him to be allocated to a classroom. In some respects, he was ahead in his knowledge but not in his nine years, but eventually he settled down. For his 10th birthday he received a bicycle and was overjoyed. Margaret was doing well at her job and was making new friends at work.

Audrey had organized a netball team, from the local girls. She trained them, organized their uniforms, called them "the Emeralds" and joined them into the Midland Association which was the closest one. They qualified as "C" grade, became B after the first year and A after the second, although they did not win the trophy. They had fun and Audrey as captain always tried to keep it more as fun than competition.

She resigned after the second year feeling that she needed to move on.

Audrey was just seventeen when a vacancy became available on the switchboard. She had never been in that room but knew where it was located. A nurse on that floor told her one of the four girls was leaving. She immediately wrote a note to Mr Griffiths, thanking him for giving her the perfect job that had allowed her to know the administration and many functions of the hospital. She said she had heard of the vacancy and please could she be considered for it. She would not let him down. She told again of her experience and knowledge of PBX and PABX boards and begged him to check on her progress to date of the tasks she had been assigned.

She was overjoyed when she had a call from the personnel department telling her she could start as a telephonist at the beginning of the following month.

Mr Griffiths Gets Audrey a Job

When she reported for her first day at 9am she moved into a hostile environment. The first thing she was asked was her age. Her answer was obviously unacceptable. The two girls on duty said they were over twenty-one and not here to wet- nurse someone who was young and inexperienced.

Audrey immediately told them of her experience. She was familiar with the switchboard and asked only for a list of all the 350 extensions so that she could learn them. This mollified them only a little. One girl left for morning tea and the other girl sat down next to Audrey. Audrey had been told that two girls operated the board between 9 am and 5 pm. One girl started at 7am and finished at 3pm. One started at 3 and finished at 11. Then a male night shift took over until 7am. Everyone worked 5 days with two days off. The fourth girl filled in for these days which varied all the time.

It sounded complex but Audrey could see how it would work. Rita, the girl sitting with her said she had to go to the toilet. She gave Audrey the list of extensions, told her that she seemed to know how to answer and connect a call and would be alright on her own for a few minutes.

Rita had barely left the room when Audrey answered a call. 'Bones' was the request. Audrey said "One moment please. I will connect you," trying to find some time to look for 'bones' on her list. It did not appear. She thought about it and then connected the caller to pathology, trusting that if it wasn't the right extension, they may tell her where to put the caller. A flashing light which she answered with "switch" had an irate person who said "Switch, take this call back!"

Audrey said "hello" and got "Bones!! Is that Bones??" "One moment madam I am trying to connect you!" Back to the list. There was nothing. She took a chance and connected her to the Theatre only to have another flashing light. No help there. Audrey went praying that one of the girls would reappear. There was nothing that seemed to be correct on the list except maybe the Mortuary Dept. She connected the call. It seemed to be alright, so she went on answering and connecting calls. It was a very busy switchboard. During a brief respite, she clicked a key over to see how her 'Bones' lady was getting on. The woman was talking to Frank the mortician.

"We can discuss his remains…his bones, later madam; in the meantime, could you please give me the name of the deceased?" Frank sounded exasperated.

"I knew he wasn't the best, but I didn't think it would amount to this!" the lady continued.

"I'm so sorry for your loss, but if you could just give me the name, madam?"

"I don't know how I got into this…It just started off with the blanket!"

At this time Rita returned. Audrey asked her for the extension number for "Bones."

"Just tell them wrong number," she said.

Audrey was puzzled. "Why would I do that?!"

Rita smiled. "Our number here is BF 1321. Boans, a Perth Department store is BF 1231. We get a lot of wrong calls." Audrey was horrified. "But she is talking to Frank and now she thinks someone has died."

Rita laughed, "Go on the line and straighten her out."

Frank was still trying to make sense of the call. "Please lady if you will just…"

Audrey said "Excuse me Frank; I need to take this call. Hello?" The lady said "Is that Boans?? Please I just want Boans!! I just need to have the blanket department!"

Audrey apologised and explained the wrong numbers. She was tempted to connect her to the Department store, but she knew Rita would frown on her taking up an incoming line which may be urgently needed. She explained it was her first day and asked to be forgiven. Then she rang Frank and thanked him for his patience and explained the mix-up. He laughed, said it had made his day. He was completely forgiving.

It took Audrey a week to be at ease with quickly finding the extensions but at last she was competent and just as quick as her colleagues.

The different shifts added variety to her days; however, she did find that the bus timetable schedule featured in a large part of her life.

CHAPTER 35

The Beginning and End of a Career

Audrey had met a boy at the shops. His name was Tony and he was from London. He carried some heavy groceries home for her one day and then asked her out. They went to a movie.

It took six weeks of occasional dating before she decided she didn't want to see him again.

She told him gently. He still kept coming around to the house. After the fourth time, as she saw him coming down the street she fled over the fence, to Katherine next door, telling her family to say she was not at home.

Margaret inevitably got the job of dealing with him. She let him sit in the lounge and talk and eventually they started to go out together. It seemed to be getting serious. Audrey was relieved.

Audrey met a good-looking, polite young man at the Embassy. His name was Mason Butler and he was a very good dancer. He came back time and time again for another request and eventually Audrey resigned herself to being his sole partner. He was doing a five-year apprenticeship as a fitter and turner; he had eighteen months to complete. He was 19 years old.

He took her home in an old red Ford car. Audrey found it strange. The windows came out, the roof could disappear and altogether it was a very draughty rattler of a car.

He drove her home and offered to pick her up the following Friday to take her dancing again. Audrey was happy, anything to save another bus ride. This continued for the next month, then it was a date for the pictures; a picnic in the hills, then after six months, on a Sunday he took her to his home to meet his parents.

Mason's grandparents had gone from England to India many moons before. Mason's parents had left India for Australia when Mason was ten years old. His only sibling was a brother called Kevin who was 18 years old.

Audrey got along well with his family, eventually meeting some aunts, uncles and cousins. After a while she stayed for weekends and they taught her to play bridge. She got used to eating hot curries always with potatoes as she did not care for rice.

They often did a Ouija board. They liked her to participate in this and it always behaved better if she joined in. Audrey was neutral about this. She had no views either way and did not object to participating.

The house was a two bedroom with a rear sleep-out on a covered in veranda. It had a laundry and toilet at the opposite end. Audrey slept in the sleep-out, although she found this very warm as summer approached.

One Saturday, in the early hours of the morning she awoke to find Mason in bed with her. His hands seemed to be everywhere and although their petting had gone some distance she was still ignorant of the complete sex act. That evening ended it. It was very sudden; over in a few minutes, with Mason happily panting away and Audrey feeling that somehow this should have been prevented. She was aware only of a wet sticky mess that she tried to clean up after Mason kissed her on the cheek and crept back to his own room that he shared with his brother.

She went home early on the Sunday, reluctant to spend time with his

The Beginning and End of a Career

family or Mason. She was thoughtful on the drive home, preferring not to talk. Audrey felt she couldn't blame him; she could have called out, hit him, etc. She was busy sorting out her responsibility in this event, trying not to include blame or shame in the calculation.

In her imaginary talk with Dr. Gordon she said, "If you were here you would point my nose, now I have to work out where you would point it…"

"Hasn't it always been at you? Isn't that where you have always insisted, because that places you in control and then you feel you can handle anything? Does this still resonate with you?"

"Yes of course! It is just that I didn't really feel I participated in this, almost as though I didn't choose it. What am I missing here?"

"Could it have happened if you had not been there?"

"Oh, aren't you clever. Of course, just my being there by choice, makes it a co-creation. How could I miss that? One can always take responsibility for being in any place at any time." She felt him smile. "It isn't so easy when you are part of the event. By the way, the only clever part was me giving back to you what you taught me long ago!"

She mentally gave him a hug.

They had arrived at her parents' home. She leaned across the seat, kissed Mason's cheek and said "Everything is ok! See you on Friday. Will we go to the Embassy again?"

Mason nodded. He looked relieved.

When Audrey entered the house her parents were in the kitchen looking at a road map. They showed her a letter that said the family would be moving to a brick and tile home in Como within the next month.

Audrey studied the map and found it perhaps placed her a little closer to Mason's home although it wasn't easy to work out by bus or car.

The family moved to a better home that did not transfer noise and communication through the walls. It felt solid and you couldn't see through its underside. However, because the block sloped from the front to the rear there was a door in the limestone foundations at the back which could act as a small storage area for the gardening equipment. This pleased Fred. The rooms were bigger also, which pleased everyone.

Charles had to change to another school, but he was due to go to High school after the Christmas holiday which started in three weeks, so that worked very well. Buses were closer and more frequent. Fred was considering buying a car, which seemed a necessity in Australia.

Katherine and Simon had bought a car when they had been in Australia only six months, saying you really couldn't survive without one. They were sorry to leave their friends but promised to visit each other.

Moving was a big event. It took almost two weeks to find out where they had put everything, particularly in the kitchen. It always seemed to be someplace else. Eventually they rearranged their possessions into a workable and orderly sequence. A telephone was installed, the first they had in Australia.

Audrey continued to see Mason. She wasn't sure about this relationship. She did not know whether her thoughts were because she was being unfair or because he wasn't the man for her after all. It was a confusing period of her life and she was dejected at being unable to sort it out whenever she brought it to mind.

Audrey did not share these thoughts with Mason. Mason seemed to feel that once the ice was broken so to speak, that sex should continue to be a part of their lives. Audrey tried to avoid this, not liking the deception, having to be careful and to be truthful, not enjoying it most of the time.

CHAPTER 36

Lectures at The American College of Personal Efficiency

Fred saw an advertisement in the paper from 'The American College of Personal Efficiency'. It promised five free evenings of lectures. The college was in Mount St Perth. Fred said he considered everyone ought to be more efficient and that the family was going to attend. The family had mixed reviews at the end of the course.

Fred thought it was alright but was not interested in going further, particularly as it cost money. Margaret was concerned about washing her hair and getting her clothes ready for a coming Saturday date. Dorothy politely smiled through most of it as the lecturer had a rubber face and brilliantly acted everything out. He was proficient and very amusing.

The lectures were mostly over Charles' head. He yawned through most of it and once fell asleep.

Audrey was entranced. She loved the philosophy. She learned about the three universes: one's own, another's, and the physical universe, and how they interacted. She learned that three components, Affinity, Communication and Reality, equated to understanding, and how they all affected each other. She learned about the Cycle of Actions, the Cycle of Control, and so much more. Audrey would have so enjoyed sharing all these truths with Doctor Gordon.

She decided to continue, but first of all she wanted to make sure that she had the first course off pat. She did it three times and at the end felt that she could teach it.

Margaret announced that she wished to marry Tony. Fred said, "It's not happening. You're too young. I don't want to hear any more about it, and you tell him so too!"

In September, Audrey resolved to end her relationship with Mason at the first right time.

In October she found out she was pregnant. This was a shock to both of them. Condoms had been used and were not thought to ever be ineffective.

The Doctor she visited confirmed her condition, saying the baby would be due early April.

There was no doubt about what was to happen now. They had to get married. That is what always happened. Parents had to be told.

There was uproar from Fred, quiet resignation from Mason's family. A wedding had to be arranged.

Audrey was told she couldn't wear white. She took her savings and bought some lovely blue and silver fabric and designed a dress with a matching headgear for the lady up the road to make. Mrs Flatbush was a good dressmaker and had already made clothes for Dorothy. She produced a beautiful outfit for Audrey.

Fred said, "She has to be married from home and have the reception here, I'm not spending money on a has-to-be wedding." He instructed Dorothy to make a cake and bake some sausage rolls.

The day came. Audrey was to go with her father to the Church, a neighbour having taken the rest of the family.

Before her father started the car, Audrey said, "I don't want to do this. I don't want to marry him."

Fred said, "Stop this nonsense. You can't get cold feet now. You've made your bed, now you have to lie in it. Don't for one moment think that you can stay here and have us look after you because you couldn't be more mistaken. It's not going to happen."

He started the car and drove to the Church.

Within the hour everyone was back at the house, eating sausage rolls.

The honeymoon consisted of a long weekend at a guest house in the country. It was decided that the newly married couple would live with Mason's parents. Keith was to be in the sleep-out, Audrey and Mason in a new double bed in the boys' room. Audrey continued to work. She did not suffer from morning sickness, but she lost her energy and felt tired most of the time. On one of her days off she visited Doctor Elton whom she had seen previously. He was nice, non-judgemental and interested in what she had to tell him. He took blood samples and saw her again a week later. She had fainted a few times, which she was inclined to do with any exertion. He went through her results; the anaemia was back, quite severely, necessitating an injection once a week. Audrey was relieved to find that eating raw liver did not have to be part of the treatment.

Dr. Elton insisted that she gave up work immediately for her sake and the baby's.

Once a week Audrey visited her parents and the Doctor. She had always been friendly with the people next door. Esme was kind and when Audrey asked her what it was like to have a baby she did her best to inform her. Esme and Frank had a little girl called Jillian. Audrey often took her for a walk to the Doctor's. They bought an ice-cream on the way back and became a familiar sight in the street holding hands.

Audrey's feet began to trouble her. She had to wear special rather ugly looking shoes to support her arches. Her legs and feet began to swell. Salt was banned from her diet. The no-exertion rule was irritating. She had always moved quickly even doing the smallest task and it was difficult to slow down.

Pushing a lounge chair into a different position made her feel faint.

Although she was not enjoying her pregnancy, she also felt detached from it. Almost as though she had taken the position of the spectator that had always been present but never as palpable as now.

Audrey wanted this to be over. She felt she needed to reorganise her life. This was like being in limbo with lots of realities to choose from but none in this time were applicable. Mason seemed to take little interest in the event. He felt it would eventually be over and sex would be back on the agenda, and Audrey could go back to work. His parents worked each day. His father was a fitter and turner at the same government workshop that Mason had done his apprenticeship. His mother, a former nurse in India, acted as a companion nurse to a lady in a suburb on the opposite side of the City.

Audrey was left to her own devices for most of each day. She did some light house duties and prepared ingredients for the dinner. Reading became her favourite pastime again. The Butlers' had a well-stocked bookcase and Audrey systematically went through it.

Margaret had finally won Fred over and on April 1st she married Tony. It was just six days before the birth of Audrey's baby.

CHAPTER 37

April 1954—Dwayne is Born

Audrey awoke just after midnight feeling pains in her back and stomach. She decided to try and sleep some more but at six o'clock she woke Mason and said perhaps she should go to the hospital, which was close to her parents.

He drove her there and left to go to work.

It was a private maternity hospital that Dr. Elton had recommended.

However, Audrey did not feel it was very welcoming. She was told babies took a long time and she should keep walking round and round the outside veranda, until someone came to get her. She spent some time sitting in a cane chair as the walking was exhausting her.

Eventually she was taken indoors, given an enema, taken to the toilet and told to stay there.

After about half an hour she began to feel faint. She pushed a red bell, no-one came and soon she fainted.

She came to but after a while she fainted again; she was hot and sweaty, then cold. She pushed and pushed on the bell and eventually a disgruntled nurse asked her what she wanted.

She explained what had happened and about the anaemia. The nurse took her to a room and she laid on a stretcher type bed. She was asked if her waters had broken. Audrey said she did not know. How could she tell, because she had been on the toilet for so long? The pains were getting hard and frequent and although she was trying to be brave, the moaning and grunting could not be controlled. She gave up after a while and let the screaming that seemed to belong to someone else emerge. The matron came in after a while, peered between her legs and said to an accompanying nurse, "Send for the locum." Audrey didn't know what a 'locum' was, but said "I want Dr. Elton, he's my Doctor."

The matron said, "He's away on holidays. It is Easter you know."

They went away again.

In between passing out, Audrey was in severe pain. She was left alone. She came to hearing a voice saying, "Why wasn't I sent for before this?", then kindly "Audrey, I'm going to cut you, we need to get this baby out. I'm sorry. I'm going to give you an injection." It was the last thing she remembered.

She woke many hours later. Her mother in-law was sitting by the bed. She smiled and said "Hello, how are you feeling?" Audrey said, "I don't know, she was silent then she said, the bed feels all sticky."

Mrs Butler threw the sheets back and gasped. She rang a bell and a nurse appeared. She said to the nurse, "Send for the Doctor immediately. This patient is having a haemorrhage!" In the meantime, Mrs Butler stripped the bed, got some pads from the nurse and began to clean Audrey. The Doctor arrived, arranged a blood transfusion, and was obviously very cross with the hospital staff. Audrey and her mother in-law could hear him belabouring them about their duties through the door. Audrey felt dazed. She was unsure of her whereabouts. She didn't know whether the baby had been born or not. She only appreciated the freedom from pain and some caring that was being issued. All she wanted to do was sleep.

She awoke when it was dark. She was thirsty and rang the bell. A nurse came and gave her some water. She asked about the baby. "It's a boy, seven pounds two ounces, born at 1.15 this afternoon. You can see him later after

April 1954 – Dwayne is Born

the Doctor has been." Audrey slept on until the Doctor came in the early morning.

He enquired how she was and encouraged her to eat something. She didn't tell him that nothing had been offered…and then he explained that he had cut her on the outside near her vagina necessitating fourteen stitches and that she had ten stitches on the inside that would eventually dissolve. She asked him to explain all this to Dr. Elton who was treating her for anaemia. Looking a little grim, he promised to do this; he said Doctor Elton would return from his holiday in three days and that Audrey would see him then.

That evening Mason came. Audrey had seen her son, had her face and hands washed, her hair combed and was looking better. She had spent an hour with her son in her bed, had eaten two meals and was feeling much better.

Mason stared at his son, held him awkwardly for a moment then placed him near Audrey on the bed.

She was told that her mother had phoned, been told of the baby's arrival, and that Audrey needed rest and quiet for at least one more day.

She had marvelled at the tiny creature that she had given birth too. Having no idea of the normal hospital procedure she was without judgement, mainly feeling that this was not an event that one could relish or hope to experience again.

Mrs Butler came the next day saying that Audrey was not staying in this hellhole any longer and that she was taking her and the baby home. Everything was got ready and soon they were in a taxi and on the way home. Mrs Butler called Dorothy and filled in the details. Dorothy was shocked, saying that Audrey would have been better off with a midwife.

A week later Audrey visited Dr. Elton for her injection. He told her that the hospital had changed hands a few months before her visit and that he had not had the occasion to go there since. He was appalled at the report from Dr. Mills, the locum, and informed Audrey that the hospital was being reported to the authorities.

Eventually Audrey heard that it had been closed down.

Audrey tried to take stock of all that she had experienced once she was home.

She felt somewhat detached from all that had happened. She had been told that the birth of a baby was a wonderful experience. She went looking for the wonderful. All she could find was the marvel of seeing this tiny creature with its fuzz of white golden hair and blue eyes.

She didn't feel that she had produced it but was very happy to care for it, protect it and love it. She did not feel like a mother, but then she did not know how mothers were supposed to feel.

Now he lay in her arms and she gazed at her baby. It looked like her; she could not see any resemblance to Mason or his parents. Now, she had to decide on a name. Mason, when asked had no views and seemed uninterested; but Mrs Butler said Roland had always been a family name. It was Mason's second name, what about making it a first name.

Audrey considered it, but it did not make her smile. She wanted Paul as a second name. Finally, Audrey decided on Dwayne as a first name.

The family were disappointed but passed no judgement. Fred snorted and said, "I don't suppose you even considered naming him after me?"

Audrey said, "No one could ever take your place. Only one Fred is allowed in any family!"

Fred wasn't sure what to make of this but stayed quiet. Dorothy smiled.

A few weeks later Audrey complained to her Doctor about irritation and itching all around her vagina. She also was aching just above her pelvic region.

She had an infection that was creating a discharge. Antibiotics did not seem to fix it. Eventually she had to have a DNC, a minor operation that involved cleaning tissue from the uterus lining; probably caused by the heavy bleeding that had ensued after the birth.

Mason was not a happy man. His sex life had been non-existent for some time, and it seemed to him that the baby had all the attention.

He complained loudly and often, and no amount of Audrey's explana-

April 1954 – Dwayne is Born

tions seemed to mollify him. Audrey felt that he considered she was to blame for the pregnancy and the subsequent happenings. His behaviour led her to be more and more detached.

Mason finished his apprenticeship. He applied and got a position with a large earthmoving company.

His parents decided to leave Australia and move to Africa. They intended to rent their home at a figure that Audrey and Mason could not afford. They had to move. Audrey went to the State Housing Commission. Their name went on a waiting list for a Government house.

During the next two years they lived in three different houses, each one in a worst condition than the previous one, necessitated by Mason having six different jobs. Always it was because the boss had no idea how to run the place or how Mason was supposed to do his job. Mason was always right and the boss wrong. If Audrey pointed out that the firm had existed for countless years and therefore it must be doing something right, she was in trouble for not supporting her husband.

Suddenly the clouds had a silver lining. A State Housing Commission house in Nollamarra was allocated to them. They moved. One month after they had moved in, Mason's brother arrived on the doorstep asking to stay for a while as he had lost his job and was on the 'Dole'. He contributed nothing to the household expenses. He expected to be fed and have his washing and ironing done. He didn't even clean his room.

Keith was a liability. At twenty-three, he was a drinker and a gambler and had no intention of getting a job.

Audrey had been very caring and loving towards him in the beginning. Finance was tough. It often took a few weeks for Mason to get another job. This meant no money was coming in to pay the rent and buy food. One day there was just one egg in the fridge. Audrey intended it to be for Dwayne.

She went to the local shop to buy some milk; all she could afford, and when she returned Keith was eating the egg.

When Mason returned home, she told him that Keith had to go, and immediately; enough was enough. After a fierce argument, she won and Keith left.

CHAPTER 38

Mason and the Ultimatum

Audrey took stock of her situation. She had never lived like this. When she was working, she had some decent clothes and shoes and was in charge of her life. Now she was down to two dresses and one pair of shoes because she had sold most of her possessions to survive.

She decided to get a job. Not an easy task. Single girls were employed but not married women.

Mason immediately protested the idea. Married women stayed home and looked after children and did what they were told. Husbands looked after their wives who were supportive and grateful.

He couldn't have stated his case better for encouraging Audrey to look for work. She didn't agree with any of his utterances and said so. He immediately accused her of disrespect. She pointed out that respect had to be earned and he wasn't doing anything to promote this.

After a fierce battle they went to sleep in an icy silence.

The next day Audrey went through the wanted ads and found three possibilities. She asked the lady next door, Pauline, to care for Dwayne. She also asked her if she could borrow a few shillings until the end of the week. Pauline had some idea of what was happening and was happy to oblige. She liked Audrey and loved Dwayne.

Audrey went to town and to the first employer on the list. She was refused an interview but filled in a questionnaire.

The second employer finding out she was married, refused to interview her.

Audrey appealed to the angels for help. They answered. During the third interview the Proprietor, a Dutchman suddenly said, "I like you. Can you handle this job, even though you don't have any experience in running a restaurant?"

Audrey smiled and said with sincerity, "I am almost twenty- one years old. Everything I have done for the first time this lifetime has been without experience. I'm very fast at learning. I'm enthusiastic. I would love this job. I'm willing to take the chance that I will do it well. Will you take a chance on me?" Abe Bakker started laughing, "Yes alright, you can start next Monday. Come in at 11am. You can leave at 8pm. It will be for five days. I cover the rest but if I need a weekend off you will have to work and have two days off during the week. How does that seem to you?"

Abe continued. "Because you are working long hours the pay is good. After the first month, if you are doing well, I will give you a twenty five percent rise. If you are doing badly with no sign of improvement I will fire you. Does that seem fair to you?"

Audrey nodded, she stood and shook hands and thanked him and went home more joyful than she had felt for a long time.

At last she was back in control of her life. She never wanted to hand over her welfare to someone else ever again.

The next day she went through the telephone pages looking for nurseries that would take Dwayne.

Eventually she found one on the outskirts of the City that would take her son from ten thirty until four thirty at a reasonable fee. She inspected the premises and the staff and found both more than satisfactory.

Audrey figured that Mason's jobs always seemed to start around seven or seven thirty and finish around three or three thirty. She decided that

Mason and the Ultimatum

Dwayne would be picked up by his father, taken home, bathed, fed with the meal she would leave them both in the fridge or the oven, and eventually Mason would put his son to bed. It was an opportunity for Mason to get to know his son.

She knew she may not see Dwayne in the evening except when he was asleep; but she would be there to greet him in the mornings when he awoke and also spend time with him. This would have to do. Also, it gave his father time to really know his son, as he paid little attention to him if Audrey was there to look after him. When told of the arrangement Mason again objected; but Audrey was adamant and soothed him by dwelling on the extra money that would take care of the unpaid bills.

The arrangement worked well. Audrey got her rise in pay; the marriage appeared to be more acceptable, probably because there was little time they spent together, other than the weekends. Even this time was limited as Mason was a keen hockey player and away on matches on Saturday afternoons. He trained one evening a week and Pauline looked after Dwayne from five pm until seven pm.

Everyone seemed to be doing what made them smile so the atmosphere was more conducive to good humour until one fateful morning when calling visitors changed all their lives.

One Sunday morning Mason brought a man and a lady into the lounge. He called for Audrey and introduced them as Jean and John saying that they had some news about God that would be useful to the family; and how about putting the kettle on.

Audrey looked at the visitors. They were in their thirties, were nicely dressed, friendly, and had a knowing air about them. Audrey hadn't had a philosophical discussion about anything, certainly not about God, since she had left the ship. She looked forward to hearing their views.

A LIFE of Enlightenment

Jean and John were Jehovah's witnesses. Audrey had never heard of them. They gave her a Watchtower pamphlet and a small book and asked both of them to read it before they returned the following Sunday.

Mason said he would look at it later and went back to his gardening at the front of the house. He said they just arrived and started chatting and he agreed with much they had said at the time.

Audrey sat down and eagerly started to read. She read the pamphlet and then the book. She decided that the book was more complex than she thought or that she had misunderstood most of it. She read it again. She hadn't misunderstood anything in it. She was shocked that any woman could take this seriously. The implications should be appalling, yet these people to all Watchtower accounts had a huge following. She wondered if most of them could be men.

She awaited their return with interest.

When questioned, Mason said he had only scanned the book but that from what they had told him the week before he was in favour of it and wanted to join.

Jean and John turned to Audrey with a friendly enquiring look. Audrey said, "I want to make sure I have got something straight before I give you my decision."

They nodded politely and approvingly.

Audrey enquired. "I have read the book twice to make sure I understood it correctly. It seems to me that the husband as head of the house is responsible completely to God and his wife is protected providing she follows all his instructions." Mason was nodding and had a small smile on his face. John smiling said, "You have done well: you really seem to have understood your reading!"

Audrey went on. "As an example, if Mason told me to stick my head in the gas oven and turn it on, I would not be in any trouble with God but *he* would. He has to answer to God, but I don't. Have I got this right?"

They all looked at each other. Jean said "Well, that's a bit extreme but generally yes; you are correct."

Mason and the Ultimatum

Audrey smiled saying, "There is no way I am giving my life or indeed any control over it to anyone at all, particularly to my husband who would like nothing more than a subservient wife." Looking at Mason, she said, "No wonder you are so eager to join." She rose and left the room.

After they had left, Mason came into the kitchen where she was preparing lunch.

"I think it's good to be religious anyway, so I'm joining. I'm going to be baptised in a couple of weeks. Think it over because if you don't you will feel left out."

Audrey stared at him. "You can't be serious, you never really read the book. You know nothing about it. You just want it to use as a weapon against me."

"Well, someone should keep you in line; it might as well be me."

Audrey had nothing to say. She was quiet and thoughtful. As usual she was finding her way philosophically around this event.

Audrey never looked back. Always her look was forward and long ago she had said that there was not a single happening that appeared to be a liability that you could not change into an asset. It was a matter of changing your viewpoint.

She did not question marrying Mason or having Dwayne or her life as it had been to date. None of this could have happened without her being present and that premise allowed her to be responsible for her life. Now, she needed to use her definition and "respond with ability" to take care of her life as it unfolded.

Two weeks later Mason got baptised. Audrey was working for one of Abe's weekends off. She was glad not to attend the ceremony.

After this the radio was banned. If Audrey turned it on, Mason turned it off.

She listened to it when he was not present and then hid it as he threatened to give it away or destroy it.

Audrey was not happy. It seemed that the witnesses were always telling Mason how difficult and ungodly she was and generally turning him against her, not just as a wife but also a mother. This was difficult to circumvent, and Mason was not a willing listener.

She grew thin and her normal smiles grew as thin as her body. She developed boils, one on her shoulder that turned into a carbuncle, so she was unable to wear a bra. She did not sleep well.

One evening Mason jabbed his finger at her and said "You are my wife and I demand my rights as a husband. Now get in there and he pointed to the bedroom."

She said nothing. She walked to the bedroom. Shut the door and turned the key in the lock. He hammered at the door, but she ignored him and eventually he left the house, no doubt to relay his latest victimhood to a witness colleague.

Easter was approaching and also Dwayne's second birthday. Audrey arrived home from work on a rainy Tuesday to find her parents in the lounge room.

She was surprised.

Mason said, "I sent for your parents to take you home for a rest over Easter. You look ill. You need a change." Audrey was amazed, this was the first time he had shown her any consideration for weeks.

Even Abe had said, "Look, take a few days off, have a rest, see the Doctor and get a tonic, you look all in!"

Finding her parents there seemed interesting synchronicity. Her mother said, "If you are not working for a few days, come home with us and have a good rest. You don't look a bit like yourself."

Her father said, "Get your things. If we are going to do this thing, we need to go now. We've been here over an hour as it is."

Audrey said, "Wait a moment I need to get Dwayne and pack a bag for him."

Mason and the Ultimatum

Mason said, "It's pouring. Don't take him out in this, if you want to take him, come back later sometime. He's already got the beginnings of a cold. Don't be stupid. Anyway, I can look after him for a few days."

Audrey looked at her father, giving an almost imperceptible shake of the head. "Alright I'll bring you back tomorrow, now let's get going." Fred stood up.

She packed a few things and climbed in the car, experiencing a huge feeling of relief at leaving the house.

In the car her father said, "Well, are you going to tell us what has been going on? Since you had the baby you have hardly talked to us; not since your in-laws left! At least you now have a government house and Mason is working again! So what's the problem, and don't tell me there isn't one. You can cut the air with a knife in that house."

Audrey hesitated. She was a private person. Events that were usually considered negative were not to be focused on, as that to Audrey seemed to make them even more prominent. Sympathy, which she never wanted or looked for, was another way of agreement that one was overwhelmed and couldn't cope. Support was always good. To Audrey this was someone saying, "How do you want to go about dealing with this, or what advice would you give someone in this situation?" It put the person back in charge of their life, taking the victim idea away.

Now, she deemed it wise to say to her father, "Mason has become a Jehovah's Witness. I did not wish to join. This has created conflict. They have a rule that the wife must always follow the husband in his wishes; this even included sticking my head in the gas oven if he told me to do so. I know that sounds far out, but I checked and it is true. I don't think he understands this religion at all, but it serves him to assist in controlling me. Apparently, only husbands are answerable to God. Wives are safe providing they do as they are told."

Fred said, "I could have told him that you wouldn't wear that. You've never done what I told you to do. So what chance has he got!" Dorothy said, "Never mind, leave it alone now. She needs a rest after all that!"

CHAPTER 39

The Disappearance of Dwayne

Audrey spent that evening and the next day resting and allowing her mother to look after her. It was a welcome change.

On the Thursday, after her father finished work, he took Audrey back to her home. There was no one there. The blinds were drawn and when she looked in her purse, the key to the house was missing. They decided to come back the next day.

The same situation prevailed. They finally broke in. Fred managed to force a window and Audrey was hoisted up on his shoulders and then through the opening. She let her father in through the front door. The house was empty. All that remained was Audrey's clothes, a few of her personal items in the bathroom and an old treadle Singer sewing machine that her mother-in-law had given to her before she left for Africa. There was an old suitcase on top of the laundry cupboard. Audrey used it to pack everything that was left. After saying, 'the little bastard', a grim silence emanated from Fred. Audrey was a little stunned. This was unexpected.

Where was Mason? Where was Dwayne?

She said to her father that they needed to go home where she could use the phone and find Dwayne.

A LIFE of Enlightenment

That evening and the following day, she made many, many calls. She rang and asked to speak to Mason as though she knew he was where she had called. She phoned every one of his relatives and a couple of friends. She did not ring many of the witnesses; indeed, she only had heard of one or two and had to phone Enquiries for their numbers. She found all the answers were polite and puzzled. Audrey offered no explanations. She came to the conclusion that Mason and Dwayne were not to be found in any expected places.

It was now Easter Friday 31st March.

On the Wednesday, as the holiday finished, she rang his work, only to be informed that he had resigned and had not been there since two days before Easter. She asked to speak to Accounts to find out if they were sending any pay to an address, only to discover he had called in and picked it up before the holiday began.

She had to go back to work, but before she started at the restaurant, she went to the police. She was surprised and disappointed to discover they could not help. In fact, they were sympathetic but not interested in what they classified as 'a domestic'. They suggested Audrey see a solicitor.

John Billett, the solicitor, was a short, intelligent looking man in his thirties. He wore large dark rimmed glasses, too big for his face. He was attractive, friendly and concerned about her plight. He made notes as he listened intently to her story. When she had finished he leaned back in his chair and gazed out at the river view behind his desk.

Finally, he swung his chair around, and said "Audrey, this is what we are going to do. Firstly, I will check with all the people you have telephoned and anyone else that you may think is appropriate. It is pointless to check the electoral roll until at least we are closer to the next election when it should be up to date. I will also contact the Jehovah's Witness organisation. When they realize they are talking to a solicitor's office they may be less reluctant to give me information. I don't suppose you can afford a private detective?"

Audrey shook her head. "I did think of that, but they cost so much to start and then a large sum per day."

Mr Billett nodded. "Audrey, the legal position is this: A child belongs to the father until the Court legally awards it to the mother. You look shocked, as well you may be. There are protests that may eventually change this law, or at least consider the different circumstances of each case, but that is how it currently stands. If Dwayne is out of the country, there is nothing you can do, unless he returns within the next six years. Of course, he may still be in Western Australia or in another State. Do you have any in ideas about this?"

Audrey gazed off into the distance looking as though she was giving the question serious thought. It was quiet in the office. Finally, looking as though she had arrived from some far-off place she said, "I cannot feel Dwayne's energy anywhere around. I have the feeling he is not in Australia anymore." "What about his father?"

Audrey looked apologetic, "I'm sorry, I have got so detached from him that I didn't pick anything up."

John Billett smiled, "You are doing very well. I don't know anyone else who locates people by their energy."

Audrey said, "Lots of mothers would disagree; they may not have words for it, but it is something they do all the time."

He smiled, "Audrey, I will contact you in a day or so and tell you any news."

She left feeling confident that he would do his utmost, yet feeling in her heart that Dwayne was not to be found at this time.

She went home to her parents.

Now that Audrey had done all that she felt could be done she relaxed. Then the grief came. It started almost like a hiccup, slowly growing into stomach wrenching sobs that she could not control. After a while she found she was taking great gulps of air to avoid running out of breath. Her throat pained and her stomach felt as though it was tied in knots. She sobbed and sobbed.

She was glad that she had the house to herself. She was alone. There was no-one to hear her or question. She knew Dwayne had gone and the void that the leaving reflected seemed enormous. Even when some of the grief had dissipated, and she had washed her face, and combed her hair, sobs would suddenly escape as though they had a life of their own.

She felt exhausted. She lay on her bed wanting to play her glad game but finding little to be glad about. Eventually she fell asleep knowing that when weariness was not around she could take a more rational view of the situation.

John Billett called two days later. He had no news. Every avenue had produced nothing new. John said the sect were sympathetic and willing to help, and that they would never condone Mason's current behaviour. However, they had made enquiries and no-one in the sect had seen or heard from him since before Easter.

Audrey rang Abe, her boss, and briefly filled him in with the current events. She said, "You have been so kind and caring. I don't feel as though I can do you justice right now and you do need someone who is competent, please let me resign. It may take some time to sort this and myself out and it wouldn't be fair to you to wait."

He reluctantly agreed, leaving Audrey free to deal with her grief.

For two weeks she cried off and on. At the end of that time she took stock of the whole event, her feelings and actions, deciding it was time to get on with her life.

CHAPTER 40

A New Job, a New Romance

She found another job as a receptionist with a firm of trichologists. Audrey asked Dorothy for information about trichology before her interview. Dorothy had told her it was about infectious diseases of the hair and scalp and named some of them. Audrey felt this small knowledge had helped her to get the position.

It turned out that there was only one consultant. His name was Steven Dempster. He was tall, very good-looking, with a wonderful head of hair. Although he was only thirty-five, he had tiny wings of grey at the temples against a wavy thick mop of dark brown hair. His smile reached his blue/grey eyes. He was altogether charming, friendly and gave his clients the impression that he was more concerned about them than anyone else.

He showed and told Audrey what was expected of her. The office opened at ten and closed at eight in the evening to allow clients to call after work.

Audrey was used to long hours and was in no hurry to go home. Sometimes they shared a meal together after work.

After a while he taught her how to interview a client. It was a set routine and patter. The clients were given a kit of small bottles filled with various coloured liquids which they rubbed into their scalps, returning one month after this treatment. Audrey wasn't sure what was in the bottles and Steven did not seem to know. They arrived from Head office each week. Audrey began to think that perhaps this was all a scam, but she got confused when clients began to show her how they had grown hair or cleared up a rash or dandruff.

She became an expert salesperson. To the clients she seemed as genuine and sincere as Steve was. She got a raise in salary, and even after paying her parents board she managed to start a decent savings account.

Steve told her he was married. His wife was called Daisy. He said they were not happy and they really needed to part. Daisy appeared in the office now and then. She was tall and willowy, wearing gold framed spectacles on a plain face. She had black hair with an olive skin. The mustard colour she often wore did nothing to enhance her. She treated Steve almost as a stranger and Audrey with derision.

One late afternoon, Audrey was sitting in the clients' chair in Steve's office when he said, "Although you are generally a happy smiling person, I have a feeling that you have a hidden cloak of sadness about you. I may be wrong. Because you have dimples you often look to be smiling and enjoying life when I don't think you mean them to show! Am I right?"

She looked away. "Look, he said, I don't mean to pry, but I feel if you talked to me it may help and some of the sadness might fly out of the window. Now, what say you?"

She said, "My son, who is just two, got kidnapped by his father last Easter. I don't know where he is. I haven't seen him since." Steve's queries about what had happened soon brought forth the whole story. She managed it very well but at the end she began to cry.

Steve came from behind the desk, locked the door, knelt in front of her and took her in his arms.

He held her, stroking her back, until she stopped. Then he pulled her to her feet, wrapped his arms around her, stroked her hair, and kissed her forehead, occasionally saying, "Better now?"

Audrey said, "Thank you. I never knew anyone so kind."

A New Job, a New Romance

"You make me feel as though I want to look after you, not just now, but all the time. There is something so vulnerable about you despite the enormous strength that shines through. You are also very lovable. You are not aware of any of this are you?"

She said, "I have been told this before. I'm just not good at looking at me!"

He smiled. "That's alright, you don't have to be."

Audrey smiled back. He bent his head and kissed her. It was a very gentle kiss. He followed it with another and another until she began to kiss him back. It was the first time that Audrey had felt a kiss that stirred her. She had quivering in her stomach and for the first time she wanted to feel a man's hands all over her body. She gave a small moan of desire.

He took off her white uniform, then her bra and panties and still holding her close, he slipped out of his white coat and then his trousers. He laid her gently on the floor with his jacket under her head. Kneeling over her legs he began to run his hands over her body murmuring, "how beautiful you are, such a soft skin…"

She pulled him down to kiss him and with one hand his undergarments were gone and he lay naked beside her. He went on kissing and touching her, and she held him and stroked him, until she pulled him to go inside. She opened her legs and for the first time felt she was willing and happy to have a man inside her.

He was careful and slow until she arched her back and began to match his rhythm. Her first orgasm was a delightful surprise. She didn't quite know what to make of it; only that it was wonderful, very intense and felt as though she had been loved and not just used.

He wrapped his arms around her and said "that was wonderful, you are wonderful and lovely, and I think I could love you with no effort at all. Now I am a little concerned because we did not take any precautions." She said, "my period is due in two days; does that help?"

"Very much so." He grinned at her. "Would you like to do that again?"

"Yes please," she said, laughing. And so they did.

They became lovers, with precautions. Audrey was amazed at her appetite for sex. Some sleeping giant had been awakened inside her and couldn't wait to devour and be devoured.

She was happy. She loved Steve and believed he loved her. They spent many hours just smiling at each other, before the look became not enough. They got used to the floor. Audrey bought some cushions for the waiting room chairs, but these mostly lived in the office as headrests.

Their happiness created an atmosphere for the clients. The clinic was busy and the clients did well and were happy with their results.

Even Daisy's occasional visit did not cast any gloom. They simply smiled through it.

Steve said, "She has no wonder, and is the least curious person I know. Only her Catholic upbringing stops her from divorcing me, but I feel she might come around soon; we are living a lie and that must get to her eventually."

Audrey asked him why they had married in the first place. "We were childhood sweethearts and it seemed it was inevitable. We were very young; I was eighteen and she was seventeen. Our parents, who had been friends since they too were young, were overjoyed at the match; we seemed to be swept along in the flow. It took a few years to realise that we had different goals in life, different views and principles; we had so little to discuss. When we were in high school there were some similarities and we could converse, but in later life there is little we have in common."

Audrey thought about comforting Steve but there seemed to be little cause to do so. He had no air of conflict or sadness. His discourse was matter of fact. The situation had existed for a long time and it seemed to be a part of his life that he had placed on a shelf. It seemed unworthy of his attention.

She did not feel guilty about the love making. They were both still married and unhappily so. They seemed right for and to each other. She went on enjoying the relationship.

A year passed. An announcement from head office requested that the

A New Job, a New Romance

Perth office be permanently closed. Steve was to open a second office in Sydney. Daisy decided not to go. Steve invited Audrey. He checked with Head office, praising Audrey to the skies and finally got an okay for her to act as his receptionist. However, she had to pay her own fare. Steve wanted to treat her but it was difficult as his account was a joint one with Daisy. Audrey had saved just enough for the air fare and was thrilled to go.

When they arrived, Steve was given a small apartment which Audrey could share. It was an idyllic time. She cooked for him, they went out together with no fear of being caught and made love any time of the night and morning.

Steve jokingly said, "You are going to wear me out!' Audrey kissed him until he changed his mind.

The company decided after a year or so to leave Australia and open in South Africa; at the same time, Daisy demanded Steve's presence back in Perth as his father had had a stroke.

Steve had told his manager that Audrey was actually a good consultant and could easily run her own clinic. Nothing had eventuated, but now they offered her a post in Durban. They were leaving within the week.

Audrey was torn. She did not know if Steve would return to Sydney. She felt he would not go to South Africa if his father was ill.

A letter from Dorothy settled the matter. She wrote that Fred had cut off his thumb and first finger and part of the second one on his lathe in the shed at home. Because it was not done at work there was no compensation. The hospital and Doctors bills were enormous. Could Audrey help with some funds.

Audrey had not been paid for a month. She went to Head office and asked for her pay and holiday pay up to date. She was told it was not a problem; but it was late on Friday, so she should come back on Monday and her cheque would be ready.

On Monday the office was closed and locked. She spoke to the office people next door. They said everyone had left for South Africa on the Saturday. There had been a farewell party on the Friday night. She contacted the owners of the office block, only to be told there was three months' rent owing and did Audrey have a forwarding address. Audrey did not.

Later that day came a visit from the landlord of her apartment. She explained that Steve had been called away to Perth. The landlord was not interested. The firm had rented the apartment for the two of them. The rent had not been paid for three months, always with excuses. As Audrey was and had been living there, as the tenant she was legally responsible.

Audrey explained about her lack of money, her lack of a job, Steve's absence, her family' predicament. He was courteous but firm. She was to sign a paper stating that she would take responsibility and pay the rent at so much a week until the debt was cleared. He gave her two weeks to find a job but only one week to move out. Then the first payment was due.

Audrey sat down and started to read the help wanted ads. Within a few days she had a job as a receptionist at Ushers hotel in the City. She chose to have and keep the seven thirty morning shift, as the money was better than the nine to five one. Within a few days she heard that Australia Hotel almost opposite was looking for someone for a similar job. She applied and got a four pm to eleven pm shift. This gave her an hour to herself. She found a room in a boarding house that also included breakfast. She felt she was organized. She divided her pays to include her rent, her rent arrears, some living expenses and money to send to her mother.

She invested in an alarm clock, rising at 6.30 am, leaving at 7am—usually with her toast in her hand—catching her bus and arriving at Ushers by 7.30am. She seldom got home before midnight as the buses were less frequent. Sundays she had off. She shopped, washed and ironed and cleaned her room, occasionally treating herself to a dinner at a cafe.

Audrey felt lucky that each hotel gave her a meal. This saved her shopping time and her funds.

After two months she had paid the rent arrears and could send extra money to her mother. Her father was expecting to go back to work soon. The skin grafts had taken time and expense.

Audrey eventually sent Steve a letter informing him that the firm had

A New Job, a New Romance

gone to South Africa, closed down all the branches in Australia and that for financial reasons she was staying in Sydney. She trusted that his father was back in good health and sent her regards to him and Daisy. She wrote it with her address on the notepaper but gave no details of her work or the finance requests she had to overcome.

CHAPTER 41

The Divorce Plea

A few weeks after starting her two jobs she came home to the boarding house one Saturday night to find Richard, another boarder, who was also a very nice homosexual, waiting for her. He said Mason, her husband was coming to see her in the morning and that he had already agreed to help Mason out with a project but only if Audrey agreed. Audrey was puzzled and wary. Richard said her husband would give her details.

The next day it was a shock to see Mason in the small sitting room all the boarders used. She had not seen him for almost eighteen months.

He told her that he had met a very nice girl who was a nurse and also a flight attendant. He wanted to marry her as she was a Jehovah's witness. He was not allowed to be the guilty party in a divorce, so he had already had a chat to Richard and was paying him twenty pounds, a great sum, just to be caught in bed with Audrey. You only have to be in bed together when a photographer bursts in and takes a picture of you. You don't have to be doing anything.

Audrey said, "Where is Dwayne?"

"He's okay. He has been with my parents in Africa. I brought you a few pictures and there's an old letter that I will read to you."

The letter read: *'Dwayne has been asking for his mother. We didn't know what to tell him as it seemed unlikely that you would get together again as Audrey is now living with her parents. So we told him that his mother was now in heaven and we made it a lovely place. He seems to have accepted that, so I hope you do too.'*

Mason stared at her. Audrey was appalled. She was dead to her son. She didn't see that anyone could say such a lie and have a clear conscience.

She was disgusted with Mason who seemed to think that it was a wonderful idea. 'Tied up loose ends', he told Audrey.

He said "If you help me out I will pay for you to go back to Perth. That's expensive, and Richard told me you work two jobs because of your father cutting his hand off."

She did not correct him.

"I will give this some thought. Where are you staying, do you have you a phone number?"

He gave her a piece of paper.

She said, "I will let you know in a few days."

"What's the matter with now?'

She repeated "A few days!" and left the room.

Later she talked to Richard. He said "Only if this is okay with you! I could use the money but I will not do anything to upset you. We are friends."

She telephoned Mason. "I suppose that as you are getting married, Dwayne will be coming back to Perth."

"Of course."

"When?"

"As soon as you sign the paper. I can make the arrangements for his flight. Adultery does not take so long for a divorce. In NSW it is very quick and as we both live here at the moment I can start the arrangement as soon as you sign the paper and I collect the photos."

She knew that as the guilty party there would always be a stigma to her name. Divorce, particularly for adultery was a matter for more than tut-tut's and shaking the head with eyebrows raised. The guilty party was scorned.

Audrey looked this over very carefully. There was another side to this event.

She would be rid of Mason completely. This was something that made her smile, even though the way she was going to go about it didn't make even a glimmer of a smile.

Audrey wanted to have Dwayne.

She telephoned Mason. "I will only sign these papers when Dwayne is back in Perth, and not before!"

"What are you going to do, he thinks you are dead."

She said "I will handle that carefully if at all, and not until after I see him. His welfare matters more than anything. These are my conditions."

There was silence, so she hung up the telephone.

A letter arrived from Steve. His father after a long battle had suffered another stroke, later a heart attack and now had died. He had not written because he did not know until now what he was going to do. As soon as he had finished the arrangements in Perth, he was coming to Sydney and together they could work out a future. Daisy had agreed at long last to a divorce, listing separation grounds. This could take three years. It may be able to be back-dated as no conjugal rights had taken place for a very long time. It was complex, but it would work out. He told Audrey how much he loved her. He would come to her as soon as he arrived. Did she have a phone number? Would she call him at home? He listed his number.

Audrey telephoned Steve and gave him the phone number of the boarding house. She didn't want to discuss all that had happened and what was happening in her life since he had left Sydney. She wanted to wait until he arrived, be in his arms and then bring him up-to-date.

A few days after her last conversation with Mason, he rang and said that Dwayne was on his way from Tanganyika. A friend of his grandmother's was flying to Australia and offered to look after him on the plane. It was an opportune moment. Mason had arranged for Lisa, his bride to be, to pick him up at the airport. Mrs Butler had sent a message that Dwayne had not been well but seemed to have recovered from the flu, and it would be wise to have him checked by a Doctor as soon as he arrived.

Audrey signed the divorce papers. Two evenings later she lay in Richard's bed, waiting the inevitable. The door burst opened. They were blinded by flash bulbs going off. The door closed. It was over.

The next day Mason told her that Dwayne was in Princess Margaret hospital in Perth, but it was not critical.

He gave her a ticket for her journey home. Audrey had expected a plane ticket but this was for a ship that sailed the next day. It would take ten days to get to Fremantle. It could not be changed.

Mason was surprised at her crossness. "It gives you a holiday too. I'm looking after you. Why don't you show some appreciation for a change? You always think I'm wrong!" Audrey said nothing. She went to see the Managers at both the hotels and explained that her son was in a Perth hospital and that she had to leave right away. They were a little put out, but understanding. She was well liked and efficient, so they gave her wages and her holiday pay and wished her luck, adding that if she returned to Sydney, to call on them and that if there was an opening they would be glad to employ her again.

Audrey packed her bags. She called Steve. There was no answer. She called her mother and gave her arrival details. She tried Steve that evening and the next day before she had to board the ship. Perhaps he was at the funeral? Audrey had no idea how close he was to finalising his arrangements.

She concentrated on enjoying the journey home, but she was eager and impatient to be there. Audrey thought about 'impatience.' It was like saying that 'the moment you were in, was not good enough. You needed to be in the next one.' She mentally shared the thought with Dr. Gordon and felt his agreement with her definition.

The ship arrived. It was a Saturday. Her parents were there to meet her.

Once she was in the car, she asked Fred to go to Princess Margaret Hospital. She intended to collect Dwayne and never let him go.

Once there, she asked if he was still a patient. They could find no record of him ever having been there; they checked the records for the past year.

The Divorce Plea

There was no other children's hospital and the adult ones never admitted children under fifteen.

From her parents' house, she checked the airlines. No-one would give her any passenger information. Audrey called John Billett. He was pleased to hear from her. She explained the arrangement with Mason and the fact that she could get no information on Dwayne's whereabouts; that she understood he was somewhere in Perth or maybe Sydney because his father was getting married again etc.

John promised to check the airlines and the hospital again. There was no record of Dwayne's arrival.

There was no evidence that Dwayne had ever returned to Australia.

Audrey gave her parents only the information that she had heard that Dwayne was in hospital and she thought she should see him. She simply said that it turned out not to be true.

Telling them all that had happened was just inviting Fred's wrath, judgement, and promised violence to Mason. Audrey had experienced enough traumas to last her a lifetime, without inciting any more. She knew that confiding in her mother was comforting but nothing was safe from Fred's inquisitiveness and Audrey knew Dorothy would not stand up to Fred's questions for very long.

Now she had to come to terms with Mason's deception once again.

Audrey could see that here was a lesson in discernment. At the same time, she could see that ability was ability, no matter how an event evolved. All the work that had gone into making her believe without checking all that she had been told was impressive. She once read that a victim at some point always admires his executioner. She began to see that it could be true.

She also felt that there comes a time in life, that the victim takes his head off the block and hits the executioner over the head with the axe.

At the moment she relished that thought; but then she also remembered 'the horse incident.' Matching vibes was not the answer. It reduced you to the level of the assailant, and made you a victim. Audrey knew that it was important to go on being *you*, no matter what. It was not appropriate for someone else to determine who you were. You had to go on being the very best person you could conceive yourself to be. Nevertheless, her thoughts previous to these conclusions had shown her that she could be a force to be reckoned with; she was rather amazed at how much havoc she could have created.

Revenge however was not the answer. In her heart this she had always known. The answer was to move on.

She called Steve, again no answer. She rang the boarding house. Yes, a message, yesterday. Steve was on his way to Sydney. She asked that he be given her number so that he could call her the moment he arrived.

Audrey waited. When there was no call she spoke to Richard. Steve had not arrived at the boarding house, however in their street a taxi had collided with a bus. He would check the hospital. Audrey gave him details.

Within a few hours, he told her that Steve was in hospital, seriously injured and that the authorities had sent for his wife. Audrey rang the hospital. Using Royal Perth hospital data as an entrance she eventually talked to his Doctor. She told him who she was and asked him to give Steve her love. He said Steve was conscious, but that his injuries were severe. She asked his doctor if she could call him again. He was sympathetic and suggested she leave it for a few days. Audrey agreed.

The next day a telegram came. It simply said, 'My love until the Twelfth of Never, Steve.'

Audrey was puzzled. Why the twelfth? Why never? She did not hear Johnny Mathis singing the song on the radio "The Twelfth of Never" until ten days later.

She called Steve's doctor after five days. He was kind and sympathetic. Steve has passed away the evening before. His injuries had been too severe. The doctor said that if he had lived he would have been crippled for life.

Audrey felt as though her world was collapsing around her. She felt it was in little broken pieces all around her feet. She wept; for Steve, for what might have been, and for herself.

She felt she had to be alone. Even though she felt she must be cried out

The Divorce Plea

considering the past few weeks, she knew there was more to come. She couldn't do that here. She rang Ruth, a girlfriend who had a flat in West Perth, and asked if she could spend a few days with her. She was going away for a long weekend, Audrey would be alone. Would that matter?

Audrey was pleased. It was perfect. Leaving a note for her family, she left for Ruth's home.

It was quiet, peaceful. She cried until she was exhausted. Afterwards, Audrey slowly began to relax.

It took two days before she realized that she was feeling sorry for herself. This had to stop. She began to put the broken pieces of her world around her feet back together again, almost like Humpty Dumpty.

After all she was still here. As a being, she existed. She had existed before and always would. This was just one life for her to live.

No-one else was there to dictate her feelings, her thoughts or her life. She was creating all these considerations and it must be by choice. There was no one else present. People created or co-created events. How she responded to them was her choice. She could see that she had reacted rather than responded. Lately she had seemed to do this, and it took her a little while to come to terms with each event before she felt she was cause again rather than effect. She remembered her own definition, 'taking responsibility meant responding with ability.' Why was she delaying in applying her own wisdom? It was time to take charge again.

She went for a walk. There was a park nearby and she did a slow stroll around it, concentrating on the trees, the flowers, the grass beneath her feet. Thinking was often wandering in condensed spaces. So, no thinking. She began to feel better and part of the world again. Seeing newsagents, she called and got a newspaper. It was time to get a job.

CHAPTER 42

Audrey Joins a Real Estate Firm

Audrey decided to return to the American College of Personal Efficiency and do some of their advanced courses. On arrival at the building she found it had changed its name to 'Scientology'. She asked what the name meant. Ology means "study of", Scio means "knowledge", so Scientology means the study of knowledge, the receptionist informed Audrey.

While nowadays a lot of people tend to hold a negative opinion of Scientology and view it as a cult, at the time it was merely a personal development philosophy which Audrey felt she could benefit from. She decided that it would be wonderful to be more knowledgeable or knowing, and enthusiastically told the receptionist how she had enjoyed the four times she had done the beginners course and what she had understood and applied to her life. She detailed the philosophy she had applied to make the events in her life less traumatic. The receptionist asked her to wait and soon Stanley Richards who had taught the earlier course appeared and invited her into his office. He invited her to a seat opposite his desk.

They talked for some time. Then Stanley asked her to hold some empty cans in her hands. The cans had clips on an open top and the wire from them was connected to a blue meter. Audrey could only see the back of it.

Stanley asked her to assist him in trying out a process. Audrey knew what processing was from her earlier course and readily agreed. He asked her to be comfortable and not move the cans around and to just follow his instructions and later tell him what she had experienced.

She sat back in the chair, relaxed and closed her eyes.

Audrey heard his voice say, "Be three feet back of your head! Now tell me what you see?"

"I see the back of my head."

"Good, now be near the sun…"

Then it was the stars, the moon, etc.

Audrey was giving detailed accounts of what she was viewing at the same time being intrigued by all that was occurring.

Then there was the command, "Be near your body, return to your body!"

She opened her eyes, and looked around the space she was in.

She said, "Well that was interesting…quite enlightening."

She smiled at Stanley.

He was looking at her thoughtfully. "It is unusual for someone to be able to do what you have just done."

Audrey said, "Why is that?"

"I'm not sure. Perhaps it is a question of trust. One needs to have trust in one's auditor."

"What do you mean by auditor?"

"An auditor is 'someone who listens.'"

Audrey thought about this for a moment. "Perhaps it is a lack of trust in their own power…Could it be that?"

She applied for a few situations over the next few days, eventually being offered a job at a Real Estate office, as an assistant to the accountant. Mr Bannister, the owner, felt that although she had no real estate experience, she would be quick to learn. She took the position because he was kind and

Audrey Joins a Real Estate Firm

she knew she could work closely with him.

Audrey was happy to learn a new skill. She had to type. Her first attempts were pathetic. Keys bunched together and had to be separated by hand, which meant she had to continually wash her hands. Audrey was sharing a large office with Mr Bannister; she typed with her back to him, so she missed the amused looks he gave her attempts.

He was patient. He gave her a book showing what fingers to use on the keyboard. She tried this but soon found it was quicker to use just a couple on each hand. The office letterhead was on blue paper, so rub-outs were obvious. She got used to retyping letter after letter, finally managing to do this only occasionally.

It took her very little time to handle the trust account. Her debit and credit lesson at the architect's office stood her in good stead. She balanced the accounts with ease at the end of each month. She also got good at forming the letters to Solicitors requesting mortgage funds for clients buying houses. They got used to her phone calls and were always polite and courteous.

Mr Bannister gave her more and more responsibility. She responded with efficiency, pleasure and smiles.

Audrey went back to the Embassy Dance Hall. Her sister Margaret had a girl, now three years old and was pregnant again. So, Audrey went alone. She met an Insurance agent named Trevor. He appeared for every dance. Every three weeks he had to go away for two weeks to the country. He introduced her to Clyde Hill, a friend of his, saying "he will keep you company while I am away." She liked Clyde, they danced well together, and he always took her home.

After a few months Trevor told her that he wished to take her to meet his uncle. On a Sunday he took her to a monastery in North Perth and introduced her to Brother Paul. They sat on a park bench in the grounds.

Trevor excused himself, saying he would leave them alone to chat. The monk was dressed in a long, dark brown garment with a hood and a thick tie around his waist. He slipped the hood off and smiled benevolently at Audrey. He chatted small talk about the gardens, her going out with Trevor.

Finally, Audrey asked, "Why am I here?"

He asked her about her religious beliefs. She said, "I have a lot of questions, not so much about religions but about God." He was pleased. This girl had possibilities. She may already have leanings towards the church.

She asked him if he considered that the Bible was true. He said, "Generally yes. It is a good book to follow!"

Audrey pointed out all the contradictions she remembered. There were many. She finished by saying, "Even a pavement painter wants nothing more than to be believed in, but he does not exact revenge if the public ignore him. You want me to understand that God who is supposed to be all lovable, will reap fire and brimstone on my head if I don't believe in him. I'm not saying that I do not believe in a creator who created all this. She waved her hands at the gardens and the sky, but I refuse to believe in the God that you do with all his fire and brimstone. Did Trevor bring me here to see if I would become a good Catholic?"

He smiled. "Trevor wants to marry you, but he can only marry a Catholic!"

She laughed and said, "You see what I have been saying Brother Paul, do you really think God would not allow two people who may love each other to be together? Can you really see God objecting or making conditions about love?" Then, more gently, because she could see he was a little defensive and she did not wish to offend him, she said, "I'm sorry, I cannot ever go along with this. All this stuff is man- made and has nothing to do with God; I will not ever be a part of it. I'm sorry if what I have said upsets you, but someone needs to say it, not just to you but to all religions who think they may have a monopoly on the Creator. I'm sorry I find this idea so unpalatable."

They both stood at the same time.

Audrey thanked him for the talk and gave him a hug. She saw Trevor in the distance and beckoned him to take her home.

On the way she told him in detail of the conversation with his uncle. Trevor said, "What were you trying to do, unfrock him?!"

She was shocked. She told him that she would never be a Catholic and that he should look elsewhere.

They talked, but she was adamant. He was going away the following day and Audrey thought that was a good idea.

She went back to the Embassy and to Clyde. Because Trevor was his friend, she briefly told him what had happened. He seemed pleased that now he could ask her out, without treading on Trevor's toes.

Audrey wasn't sure about this, but she was happy to see Clyde.

CHAPTER 43

The Marriage Proposal

Audrey and Clyde Hills went out for four years. During this time, he often said that if she married again it needed to be to a professor who could keep up with her. She laughed and told him that she would find him a rich widow.

She had shared most events of her life with Clyde. He was very non-judgemental, very caring. Eventually they gazed at each other one evening and he said, "Why don't we get married?" She smiled and nodded and together they went to choose wedding rings.

Clyde worked in a Bank and was being groomed for a top position.

They were earning good money and paid for their own wedding.

When they went back to the Saint Peters Church of England that had married Audrey previously, they refused on the grounds that she was divorced. Clyde's parents were not too happy about a divorced wife for Clyde but would accept them more willingly if they got married in a Church.

A Methodist Church offered to do the honours for them. Her employer Mr Bannister officiated as the Master of Ceremonies, Clyde's sister as bridesmaid and Danny, Clyde's best friend, as best man.

It was a lovely wedding and they went to Caves House in Yallingup for

A LIFE of Enlightenment

their honeymoon.

A week after Audrey returned to work Mr Bannister announced that he would retire at the end of the month. Management immediately offered Audrey his position but with no increase in pay. The company was in North Perth.

She promised to think about it. She decided that she deserved an increase in pay for shouldering a great deal more responsibilities, but management did not see the need for a raise. She decided to look elsewhere for a higher more well-paid position.

In the end, seeing a position as finance officer for a Real Estate firm in the city, she applied for and got the job. She was to arrange finance for existing homes sold and for new homes to be built for their clients.

She started at her new post two weeks later. It was a large office in Saint George's Terrace, employing some fourteen people. The staff was friendly and welcoming to Audrey.

She wasn't sure how the mortgage money lenders would respond to a lone female asking for funds. She made appointments with all the solicitors, lawyers, and building society managers in charge of funds and simply appealed to their goodwill. She asked them for specifics of what each of them required in a letter of application, including inspection fees, keys, etc. and followed their instructions to the letter, including any further relevant data regarding the clients.

Because Clyde also worked in the City it was much more convenient for picking Audrey up after work. They had found a rental apartment in West Perth, bought some furniture and were happy there.

Clyde was eligible for a housing loan at a reduced interest rate and minimal deposit. In a short time, they purchased a block of land at the high point of Mt Pleasant. Hiring one of the two builders used by Audrey's firm, they started to build a home from a plan previously used by the builder. Audrey made some alterations as the house progressed. As it manifested it was easy for her to see how it could be improved.

She did well at her job. Soon she asked for an expense account and three

The Marriage Proposal

times a week took one of her lenders to lunch. When a credit squeeze happened, she always got funds for her clients, whether from deceased estates handled by the solicitors or from one of the two building societies. She wrote thank-you letters whenever they helped one of her clients and always ensured they had all the data required including an available key for inspections.

As much as possible, Audrey always made sure that the clients fully intended to repay their loan and were capable of it.

If a Bank Manager refused an application because it did not comply with policy, she pointed this out and simply asked what had to be done to make it comply with policy. Inevitably the Bank manager would talk himself around to saying 'Yes' in the end.

She did not know this, but the accountant who often knew from the papers previously viewed that a refusal was imminent, would have bets with the rest of the staff that the 'No' would not stay by the time Audrey appeared from the office.

Clyde was relieving managers who were taking holidays, so he was often at different branches of the Bank. He told Audrey she was not to ever approach him for or with her clients. "Just let me be a husband and that is all. I don't want to deal with you on the other side of the desk. Just stay with persuading my colleagues for loans for your clients."

She enjoyed her job. She shared a large office with the building consultant, a middle-aged man called Samuel Beardson.

She had little hassles with him. He often wanted her to finance impossible deals because he was working on commission. When Audrey refused he threatened her with management. Audrey simply told him to do his best, knowing she was well liked, respected and efficient at her job.

One day he received a phone call saying his teenage son had broken his back on a boy-scout exercise. He went home.

A LIFE of Enlightenment

Management asked Audrey to take over his section until he returned, despite the fact that she knew nothing about his job. The next day a man and his wife in their thirties arrived, asking to see some plans for them to build a new home.

After asking them a few details, Audrey started looking in the file cabinet. She couldn't read plans well at all, so she was slow in finding anything that looked remotely like complying with their request.

After lots of shaking of heads and 'no thank you', Audrey gave up.

Playing for time and also to get a better idea of what was needed and wanted, she sat behind her desk and asked questions about every room in the house. She had an epiphany when room sizes were being discussed. Size was unimportant. What one needed to place into a room, must be the minimum deciding factor of size. She shared this thought with the clients who thought it made sense. They gave her a list of contents for each room; also the placement of the rooms on the block etc. She remembered the Fremantle doctor, a south-westerly cooling breeze, and together they decided optimal placements. All of a sudden, she had a very clear picture of the layout of the house. On her large blotting pad, she drew a bird's eye view of a plan which she felt complied. Audrey was amazing herself.

She turned the plan round and they studied it, before declaring that it was exactly what was required. They were pleased and excited. Audrey asked them to close their eyes and get a picture of how the house would look from the outside. They willingly shut their eyes.

Across the desk, suspended between Audrey and the clients appeared a coloured picture of a home. It was white with a green roof and yellow shutters. It was like looking at a slide that was viewed through a projector. It was a huge picture, and as clear as a bell.

Audrey was fascinated. They opened their eyes. Audrey said, "How did you do that? It was magnificent!" They looked puzzled.

Audrey said, "You sent a picture of your house across the table; it was white with a green roof and yellow shutters. Is that right?"

They nodded. She continued: "Oh, I would like to know how you did

The Marriage Proposal

that; I would love to be able to do it too!" They looked surprised.

"Well, we just got a picture of the house, that's all," they almost said in unison. "How much will the house cost to build?"

Audrey said she needed to see the builder. Did they have a plan of their block? They gave her this and when asked to return the next late afternoon, they said of course they would and told her how pleased they were.

The office had now emptied of staff. It was six o'clock. Clyde was going to training. He was a football umpire on Saturdays. Audrey always caught the bus home on training nights.

She sat at her desk, looking at all that had occurred in the last two hours. She was amazed at what she had learned.

She found a piece of graph paper and started to draw the house to scale. All of a sudden, she knew how to do this. She knew what size a passage or a doorway should be; how to show windows in a room and so forth. She did not question anything; she simply went along with the flow. She even drew a section. She thought of drawing a roofline, but could only think of flat roofs or domes, not ones she had seen on ordinary houses; somehow she knew that was out of her capabilities at this time.

It was ten o'clock when she finished. Alfred Parker, the builder never went to bed before midnight.

Audrey rang Clyde, told him she was catching a taxi to the builder's residence; she needed a price from Alfred before four o'clock tomorrow. Clyde offered to pick her up from there within the hour.

The builder stared at her plan. He said, "I didn't know you could do this?"

Audrey said, "Neither did I…Is it alright?"

Alfred said, "Yes, it is good, except for this section. The footings on this would hold up a bloody castle!"

All of a sudden in front of Audrey's eyes, castles and cathedrals started marching past like a herd of elephants. She stared at them, suddenly realising that she did not know how to draw a roof line for a domestic house, because this was not something that was familiar to her.

She sighed. She was suddenly aware that she had been looking and operating from a past life.

To Alfred she was gazing at something in the future, not the past. He said, "Look, you are tired, you need to be in bed. Is your husband outside waiting for you?"

She nodded.

"I will ring you tomorrow with a price, and we will take it from there. You have done a lovely job, far better than anything Sam ever produced. Are these people keen?"

"Very," she replied.

"If they like the price, get on to Jack Emery, the draftsman and he will do the working drawings. I will meet the clients and do the specifications. Sam never got them right anyway. I have a feeling after talking to him that he won't be coming back."

Two days later Jack Emery called at the office. Audrey was a little concerned at giving him the plan she had designed. After all, here was an expert. He asked why he wasn't seeing Sam. Audrey explained his absence, stating that Sam's return was undecided.

He gazed at the plan, saying, "Did you draw this?" She nodded. There was a moment of silence "Well, I'm used to getting scribbles on a piece of paper or even on the back of an envelope, with no sizes and no scale. This is wonderful, quite a contrast When do you need this plan?"

"As soon as you can do it, please!"

He smiled. "I'll call you. What is your name again?"

Then he was gone. She liked him. He was friendly and accepting. He was of medium height, with sandy hair, very blue eyes.

Jack also had a lovely smile. She immediately felt they could be friends.

He returned in a few days with the completed plans. Audrey got some copies and delivered one to Alfred, so that he could do the specifications and make out a building contract.

She rang the clients and Alfred joined them to go through the plans, specifications, and sign the contract. They paid a ten percent deposit. Half went to Alfred and the firm kept the other five per cent as commission. Audrey was given ten percent of this as a payment for her hard work as well as her normal wage.

Sam never came back to work.

Audrey took over the building section. In the beginning, she also handled the finance as before, but after a while it became too busy and she only financed the new homes.

Because the routine she did with her first clients worked so well, she changed nothing. Finding out what was needed and wanted with all its specifics worked beautifully. The clients had never been cared for in such detail and felt that if anyone could produce their wishes it would be this firm. Audrey found it easy to draw sketches on graph paper to a scale. She knew she was drawing from old data and experience that she was recalling from somewhere, but she kept this to herself, feeling it would not be opportune or acceptable to share.

Eventually she talked to Jack about angles and hips and valleys for roof design. He drew simple diagrams showing her how to link together the different triangles and squares. She soon learned this new skill. Always she left the pitch of the roof to Jack, feeling this was something that needed to vary with the design.

Keith Templin, the other builder, showed her how to do specifications one day when he was waiting for a late client. The two builders took it in turns to build a job. Audrey got along very well with both of them and learned much from their helpful comments.

CHAPTER 44

Audrey Learns a Rescue Remedy

The manager of the firm Audrey was working for was a young man in his early thirties called Kevin Bury. He looked much older than his years, almost as though he was seeing life through a grey fog that seemed to cover his face and neck. He strolled through the office glancing from left to right but giving Audrey the impression that he saw nothing. Audrey had little to do with him, but she felt there was something seriously wrong. He reminded her of two stretched wires that may snap at any moment.

One late afternoon as she was seeing her clients from her office, one of the girls came to ask for her assistance.

"It's Kevin," she said, "He is under his desk again and we can't get him out."

Seeing Audrey's look of amazement, she went on.

"He does this periodically, no one knows why. We usually leave him and eventually he comes out on his own and behaves as though nothing has happened; but this time he has been there for almost an hour with the door shut and he keeps barking like a dog! Now it is almost five o'clock and the girls need to leave. All the salesmen are out on jobs and won't be back, so I thought I had better come to you!"

Audrey thought rapidly, "Look, all of you go home, I will take care of it."

She waited until the office was quiet then went into Kevin's office. He was on his hands and knees under the desk, emitting short barks at intervals. He did not seem to notice her presence.

She remembered some of her training. Ron Hubbard had said that even someone in an asylum that had not communicated for years would do so, if you sat opposite him and mimicked all his movements without saying a word. Audrey took a pen from the desk, holding it so that it could not be seen. She got down on her knees under the desk, duplicating Kevin's position, the angle of his head, his expression as much as possible, and imitated his bark as soon as he made one.

After a few minutes noticing her, he suddenly said, "What do you think you are doing?"

She held up the pen. "Found it!" she said, triumphantly. "Is this what you were looking for?"

Kevin took the pen from her, looked at his watch and said, "Time to go home!" in a perfectly normal voice.

Audrey talked to Stanley Richards at the Scientology Centre a few days later. His only comment was, "Well done, especially with the pen, you didn't make him wrong. That was important. You will make a good auditor."

A few days later, on a hot summer's day, the air conditioners in the office failed. It was forty degrees Celsius outside. The office was mostly in a basement with little window space and it got extremely hot.

Audrey was tidying her desk prior to leaving when one of the girls came in and said, "We think Kevin is dead. None of us can wake him up. Should I ring the police or an ambulance?" Audrey said gently, "Go home and tell the others to do the same, I will take care of it."

She went into Kevin's office. He was slumped in his chair with his head thrown back and his eyes open. The open eyes were disconcerting. Audrey felt for a pulse on his wrist and in his neck. Nothing. She was not convinced. This felt like the last straw. Since the barking dog episode, he had had his stomach pumped out after he had taken an overdose of a few hundred

Audrey Learns a Rescue Remedy

aspirins. One day at the office, Audrey had suddenly left saying, "Kevin's in trouble. I need to go to his home. What's his address?" When she got there, the mattress was smouldering from a cigarette he had dropped from a drunken stupor.

Now there was this to handle. How to be sure he was dead? She got a mirror from her purse and held it to his mouth. Nothing happened. She found a bucket half filled it with water and poured it over his head: because it was suffocatingly hot in his office, he lightly steamed but otherwise there was no response.

She picked up the phone and rang Stanley, remembering a talk in the original lecture where he had said that processing was so powerful that it would probably revive the dead.

When he answered she wasted no time: "It's Audrey. I'm in the office. Kevin, my boss (the barking dog man) has died. Now what process do I run on him?"

There was silence. She waited. It seemed a while but she felt he was mentally looking through a large file to choose the right one.

Finally, she said, "Are you still there?"

"Yes."

"Look, you could try 'give me that hand, thank you!'..."

Audrey was more than surprised. "How do you expect him to do that when he is dead? I have questions. Can I close his eyes?"

"No," Stanley said. "Do not move him at all. You ask him to give you that hand and *point* to it, when he doesn't you pick it up and say 'thank you' as though he did it by himself. You keep running this process first on one hand and then the other. Now, if it works, you will need to lead him around the room asking him to touch things like the wall, a chair, the desk etc. Keep him moving and after each command place his hand on the object and say 'thank you' as though he did it himself. Eventually he probably will."

Audrey asked, "Why do you say 'If it works'? Don't you mean when?"

Stanley was stunned, but replied, eventually, "Audrey, ring me when you are through and let me how you got along. It doesn't matter what time

A LIFE of Enlightenment

it is, call me."

⁓

Audrey stared at Kevin. "Don't move him…that's tricky."

He was sitting at his desk with little space between his body and the desk. Audrey finally sat on the desk facing him with her legs down between his knees. (Why did men always sit with their knees apart? Today she was glad). She leaned down, pointed to his right hand and said, "Give me that hand." There was no response, so she picked it up, held it for a moment and then returned it and said, "Thank you."

She did the same with the other hand. Audrey continued this for some considerable time, with no change.

She heard Clyde come in to pick her up and knew she had to go out to see him. Having no idea how to put in a session break, she tapped Kevin on the head and said, "Don't go away. I will be back in a minute."

She went out to see Clyde. She explained the scene to him and he stared at her in disbelief. "Are you sure he's dead? Let me see him!"

Audrey said "OK, but you mustn't touch him or say anything or move him." Clyde nodded and went into the room. He emerged a minute later saying "Heh! He really is dead. You need to ring the ambulance You can't process someone who's dead."

She explained that Stanley had said: "Processing is so powerful it could revive the dead!"

Clyde said, "But he wasn't serious, it was just an expression." "No, it wasn't. I rang Stanley and he told me what process to run and I'm doing that. Will you wait for me?"

Clyde looked shocked and crestfallen at the same time.

Audrey kissed him and said, "I won't be long I hope. It is so hot in here. The Air Con has broken down. Please leave the doors open to get some air."

She returned to Kevin who looked exactly the same. The eyes still looked like a dead fish. She climbed on the desk, saying with emphasis, "I'm back.

Audrey Learns a Rescue Remedy

Now!! Give me that hand."

After another ten minutes of this, she was beginning to feel exhausted. Her back was aching because of the angle and the leaning she had to do to take and return the hands. It was unbearably hot. Audrey considered any temperature over 75 degrees Fahrenheit intolerable.

She stopped and said to Kevin, "Now, I expect you to respond to this so please stop messing around. I am going to do this for just five more minutes and after that you go to the undertakers and that will be that! Now, give me that hand!!" The five minutes went by, she continued for another five, reluctant to give up.

Suddenly Kevin made a horrible noise. She dropped his hand and shot to the back of the desk. She realised that the noise was because he was sucking in air. He closed his eyes, which was a great relief to her.

She remembered what Stanley had said about stage two. Hauling him out of the chair she began to drag him around the room commanding him to touch various objects and doing it for him when he resisted. He was heavy, and it crossed her mind that maybe she should have allowed a recovery time. Too late now! She continued.

Suddenly, he pushed her roughly aside and said "What do you think you're doing? Look at the time. It's after seven o'clock. I don't know about you, but I am going home." Picking up his car keys he walked out of the office, past a very surprised Clyde.

Audrey was stunned. She realised that he didn't even know he was dead or had been. She was confused, tired, hungry and wanted nothing more than home, a meal which she would cook, and then bed.

It was ten o'clock when they went to bed. At a quarter to twelve the phone rang. Clyde answered it and came back to bed saying, "It's Stanley on the phone. You were supposed to ring him."

Audrey said, "Hello Stanley, I'm sorry I forgot to ring. I was tired and just wanted to come home."

Stanley said, "Tell me the result on Kevin…?"

Audrey replied, "Well, he got annoyed, pushed me away, and said it was late and that he was going home. Do you know he does not even know that he was dead?" Audrey sounded a little outraged about this. "When I see him in the morning should I tell him?"

"No! You sound a little upset Audrey; I want you to come to see me tomorrow lunch time so that we can talk. We can fix your upset." Audrey was annoyed. "*He's* the one who is upset! He just pushed me away. He was annoyed. I'm not upset!"

"Alright, come to see me anyway, I need to know exactly what happened." She agreed and made a time to visit him.

The next day, Audrey just arrived at work when Kevin also arrived. He strolled through the office nodding and saying an occasional 'good morning', leaving shocked expressions on the faces of the staff who thought he was dead.

As he went into his office everyone clustered around Audrey. There was a chorus of voices saying "What did you do? We know he was dead!" and so on. Audrey wasn't too sure what to say that would be acceptable, she smiled, and nodded at some of the comments and finally she put her finger on the tip of her nose and wriggled it from side to side (like Samantha in the TV series 'Bewitched.')

The girls stared at her. She said, "Come, let's go to work," and disengaged herself to go to her office.

At lunchtime she went to see Stanley. She told him in detail of the whole event and ended up by saying, "I don't wish to offend you but, I really didn't think much of that process. I thought you said previously that the way to improve someone's ability was to get them to do something they could do and get them to do it better. I think we should have run 'Sit In That Chair' or 'Play Dead' or something. It may have been quicker. The one you gave me took an awful long time, over two hours."

Stanley stared at her, then smiled. "Audrey, you did very well. You knew only the rudiments of processing, so I do congratulate you, especially on your inventiveness. You will learn the correct way to put in a session break and so much more. You really will be an excellent auditor…Now let's spare

Audrey Learns a Rescue Remedy

a few minutes on what you need to handle from the session." Audrey left feeling happy and clear of any emotion connected with the event.

A few weeks later, one evening Kevin arrived at her home. He looked terrible, even worse than usual. All he said was, "I've killed a man, I've killed a man, I've killed a man!"

Neither Audrey nor Clyde could get any sense out of him. Clyde gave him a stiff brandy. Audrey put him to bed. The next morning was Saturday and finally Kevin told them that his car had been confiscated by the police because he had run over someone on a crosswalk. It turned out that the pedestrian was drunk and had staggered over the crosswalk. Just before reaching the other side he had staggered back again right into the path of Kevin's car.

Audrey did not know how true this story was. Kevin had in the past driven his car down the wrong side of the causeway, terrifying some motorists.

He stayed for the weekend and Audrey took him to work on the Monday and hired him a car. She rang John Billet the solicitor and took Kevin to talk to him.

Later Kevin was charged with manslaughter. Audrey was asked by John Billet to go to court to verify Kevin's strange antics.

On the court day Kevin did not appear and could not be found. The case continued without him.

The aggressive prosecutor kept putting things to Audrey, all seemingly negative. She had some training in communication and handling 'comments' which qualified his tirade.

She let him finish and then said, "What is the question?"

He was nonplussed. "Is it true?" Audrey said "No."

At one stage he pointed out that she was not a qualified psychiatrist and that her statements about Kevin's mental health should be ignored.

Audrey appealed to the judge, "If I got under your bench and started barking like a dog would it not be prudent for you to consider that there was something wrong with me?" The judge smiled and nodded. Audrey looked at the prosecutor and gently said, "Next question if you please?"

In his absence, Kevin was convicted of the manslaughter charge. Audrey did hear that he had gone to Melbourne the night before his court day and had not been seen or heard of since.

As court finished, John Billett said, "Audrey, I wish I could have you in the witness box for all my cases."

Audrey simply replied, "No thank you, it doesn't make me smile."

It was good to return to the office, knowing that no further events concerning Kevin would be arriving. It was peaceful.

CHAPTER 45

A New Opportunity

When she had been in charge of the building section for just over a year, both builders told her they were leaving the real estate company and setting up on their own. They had been friends for some time. They did not however, wish to work together. Each one offered her a position at a far better salary than her present one, even with the commission.

The requirements were the same. Find an office in a good position on St. George's Terrace, set up and furnish an office, hire a secretary, advertise for clients, provide the builder with plans and specifications, and the rest would be done by the builder.

Because Alfred had built Clyde's and Audrey's home, Keith and Alfred expected Audrey to choose to go with Alfred. The remittance they offered was identical.

Alfred said to her, "Look, I know what Keith is offering. I want you to work for me, so I will give you fifty per cent more than his offer."

For Audrey, that was the deciding factor. She chose Keith because she did not appreciate Alfred's ethics or integrity when Keith was also his friend.

In six weeks' time they opened a front ground floor office. There was another building firm on the first floor and another one at the back of the building. Keith said, "Is it alright to be in a nest of them?" Audrey said, "I think so; it is more convenient for the clients especially if they know they have a choice of three. I need to make sure that the advertising makes us their first visit, and if I help them and care for them really well, we should be their last. Even if they go upstairs or to the firm at the back, I feel they will return if I have done my job well."

Keith, unlike Alfred was a man of few words. "Alright, I will leave it to you."

Audrey hired Kaye, a very attractive looking girl who was also intelligent, efficient, and could type. A blessing for Audrey, who had never loved the typewriter.

Kaye did not mind making coffee, going for lunches and generally looking after the office supplies and admin. They got along very well together. She contacted Jack who became her draftsman and taught her many things about roof design. They became firm friends and often he stayed in the office for a long chat.

Audrey had never done any advertising, but she knew that, like everything else, it had a purpose, an action, an audience and a buying consequence.

She placed herself in the viewpoint of the reader; "As the reader, what do I want to know?" From this viewpoint she wrote an advertisement.

She did not realise that by doing this exercise she had avoided the pitfall that most advertisers made, which was *"What do I want the reader to know?"*

The ads paid off. She was busy from the first week. Audrey signed up client after client during what was considered a quiet time in the building industry. She did not know it was a quiet time. Keith did, and he was ecstatic about the work that was pouring in. Audrey was pleased.

A New Opportunity

After the first year she asked him why he had not given her a raise. "You didn't ask for one," was the answer. So she did and got one. Audrey also gave Kaye one as she often worked later if required.

After two years of this, Keith took Audrey to lunch one day to have a serious talk. Keith told her that he only wanted to do forty-five jobs a year, otherwise he would have a serious tax problem as well as no holidays or time off.

Audrey said, "How many a year am I signing up?" He replied, "Well over the sixty mark in the last twelve months. I want you to slow down. Think of some way of doing this without harming our reputation."

So, Audrey began to send the clients to the first floor and the back office builders. This was hard work as Keith and Audrey had been recommended. Often, after visiting the competition they came back and said they would wait until they could be handled. Audrey began to put in more and more delays on being able to start jobs. She found this irksome, but Keith did not want to expand.

On Wednesdays, Clyde's training nights, Keith picked her up from the office and took her to his home for dinner and to go over the jobs in hand. His wife was called Eliza. They had a son called Keith Jnr. and Eliza was pregnant again. The three of them liked each other and socialized well together.

One day Eliza telephoned the office wanting to know Keith's whereabouts. Keith usually came into the office late Friday afternoon. Jack, Clyde and Kaye would then usually meet with Keith and Audrey at the Adelphi hotel opposite the office. They talked and had a drink or two. They chatted together sometimes about work. Jack had a dry wit. One evening as he was going to the men's toilet he said, "Well here I am, off to shake hands with the unemployed." Audrey made a cardboard ring that she could place round her glass that read, 'gone for a wee walk, do not remove'.

Apart from Friday evenings and the Wednesday nights, Audrey seldom saw Keith.

Now, Eliza had started to have the baby. Audrey told Kaye to ring some of the current building suppliers to see if Keith could be found, but she did not hold much hope. Keith had supplied Audrey with a small car. She hurried to Keith's home and took Eliza to the hospital. She stayed with her for a few hours, until Keith finally arrived just in time, after finding a message at home.

A little girl was born that evening. Keith and Eliza called her Joanne and a few days later Keith asked Audrey to be her Godmother. She was thrilled and pleased but had little idea about how to be one. Audrey was a Godmother to a friend's son in England who was born after she arrived in Australia. She possessed a few photos of Peter and often wondered if she would ever see him in the flesh. This new little girl, Audrey could see every Wednesday. She could hold her, talk to her and eventually she could feed Joanne. She was happy with her new role.

CHAPTER 46

Entertaining Guests and the Tomato Sauce Cake

Clyde and Audrey were in love and a very happy couple. They went to many Bank functions and were promoted as the ideal couple. Audrey had to do quite a lot of entertaining of Bank managers and many executives from the Staff office where Clyde was presently training.

Audrey liked cooking. Indeed, she liked anything that was creative.

One Saturday, expecting two Bank managers and their wives for dinner, she decided to give them Veal steaks.

It seemed a good idea to partly precook the veal as she had not used this meat before. When she placed it in the pan in a very short time it had curled around the edges leaving only the centre in touch with the saucepan. Audrey turned it over and flattened it, only to have it do the same on the other side. She took scissors and prinked it around the edges, but that helped only a little. Audrey gazed at it for a few moments, and then decided she would create some pond lilies. Cooling the meat, she rubbed a little soy sauce and some herbs into it, trimmed the edges with some scissors so that they looked more like petals, and placed the curling pieces on a tray to put in the oven. She made some mashed potatoes. She separated six yolks from the eggs and prepared some orange glazed carrots and minted peas. The guests arrived and while they had drinks and snacks, Audrey finished cooking the covered veal in the oven until it was tender. Placing the mashed potatoes into a piping tube, she piped it around the inside top edges of the veal, placed a yolk in the centre, laid them on an elegant tray and returned them to a warm oven until the yolks were mostly done.

She served them with the glazed carrots, minted peas and some sliced mushrooms that she had softened in brandy and cream.

Her guests stared at the flowers on the tray. Sylvia, one of the wives, said, "That's beautiful; does this dish have a name?" Audrey smiled. "Waterlilies."

"How did you get this meat to go into that shape"

Audrey laughed and said, "Actually it is quite hard not to!" There was a moment of disbelief then the serving and eating began.

One Saturday afternoon when clients were due to come to her home to view a plan she had drawn for them, Audrey realised as she was shopping that she had not made a cake for their afternoon tea. Package cakes had been on the supermarket shelves for a short time.

For speed, Audrey decided to try one. She found an illustration of a large tall picture of a cake called 'Old English Spice'. She decided to try it. However, she did not want a cake so tall so she only used half the packet mixture. When it was whizzing around in her mixer she thought it looked a little sparse, but then perhaps being a package cake it was different and would rise to at least half the size shown on the packet.

Audrey did not like the colour. It looked like diarrhoea. She looked in her cupboards for something to add to change the colour but found nothing but tomato sauce. It was in a glass bottle and stubbornly refused to pour. Audrey hit it well on its base and a large blob spurted out.

It seemed to make little difference to the colour. Audrey cooked it and was amazed when it came out of the oven. She had cooked it in a small

Entertaining Guests and the Tomato Sauce Cake

tin, so it did not have a large diameter; it looked alright, but it was only the height of about three thin fingers. She stared at it for a while. Then, she covered it with some jam; she found a tin of apple, which she chopped into smaller pieces, and used this to cover the top of the cake. Whipped cream finished the top with some fine grated milk chocolate as a final covering. It was now quite high and looked interesting.

These were the days of fruit cake, butter cake, chocolate cake and so on; nothing exotic or different.

After the clients had looked and approved the plan. Audrey put the kettle on and asked them if they would like some cake. They never ate cake, but a biscuit may be nice, they said.

Clyde, returning from his early umpiring, joined them. Spotting the cake, he said, "Am I allowed to have some of that, whatever it is?" Audrey laughed and said, "Yes of course." She cut him a large piece and as she did so the clients could see the inside of the cake. The lady said, "That looks interesting, that is a lot of fruit I see, what sort of a cake is it, what is it called?" Audrey thought quickly. "Continental cake!" was her response. "We will try a piece," she said as her husband nodded approval.

Audrey cut them each a large slice and then went to answer the telephone. Knowing she would be a while, she apologised and asked Clyde to look after her clients.

When she returned, all the cake had gone.

The lady said. "That was absolutely delicious. May I have the recipe?" Audrey hesitated, then decided to take the plunge. "You take half a package of 'Old English Spice' and when it is whizzing around in the mixer you add a good blob of tomato sauce." The lady stood. "Audrey, it is alright if this is an old family recipe, don't worry dear, it was delicious. The plan, like the cake, was lovely, and now we must go."

Audrey started to protest but she was kindly waved away with some amusement from the husband.

After they left, Clyde said, "Were you serious about the sauce?" She nodded.

"Why? Whoever heard of putting tomato sauce in a cake; what possessed you to do that?"

Audrey said, "The colour was awful. It looked like diarrhoea!" Clyde stared at her. "I know you never follow any recipes when you cook, not that I mind because it always turns out so well, but perhaps it would be wise not to share some of the things you do with others!"

"Even if they ask?"

Clyde said with some merriment, "Did you see her face when you mentioned the sauce?"

Audrey said, "I wonder if it did make a difference. Could you taste it?" Clyde shook his head, "No, it was delicious, particularly the bottom bit."

She smiled. "Maybe it does something. It didn't change the colour much. I will make the cake again without the sauce, and you will have to check it out, as I didn't get any."

Audrey made it again a few days later, without the added sauce. The cake bit was disappointing. Clyde said it was dry and not as soft as before.

From that day on, tomato sauce went into all of Audrey's cakes. She told her close friends about it who were used to her quirky ways. However, she used her discernment with others. One of her country clients from Williams, who always won the Country Women's bake-off, used it in her sponges and jam rolls and said the sauce prevented rolling breakages and made all her sponges as light as air.

One of Audrey's best talents was turning any liability into as asset. It didn't really matter if it was cooking, a life trauma, a loss, or whatever cropped up. She was also good at doing this for others. As they complained or were venting, she would always find something for them to be glad about even if it was only gently saying, "Now you can say, 'been there done that'. Never again will you ever feel underprivileged about something like this." Audrey could usually say the right thing that would get them to smile.

She went on with her training and some auditing until she had finished all her local organisation had to offer. It seemed easy to help others with the technology, even just by communicating whatever was applicable at

Entertaining Guests and the Tomato Sauce Cake

the time. Even her own philosophy *"for what purpose?"* and *"Does it make you smile?"*, turning a negative into a positive, a liability into an asset, had become so much a part of herself that it was easy. Learning to play the glad game had become so much a part of her make-up that she used it without thought or even awareness.

She was not aware at the time that the processing she had done with Kevin had installed so much confidence in her that auditing another was done with ease. After all, she knew that even if she killed them, she knew how to fix it.

CHAPTER 47

The Unexpected Affair

Clyde was now the Assistant Staff officer at the Bank. This meant even more entertaining for Audrey, but she was happy to comply.

Clyde told her that a new girl called Tiffany in his department was difficult to deal with and that she was always giving him flashback, even in a light-hearted manner. Audrey suggested various methods of dealing with this and it seemed to somewhat calm the waters.

However, one evening Clyde told her that Tiffany had been crying in his office. She was pregnant and her parents were about to throw her out. Her boyfriend was seventeen, only one year older, and was scared to talk to his parents. Tiffany had asked Clyde if he knew anyone who could help her get rid of the pregnancy.

Clyde was aghast at this and said he would talk to his wife. Audrey said, "If she has nowhere to go, you had better bring her here. I will talk to her. An abortion isn't the optimum answer."

Tiffany came home with Clyde the following evening.

She was tall, dark, and very beautiful, with a slim body. She could have been a model.

They talked for a long time. Eventually Audrey, after talking to Clyde, invited her to stay with them. They had spare bedrooms and the following weekend Tiffany moved in.

When Audrey was busy around the house or cooking, Tiffany half-heartedly offered to help.

She was superb at presenting herself as a beautiful girl. The hair, the makeup and her dress were faultless. She presented a flawless image.

Audrey was amazed when it came to anything practical…Tiffany was the most useless female she had ever met. She couldn't cook at all, she couldn't iron, sew, wash, dust, vacuum or do any of the things that most girls are shown. No wonder she was half-hearted when it came to assisting.

Audrey took her in hand. She taught her all these things although she gave up on the sewing. A button was all that could be sewn on without a disaster occurring.

When Tiffany had been living with them for six weeks, she went out on a Saturday morning, returning some few hours later, clutching her stomach and crying.

Audrey said, "What have you done?"

Tiffany had been to see some lady who had interfered with her pregnancy and now she was bleeding rather badly.

Audrey sent for the Doctor and put her to bed, changing sanitary towels often. On one of them she saw what she felt could have been a tiny foetus, so she kept it for the doctor. On his arrival, he listened to the story. He feared infection, so he sent for an ambulance. Tiffany was taken to hospital and given a D&C. She returned after two days.

Tiffany continued to live with Audrey and Clyde or "the Hills" as she used to call them. She was slowly learning the things that Audrey could teach her. Clyde thought she was a giddy, dizzy female. Tiffany found it difficult to communicate on any intellectual level, preferring her adaptability at acting something out with body language and facial expressions. She was flirtatious and playful, seldom talking without moving her hands or shaking them in playful excitement. She was an amusing boarder.

Audrey liked her and felt that as Tiffany matured, she would really create who she would like to be.

Clyde said she was efficient at work once she was focused and could be a valuable staff member. Audrey shared much of what she had learned from the American College now called 'Scientology' from the beginning course and others that she had studied.

The three of them spent time and outings together. Tiffany became and was treated as part of the family.

Clyde and Audrey had been married for six years with Tiffany sharing their lives for the last eighteen months.

Although there was nothing except Audrey's feelings to influence her thinking, she felt that Tiffany and her husband for the last few weeks were having an affair. Relations between the three of them were the same. There was no awkwardness, no subtle looks or innuendo.

Audrey had no evidence of any kind. She felt that for the first time she was becoming a jealous female and couldn't come to terms with it. She invalidated herself and her thinking and was ashamed of her thoughts. Audrey tried to change them, ignore them, get rid of them and nothing worked. She did not like what she seemed to be becoming.

After a few weeks she decided to go to the Advanced Scientology College in England to see if she could straighten herself out. They had counselling as well as training courses. Audrey decided on the training. She talked to Clyde about spending the money. He was agreeable and in June 1967 she caught a ship bound for the port of Southampton.

She spent a week in London with her Aunt Dolly and Dennis her son. Dennis helped her to buy a small car. Audrey's mother had insisted that she call on her relatives and also see Dr. Gordon. Audrey was a little reluctant to do this. She felt that after sixteen years he had probably forgotten all about her and would not welcome this intrusion in his life. Her mother was astonished. "He will love to see you; you must call him! The relatives will tell him you are with them. He will be so upset if you don't contact him."

Audrey conceded. She drove to her cousin Joan's home and after settling in and spending two days with her relatives she called Doctor Gordon's surgery.

The receptionist said he was with a patient; could she say who was calling? Audrey, smiling to herself, said, "Tell him it is his former fiancée!"

There was silence and then suddenly a warm excited voice said, "Audrey, where are you?!"

Suddenly nothing had changed. The years melted away and the old comradeship was re-established in the twinkling of an eye.

He said, "Look I have to go to a short seminar this evening, then there is a dinner. I would like you to come. At last you could meet Marjorie. How do you feel about red hair these days?"

Audrey laughed. "It's fine. No problem. Yes please, and where do I come?"

He gave directions and told her that the doorman would expect her and let him know she had arrived.

Audrey dressed carefully and turned up at the appointed time. She waited and then there was Doctor Gordon striding to meet her with a beaming look on his face. Watching him arrive she was ashamed of her conversation with her mother. How could they ever forget each other? She threw her arms around him and he hugged her close before pulling away and gazing at her, saying, "I knew you would grow up to look and be someone special. You are beautiful and I'm sure that it is inside and out. Tell me, did you ever sort out your quest for God? I remember it as an unfinished question."

Audrey smiled, and taking his arm as he led her into the room, she said, "Yes, it was easy. If he is everywhere like you said, then I must be included in his space."

He started laughing. "Of course. The answer knowing you would be simple. Well done my dear. I'm so looking forward to having a long talk and catching up. There is so much to say." They had arrived at a table. Three other couples were introduced and then there was Marjorie, his wife. Audrey shook hands. Marjorie was affable. Doctor Gordon briefly filled in the group about his past times with Audrey and she was looked upon with interest. Then he turned to her and soon they were chatting like old friends.

The Unexpected Affair

The others started talking among themselves, but Audrey was aware of wary concern emanating from Marjorie. It took but a moment for Audrey to realise that when Doctor Gordon was engaged to an eleven-year-old girl, it was endearing and nothing to be concerned about. Now here she was, in Marjorie's eyes a thirty-two-year-old very attractive woman who her husband obviously thought was something very special.

Audrey, always sensitive to energy from others, realized she needed to leave and that there was no way she could keep the appointment Dr. Gordon was trying to make for lunch the following day.

Eventually she made her excuses, told him she would call him first thing in the morning and allowed him to accompany her to the exit and get the doormen to call a taxi.

She rang him early morning, told him that unfortunately she had to leave earlier than planned, and validated how much she enjoyed seeing him again. She packed, said goodbye to her cousin Joan thanking her for her hospitality and climbed in her little car, ready for the next phase of her journey.

She drove to Sussex, ready to start a training course to learn how to counsel herself.

Audrey was surprised on arriving at Saint Hill in East Grinstead to find that after she checked in and was announced as a new student, a few of the staff and some of the students came up to her over the next few days asking, "Are you the one that audited a dead person and brought him back to life? What process did you run, did you use an E meter?" and so on. She did not know how this event had reached half way across the globe or why it was considered remarkable.

Audrey had been on her course for two weeks when a letter from Clyde and one from Tiffany arrived simultaneously.

She found them in the student box at lunchtime, opened one and began to read, before putting it away. Audrey went to the course supervisor and requested the rest of the day off. She had to tell him why. He immediately advised her to have some counselling, but she pointed out that she was on a solo counselling course and wanted to handle this by herself. He was dubious as the course had four more weeks to run, but Audrey was so confident and persuasive that he finally relented.

Audrey took her lunch, a bottle of water, a box of tissues and the letters, going quickly into some nearby woods. She settled under a tree and started to read. The letter from Clyde detailed the affair that he had been having with Tiffany for the last few weeks. Tiffany's letter was much the same. Both of them said how much they loved her and that they really couldn't help themselves. The letters were very detailed, yet asked nothing. No goals, no solutions.

Audrey was in tears. These were people she loved. She wasn't sure what to do. She looked at all the lessons she had learned. This lifetime, they had been considerable. Now, because of the crying, it was hard to think. She took in big gulps of air as she asked for some divine intervention. Then she remembered earlier data she had learned. *'What turns it on will turn it off!'* *'The way out is the way through!'*

She went on reading the letters, one after the other, sobbing her way through them, until the weeping became less and finally stopped. She felt exhausted. She rested for a while, sipping her water, and slowly eating a little of her sandwich. She found another maxim. *'What you put out you get back'* and *'What goes around, comes around.'*

Audrey began to look in her past for a time when she had done something similar. Firstly, she remembered the affair with Steve. She went through it in detail, finally spiritually asking forgiveness from Daisy and from Steve, and finally forgiving herself. Without looking, another past life incident cropped up. It was during the days of Camelot. It was so real that it put paid to the thought that Camelot was a myth or a legend. Audrey found an incident when she, as a male, had an affair with someone else's wife. She handled this the same way as the earlier incident. At the end of these events she felt almost normal. The trauma was drifting away just the same as the bathwater disappeared when the plug was pulled.

It reflected that the way out, was the way through. It was time to look at Clyde and Tiffany. Audrey considered that they must be on tenterhooks wondering what she was going to do. She drove to the post office. She sent them a telegram writing, "I understand. Thank you for telling me. What do you want to have happen now? Love, Audrey."

Driving to the flat she was renting, Audrey suddenly realized that some of her upset came from the invalidation of her own knowingness. She made a mental note to always follow her intuition from this day forth. She smiled looking at the words 'inner tuition', finding the blending well named.

She spent what was left of the day bathing her swollen eyes and resting. After an early night she was ready to go back on the course. Her course supervisor questioned her at length, before finally congratulating her on handling the situation and allowing her to continue.

CHAPTER 48

Meeting Brian

On her return to her course, Audrey was sitting next to a student from Swaziland in Africa. His name was Brian O'Donohue. He was very tall and Audrey felt he would be at least ten years older. Born in England about fourteen miles from where she had lived, she was aware that he was well educated. He had an attractive and cultured voice and looked like a professor. Brian had done many of the beginning and intermediate courses at the South African Scientology Centre and had even travelled to London to do some courses under the founder. Brian gave the impression of being very intelligent, very kind and peaceful in demeanour. They had much in common and found it easy to discourse about the course and life.

When he invited her to have a meal later one evening she refused, but instead invited him to her flat the following evening. She shared the flat with Lorraine, a staff member from Melbourne. Her promise of a roast dinner made Brian's eyes sparkle. The three of them had a pleasant meal. Lorraine went back to the college to catch up on her work after they finished dinner. Audrey and Brian sat and smiled, very much at ease with each other; almost as though they were already old friends.

Brian reached across the table and held her hand as he gently asked, "I noticed your absence on Monday, also your long conversations with John, the course supervisor. I'm here to help, commiserate or share whatever it is you would like to tell me. I have watched you for the last two weeks, helping other students who are having difficulty with some of the data. You are friendly, kind and always you tell them how smart or intelligent they are; you validate them, so that they learn faster, rather than allowing them to wallow in the concept that they are dumb. That is an Art. You would make a wonderful teacher. Is that what you do?"

Audrey shook her head. "No, I'm a building designer and consultant in Perth; and you? What do you do in Swaziland?" "I manage an Agricultural Research Station in a place called Malkerns! But we have got off the subject. Will you allow me to help you?"

She smiled. "Bless you! For me it is handled. Now I await decisions from others involved."

"I have the feeling that you have a husband who is perhaps involved? I noticed you had more than one letter and I did ask John if your absence was to do with marital troubles. He declined to comment, but somehow I knew it was so... You seem to be a very private person, also very vulnerable. Your energy gives off certain vibrations. Even though I am aware of knowing you before this lifetime, it is not my intention to pry. I feel so connected to you; it is as though the essence of what you are handling becomes mine. Am I making sense?"

Looking at him thoughtfully, interested in his discourse, Audrey was not sure what to say. There was a sense of relief and some joy in thinking that here was a being who perhaps understood her like no one had ever done before. Even looking at him now she had the feeling that he could climb into her skin. From the beginning there had been something familiar about him. Audrey's head gave her question marks. Her heart told her it was true.

She smiled. "Thank you. I like what you are saying without quite knowing how to answer it. I have had a very busy life, with lots of events happening. I have lots of experience handling all these events. I trust I'm im-

Meeting Brian

proving in my handling all the time. Sometimes it seems as though I have already had three lifetimes and yet there have been only thirty-two of my years on this planet: but enough about me; tell me about you and your life to date?"

Brian had such a soft, gentle, loving look on his face that she wanted to hug him or cry.

He said, "Please do not change the subject. Could you share some of your thirty-two years on this planet, particularly the last few weeks?"

She leaned back in her chair. She told him the happenings from the time Tiffany had come to stay at their home until present time when she was waiting for an answer to her telegram.

He listened with compassion, reaching for her hand again as she neared the end.

"I trust the decisions you await will also be the decision you wish for yourself?"

Audrey said, "In a way they always will! Their decisions don't really come into conflict with me. I have never seen the point of asking anyone to keep an agreement that they no longer wish to keep. What sort of a relationship would that make even if it was with a casual acquaintance, not to mention a spouse or business partner; it seems so inappropriate to force that an agreement be kept. So, whatever they want is okay with me."

Brian said, "Do you do all your thinking outside the square, or is it that you have learned to have such a philosophical outlook from courses you have done, your experience in life—or lives for that matter—or have you really dropped in from some other planet?"

Audrey started laughing. "I don't know! I am constantly told that I think differently from others, but I have never considered that to be true."

Brian asked, "Well what *do* you think?"

Audrey said, "Well…I just thought that others thought differently."

He started laughing. "I could talk to you for hours. You seem to get or decide on a datum for all the basic premises for living and then evaluate them into simplicity for everyday application. I've never seen anyone do this or even *consider* doing it before. It's useful, amazing, and entrancing. I find you enchanting! Now you are looking embarrassed. I'm sorry, I did not intend to make you uncomfortable."

Audrey sighed. "I am often told similar things, perhaps not as detailed or as profound as this. I have never figured out what all the fuss is about. Something pops into my head and it is out before I give it much thought. Everything happens quickly with me and often intensely. She smiled at him. Sometimes I look around this planet and it is like watching everything going in slow motion. Occasionally I think I can't stand it, but in my heart I always know that I can. And I do! I have had a very busy life, with lots of events happening…I have lots of experience handling all these events. I trust I am improving in my handling all the time. Sometimes I feel as though I have already had three lifetimes on this planet. But enough about me; tell me about you."

He told her that he had been married for 14 years and divorced for a long time. He simply said the marriage had not worked because they wanted different goals, particularly in a spiritual life. His wife had wanted more and more involvement in the Catholic Church. Brian said that he had been brought up as a Catholic but even at school had received the name of 'little heretic'. He had read a book called *Dianetics* in 1956. He said, "I knew on the way home that this would be the end of my marriage. My wife, Enid, never realized that the rituals and practices of the Church were manmade and therefore subject to discussion and even challenge. The subject of past lives, mentioned in *Dianetics*, was considered blasphemous. I wasn't about to have my life curtailed by limitations and negativity, especially by a religion that considered every other religion or spiritual idea was wrong unless it emanated from the Catholic Church. That was biased, unforgiving, lacking in compassion and against everything that Jesus would have taught or practised. So we parted company, with some effort of goodwill, but disagreement on both sides on the way to live." Brian continued. "I have my degree from the Royal Agricultural College in England, so I can work almost anywhere. I have managed farms for Lord Delamere in Kenya. I've

Meeting Brian

been a manager in South Africa on various farms and have been managing an Agricultural Research Station in Swaziland for the past few years. I need to return there in two weeks. I would like to invite you to visit me, but I am aware of the situations that need to be sorted out in your life. Perhaps when my long-service leave is due, I will come to visit you instead."

They talked until late in the night and for the next two weeks they spent time together when they were not on course. Brian came to her one evening to say goodbye as he was leaving the next day. He offered to write. Audrey offered to reply. They had a long cuddle; Audrey with her nose on his tiepin and Brian resting his chin on her head. He bent his head and kissed her forehead. She laughed and said "I need a stool." There was another long gentle hug and then he was walking away. Audrey watched him go, wondering if she would ever see him again.

The letters from Clyde and Tiffany had arrived at the end of July. When the end of August was approaching and Audrey had no reply to her telegram, she telephoned and asked them what they wanted to do. The only answer from each of them was "I don't know."

She urged them to think about it, adding that she was not cross and that whatever they decided was alright with her, and that she would honour their decision. Audrey had the feeling that this was more upsetting than anything else she could have said.

She finished her course and went on to two more advanced courses which she completed in quick succession. She spent some time with a Perth friend who was on staff. One evening in November, Linda told her that she had to go to the Scientology Organization in Paris and asked how would Audrey like to come for a holiday. They left the next day, leaving by ferry from Dover and then by train from Calais. When they emerged from the station, Linda suggested they take a taxi to the college. Paris was overcast with grey clouds emitting a fine continuous drizzle of rain. Audrey asked for the name of the street they needed. Linda said "Londres Street." Audrey said, "We don't need a cab it is very close," and leading the way, walked around a corner. They arrived in just a few minutes, barely wet. Linda asked, incredulously, "Have you been here before?"

"No…at least not *this* lifetime. I have the feeling that I may know my way around the old part of Paris." Linda smiled, having no problem with the concept of past lives.

Audrey sat in reception while Linda went into a long meeting with other executives of the Organization. A man around forty years of age, dressed in a smart suit, smiled at her and said with the delightful accent that only the French have, "I also am waiting for a friend!"

They introduced themselves. Pierre was delighted to talk to someone who had done two more advanced courses than he had achieved. After a lengthy talk, he offered to show her around Paris and take her to lunch. They left messages with the receptionist. As they stood on the outside doorstep, they were joined by two students who, gazing at the sky, commiserated with each other about the weather.

Audrey said, "Let's be positive! You know the saying 'where two or more are gathered in my name'…Now let's all look at these low-lying clouds, send them lots of love, and decide to dissipate them with our energy. On the count of three…one, two, three…Start!"

Four sets of eyes beamed love at the clouds with lots of intention. Slowly it began to work. The clouds started to lift and then part. The rain stopped.

One of the students said "Wow!" Audrey said, "Keep it going." The clouds parted some more and then the sun came out. The blueness of the sky started to spread.

Audrey said, "Well done…ten gold stars to all."

The students were excited, wanting to know what levels she had attained. Audrey pacified them by saying, "You are all on the way to do something similar. Just relax and enjoy the journey. For me, this is a new experience and I need to assimilate, relax, and enjoy it too!"

Audrey and Linda stayed overnight in Paris, intending to leave for England late the next afternoon. Linda was able to join Pierre's tour with Audrey for a few hours after lunch. They strolled through the Louvre and wandered through the gardens of the Versailles Palace.

Linda was enchanted. To Audrey, the surroundings were familiar, an echo of long ago. She didn't try to chase it down; simply allowed it to be.

When Linda said they needed to check the train time to go home, Audrey said, "No, we need to go to Switzerland!"

"Why? Audrey, I have to go back to work. I can maybe take one day more, that is all. Why Switzerland…what is going on?" Audrey said, "I don't know. I have this incredible pull to go to Zurich. I feel I must follow it. Will you come even for a day? I know strange things seem to be happening, but I have no urge to stop or question them; just to go wherever they may take me. I can't say I understand them, they are as quirky to me as they are to you!"

Linda stared at her, reflectively. "If it was anyone else…sigh…Alright, we go there as soon as possible; I spend one day with you and the next day I leave for England."

"I will pay for your plane ticket. It is less than an hour's flight. We can use our return train tickets to go to Switzerland."

Audrey wrapped her arms around her friend and gave her a warm hug.

CHAPTER 49

Zurich and Gabriel

They arrived in Zurich in the early evening. They found a bed and breakfast right away, had dinner at a restaurant, and went to bed early.

The next morning, Linda said, with a smile, "OK! What's next my little adventurer?"

Audrey said, "We need to walk over there and choose a bank." "Are we going to rob it or deposit something?"

"I don't know. I'm just going to play it by ear!"

They walked over the bridge to a street called Bahnhof Strasse.

Linda said "Which one do you want?"

Audrey pointed a finger and said "That one." They crossed the road. A doorman opening the door wished them 'Guten morgen' in German, and when they answered with 'Good morning', he switched to English, asking them how he could be of service.

Audrey said, "We are from Australia. We wish to speak to someone who speaks English and can talk to us about the differences in Australian and Swiss Banking. The doorman nodded and smiled, "Please wait. Someone will be happy to speak to you. I will make a phone call."

A young good-looking man who introduced himself as Otto Klemmer took them to a small office. He asked them to be seated around a small round table.

They spoke only briefly before he suddenly stood and said, "You need to be talking to my friend Gabriel. He even worked in Australia for a while. Please excuse me. I will fetch him."

As he left Linda said, "Is this going the way you envisaged?" Audrey shrugged. "I really don't know what is going to happen next. I'm just going along with the events as they unfold…"

The door opened. A man in his early thirties entered the room, hand extended. "Good morning. I am Gabriel Holzer. It is so wonderful to meet someone from Australia. Are you from Sydney?"

Linda said, "No, we are both from Perth. My name is Linda Martin and this is Audrey Hills."

Audrey stared at him, noting that he was very intelligent looking, with one of the kindest faces she had ever seen. He had brown hair peppered with grey, brown eyes and a young unlined face. Suddenly she knew why she was in Zurich. It was to meet this man. Audrey wasn't sure why, but already she felt a strong pull of attraction and a connection that was not new. They sat at the table and talked. Gabriel had been in Australia for some time, working for Ansett Airlines. He loved Australia and hoped to live there someday. Except for saying he was in the 'Securitas' department of the Bank, no other discussion of Banking cropped up. It was as though the initial contact had never occurred; now it was about getting to know each other. He was sincere in his politeness, always making sure he included Linda in the conversation, although his main focus seemed to be on Audrey.

Linda, looking from one to the other, was smiling. She knew what this was about also. The energy of the room had changed just after his entrance. Audrey had a glow to her face that she had not seen for some time, and Gabriel looked as though he had swallowed the canary and the cat along with the cream.

Eventually he asked if could take them to dinner that evening. They

Zurich and Gabriel

enthusiastically agreed. He called for them at the pension and they went to a nearby restaurant. They had a wonderful meal, although Audrey and Gabriel didn't really seem to notice the food as much as each other.

As the meal drew to a close, Linda said she had to return to the bed and breakfast and make a record in her diary of her visit to Paris before she left for England the next day.

Gabriel insisted on taking her back to the pension, begging Audrey's leave for a few minutes.

When he returned, he was a little out of breath; smiling at Audrey and saying he couldn't wait to get back. Audrey, already entranced, leaned over the table and kissed him on the cheek, saying "Thank you! I missed you too!"

They held hands and talked until the restaurant was closing. Gabriel asked her if she was married, so she told him everything of her current situation and a little of her past. He hugged her as much as it was possible while they were both sitting in chairs. Audrey had the feeling that if he could pick her up and put her somewhere safe and preferably beautiful he would do so. She felt he would feel protective, irrespective of her demonstrative spiritual and mental strength. Audrey had never felt vulnerable and did not know how she ever gave that impression. The behaviour of most men around her seemed to indicate otherwise.

They left the restaurant arm in arm, walking slowly, looking and smiling at each other. They came to a street vendor selling roses, obviously about to leave the area. Gabriel stopped and bought Audrey a dozen red roses. She hugged them to her breast. The perfume filled the air between them as Audrey leaned across them to thank him with a kiss. Gabriel cupped her head in his hands and gently kissed her forehead, her cheeks and then her lips.

He leaned back, smiling at her as he said, "I'm so glad you came into my life. May I see you tomorrow?" Audrey nodded "Yes please!" and smiled at him.

When Audrey entered the pension room she was sharing, Linda sat up in bed saying "Look at you! You look beautiful. I think you may be in love! I'm so pleased for you!"

Audrey laughed, "Yes well, I'm seeing him tomorrow; is it alright with you if I don't return with you? I may stay for a couple of days."

"Of course! We need to find something to give water to those roses. Audrey, ask the landlady in the morning."

Linda left by plane the next day. Gabriel collected Audrey after work. It was winter and already dusk, but they went for a walk over the bridge. He told her that Bahnhof Strasse meant 'Railway Street', as it led to the station. They found an intimate restaurant and chatted over a meal that got very little of their attention.

Gabriel and Audrey played no games. They were not careful with each other. There was no deliberation on what to say next or how to behave. They were completely themselves, no pretence. They shared their lives, their viewpoints and their considerations about so many subjects; yet it seemed they would never run out of conversation. The empathy grew and grew. The conversation slowed as they began to almost read each other's mind.

Audrey stayed one more day. It seemed important to return to Sussex and sort out her life before getting too involved in a new relationship.

When she arrived in England, she called her home in Australia and again asked Clyde and Tiffany what they wished to do. When she got another 'I don't know' she simply said, "Well I do! It is over. Sell the house, and any shares we still have. When that is done I will come back and arrange a divorce." She gave them a figure for the house, and wished them good luck.

There was a sense of relief after doing this. Always Audrey had preferred full stops rather than question marks.

She found a card that said on the front 'You are just my cup of tea' and

Zurich and Gabriel

wrote Gabriel a thank-you note for his hospitality and his caring, and ended it by saying, "I loved the time we spent together; a little of it has gone around with me ever since and makes for very pleasant company!"

Audrey received a letter four days later.

Dearest Audrey,

I hope your journey was pleasant and that all will be well with you when you have done whatever you think is a fair thing in regard to Clyde and Tiffany. I would not dream of interfering or influencing you, but I would like to be with you to hold your hand from time to time to comfort you.

Thank you so much for saying I am just your cup of tea and for your lovely message. So much of you remains with me and yet I miss your physical presence. Unfortunately, I have been sick which necessitated calling the Doctor. He is not certain what is wrong with me (maybe it is caused by being in love). His cure is to rest until I am better, eat more fruit and vegetables, limit my consumption of alcohol and drink more water.

Dearest Audrey, I feel that your presence would immediately make me well again but now it seems you are far away. I miss you.

Yet when I think of you I feel you are here, even though I know you are in England. Although we have just met I feel close to you as though we have always known each other. All my thoughts and feelings feel strange to me. I have been in love before; yet, it has never had these implications or this heart rendering warmth that arrives at just the thought of you.

The connection I feel and treasure is so strong; I adore you.

Dearest Audrey, please send me your telephone number so that we may at least talk from time to time.

Yours,

Gabriel.

Audrey was delighted with his letter. She loved his quaint way of writing. 'Cut down on alcohol', became 'limit my consumption of alcohol' and his English phrasing gentle yet so exact made her smile.

She was so looking forward to being with him again.

She felt that the Universe had given her a present. Here was someone who adored her with a love that she could reciprocate.

Audrey replied, sharing all her feelings with him, holding nothing back; sending her phone number and times when she could promise to be in her flat.

He called as soon as he had her letter. He was ecstatic about all that she had written, but confessed to be a little overwhelmed. He said that he had never been loved so openly, so honestly; he felt he wanted to reciprocate the same way, but could not shake off the notion that caution perhaps should be the order of the day.

Audrey laughed and asked him what he considered would happen if he threw caution to the winds?

There was silence, so she went on saying, "Caution, worry, anxiety, wariness, being careful, are just different degrees of fear; I have found that the only way to deal with fear is to confront it head-on. Then it just melts away as the word and the letters of 'FEAR' stand for 'False Evidence Appearing Real.' There are only two categories in life that everything falls into. One is fear and the other is love! What would you like to choose?"

Gabriel asked, "Tell me, how did you get to be so wise?"

"By living. By just going with the flow. By knowing that I create my own reality and no one else is involved except when I am in the right place at the right time for a co-creation; this is what has happened to us. It's a wonderful co-creation. I'm so happy to have met you. So happy to get to know you and to love you! How does all this seem to you?"

Gabriel said, "Right now I'm speechless." Audrey waited.

Then gently, "If it is a necessity for me to choose, then I choose Love. Love means you and I don't believe it could ever be otherwise. I do not know how to love you more."

Zurich and Gabriel

Audrey was quiet.

"Are you still there?" he asked.

She said, "It's alright, I'm just melting!"

He said after a slight pause, "This is where I wrap you in my arms and tell you how much you mean to me, how much I adore and love you. There is no fear. I wish you were with me. When is it possible for you to return?"

There was no hesitation. "I will be with you for Christmas. I'm ordering a white one. It is so many years since I saw snow. I would love to walk in it, maybe make a snowball again and feel it falling on me, in the gentle fashion that I remember." Gabriel almost sounded apologetic as he explained, "Unfortunately it very seldom snows at Christmas. Usually it is middle to late January, but I also will place a requisition slip in the suggestion box for you."

Audrey told him of her conversation with Clyde and Tiffany and her decisions.

He was concerned that her decision was in no way influenced by her contact with him. Audrey assured him that it wasn't. She could tell by this that he had much to learn about her, but this would come as she would learn to know and understand him. This was an exciting time.

She reflected on the adventure of first acquaintances when you could be light hearted and entertaining for a new friend as never quite the same for those who knew you well.

Always there was the excitement and mystery of the unknown; to find out and to be.

Audrey promised to call him with a date in December.

She wrote Christmas cards to all her family and some of her relatives in England. Bright newsy cards giving no details of her current life.

She considered that it would be best to have her life more settled, the house sold, the divorce underway… Her current abode. Where would she be living?

There was Gabriel. There were other courses and levels to do. Some she had to do in Scotland. She needed a trip to Perth once the house was sold and she had to handle the divorce details.

In some instances Audrey felt her life was in limbo. She was floating with lots of realities to choose from, yet more data and time was needed to make a valid choice. She was not concerned by these feelings or these events; it was another adventure and she had the advantage of identifying and knowing exactly what was happening in her life; she was happy to go with the flow.

For the next two weeks Audrey helped other students on course. A letter arrived from Brian in Swaziland; a long friendly letter that asked her what was happening in her life. She replied bringing him up to date but did not mention Gabriel, feeling that the contact needed to be more established before this kind of sharing.

All December, she exchanged letters and phone calls with Gabriel. She began to know his thoughts and he hers before they were voiced. It was a smiling time.

Audrey wrote to her parents, a breezy letter that omitted to inform them of the Clyde/Tiffany situation. She decided that it was time to tell them only when the divorce was going through.

Soon it would be Christmas. She rang Swissair and booked a flight to Zurich on the 23rd December. She called Gabriel with her arrival time. It was only a one hour flight, so delays were unlikely.

To supplement her wardrobe, she bought a pale camel overcoat with a brown fur collar and cuffs and two new dresses; a red one with white trims for Christmas day and a pink lace one for any special occasion.

A student going to the airport gave her a lift and soon she was on the plane taking her back to Zurich and Gabriel.

He met her at the arrival area, picked up her suitcase and established her in the car, leaning in to kiss her and hug her before moving round to the driver's seat.

Zurich and Gabriel

He did not start the car. Swivelling round to face her he said, "Dearest Audrey, I have not booked you in anywhere; at this time of year it is difficult but if you need to be comfortable we will persevere."

"And the alternative, Gabriel?" she asked.

"To stay with me." He looked at her with a half smiling concern.

Audrey looked thoughtful for a moment and then said, "Gabriel, I shall enjoy staying with you!"

He gave a happy laugh, leaned over to kiss her and said, "I'm so overjoyed."

They held hands as he drove.

He told her that his sister owned a restaurant on the ground floor of his apartment building. They went there for dinner and she met his sister and her husband the chef. They had a lovely meal in good company, with Gabriel acting as the interpreter, as Klaus and Ingrid had little English.

Gabriel's apartment was on the first floor. It was medium sized, beautifully kept, very clean and quite aesthetic for a bachelor pad.

Gabriel immediately pointed out there was only one double bed and waited for her reaction.

Audrey wrapped her arms around him and murmured in his ear. "Everything is alright. I love you!"

He sorted some space in the wardrobe and a large empty drawer to take her clothes. There was a spare cupboard and drawer in the bathroom, and in no time she was settled in.

They sat on his large couch, whispering love and kissing each other, until it became too much so they stood and pressed their bodies together. She asked to clean her teeth and remove her make-up and he waited until she returned. Gabriel wrapped his arms and his love around her and then very gently and carefully removed her clothes.

He led her to the bed, laid her on it with tenderness, and then disappeared to the bathroom.

CHAPTER 50

A Meeting of Souls

She lay naked on the bed, listening to the sounds of water running and teeth being cleaned. She had an urge to hide her nakedness by pulling up the sheet, but he had undressed her and laid her there so gently and with such admiration and tenderness that she felt it would be untimely to cover her body. She knew she had a curvaceous figure when standing, but now she began to wonder what it looked like when she was lying down. She tried to imagine looking at her body from the ceiling; wondering if it spilled sideways, losing its shape, but she found she was too emotionally in the moment to continue this train of thought.

Instead she started looking at the advantages of having mirrors on the ceiling. With her eyes closed and a small smile of entertainment on her face at these imagined reflections, she was unaware of his arrival from the bathroom until he said softly, "Hello, my darling," and kissed her tenderly on the mouth.

He climbed onto the bed gently raising both her legs so that her knees were bent, then moved between her legs, sitting back on his heels. She immediately felt too open and vulnerable. She valiantly tried to relax. He gazed at her face with a loving reassuring expression and said as he stroked the sides of her waist, "You have the softest skin; it is like velvet; just touching it is a delight." Leaning forward he gently stroked her hair and her face; then his hands lightly began to trace the outlines of her body. He traced a path over her shoulders, down her arms, caressing each fingertip then continuing up the inside of each arm, down the sides of her body, then the outside of her legs and feet before tracing all her inside curves. His hands soft and gentle caressed the front of her body moving around her breasts; her shoulders, her face and hair before tenderly starting their journey once again. Under his touch she began to relax. If ever hands could feel respectful it was these hands. The tracing changed to a light stroking; her body felt honoured by his caress. She gazed with love at his face. His expression was tender, happy and devoted. She felt adored in every way.

Since their first meeting she was aware that here was a man who was confident of his manliness. There was no need for him to hide his desire to show love, tenderness and consideration wherever and whenever it was appropriate. On their first evening together after a romantic dinner he had presented her with some beautiful red roses bought from a street vendor as they walked back to her hotel. Their first kiss was filled with perfume as she leaned across them to thank him. He was the most romantic beautiful being she had ever had the pleasure of knowing.

She was filled with a deep feeling of love. Now she loved not only him but also all that his body was doing. She opened her eyes. She was about to tell him of her love forgetting how well he could read her thoughts. During this time he had been gazing at her face. Now he leaned forward and kissing her deeply on the lips he said, "Thank you, I love you just as much!" She smiled, reached for him, but he gave an almost imperceptible shake of the head and said quietly, "No, my darling, this is for you."

The gentle stroking continued; she could feel her body coming alive under his touch. She felt as though her skin was rising in anticipation ahead of his hands. When he tenderly stroked around her breasts she arched her back reaching for his caress.

He smiled lovingly as she moved under his touch. He was entranced by the beautiful soft skin and her femininity.

When they had first met he had appreciated her open honesty and vulnerability, which confirmed her strength as she shared the events of her life. Unknowingly she brought out all his protective instincts. He admired her courage as she told him of her current situation that would have led anyone else to be in a troubled and unsettled state. He saw in her no trace of playing the victim or feeling sorry for herself, despite the betrayals she had recently experienced.

She remained self-sufficient and independent without losing any of her femininity. He was attracted by her compassion and understanding of the people involved when resentment and revenge would have been a normal reaction. She was to him unique in many ways. He loved her sense of humour; her happy smiling face and he found her unusual way of thinking about life to be enlightening. Now he was lost in the softness of her. He felt privileged and honoured by her complete surrender to his care. The happy glow on her face made him feel infinitely tender and romantic. He adored her. He wanted to care for her always, be with her always, and love her forever.

He began to kiss her; gentle but deep kisses that seemed to penetrate her flesh so that she felt all her cells were coming alive and longing for his touch. He moved to the side of her, leaning on his elbow with his hand gently stroking under her neck, he caressed the front of her body with his other hand while his mouth found her breasts. Her body became so alive that she was aware of the slightest movement of his hands, the erotic motions of his lips, then his finger as it slowly slid into the warmth of her; and then the palm of his hand as it rested on the outside. She felt the finger curl as it began to slowly explore her depths; she gave a little gasp as he found her sacred spot and began to tenderly stroke it. The sensation was breathtaking. She reached for him, but again he shook his head and murmured a gentle, "No, my love, this is for you!" The finger continued gentle but slowly stroking, his palm pressed and released; the kissing remained soft, yet tenderly passionate. She could feel the mounting sensation craving for release. When it came it started in her lower body, moved unhurriedly through her torso to her chest, and seemed to exit through the top of her head. It was not like anything she had ever experienced. It was an exquisite sensation that was long and slow and deep. Her body seemed to be taking deep breaths that carried the sensation along; as it slowly subsided she felt a warm loving peace towards him; she opened her eyes. Looking into his, she said simply, "Thank you," from her heart. He smiled and gently planted kisses on her eyes and then all of her face, saying softly "If you only knew just how much I adore you."

She held his head between her hands and covered his face with soft lips telling him how much he was loved. She felt her whole heart had opened and that it was totally safe to be vulnerable and expose all her feelings. She felt his delight and total acceptance of all that she had to offer. She felt joyful, relaxed, and a little playful. She became aware that his finger was still deep inside her. She spoke with merriment, recalling a line from a verse, "The moving finger writes and having writ moves on… But it seems this one hasn't."

He laughed softly, "Omar Khayyam; one of my favourite writers…let's see…'The moving finger writes and having writ moves on; Not all thy piety nor wit shall lure it back to cancel half a line; Nor all thy tears wash out a word of it!'"

Audrey gently said "In other words, what is done is done!"

He was silent, gazing at her with a small smile. "You have an enchanting ability of summing up paragraphs written by well-known philosophers into a single sentence, making you appear very wise or the philosophers very complex."

She smiled. His spontaneous profound remarks never failed to please her.

She decided that this one required no comment, other than the smile. She went back to kissing him. His body was warm and inviting. She wrapped her arms around him and nuzzled his face and neck. Her heart opened to love him even more.

A Meeting of Souls

The finger started to move again!

This time her body came alive with sensation almost immediately. He changed position and whispered, "Guide me in my love." His entry was gentle and unhurried as though he was exploring his journey into her loving warmth. He just as slowly and gently withdrew to a point where she thought she would lose him. After a few movements partly to hold him there and also to give him pleasure, she tightened her pelvic muscle, as he was withdrawing.

He gave a sudden gasp, froze for a moment, rested his head on her shoulder and took a deep breath, as she said, "Ooops" and stifled a small giggle. She had not expected such a large effect; now she still felt loving and playful but a little out of the moment.

He lifted his head and looked at her. She tried to look contrite but realized that she had failed miserably when he said, "You have mischief dancing in your eyes. That was very exciting my love, but you also know that it will be my undoing." She nodded. He gently kissed her nose and whispered, "Don't be sorry, I love your sense of fun." Smiling, she wrapped her arms around him and hugged him close.

They moved back into the moment in complete accord. Stroking and cradling his head in her hands she kissed his face and lips with passion.

She began to match his rhythm!

She felt loved, honoured, admired and completely accepted by this wonderful man whose consideration of all that she was experiencing seemed like a lovely gift. She felt for the first time almost overwhelmed by the love she was feeling and the sensation that was getting so intense that even her cells seemed to be vibrating.

He said, "Darling, look at me."

She gazed into his eyes and became lost in the loving depths of them.

Suddenly she was transported into space! Still aware of their bodies; feeling every movement and every sensation: she felt detached but with a strong communication line to her body. She felt she was dancing in the Universe with him in time to the rhythm of their lovemaking. She was aware that this was a meeting of souls. The realization was filled with joy and love. She sensed that he was feeling this too! This was a unique and beautiful blending of two beings that had recognised, found each other and now blended in complete harmony.

When their simultaneous climax happened, it moved through their bodies and became a poignant exchange of energy. There was exhilaration, incredible joy and love such as she had never known. She felt as though the whole Universe had joined in and celebrated their joy. As a being she felt totally integrated with him. She felt that this was home. She allowed herself to be completely immersed in the experience. It slowly changed into a feeling of utter peace. The feeling of immense love remained.

When she opened her eyes, she was surprised to find tears of joy trickling down her face. He was gently wiping them away. He did not query them; it was as if he knew they were just a release of intense emotion. He was lying on his side, propped on an elbow, with such a soft gentle look of adoration on his face that she wanted to cry. Instead she took a slow deep breath and said, "I love you with every fibre of my being."

He replied, "And I love and adore you with all my heart and soul." They smiled at each other, happy with themselves and the world.

He said as though to confirm their experience, "Now that the Universe has settled down, perhaps we should do the same and have some rest." He kissed her tenderly on her eyes, her cheeks, her lips; he held her close and softly kissed her neck and throat before slowly relaxing and turning onto his back. She moved onto her side, draped a leg across his, and rested her cheek on the side of his chest. She gave a soft happy murmuring sigh. As they drifted into sleep he said, "Thank you darling for this wonderful night. Since you and I derived so much happiness from our lovemaking, let us not settle for anything less than this in the future." She nodded. He added, holding her close, "We must not allow anything to ever change this."

Although she agreed, she went to sleep with the knowledge that from the moment she was born she had slowly become aware that the only constant you could count on in this Universe was change; and that is, was and always would be inevitable!

The next morning Audrey awoke feeling happy and full of anticipation for all the moments ahead. She smiled at the thought of last night and even more at the thought of Gabriel. She was alone in the bed, but she could hear crockery sounds in the kitchen. She stretched, feeling luxuriously lazy, becoming aware at the same time that she was naked. She wondered if she had time to make a dash to the wardrobe and reach for a robe.

The kitchen noises ceased, making the decision for a dash out of the question. Wrapping the sheet around her chest she sat up in bed against the pillows, wishing she had awakened a few minutes earlier to clean her teeth and grab some covering for her nakedness.

Gabriel came into view wearing a burgundy paisley robe, carrying two mugs of coffee.

He smiled saying "Good morning Audrey, are you well rested and happy to greet the day?"

"Good morning Darling. You are a good soul to waken me with a cup of coffee."

"Audrey, why are you smiling? Is it something I said or the way I say things that make you smile?"

"Dear Gabriel, I love the way you construct your sentences, I find them quaint and lovable, but then I find I love everything about you that I have discovered to date. Yes, I am happy and rested, but first I want to clean my teeth, if you would kindly hand me my dressing gown; then I would like to kiss you good morning. I'd like to make you aware how much you are loved!" Gabriel smiled, placing the coffee on the bedside table he leaned forward taking her in his arms. He held her gently and with such tenderness that she could feel it going through her skin. He kissed her head and neck then gently disengaging himself he went to the cupboard and returned holding out her robe. She slipped her arms into the sleeves and turning said 'thank you' with a smile, placing her hand on his cheek before heading for the bathroom.

Once there she decided to shower. While she stood enjoying the water flowing over her body, she deliberated about her feelings about Gabriel.

Audrey was confused. She had not experienced such depth of feeling before. It seemed paramount. What was the importance, the significance of this connection?

Maybe Gabriel was like a loving reward for her handling of the events that had happened in her life over the last few years.

Here was someone who loved her warmly and it seemed deeply, which she reciprocated despite their relative brief acquaintance.

Audrey had shared much of her life with him except for the Dwayne incident. She had felt that it was too much information at once, but it had to be told eventually.

Did it? Was she planning a life with Gabriel? This was all too new. She intended to go to Scotland to do other Scientology levels at the College; until then she did not know what the next event in her life was to be. Her divorce had yet to happen and although there was no doubt of it happening, time was required for a conclusion. A visit to Australia to tie up all the loose ends would also be mandatory.

Audrey turned off the water as she decided to just stay in present time and go with the flow. Let Gabriel start and continue the pace and she would follow, enjoying any and all the happiness available.

He smiled as she entered the bedroom. "I will make you a fresh coffee and shower and shave while you drink it." As he left for the kitchen he called "Please don't get dressed yet, there are things we need to do to start the day correctly."

He was back promptly with the coffee and gone just as quickly.

She sat on the bed, deciding that he meant making love was the next event.

She willingly accepted the thought.

A Meeting of Souls

Looking at her clothes she wondered what to wear; but this depended on what was expected of the day's events. Perhaps this is what he really meant. On returning Gabriel took her hands and pulled her upright and into his arms. He held her gently but firmly murmuring, "I don't ever want to let you go; you belong here! I didn't think it was possible to love so much and at such short notice. Do I alarm you or do you have similar questions and feelings?"

Audrey said, "No to the first and a big Yes to the second."

He kissed her, warmly and deeply. She responded in the same way.

Taking the initiative, she slipped the dressing gown off her shoulders and untied his belt and helped his robe to slip to the floor.

They stood enjoying the closeness and the feel of their bodies. Their hands found warm skin to explore and loving parts of the bodies began to warm and respond to each other's touch. The kissing was wonderful but not enough and Gabriel picked her up in his arms and placed her on the bed.

He bent her knees as before and knelt between them. Holding her legs, he raised them and placed them over his shoulders, automatically this pulled her closer to him. He ran his hands over her thighs, up her torso and up, around and over her breasts, pausing to gently tweak her nipples.

Audrey grasped his head between her knees as wanting him grew stronger and stronger. He smiled lovingly and lifting her hips he maneuvered her onto his erection. She gave a small murmur of approval and gave herself up to the moment. Her breath quickened, the sensation intensified, she wanted to kiss him, but from her position she couldn't reach him. She surprised herself, hearing deep low moans as release came.

Gabriel watched her with love as she regained her breath and began to relax. Audrey smiled at him, saying "Your turn now!" He slid her legs from his shoulders and carefully bent her knees to each side of his body. He took her hands and pulled her upright so that she was sitting on his thighs. She bent her knees, wrapped her arms around him and began to kiss him over all his face, lingering on his lips.

She was aware that they were still connected. She whispered in his ear, "What would you like me to do now?"

His answer surprised and amused her. "Ride me."

She began to bounce up and down, while he clung to her with his face in her neck, nibbling her ear and kissing anything available. It took a very short time for him to emit long shuddering sighs and moans as he climaxed, and she joined him.

Audrey was delighted; she felt that this was something she had caused almost by herself. She hugged him, saying, "Oh, I love you so, you are so dear to me, would you like me to do that again?"

Gabriel laughed, "Not for some time, there needs to be a recovery period my love, but thank you for the offer."

She said, "Of course honey. What am I thinking?"

Holding her close he asked, "Why don't we have another quick shower together, get dressed and then I have in mind a restaurant on top of a mountain called Arosa where we can have brunch?"

She laughed and said, "What a lovely idea! We seem to be living on love, but I am not complaining."

Gabriel laughed and said, "Neither am I, but my stomach is now deciding otherwise."

The circular road going up the mountain was a breathtaking experience.

The road to Audrey seemed very narrow. The up traffic was on the edge looking down into the valley, whilst the down traffic seemed to hug the side of the mountain whenever cars passed each other.

The hotel was interesting, the food was good. They ate in comfort looking through lots of glass at wonderful views. Gabriel told her it was reasonably popular for skiing in the season and pointed out the slopes when they went for a walk after lunch. They held hands walking in a companionable silence. Audrey felt him gazing at her, but then he looked away when she noticed him. Then she would watch him until he felt her gaze and turned his head in inquiry. Suddenly they both started to laugh.

Gabriel said, "What is it you wish to know?"

A Meeting of Souls

"I have statements and questions; you may consider them a little personal, so you have no obligation to answer."

"Please go ahead, I am happy to answer all your questions, personal or otherwise, I cannot conceive of you ever being offensive by choice; you are too much a dignified lady for that to arrive."

She started to smile. She was getting used to Gabriel's quirky sentencing; it actually gave her pleasure.

Audrey holding his hand and turning to face him said, "I want to thank you for pleasing me so much in the lovemaking department. I don't know if this has come from lots of practice; from books or maybe a course you did, but I am happy to acknowledge that I have the pleasure of loving not only someone I adore but an expert in the field." She could feel a blush mounting and did her utmost to hold it at bay. She gazed at the ground waiting for his comments.

Gabriel tilted her chin, looking into her eyes he murmured, "Don't look away. You are such a mixture of daring and shyness. We can discuss anything; all aspects of making love; the ins and outs of it, the techniques of it; how it is for you; for me; what is preferred and so on. I would delight in having this discussion with you. I confess it would be a new hallmark for me, as I only ever had surface talk with a member of the opposite sex before."

Seeing Audrey's question mark in her eyes, he clarified, "Just likes and dislikes from a female viewpoint, is as far as I have questioned."

He smiled at her, as he continued. "You hide nothing. Your face and your expression and your eyes say it all. I never have met anyone so open, so honest in feeling. It is one of the many things I love about you! Let us have a frank discussion. You have questions about other relationships I have participated in?"

She gave him a hug. "Have you been in love often? Did you have many relationships? Where did all the expertise come from? This is not really very important…mainly female curiosity!"

He laughed. "Alright. Let us answer these questions and perhaps give you even more important information at the same time. You have said you prefer full stops rather than question marks, so let us supply full stops for both of us. Yes my dearest Audrey, I am thirty-three years old and I have had many relationships before. All of them have been pleasant and where it has been applicable I have participated in a sexual manner and have enjoyed all of it. Always I have been honest with my partner; sharing my feelings, so that there can never be any misunderstanding about this being 'The One' when the lady in question has considered that it is 'The One' for her, I have gently ended the romance, so that her time will not be taken by someone who does not deserve it. Have I loved before… Yes, but until now I did not know that I could love so deeply, with all my heart and soul. You have taken me by surprise without doing anything but simply being there. I confess I am still coming to terms with it. I can hardly conceive of a life without you in it and I am sure the speed of all these deep feelings must leave you just as breathless as me. I feel I know you in the fullest sense of the word and yet I cannot wait to know more of you."

He pondered for a moment.

"Sometimes it feels as though there was a time when you were gone from my life and now I need to know what has happened since you went away. Do you understand?"

Audrey was overjoyed. She threw her arms around him holding him close, gently kissing his neck, then his face and lips. She pulled back, gazing into his eyes she said, "You are so right. We have been together before, now we are together again. We don't have to catch up on all the absence, maybe just this lifetime. I know why I came to Switzerland. You are the reason. You are my love of long ago and meeting you again has been the best thing that has ever happened to me this lifetime. I do not know how to love you more, but that will happen." Gabriel had tears in his eyes as he held her close saying, "Oh, my love, my dearest one. I love you so!"

They sat on a nearby bench, Gabriel's arm around her shoulders, her hand in his. For a long time they said nothing, just letting the loving silence envelop them. Eventually he turned her head kissing her softly as he asked,

"Shall we discuss the lovemaking now?"

She nodded.

"Alright. Have you heard of 'Kama Sutra'?"

She replied, "No. Who is he? He sounds like an Indian man." Gabriel laughed. "It is the name of a book! You are almost correct; the author is an Indian man called Vatsyayana. It is a book about sensual love and relationships."

Audrey asked, "Is it in English? May I read it?"

Gabriel smiled. "My copy is in German, but it does not affect your understanding, because there are pictures of sexual positions which are easily understood, but not always achievable unless you are a contortionist. I am happy to translate the text for you."

"Gabriel, how many languages do you speak?"

"Five or six... French, Swiss German, High German, Italian, Spanish, A little Swedish and English. And you?"

"English, Australian—believe me it is a whole new language— and a little school French. Tell me, how many sexual positions does this author describe?"

"Two hundred and forty-four if I remember correctly." Gabriel smiled at her with raised eyebrows.

Audrey said, "I don't think I can stay so long." They started laughing.

She said, "When we have made love so far, I do not feel as though I have contributed very much, so I would appreciate you telling me what you enjoy..."

Gabriel gave her a hug. "When someone is as desirable as you are, little stimulus is required. Whatever you would wish to kiss, stroke or touch is wonderful, but that would also be dependent on your ability to reach it.

You are a wonderful lover; now don't raise your eyebrows at me, I don't think you are aware of some of the things you do. Your kisses are superb; gentle, sensual and then passionate as you get aroused. When you climax, you have the most powerful pelvic muscles I have ever accounted. I feel as though you are milking me. It is an intense sensual feeling. It takes tremendous will power on my behalf not to join you at that exact moment. I wish always to give you at least two orgasms before taking my own, so I need to bear that in mind. When I join you, it becomes a spiritual feeling as well as physical sensation. I feel uplifted and at one with you, and even with the world. I have never experienced this before, so you see you contribute a great deal to our lovemaking. You are so aware, and yet not self-aware when it comes to all your virtues and enhancements. You are aware of issues and you deal with them until they no longer appear. You are very brave and very strong and this I admire."

She pulled back a little. "Audrey, why did that not please you?" She said, "It is just the word and the concept of 'admiration' which I would prefer not to have, especially from you."

His expression was puzzled.

"Admiration implies distance, and all I want is to be as close as possible to you."

He stared thoughtfully into the distance. "You are correct. It is hard to admire something under your nose. You need to stand back and look at it with some distance between it and you. I thought for a moment you were splitting hairs, as the English say, but I like your exactness of meaning in all that you say. It upholds your honesty and sincerity.

Thank you for pointing that out. I shall think of a truer concept for my feelings."

Audrey laughed and hugged him. "Sorry, it isn't really so important. These things come into my head, and out they come without any delay."

Gabriel enquired, "Who was it that said 'The Unexamined Life is not Worth Living'?"

Audrey replied "Socrates!"

Then, with a smile, she added, "Shall we leave soon? I'm rather eager to read this picture book you have at home!"

CHAPTER 51

Meeting Gabriel's Family

Gabriel had always visited his family on Christmas Eve. He told Audrey that his twin brother and his extended family always met at his mother's home, went to Church, came home to open presents, had supper and stayed the night or drove home.

He asked Audrey if she would like to join them and she readily agreed.

His mother lived some distance away; towards the mountains, so they left around four thirty. Gabriel organized the presents and some flowers that Audrey could present to his mother. He suggested that they return home the same evening. Audrey wanted to spend as much time with him as possible, so the suggestion made her smile.

They arrived only to find the family ready to leave for Church. Gabriel raised an eyebrow to Audrey who nodded. She had shaken hands with most of the family and was concentrating on remembering a few names.

The Catholic Church was crowded. Audrey simply followed Gabriel; doing whatever he did, being aware of the genuflecting and kneeling with bowed head which was taken so devotedly by all the family. She understood nothing of the service; some seemed to be in Latin, some in German. However, she paid special attention when she heard that Premier Harold

Holt of Australia was a drunkard. She stared at Gabriel who whispered, "So sorry, Audrey."

When they emerged from the Church she said to Gabriel, "I do not know the Prime Minister well, but I'm pretty sure he is not a drunkard."

Gabriel smiled, "Oh my dear, the priest did not say he was a drunkard; that is the German word for drowned. Apparently, the prime Minister went swimming and never returned. After four days of searching he is presumed drowned. I'm so sorry for your loss and so is my family. My mother says the Father often talks about world affairs, so she is pleased that Australia was mentioned for you."

They walked to Gabriel's mother's home. Gabriel's twin had a little girl around three. She had been staring curiously at Audrey and when Audrey found she was walking beside her, she offered her hand. A small fur-mittened hand and a smile made them instant friends.

It seemed Gabriel and his twin brother were the only ones that spoke English. His brother was not very fluent. Audrey decided to smile and pantomime her way through the evening. The table was already laid. Hot dishes began to appear from the oven and everyone was told to sit down and eat.

The atmosphere was friendly with many curious glances directed towards Audrey, until Gabriel's mother in a querulous voice pointed to the ring finger on her left hand and then still pointing at Audrey began to berate Gabriel. Audrey heard the word 'Catholic' and knew she was condemned. There was no doubt that a non-Catholic married woman was taboo.

Gabriel remained quiet and calm, answering his mother in a placating tone. The rest of the family was regarding Audrey and the mother with dismay.

Audrey felt she was ruining the evening. She held Gabriel's hand under the table and whispered, "Perhaps we should leave?"

Meeting Gabriel's Family

Gabriel squeezed her hand and said in a normal voice, "When the meal is finished. I am sorry for this occurrence. My mother is very religious and very much of the old traditional school. Please forgive her; she is normally hospitable and welcoming. Before you took your gloves off and she noticed your hand, she told me how pretty you were and that you seemed a lovely girl. She was impressed when Heidi took your hand walking home.

Hearing her name, the little girl climbed down from her seat, came to Audrey, and clambered up the chair and onto her knee. Audrey kissed her head and said 'Danke', feeling that she had escaped total condemnation because a little three-year- old found her acceptable.

Heidi's mother called her away, but she shook her head and snuggled into Audrey's chest.

The meal finished. Gabriel placed the presents on a side table and gave his mother the flowers saying they were from Audrey. She glanced at them, put them aside and started protesting again to Gabriel. He wrapped his arms around her, soothed her and said his goodbyes to the rest of the family. Audrey went to his mother, took her reluctant hand and thanked her for her hospitality. She said a general goodbye to the rest of the family and waited for Gabriel by the front door. On the drive home, Gabriel talked about the fact that perhaps it had all been too soon. The family needed time to get used to the idea. They would find how wonderful and what a beautiful person Audrey is given time. Audrey contented herself with holding hands and saying nothing.

She was thoughtful, looking at how quickly an atmosphere could change and over something which she had expounded her views constantly in the past. She looked at what she would say if Gabriel asked her for her views of Catholicism or the Church. For Audrey nothing had changed. This evening had only confirmed the viewpoints she held to be true. She felt it was a pity that no one had considered what Jesus would have to say about any religion that perpetuated restrictions, judgments, condemnations, negativity or limitations supposedly in his own name.

When they arrived home, she hugged Gabriel, put the kettle on and taking her dressing gown into the bathroom removed her makeup, showered and washed her hair. Symbolically she felt she had washed away the disdain of the evening. When she emerged, Gabriel was waiting with a cup of coffee and looking at her freshness said, "Good idea, I will do the same."

When he emerged, they sat in opposite corners of the couch with their knees tucked under, facing each other.

Gabriel smiled as he said, "My love, we have not as yet discussed your religion?"

"That's true!"

"Would you like to talk to me about it?"

"Well…firstly, the word 'religion' in a dictionary written before 1911 means 'to go through again in thought', so you see every time you think something over you are being religious. All Church religions are manmade. I feel that if Jesus knew all the rules, regulations, doctrines, practices, limitations imposed and negativity in regard to faiths of others, and even the philosophy espoused in his name by all the religions on earth he would be absolutely mortified. By my own definition I am a Christian. That means that in action and beingness, I am creating myself to be the very best being that I can conceive of at any given time! I do not know how to do better than this, but if you can enlighten me I will be forever grateful."

She gazed at Gabriel with a smile that had a little sadness in it. Gabriel however was looking at her with nothing but love.

Audrey went on because especially now it had to be said, "There is more to the story of my life to date. The divorce that will shortly happen is a second divorce not a first one. I would like to fill you in on all this if you are interested."

Gabriel said, "Please, but first let me be close to you, I am too far away." He moved towards her; she straightened her legs as he pulled her close and kissed her cheek, "Please go on, you have my undivided attention."

Audrey relaxed against his shoulders and told him the whole story of Mason and Dwayne. In explaining she found it was necessary to tell him about Steve, his accident; his death. It took quite a while. He did not interrupt or ask questions.

At the end he held her close saying, "I cannot imagine how losing your child really felt. I look at you today and it is hard to conceive that your life has been anything but ordinary. You somehow retain an air of innocence about life yet at the same time you are incredibly wise about the process of living. Am I making sense? I am amazed at your handling of the situation. I know of your capacity to love. It is immense; it also reflects your capacity to feel. Yet somehow you rise above all the negativity of these events. I feel privileged to be in your presence. You are an astonishing woman. It is with regret that I feel and understand your loss of Dwayne and also of Steve. I am so glad that you have trusted me enough to tell me all these things that have been in your life.

I am glad Steve was part of your life. It seems as though that was the first time you were really loved not just emotionally but physically also. This is to be treasured. Now you only need to know that I truly love you. I will always be here for you as long as you need me; as long as you want me."

Audrey swiveled round, laid her head on his chest and leaning in his arms she kissed him and said, "Thank you for listening, for understanding, but most of all for loving me the way that you do. I will always love you, no matter what happens to us; no matter where I am; no matter where you are, I will go on loving you. We have a connection, a strong old connection. This life is like a reconnection, a revival of what used to be. It explains why all the love we feel for each other is so strong as well as so sudden. It didn't need time to grow; it was already there and available to enjoy. I am happy to enjoy it and you for as long as possible. How does all this seem to you?

Gabriel smiled, "My little strange love, you say things that are new to me; never included in my education; yet they ring a dim bell somewhere, somehow; so, we will accept and go along with these conceptions. In our present situation they explain much and for this I am grateful. However, you talk of times that we were not together. Is it because death comes to us all or is it a premonition of a near future?"

"Darling, I don't know. It is Christmas Eve. Let us have a happy loving

Christmas and enjoy each other. I have a present for you. Would you like to open it now?"

Gabriel smiled and nodded. Audrey took a large parcel from her suitcase and gave it to him with a kiss.

He went to the bureau and returned with a small wrapped gift box. For some reason she was reminded of Doctor Gordon handing her the box containing the engagement ring; perhaps because the paper and the ribbon were the same colour.

She smiled and thanked him saying, "You first!"

He opened the parcel revealing the fur lined kangaroo boots. Audrey said, "I rang Otto for your size. I do trust they fit?" Gabriel put them on and strolled proudly around the apartment saying, "They could not be more perfect and so warm. Thank you my darling. What a perfect and so appropriate a present!"

Audrey opened her gift to find a beautiful gold pendant watch. It had painted flowers around the edge a white face, black fingers and was a lovely work of art. She smiled and said, "How lovely. Time is the art of the Swiss and now I have a piece of it to keep. Thank you so much my love!"

They clung to each other feeling more loving than they had ever been. Cuddling seemed to be more important than making love that evening. Their closeness seemed even deeper. They went to sleep in each other's arms, feeling that this was a wonderful and a very loving Christmas.

CHAPTER 52

Do All The Golden Places Have Short Leases?

The following afternoon, Otto with his girlfriend Annette came visiting. The men exchanged presents. They talked in English and the girls got to know each other. It was a lovely interlude. Later Audrey peered in the fridge. There was little to find. Gabriel was apologetic. He only had breakfast at home, lunch in the City, and dinner at his sister's restaurant. On the weekends he played tennis, often changing and eating dinner at the club or going to a concert, show or a dance with a friend. Audrey resolved to go shopping the next day.

The four of them went to the restaurant for dinner. It was not open but Klaus and Yvette were happy to have them for a Christmas Day celebration. Two extra was little work for the chef who was an abundant cook and had prepared a traditional dinner for four.

That evening they made love again. The relationship had changed. Both were aware of it without either of them putting it into words. The excitement was all there but the love and closeness were more palpable than before.

The next day they lazed in bed, talking and cuddling. Audrey told him at length about her work and how she had risen to be a building designer.

She did not mention past lives in any detail, rather leaving it to Gabriel to arrive at his own conclusions. He told her a little of his job in securities and investments for Bank clients, of his love for Australia, and how he hoped to live there one day.

He also explained how Switzerland was ruled from the bottom up and not the top down like in most other countries. Audrey was intrigued and did not understand why this was not universal in all Western countries when it was evident that referendums were the correct order of the day.

The next day they went shopping, buying eggs, bacon, bread, chicken and some vegetables. Audrey wanted to cook for him despite his plea that it was unnecessary. It took some time to convince him that she really would enjoy cooking him a meal. Gabriel felt she should be having a holiday free from all chores. Audrey felt it was a surprise to him that she enjoyed housework and cooking just as much as she enjoyed being a career woman.

They unpacked the groceries and then Gabriel took her for a drive. They drove for what seemed to be a short time. Audrey wondered why Gabriel had asked her to bring her passport and was surprised to find that they were now at the Italian border. He suggested she may like to buy some shoes, but she negated the idea because she had more than enough and the weight in her suitcase had always to be considered.

Talk of leaving tended to sober the conversation. Gabriel had to return to work the next day and Audrey suggested that she return to England the day after. It was decided that she would leave on the Wednesday, telephone her solicitor to get an update on the divorce and perhaps be able to plan the next few weeks of her life.

They had dinner in Italy. Audrey was allergic to garlic so they concentrated on the fish menu. The chef was very accommodating, and the food was wonderful. As usual when they were not eating, they held hands across the table and played games with each other's eyes. All their hours together seemed to be full of love and wonder as they discovered more and more of each other's lives and thoughts.

The next day Gabriel went to work. Audrey read a book, went for a walk,

Do All The Golden Places Have Short Leases?

and made dinner for him.

He was delighted to find her waiting for him when he returned home and she felt he was enjoying the domestic scene. He complimented her on the chicken dinner which was plain as his pantry was bereft of spices and herbs.

Audrey looked at the idea of always caring for Gabriel this way. She did not dismiss it, but she knew that her path was not conducive to this idea in present time. Gabriel was watching her, and she felt he could read her thoughts. He said, "I cannot think of anything more pleasant or wonderful for me than to come home and find you waiting; but I feel that your thoughts are not quite the same."

She nodded. "It is the timing. I have so much to do to clear my path and generally tidy my life. You make me smile. I feel you will always make me smile. A life with you at the moment is full of question marks. I feel that in six months I will know my direction so much better; can you be content with that?" Gabriel smiled, "Of course. I understand possibly even more than what you are saying. In June I have two weeks holiday. I shall wish that you will be here at that time even if you are here before, and we will go away together on a wonderful holiday. I will show you Switzerland. I will wait for you. I love you."

They were holding hands across his small dining table. Audrey let go and sat back in her chair, the better to look at him. He was the kindest most considerate man she had ever met. Everything about him seemed correct. Beautiful manners, intelligent, handsome, well dressed, appreciative, compassionate and above all loving; and yet she felt this tiny, *tiny* doubt in the back of her mind that they were not to be. She couldn't identify it. Was it because her life needed fixing? Would it be different later on? She shelved it; something to be dealt with later?

She smiled at Gabriel, walked around the table to kiss him, and went to the sink to wash the dishes. Gabriel dried them in a compatible silence. They made coffee and curled up on the couch. Quiet, just holding hands and happy to be close.

A LIFE of Enlightenment

On the last night they made gentle tender love and slept in each other's arms. In the morning, already dressed for work, he brought her coffee, and told her he had arranged to return at four o'clock to take her to the airport.

When he arrived, she was packed and ready to leave, after already saying goodbye to his sister and Klaus at the restaurant. She had written Gabriel loving little notes and hidden them amongst his possessions.

At the airport they hugged and kissed. Audrey said, "Please don't wait for me to go. I want to watch you walk away. Will you do that for me?" Gabriel smiled, nodded, turned away, and then he was gone in the crowd. Audrey boarded the plane and settled in to her seat for the fifty-five-minute flight to England.

CHAPTER 53

Clyde and Tiffany's Visit

When Audrey arrived at her flat in Saint Hill she found Clyde and Tiffany waiting for her.

Audrey was stunned to find that they had left the house unsold and the garden unattended. It was summer in Australia and the Queensland Blue lawn grass needed to be watered every second day to survive. Audrey had expected Clyde to take much more responsibility; this seemed out of character. She asked him if he had taken leave from the Bank, only to find out that he had resigned.

Clyde had been the youngest cadet ever and was being groomed for top managerial positions. He was well on the way to great heights, excelling at all he had done to date. He had loved his job and Audrey was amazed that he had thrown such an opportunity away.

When Audrey pointed out that spending their money on a world trip for him and Tiffany was not applicable at this time and that he had failed to organise her college funds as requested, he seemed very offhand and distanced. He told her that the price she had placed on the house was far too high and all the agents he had contacted agreed. He said it was not his fault that the house had remained unsold.

She stared at them for some time saying nothing. They sat in unconcerned silence, holding hands.

Audrey said, "Alright if this is how it is, I am going home on the first available flight to sell the house and organise the divorce. You had better let me have some forwarding address where I can leave a message or call you."

They gave her three names and addresses of accommodation they had booked; one in Portugal, one in London and one in France, promising more if required. Their unconcerned distanced attitude regarding all this left her a little breathless. After they left she called Qantas and arranged a flight for the following day. She packed only a minimum of summer clothes knowing she had more in her wardrobe in Perth.

Audrey then rang Gabriel, updating him on the situation. She said, "I'm going home tomorrow to water and talk the grass into being green again, sell the house, organise a divorce, and settle some of my life. I do not know when I will be back. This will take as long as it takes. Darling, I will write to you. Remember I love you!"

Gabriel was very understanding. Audrey knew he would be, but when he offered to come to England to see her off at the airport, she refused, saying that it would be better and easier for her to just go.

It took more than twenty-four hours of flying time to arrive in Perth. Because of the time difference, Perth was already eight hours ahead of England.

Audrey caught a taxi from the airport to her home in Mt. Pleasant. It was dark when she arrived, but even in the evening light and with the lamps outside, she could see that the lawn was a sorry sight. There was a letter from Pierre in France, stating that he had something important to discuss with her and begging her to visit when en route to England or Australia, and another caring letter from Brian. She took them to bed and read them before she slept.

Clyde and Tiffany's Visit

She awoke at eight in the morning, full of energy and ready to do whatever was needed to turn the lawn green, then advertise and sell the house.

She turned on all the sprinklers, then sat on the front steps, and with lots of intention, willed the lawn to turn green. She spent two hours each day in the front garden and the same in the rear garden.

She made a list of all the furniture to be sold, and after two days when she knew the grass would be green again within twenty-four hours, she wrote an interesting advertisement for the sale of the house at a price ten per cent higher than she had given Clyde. She had it inserted in Wednesday's and Saturday's papers. She rang two auctioneers regarding estimates for the furniture.

In the meantime, she cleaned the house, polished windows and weeded the garden. She fell into bed each night quite exhausted but feeling good about her achievements.

On Wednesday, Audrey received three phone calls regarding the house, none of which resulted in an inspection. However, a middle-aged couple from England arrived on the Saturday and immediately bought the house provided the carpet in the lounge was changed for the same price. Audrey agreed. She signed them up and rang a friend to bring carpet samples. Their shop was in the area so in one hour the deal was complete. The new owners wanted to buy the furniture and move in immediately. Audrey gave them the auctioneer's written estimate which they agreed to, and she promised settlement within the week instead of the normal twenty-eight days. Her real estate experience stood her in good stead. The car was still in the garage. She rang a dealer who bought it on the understanding that she used it for up to a week.

The next day she went to her bank. The new owners happened to also use the same bank, so the bank, with the buyer's permission, made an exception and acted for both parties. The officers could not have been more helpful. It seemed Clyde's infidelity with Tiffany had already spread; Audrey was treated with commiseration by anyone with whom she had to deal. The loan and settlement officers bent over backwards to assist. Settlement was promised within three working days.

Audrey was ecstatic. Everything was going well. She called to see the new owners at their hotel, requiring their signatures for transfer and other documents, and informed them of all the good news. She spent the next few days adjusting rates and taxes, informing the Shire Water Board, Telephone Postmaster General, and Post office of all the proposed changes.

Audrey rang her solicitor John Billett and made an appointment. John told her that Clyde was not eligible to receive any monies of any kind from any sales, as he was the guilty party. Audrey had already found that Clyde had sold their shares and was obviously using the funds to finance his travels.

She deducted half the share windfall, the cost of her air ticket, and the cost of the divorce from Clyde's half share of the house sale, and instructed the solicitor to pay the balance into Clyde's account.

John objected strongly, telling Audrey that Clyde legally had to refund all the money spent and that he was entitled to nothing. A little battle ensued. He could not understand Audrey's complete lack of deserved legal abundance or payback in even the mildest form. She was adamant that her instructions be followed.

She gave instructions to the Bank for the distribution of funds, for accounts for the solicitor to pay, and the balance sent to her account in Barclays Bank in England.

The following day she moved into her parents' home and began the handling of all their questions and advice on what should have been done. Audrey knew there would be recriminations for not keeping them informed. There was a lot of shouting from Fred, sadness for Audrey from her mother. Fred stressed what an idiot she was, and why she wasn't angry like anyone who had some sense would be. He was furious on her behalf with promises of giving Mason and Clyde 'what for' if he ever saw them again.

She was mostly silent throughout the attack, only saying when it had run out, "It's important for me to go on being me no matter what is going

Clyde and Tiffany's Visit

on in my life or what anyone else is doing. It's my rule for living; no one has to agree with it or do it, but I do and that is how it is."

Dorothy wrapped her arms around her daughter and, leading her away from her father, said, "I'm so sorry things have worked out this way, yet I'm very proud of the way you have handled your life. It hasn't been easy, yet your dimples are still there to remind me that every cloud has a silver lining. Please take care of yourself. Your father really loves you. You know, he actually admires you and disapproves of you all at the same time."

Audrey said, "Yes, I know. He's a mental gymnast; an expert at holding contradictory viewpoints. I don't think he realizes he is doing it. His anger gives him all the right words and they just bubble forth."

She hugged her mother who was busy patting her with tears in her eyes. "Mum, I'm fine, I really am. I need to go. Please look after each other. I will be back when the time is right. I have my return ticket, so I will be leaving within the next day or so."

Audrey felt that everything was finalised apart from her decision on where she would go next.

She drove to the top of Kings Park. Looking at the view over the City and the Swan River, she looked at all the alternatives, aware that the decisions she would make in the next twenty-four hours would determine her life for the next few months, and perhaps even years.

Audrey changed her flight to a forty-eight-hour stopover in Paris and then on to Scotland with an open ticket to Gatwick. Gabriel would wait until she had finished another course level. She would then take a deep breath and look at the world from different eyes and see what made her smile.

Her first stop would be France. Not only would she see Pierre, but she decided she would also be buying an outfit in Paris. After all she had raised the house price by ten per cent; sold it, had saved all the commission by selling it herself, and a Parisienne outfit was to be her reward. Audrey sent a telegram to Pierre giving her arrival time and asking him to meet her at the airport. He replied immediately saying he would be there.

She telephoned the College in Scotland asking if there were any delays

A LIFE of Enlightenment

on starting her next levels. She was told there was a back-up and she may have to wait to start. It could be two weeks, possibly more. Audrey decided to count on some Divine Intervention so that she could get on with her life.

Two days later she left Australia, ready for wherever life might take her next.

CHAPTER 54

Michael's Proposition

Pierre's face was wreathed in smiles. He took her to his apartment and then out to dinner. Audrey waited patiently for the purpose of his request, but he happily made inconsequential small talk. She began to yawn towards the end of the meal. Although it was only ten in the evening in Paris it was for Audrey the equivalent of six in the morning in Perth. Audrey was tired and ready for bed after her long flight. Pierre had only one double bed. He said, "I'm sure you realised that I'm a homosexual, so we can share the bed and you will be completely safe. If you are not comfortable with that, I will sleep on the sofa."

Audrey gazed at the sofa and then at Pierre's tall form and said, "No, the sofa is mine; it was always mine; you take the bed."

Pierre with only slight disagreement agreed, and Audrey finally got to rest her head on a pillow.

After a breakfast of warm croissants and coffee, Audrey went shopping. She avoided all the designer salons, concentrating on the big stores. After two hours she found a lovely off-white coat of unborn calf. It was synthetic, and the style looked Russian. The movie 'Doctor Zhivago', set in Russia, was showing all over Europe. The coat length was down to her ankles.

There was a synthetic band of fur round the neck and this continued down each side of the front near the closure. It fastened with white silk cords which looped around the buttons on each side.

Audrey bought a silver pair of boots and a matching brimmed hat. She was thrilled with her purchases but wanted to do something about the coat length. When she put it on she disappeared and became all coat, not being tall enough to carry it with aplomb. She went to a haberdashery section and found and bought a long band of the synthetic fur trimming.

When Pierre returned from work, she asked him if it was possible to borrow a sewing machine. He went to his aunt's home and came back with one familiar to Audrey.

She shortened the lining and a good length of the coat, so that it was about three inches below her knee. She neatened everything and then made a hood from the cut off length. The cut off lining became the lining for the hood. Using the fur band, she finished off the bottom of the coat and then trimmed the hood with the balance. She attached the hood to the coat. Altogether when it was finished it made a fabulous outfit, fit for a queen.

Pierre was intrigued watching her creation. Soon however he wanted to talk about his life.

He told Audrey that he had been gay since he was a teenager. Now he was thirty-five and wondered if it was possible to change. He would like to marry and have children.

He asked Audrey about the different Scientology levels that he had yet to do. She could only tell him that he would get out of them whatever he put into them and that his intention was paramount. She told him to be sure of his real wants and only do whatever made him smile, and not what he thought he should do for anyone else's sake only his own.

The next day dressed in her new outfit she boarded the plane for Scotland. It was almost January and very cold. The beautiful, warm outfit looked perfect and very elegant.

It was only a small plane carrying around forty passengers, with two repetitive seats on each side of the plane. Audrey had two seats to herself on the right. There were few passengers on board; only half the plane was full.

She was straining to place her vanity case in the overhead locker when a voice behind her said, "Allow me". The case was neatly put away and she turned to find a much taller man smiling. "May I help you with your coat?"

Audrey said, "Thank you. I really must put some fertilizer in my shoes. I would love to be just a little taller."

He smiled, "You look perfect to me, just the way you are." Audrey replied, "That's kind", as she folded her coat and placed it in the seat near the window. She did this to discourage him sitting next to her; not that he was unacceptable, if fact he looked dignified, pleasant looking, intelligent, and was smartly dressed.

He sat down opposite, with the aisle between them. "I think you may find on these older and smaller planes that the luggage racks are slightly higher than the Boeings." The man was English, well-educated and well spoken.

"That's good. Now I know I'm not shrinking!"

He laughed. "Is this your first visit to Scotland?" She nodded. "Are you visiting family or friends?" She shook her head.

"How rude of me, let me introduce myself, my name is Michael Meadows, I have a business in England and Scotland, so I frequently have these one-hour flights each month. I am a seasoned traveller and capable of giving you any information you may require. I have just had a brief visit to Paris, which has given me the opportunity of meeting you."

Audrey replied, "My name is Audrey and I am going to Scotland to do some advanced training at the Scientology College in Edinburgh."

Michael nodded, "Where are you staying? "I haven't the faintest idea!" she replied.

"Audrey dear, do you realise that this is the Scottish New Year? You will be lucky to find any decent accommodation. Will your college have booked you in anywhere?"

"I doubt it. I did phone, but I didn't give them a definite date for my arrival."

"My dear, now you have me quite worried on your behalf."

"Please don't concern yourself; something will turn up; it always does. I'm not at all concerned."

"But my dear, you should be. The Scottish New Year is a big event, much more revered than Christmas in England."

"It's kind of you to worry about me; but really I always seem to land on my feet. I'm sure I will have somewhere to live or board shortly after I arrive."

Michael stared at her. "These courses you are doing must give you a very positive even optimistic view on life. Tell me something about them, please?"

For the rest of the journey, they chatted with Audrey doing most of the explaining; Michael asking questions. Their rapport was excellent.

As the plane came to a stop, Michael lifted down her suitcase and held out her coat.

As she slid her arms into the sleeves, he said, "Please take my card. Promise you will call me for any reason; it will be a pleasure to assist you and take care of you anyway you wish. For all your bravery and certainty, to me, you seem not only exquisite, for that is the way you look, but also vulnerable. I have this urge to take care of you. I hope this does not offend you?"

She smiled. "No, that's fine, thank you so much."

On the way to baggage claim she was thinking, 'What on earth is it I do or say that makes men in particular think I am vulnerable or need looking after?!' She didn't have an answer. Waiting for her luggage she found Michael standing next to her. "Please indicate your case so that James can take it to the car."

"James?"

Michael indicated the uniformed chauffeur on his left. "With your permission, we will drop you at your college; the street you indicated is on the way to my home, so it is no trouble."

Audrey thanked him. She was happy and amused to be arriving in style.

Michael's Proposition

The car was a dark Maroon coloured Rolls Royce. Audrey was tucked in the back seat with a fur rug and James indicated the bar and the telephone.

Michael closed the door saying, "I shall ride in the front with James to read my messages. Please tell me if I can provide anything else for your comfort."

"Thank you, I will."

Within a short time they arrived at the college. There were large glass doors that opened on to the street. Inside Audrey could see a receptionist who, seeing the Rolls pull up and the chauffeur get out, picked up a phone, and a man obviously the CEO came running down the stairs. Audrey watched this with some amusement as James opened the boot and pulled out her suitcase. Obviously, they thought she was some sort of celebrity. She was aware that her outfit gave credence to the vision.

The gentleman took her case from James, nodded to Audrey and said, "Now where did you just spring from?"

She smiled. "Paris"

"Aaaah," he said, as though that explained everything. "Please follow me."

"One moment please." Audrey walked to where Michael was standing. "Thank you so much for everything." She offered her hand. He leaned forward and kissed her cheek." Please contact me the moment you have or don't have accommodation. I do know people who may assist if needed. Will you have dinner with me this evening? Please call me so that we may talk. Will you do that?"

"Yes, if that makes you happy, I will call." She smiled at him and turned to follow her escort up the stairs. The college only had the receptionist downstairs. The rest of the courses and auditing spread out along the next floor.

Audrey managed to arrange to start her course the following morning with no waiting. She did nothing to perpetuate the idea of being a celebrity; or nothing to correct it. She was very happy not to wait.

The only accommodation available turned out to be a boarding house about quarter of a mile away. There was an upstairs room with a double bed, a chair, a table, and a meter that had to be fed shillings almost every two hours to provide some warmth. There was a kettle and a cup and saucer and that was it! A shared bathroom lived next door.

A continental breakfast was provided downstairs and the rest was up to the occupant. It didn't make her smile, but she was grateful to have anything at all. Someone from the college apologetically drove her to the door and carried her suitcase up the stairs.

She visited a nearby shop; bought some coffee, herbal tea and a small bottle of milk, and changed some money for lots of shillings. There was a boarding house telephone that took money and she used it to call Michael. He was very pleased to get her call. He arranged to collect her at six thirty. Audrey waited for him outside. He was driving himself this time. When he arrived, he looked up at the building she was occupying, raised his eyebrows and said, "May I find you somewhere more suitable?" Audrey smiled. "No thank you. This is just somewhere to sleep. I will be at the college from nine in the morning until six at night, seven days a week, so this is fine. It is clean. As long as I remember to keep up the supply of shillings for the meter, I can't go wrong."

Michael opened the car door for her. They drove to a hotel. He had booked a table and seemed to be well known. The welcoming staff was very accommodating to all his requests.

In between the three courses and after the coffee they talked. She gathered between the soup and the main course that he was married. She waited for the inevitable 'but my wife doesn't understand me' scenario, but it didn't arrive.

Instead he said, "We have an understanding. We don't get along as we should. So rather than divorce, because we are excellent friends, we have an arrangement. Yvonne does whatever she wishes and I do the same. We only

Michael's Proposition

see each other about once every three months. She is mostly Parisienne on her mother's side, so she spends most of her time in Paris. I saw her recently because she needed some advice on an investment she was considering. She seldom comes to Scotland or England. She says they are too harsh and cold for her, Paris is gentler and has a slightly warmer environment which suits her well."

Audrey smiled at him and he held her hand while he told her of this part of his life. She made no comment on his discourse. The next course, some delectable salmon in a light creamy sauce, took their attention for some time.

Michael looked at her across the table. She met his gaze with a faint smile. He said, "You have the most penetrating green eyes I have ever seen. On someone else they could be intimidating, but the dimples constantly blinking in and out completely neutralize the effect. I need to let you know that I find your conversation fascinating, your considerations on life unique; I love the way you look and altogether I find you enchanting. Now you're looking away. Have I embarrassed you?"

Audrey was saved by the waiter clearing their plates and requesting their dessert order.

While this continued, she leaned back in her chair considering Michael and also thinking of Gabriel. She had resolved to leave the question of Gabriel until she had finished her next course level. Audrey was aware that eventually Gabriel would ask her to be his wife. She was also aware that his religion was a barrier and although she felt he might even offer to give it up, the ostracizing from his family did not argue well. She did not wish to have more children, and although he had not given her an inkling of his wishes in this regard, his admiration of how well she had bonded with his niece at Christmas despite the language barrier had given her some idea of what his wishes may be. There was the divorce... another no-no. And it also had yet to be finalised.

She gave a little sigh and looked at Michael only to find him watching her intently.

"I can't offer you a penny for your thoughts, it seems like a few pounds would be more appropriate."

"My apologies, Michael. I was thinking about all the different journeys people have on this planet. I'm sorry I went so far away from you, but now, here I am. You have all my attention." "Is there something you can tell me about your visit elsewhere?" He was holding her hand again. "I have noticed you are wearing a wedding ring."

Audrey told him about her current situation with Clyde and Tiffany.

He was attentive, asked a few questions and seemed to accept the fact that she was not upset about the situation; only ready for it to be over. She did not mention Gabriel. Audrey felt that he was still looking at her with a question mark.

She smiled, "What is it Michael, please feel free to ask me anything?"

He leaned forward, "I do understand that you are no longer upset about this situation, but I'm intrigued that you have not voiced any of the usual platitudes common to this type of scenario?"

"And they are?"

"Considerations such as, 'I wasn't enough for him'; 'There must have been things I did…didn't do'; 'I should have understood him better', etc?" He raised his eyebrows at her with a faint but questioning smile.

Audrey started laughing. "Look, this has nothing to do with self-esteem, which one would need to lack in order to voice those concerns. This has to do with the purpose of relationships between people."

Audrey continued. "I need to ask you a question."

Michael nodded.

"Tell me…if you were the only person in the world, would you have any idea who you were?"

Michael pondered for a moment. "No, I guess not!" He reached for her hand again.

"I feel that is because we define ourselves by our interaction with others. We are different beings to different people, according to their reflections to us."

Michael's Proposition

Audrey went on. "A relationship serves us as long as we are learning about ourselves from each other. When that is over the relationship has lost its purpose and it is time to move on." "They don't always move on. Audrey, don't you think that people stay together out of habit sometimes?"

"Yes, but that is really based in fear. The fear that someone else may not come along. The devil you know is better than the devil you don't. Or if the relationship is over, other thoughts may prevail. *'I failed this time to make it what I thought it could be and I don't know where I went wrong'*. Then there is, *'Obviously I wasn't good enough, sexy enough, thin enough, caring enough, should have looked after myself better'*, etc. This can be male or female thought…all of them based on self-invalidation. All associated with blame, shame or regret."

He nodded. He appeared to understand what she was saying. She went on, "For Clyde and Tiffany, it was their time to reflect to each other and my time with Clyde was over. If it wasn't so, the infidelity would never have occurred. I still have a relationship with each of them, but it is a changed one. I still love them, but I also know that it is OK to love at a distance. I do not need them in my immediate space. Am I making sense with all this?" She regarded him thoughtfully.

"Very, you really seem to have it sorted." Michael was sitting back in his chair, regarding her with a question mark.

"But Audrey, what about the couples who break up and then decide to come back together again?"

"True. That happens; but it is a new and different relationship; ask any couple: if it is not sufficiently new or different, they break up again."

Michael said, "Well this has been a most interesting evening. Is it possible for us to have dinner every evening while you are here?"

"Yes, but not always at expensive places like this one. Perhaps we can eat somewhere more casual and I can wear casual clothes. How would that be for you?"

"I will enjoy whatever you wish. It is the company that counts."

Michael took her home, agreeing to call for her at six fifteen each evening at the College. They hugged at her door. She was careful to avoid any further intimacy. The dinners continued. They talked about past lives, death, how one created one's own reality, empathy, the purpose of life, doing what makes you smile etc. For Michael it was an education; for Audrey, an enjoyment in sharing.

Their dinner dates always took a minimum of three hours. They talked during courses, between courses, and over coffee. Michael was adept at holding her hand. Often, she was surprised not to have noticed until she paused at the end of explaining some data. He challenged or asked for clarification constantly. He reminded Audrey of how she still behaved towards data that seemed to be unquestionable. Every time he challenged she gave him ten gold stars. Where possible, she asked him to look at his own experience, to see if what she had put forward was true for him.

Audrey had said that everyone needed to act with responsibility to events in their lives.

Michael said, "Surely that depends on who's to blame?" Audrey said "No. Blame, shame and regret are not part of being responsible. Judgement of right and wrong comes after that fact and is basically opinion, based on belief or culture. When that occurs, we are talking of reaction to an event not a response.

Being responsible is acting as cause. Responsibility means to respond with ability. It is simple. Reaction is emotional, usual a knee jerk reaction.

Even when two cars collide with each other and have what is termed an accident. A co-creation is actually what takes place.

Each driver from a spiritual viewpoint has one hundred per cent responsibility. No one made them be there. Each had a choice to be in that place at that time. One can always take responsibility for being there. That is always applicable, no matter what is going on."

Michael said, "Aren't you being a little harsh?"

Michael's Proposition

Audrey laughed, "Good heavens no. Being responsible puts you at cause instantly and not effect. There would be no shouting or anger or blame, or regret, just the simple use of ability to sort out the details of the cars and so on."

Michael brought up other events to be analysed and examined. Each event brought about a reaction and blame, shame, and regret got assigned. It took a while to sort out the difference between having a reaction and being responsible. Eventually Audrey said, "Let's put it this way: Reaction is fairly normal on this planet. Response is still being learned."

Michael was smiling. "Is there some reason that you frequently say, 'this planet'? Somehow it puts you in the context of being a visitor."

Audrey laughed and said, "Yes, well...", her familiar rejoinder when she chose not to answer.

By the end of the week, Audrey had completed all she wished to do. She told Michael she would be leaving for England on the Monday. He was immediately concerned about where she would stay and what she would do next. Audrey explained that she shared a flat with a Melbourne friend and also talked to him about her self-sufficiency and independence, trusting that would make him realise that she did not require his protection or help.

Michael listened patiently to all she had to say, then smiling and taking her hand, he pointed out that he was only doing his manly job.

"I have always felt this way towards women, even more so when I meet someone like you. Maybe it is because long ago I was a Knight and sworn to defend the fair sex, or something similar. You know about past lives, perhaps you can explain it?"

She nodded smiling, "Maybe you were part of King Arthur's court. I do know that it is not a myth or a legend, because I viewed the actuality myself in a session when I was looking for something specific."

Michael said, "To use one of your expressions, that idea makes me smile. Perhaps that's where... I always felt that I knew you even on the plane. If we had a connection back then, it must have been a romantic one, because that is how I feel about you now. What do you think?"

Audrey patted his hand, "I feel it is preferable to stay in present time as that is the only important time in this life, for everyday living."

Michael and Audrey boarded the plane together on the Monday. Another Rolls Royce, black in colour with a chauffeur called Thomas, met them at Gatwick airport.

The drive to Audrey's flat was uneventful and they were both quiet during the journey.

Michael insisted on carrying her suitcase upstairs himself; once there he looked around and said, "Well it looks cosy and the location next to the forest is excellent."

Audrey said, "It was the butler's flat when the Manor had lots of servants. It is convenient to the College and the grounds are lovely. We get along well with our landlady who owns the Manor, and she is very helpful if anything needs maintenance. I think she is quite fond of Australians now."

Michael left to visit his factory in Bristol, after getting Audrey's phone number and telling her that he would contact her on his return.

She went to the college and brought them up to date on her progress. She checked on the students she had coached and spent some time over the next few days helping them and others. On the Saturday morning she received a phone call from Pierre. He was staying at the Crown in town and wanted her to meet him for lunch.

Audrey drove in, luckily finding a parking space nearby; the pub was always busy and crowded on Saturday mornings. She found Pierre sitting at a small table in the main area. It was very busy. All the tables were full and there was a crowd at the bar ordering lunch. Pierre rose as she walked in and handed her a single red rose. Audrey thanked him and took the only available seat opposite him.

She asked him how he was and why he had come to visit. He did not answer, just stared at her with a loving expression on his face.

Suddenly he got up out of the chair and moving to the side of Audrey he got down on one knee saying in his lovely French accent with an impassioned plea, "Please marry me. I love you. With you I know I can be

Michael's Proposition

whatever I want to be. I have in you such faith. I need you. I will to you be good! Audrey, please marry me."

Pierre had a lovely voice that carried beautifully over the space. The noise in the room had abated slowly over his speech. Now it was quiet, and the audience waited for her answer with bated breath. All eyes were focused on both of them. Audrey took a big breath and placing her hand on his shoulder said, "I'm so sorry but I cannot marry you." There was a groan of 'ooohhh' from the crowd, and some shaking of heads in disapproval. She tried to haul Pierre to his feet. He reluctantly moved back into his chair.

Audrey took hold of his hand and said, "Pierre, you know that I would be a solution to a problem. You also know from your training that all solutions eventually become problems, and believe me I'm capable of becoming a huge one. The only way to handle what you have decided is a problem is to dis-create it."

"How do I do that?"

"Well Pierre, you created it in the first place, no one else did it for you. Anything you create you can dis-create."

"Audrey, why would I create this?"

"Only you know the answer to that one, Pierre; perhaps at the time it served you in some way, or perhaps you were adding to the numbers to help homosexuality become acceptable to the rest of humanity. I do not know. You are the only one who does know? When you do some more levels, you will find the answers, when it is the right time for your journey and if you have firm intention to want to change."

Audrey was aware that some of the people close to them still had attention of what was being said.

She said to Pierre, "Look, this is not the best place to have lunch, under the circumstances. I have the car outside, let us go somewhere else were we can talk in peace."

Pierre rather remorsefully nodded and they left the hotel.

They went to a café down the road and Audrey let him talk. At the end of Pierre getting off all his considerations, she offered to run him to Gatwick so he could catch a late flight back to Paris. It was easy to change his ticket from the Sunday to the Saturday and this gave him extra time to prepare for work on the Monday.

Audrey saw him his off at the airport, thanking him again for his proposal and promising to always be his friend. She also pointed out that she was still married, therefore not available for proposals or propositions for that matter. She also mentioned Gabriel. When Pierre waved goodbye, he seemed resigned if not cheerful, but he had obviously accepted that her refusal was on good grounds.

Audrey spent the next day with Lorraine, who was anxious to be brought up to date on Audrey's progress on course and in life.

Being an avid romance novel reader, she enjoyed all the details of Audrey's love life, sharing her romances second-hand. She didn't object or commiserate to any of the traumas in Audrey's life; Lorraine felt that these had all contributed to Audrey's strength and understanding of life. She envied them in her own quiet way, because adventures were always going on and her life by comparison seemed very quiet and inept. Even Audrey's lovers were better than the ones she read about in books because they were alive and much more fun. Audrey would have been surprised to know her thoughts.

She spent the next few days walking through the woods, helping students on course and assimilating the cognitions that had eventuated and were still occurring from the most recent levels she had attained.

Michael telephoned after ten days, saying, "Audrey, please spend at least half a day or preferably a whole day with me. I want to take you to London and show you something very special. Will you do this?"

Audrey agreed, and Michael made a time to call for her the following Saturday. He arrived in the Rolls with Thomas driving. He slid the glass pane for privacy, held her hand and started talking. He was bright and eager, like a small boy. She couldn't help but join in the enthusiasm and smile with him.

His visit to the factory had gone well; better than ever. He looked and

Michael's Proposition

treated the staff differently because of all the things she had taught him. He was so happy with the response he had got. He said, "Whenever I have tried to change anything before, I have got reactions rather than response. This was so different because before starting I took the trouble to really find out what was needed and wanted, and then the workers came up with almost all my ideas. After that they were amiable to anything I suggested. It was a wonderful feeling and I am so grateful to you!"

Audrey smiled and said, "It was a pleasure," and squeezed his hand.

Michael went on. "I have had lots of time to think over the last week or so. I have lots to tell you but first of all the surprise. Unless you want to talk, we can just listen to music and enjoy the drive."

Audrey nodded. So, they held hands and Thomas drove gently forward to London.

Thomas pulled up outside some very expensive apartments in Mayfair.

Michael took her hand as they alighted from the car and led her up some steps into a very elegant foyer. They climbed a staircase to the first floor and then walked to a double entry door on the right.

He opened the doors and then stood back, beckoning Audrey forward with a small flourish of his right hand. She walked into a very beautiful large open living and dining space with large windows, doors leading to a balcony with a magnificent view of an opposite park. The furniture, window treatments and general ambience was like something from an exquisite movie set. Audrey turned to Michael saying, "This is absolutely beautiful; is it yours?"

He nodded, smiling, and taking her hand again showed her the kitchen, a bathroom, and the two bedrooms one with a bathroom including a spa, large shower, twin vanities, toilet and bidet connecting to a dressing room with long robes, drawers, mirrors and shelves on each side. The powder room which served the second bedroom and visitors was also beautiful and this bedroom had a large bed, beautiful dressing table and a walk-in-robe with a door connecting to the second bathroom. There was a small study, lined with bookcases, a large desk with a built-in leather top and matching chair. A small grand piano graced the lounge. On one wall built in cupboards and shelving housed a large TV and stereo. There were hints of gold leaf everywhere and the upholstery was exquisite. It was a luxury apartment presented to take your breath away.

Michael led her to a sofa and taking her hand again, he said, "Well, what do you think of it?"

She said again, "It's beautiful, do you live here?"

"No, we bought it a long time ago and it has not been lived in for some years. It is cleaned and aired and occasionally a few friends have stayed here; nothing permanent. I have a small apartment in Kensington which suits me fine as I live alone. I have something similar in Scotland, also adequate. My dear, this apartment has been waiting for you."

Audrey gave him a questioning look with eyebrows raised. "Audrey, I want you to have this apartment to call your own. Thomas is always available for you. I will only be here…well, less than fifty per cent of the time.

I have had time to look at our connection whilst I was away. It is something I cherish. I feel I have been uplifted, thoroughly shaken up and then set down; except I'm not sure my feet have touched the ground as yet. Being with you has been the best time of my life, despite it being such a short time. I feel as though I have known you for years; I have grown to love you. I don't want to consider you not being in my life. I know you would not like to be tied down, so I would place no restrictions on you whatsoever, only ask that here is a base for you, that you share with me when I am able to come to you.

Financially this will cost you nothing, there are charge accounts for you and an abundant bank account will be at your disposal. Caring for you in every way will make my life so worthwhile. Will you allow me to do this?"

Audrey was a little stunned. She wasn't sure how this had happened. How had she created this event? She had not even kissed Michael except

Michael's Proposition

for a quick kiss on the cheek as a thank you and a hug here and there.

She asked what had precipitated his declaration. Michael looking thoughtful suddenly smiled, "You have made me aware of who I really am, with all the nonsense stripped away, all the game playing gone; I guess it is a little like a rebirth. I don't really know what a rebirth is but that is how it feels…

To me you are the embodiment of femininity, wisdom, intelligence, caring, compassion and understanding. You would make a perfect wife or partner… I just realise that I don't know if you can cook, entertain, sew, iron or do any of those wifely things?" He looked at her smiling with raised eyebrows. "None of that matters. You can have a maid, a cook whatever makes you smile. You see how well you have taught me. The idea I have shared with you makes me jump for joy. Now I am talking too much, I am nervous about your answer. Would you like to think about this for a day or so?

Audrey shook her head. "Michael, I am not yet divorced but even if that was so, I could not accept your idea. Being a kept woman does not make me smile and no matter how beautifully it is put, that is what this idea amounts to! When you get to know me better, which I am sure you will if we remain friends, you will realise that I am completely self-sufficient and independent. I appreciate all you have said, I really do, and you have said it so beautifully that I am stuck for the right gentle words of rejection."

She got to her feet and he joined her. Audrey wrapped her arms around him and for the first time lightly kissed him on the lips. She said, "Thank you, but No thank you!"

Michael looked crestfallen. She said, "Michael, please be glad it happened. The new you is a unique being which you always were. Now you are more aware, not just about you but about life: so, don't be sad. I'm so glad it happened. I wouldn't have missed you for the world."

She was silent. "It is time to leave?"

He nodded, and taking her hand he led her away and back to the car.

They were quiet on the way back to her flat. They held hands and when she caught his gaze she smiled at him. Eventually he said, "When your divorce is through, could we get together and talk about this some more. If the charge account and the bank balance offend you, we can leave that out of the equation. It would be only that you live with me, that we could be partners. You would still be as free as a bird, especially so when I am not there. I want you in my life; you can dictate all the terms. May we look at this again at a more appropriate time?"

Audrey kissed his cheek as she said, "No, I'm sorry. In a short time, I will be leaving for America. I want to do some advanced training and that is the place for me to go. I may be away for a few years, but even if it was only a couple, I would still be returning to Australia. England was my home when I was a child; now it is a place to visit and Australia I will always call home. I'm so sorry, Michael. It was not my intention for our relationship to come to this. I really do thank you for your love, but from now on it needs to be at a distance."

They arrived at her flat. Thomas opened the door and Audrey quickly hopped out of the car. Leaning in towards Michael, she kissed him and said, "Well this is it. Goodbye Michael. Thank you so much for everything, but in particular for being you." She closed the door without waiting for a reply, and ran upstairs to her flat. She watched through a curtained window feeling that she couldn't really settle until she saw that the Rolls had gone.

CHAPTER 55

Audrey To The Rescue

Audrey was happy to be home. There was a long letter from Brian in Swaziland. As always it was bright and cheerful. Audrey felt that Brian played the "glad game' because she was aware that anything Brian would consider a liability, even momentarily, would be turned into an asset. This was obvious from his letters. She really felt that he was a kindred soul.

Audrey had mentioned her journey to France and Switzerland with Linda whom he had met at the Scientology Organization. Audrey did not know why she had not told him about Gabriel. She felt that she could; she felt he would understand and be interested. Audrey knew he would be sympathetic and that her happiness was even more important to him that his own. Audrey did not know how she knew this, but her heart told her it was so. She was perhaps reticent because deep down, she felt that the relationship with Brian would one day be important.

Lorraine was happy to see her and ready to hear all her news. They had dinner together and Lorraine told her that there was conflict with Scientology and the Australian Government. Psychiatrists seemed to resent their technology and their success and queried the status of religion granted to the Scientology Organization.

A LIFE of Enlightenment

At Saint Hill, 'New Era Dianetics' (NED) was also available as an extra course. Audrey decided to do this course. It was time to expand her knowledge and she had always been a proponent of learning the technology rather than having it as auditing.

Before she started she went to the student room and as always helped any student with checking out their understanding of the bulletins they were studying.

She wrote to Gabriel, sending him love and telling him of her current plans. His letter was loving and so appreciative of the little notes he was coming across in his home. He wanted to get a week off and visit her but felt it would be a difficult time to ask for leave from the Bank.

Nevertheless, a few days later, he sent her a telegram for her to pick him up at Gatwick airport the following weekend.

Luckily, Audrey had not started her course. She was happy to see him. Lorraine offered to stay with a friend, so they could put the single beds together in their one-bedroom apartment and have the place to themselves for a few days.

Gabriel was ecstatic to be together again, although only a few weeks had passed. They went for walks in the nearby woods. Audrey showed him the tree she had leaned against and constantly read the letters from Clyde and Tiffany. He was amazed that she could do this with no emotion. She explained how this could happen and asked him if there was some area of his life he would like to handle. He told her about the death of his father and Audrey guided him through the incident until it was cleared. He cried tears at one point and seemed to be ashamed, but she held his hand and persisted until he was through it and smiling again.

They talked. She told him about Doctor Gordon, about going to school at three with his help; her engagement to him at five and her jilting of him at 11 years old and about all the philosophical talks they had shared.

Gabriel was entranced. He encouraged her to write a book and share all this wisdom. Audrey said perhaps she would do that one day, as it had been suggested very often, beginning with her headmistress at Grammar school.

Audrey To The Rescue

Audrey had to encourage him to talk about his life, his interests, his friends, because he thought his life was very ordinary by comparison. She explained that everyone had a different journey through life. Hers was a very busy and eventful one because she did not want to return to Earth in her next lifetime, so it was important to get two or maybe three lifetimes squeezed into this one…

Gabriel stared at her. She hugged him and laughed and told him not to take her too seriously as she was only sharing random thoughts which may never eventuate as reality. She relaxed as his expression became normal again and kissed him until he started laughing.

They had fun together. They went for long drives through the English countryside that Audrey had always loved. Her little mini chugged uphill and down dale on its economical petrol consumption; she made picnic hampers and they often stayed away until dusk.

They were a little sad when Gabriel had to leave, and she drove him to the airport. This time he insisted that she walk away first.

Four days after Gabriel had left for Switzerland, just as Audrey was about to start her course, she received a letter from Peter at the Perth organisation stating that a bill would be passed in Parliament banning Scientology. Audrey decided it was time to go home and lend a hand at fixing this new development.

Two days later she was on the first available Qantas flight to Perth.

Audrey had telegraphed her mother saying to expect her but stating that she would find her own way from the airport.

She entered the house with a hidden key and unpacked the few clothes she had brought. It was summer in Australia. She was getting used to going from summer to winter and back again all in the space of a day's flight.

Audrey decided to go into the Scientology organization the next morning, rather than join them partly through the day.

She told them of her plans over the phone and one of the Scientologists who owned a taxi offered to pick her up the following morning.

She was warmly received and congratulated on having completed two levels above Clear. Other Clears were on staff. Audrey listened attentively as she was filled in on the current, now banned situation. Michael, the Guardian of the Org, told her that anyone who lectured or disseminated any part of Scientology was to be immediately arrested and jailed. The World Wide Organization in Saint Hill East Grinstead which Audrey had just left, sent messages that the staff had to continue as normal despite the ban.

However, another development had occurred. A Minister, Mr Graham of the present government, had told Michael the guardian of the Org that if someone was arrested they would be taken to Claremont Mental Hospital and given shock treatment for breaking the law. He said it was all arranged and to take care. No permission was necessary. This was a government edict.

This created consternation among the staff. They had intended to have a lecture on the Perth Esplanade on the coming Sunday, but the repercussions could be severe.

Audrey felt that she was sufficiently advanced at two levels above Clear to handle any consequences, so by volunteering she offered to do the lecture. She was told it had to be done by a staff member. Consequently, Audrey was granted provisional staff member status.

Audrey decided to talk about one of L.R. Hubbard's articles, "The Secret of Greatness." The 'secret' was about the ability to go on loving despite all reasons one should not; despite all provocations to do otherwise. The article stressed that a truly great person did not hate or seek vengeance, but simply understood and went on loving regardless. She asked for many leaflets of the article to be printed so they could be distributed among the spectators, and she needed a handful herself to handle whoever or whatever may crop up.

The lecture and the expected subsequent arrests were broadcast as news items on most of the television and radio stations.

Audrey's father said to her, "I hope you are not going to the Esplanade; this whole thing could turn nasty and I don't want you involved."

Audrey To The Rescue

Audrey said, "I am giving the lecture!" There was dead silence for a moment and then Fred went into his lecturing mode.

When he paused for breath, Audrey said, "When I was young I remember you saying that one had to stand up for what one believed in; You cannot take that back now, because it isn't convenient or because it may not represent safety. I am going so that is that. I will be back. I have the technology to handle this type of thing so don't distress yourself. I will be home around four thirty."

The taxi arrived just as she finished putting on her make-up. Audrey had dressed in a light blue sweet short sleeved dress that came up to the neck with the front covered with small lacy ruffles. She wore a matching headband and white low-heeled shoes.

Although she was almost thirty-three years old she could easily have passed for someone in their very early twenties.

As she went to leave, her mother gave her a brown paper parcel whispering "There's a pair of knickers in there and two pieces of cake, just in case." Audrey smiled and kissed her mother.

Audrey arrived by taxi at the esplanade. Steps leading to a platform had been set up with speakers and a megaphone.

Audrey saw Michael who gave her the pamphlets. She asked where the arresting officers were and Michael said, pointing, "There are four detectives and they are hiding one to each tree."

Audrey said "Do you have their names?"

He shook his head. "They are being incognito."

Audrey went to the first tree and, finding the detective behind it, she introduced herself, gave him a copy of the article, and said, "This is what I will be talking about. When you are ready to arrest me, I will be over there," indicating the platform. "Thank you for coming, enjoy the article."

She repeated this performance behind each tree, and then she climbed the steps onto the platform and picked up the megaphone.

TV cameras and news media ones began to roll. Audrey thanked everyone for coming and then said, "I would like to read you an article by

L. Ron Hubbard about *'The Secret of Greatness'*."

She read the whole article, emphasising the topic of love and understanding, and finished again by saying, "To love in spite of all is the secret of greatness and may very well be the greatest secret in this Universe!"

There was applause from the crowd when she finished. She spoke briefly to Michael and Peter and two or three other Scientologists and then found Dave to take her home in his taxi.

Michael later told her the detectives simply left.

Audrey could understand that it would be difficult to arrest what appeared to be a sweet young girl for talking about love in full view of all the Nationwide TV and media cameras.

Games always have to have opponents, opposite decisions and goals, in order for any game to be played. Imagine saying to a football team, "Go on the field, there is your goal, now play for as long as you like, with no opposition and when you are ready, you leave the field and let the other team do the same." No-one would be interested in playing.

This was a game like any other and followed the same rules. Audrey knew this technology well. All she needed to do to handle the situation was 'ruin the game.'

A few days later she was asked to give a talk within the confines of the Org. It was to be a Sunday evening lecture which was standard practise.

She was shown a small room which was generally used. She queried the size of the room. "Well, we always get twelve faithful people every week." Audrey said, "Move the lecture to the large room and put out ninety chairs. You advertise in the paper, don't you? You must not say my name, but you can state that the title of the lecture will be 'How someone can be a suppressive person.'"

In Scientology the lecturer is considered to be king, so Audrey's requirements were followed without recourse.

She arrived to find eighty people sitting in the chairs plus some plain clothes detectives sitting in the back row.

Audrey thanked everyone for coming, read out some Church notices, and then asked everyone to be upstanding whilst she read out 'The Code of Honour'. The Scientologists who had never stood up for anything in the past, stared at her for a moment, but all stood as she repeated the request. The men in the back row remain seated. She looked at each one in turn and then said. "I am sorry, but I cannot continue until everyone is upstanding." The Scientologists swivelled around to see who was not complying and the whole back row shuffled to their feet. At that time, they became part of the group rather than a separate entity wishing them harm.

Audrey read the creed, talked briefly about the technology surrounding suppressive people, and then with Michael and Peter as a panel, asked for questions. Eventually she ended the evening with tea, coffee and biscuits for all; thusly, the visitors got looked after by the attendees.

Audrey lectured a few more times. She introduced music and songs appropriate to the subject. Attendance was always good, and rumours began to circulate that the ban may be lifted. After a few weeks she began to consider leaving. It was time to move on.

She made reservations to fly to Scotland to complete the next available four levels. She wrote up the duties and functions of the job she had been doing as a temporary staff member so that others could follow any success she had achieved.

CHAPTER 56

"Darling It's Alright to Let it Go"

Audrey completed her levels in record time. It was close to summer in Europe, and although she had returned to England after Scotland, she knew it was time to keep a promise to Gabriel to join him for a holiday around Switzerland. Audrey was really looking forward to seeing him again. At the same time, she felt as though many months rather than weeks had gone by since they had last said goodbye.

She had been writing to him regularly and sending him love. Gabriel had been most concerned about her lecturing when Scientology was banned and feared for her safety. Somehow, he seemed to get access to the Australian news. This was obvious from his letters and on the day she lectured she received a telegram from him asking her to take care and sending all his love.

From Sussex, Audrey called him and arranged a flight for the following week which gave him time to arrange his two weeks leave.

He was overjoyed to hear from her and for Audrey it was cosy and warm to be wrapped in his love even though it was over the telephone.

When they met at the airport they cuddled for a long time before pulling apart enough to kiss. Audrey was swept away by his jubilation. She couldn't stop smiling with him. They held hands on the drive to his apartment, talking only about the feeling of being together again.

After a warm welcome, they had dinner at his sister's restaurant.

In his apartment, Audrey unpacked a few clothes as Gabriel indicated they would be leaving the next day. "Not all your wardrobe will be needed for the next two weeks," he said with a wicked but loving gleam in his eye.

Surprisingly, they were both a little shy and hesitant about making love.

This changed when he said, "I love you so, and now I love your body and your face as you look at me." She responded by saying, "I love you very much. I'm not sure where this will take us but for now being with you is more than enough." Soon they were two sated, sleepy, loving people with tangled limbs.

Audrey had no idea where they were going. As they went through a place she called 'Chur' and found out it was pronounced 'Hooor', she gave up on names and decided to enjoy the driving, the scenery, the different hotels and accommodation that Gabriel had booked in advance, but most of all she was enjoying Gabriel.

They travelled almost every third day. She loved the mountains and lakes…always there were lakes. It seemed that one went up a mountain, down another side, and at the bottom there was a lake and around the lake was built a town. Audrey had never seen anything so picturesque. Switzerland was rapidly qualifying for being her favourite country.

Gabriel was delighted at her response. She remembered some names. Lake Locarno, the warmest climate in Switzerland. Lake Lugano where she paddled a boat on the lake gazing at Switzerland and Italy. Lucerne, Lausanne, all beautiful lakes and towns.

They talked as though communication was going out of style. Other times they held hands or gazed at each other across a tablecloth in a restaurant in a companionable silence. It was peaceful.

"Darling It's Alright to Let it Go"

Audrey knew that Gabriel would propose marriage to her; she turned this over and over in her head. She realized that from Christmas time she had known in the depth of her being that Gabriel was not for her, and yet immediately had begun to wish he was. Now what to respond? Her heart said 'Yes'. Her head said 'No'. Trying to put the two together was not easy. She always ended up with 'I don't know'.

This was unusual. Audrey seldom had more than one thought when a decision was required, and never had regrets.

She decided to shelve the question and just enjoy the holiday. After two weeks they returned; they knew each other even better and seemed even closer than before.

As they neared home, Gabriel stopped the car and asked her if she would like to walk along Lake Zurich, perhaps across the bridge.

She nodded. They held hands. As they were nearing the end of their walk, he stopped and turning her to face him, he told her how much he loved her and said, "Why don't we get married?" The minute the words were out of his mouth she knew the answer was 'No'.

Instead she said, "Darling I am still not a free woman. There are so many things to consider; your family, religion, where to live, my career and my training in Scientology which I wish to continue in America or England; preferably the States as I have had enough of the English weather. I don't see how this could possibly work, not at this time and maybe not even this lifetime. I sound harsh, but we need to be truthful and take an honest look at what we have and where we are going. In some ways it is sad, because the timing is so bad."

In an effort to lighten the moment, she smiled, saying "that rhymes."

Gabriel looked upset. He turned his head away.

Audrey continued, "I have never loved anyone the way I love you. No matter where I am I will always love you, even if it is at a distance. I will never feel disconnected from you; a connection once made is never broken. Do you remember how we cemented the connection we already had from even some previous lifetime, in the beginning of our relationship?

That connection will always, *always* be there."

Audrey said all this calmly, but she could feel the catch in her throat and her eyes were beginning to tear.

She concentrated on pulling herself together. She reminded herself that hearts did not break, they just stretched with exercise.

Gabriel was silent. He looked crestfallen.

Audrey wrapped her arms around him and hid her face in his shoulder. She took three deep breaths. She turned his face to look at him, kissed him softly, saying, "Always you will be my knight in shining armour. We found each other when my life was confused. Your love made it orderly and more sense than it had been for a while. Even more reasons to love you, yet I only love you because of who you are and for this I thank you!"

He said, "What can I say. You have said so much and even though it makes sense, I do not see how I can want to go on if you are not in my life?"

She replied, "But I always will be, not physically but always spiritually. We can write to each other, keep in touch and if you ever come to Australia perhaps we can connect. Who knows what the future holds? Always I will love you!"

He smiled. "And I will love *you* forever." Audrey kissed him and held him close.

They went to the restaurant and then to the apartment. Audrey sorted out her clothes and packed. They still had a weekend before Gabriel had to return to work, but she knew it was best to leave in the morning and give him time to adjust.

They lay apart in bed until she slid an arm under his head and pulled him towards her, cuddling him against her body. She could feel his grief. She said, "Darling it's alright to let it go." She felt him shake his head.

He said, "I will never find anyone to love that comes even close to you; you have no idea how unique you are; you are the most wise, the most loving, compassionate, generous person that I have ever met. I don't think there will be another that comes even close to you."

Audrey said, in an attempt to lighten the situation, "Perhaps we should

"Darling It's Alright to Let it Go"

say thank you for that. One of me is probably all the Universe can stand!"

Gabriel cuddled up even further. He began to kiss her, saying, "May we make love; just one last time?"

She said, "Of course," returning his kisses and pulling him even closer. They gently made soft love but after they had climaxed they both began to cry. They wept for what might have been.

Audrey was reminded of the first time they made love, when she had shed a few tears at the end. At that time, it was a release of emotion; this time it was similar, but emotion tinged with sadness.

They had an uneasy sleep. Gabriel was up early bringing the coffee. Showered and dressed they left for the airport. When it was time to board the plane, she hugged him and said, "It's your turn to walk away." He nodded and left. This time she watched him until he got lost in the crowd. Taking three deep breaths she boarded the plane ready for the next event of her journey.

There was packing to do. Three letters from Brian awaited her, full of news and his thoughts on life. She could tell from the tone of his letters that he was more than a little fond of her. She was glad he was in Swaziland. At the moment another romantic love in her life was more than she wished to handle. Audrey wondered if it was ever really possible to have a platonic friendship with a member of the opposite sex. She remembered Jack her draftsman once saying that a platonic friendship was a play for the man and a tonic for the woman. The thought made her smile. Always he was amusing.

She arrived in England, caught a taxi to her flat, and started packing for America. Audrey booked by telephone for the Briefing course in the Saint Hill Scientology Centre in Los Angles, arranged a flight, and within two days she was at the airport and ready to depart, after a fond farewell to Lorraine and some of her friends at Saint Hill England.

CHAPTER 57

America

Audrey arrived in the USA in July 1979. It was summer; not as warm as she had expected. It seemed a little cloudy as though there was a haze over the sky.

She went straight to the Saint Hill Organization, to check on accommodation. They sent her in a taxi with her luggage to an apartment in Coronado Street, walking distance from the Org. The taxi man helped her up the steps to an apartment on the second floor. A dark-haired girl with glasses and a smile opened the door. Her name was Marilyn. She seemed to be close to Audrey's age; slim and pretty behind the large black rimmed glasses she was wearing

Audrey unpacked; explored the rest of the apartment, especially the kitchen, and conferred with Marilyn about food and grocery shopping and the nearest bank.

Armed with directions, she found the bank, changed money and travellers' cheques for American funds, and went grocery shopping. Audrey was used to supermarkets, but not like this one. There was a whole aisle devoted to cereals. There seemed to be an excess of almost everything. Twenty-six aisles were not enough. Around the checkout counters and along the walls

A LIFE of Enlightenment

where customers entered were cards, magazines, stationery of all descriptions, vitamins and health items, booths to order tickets for various events or sign up for insurance, health benefits etc. To Audrey it seemed more like a complete life store rather than just a supermarket. There were also two security guards near the entry and exits. There was not anything even close to these ideas in Australia, or England, and even in the one supermarket she had been to in Switzerland. She was intrigued.

She staggered back to the apartment, with her parcels, filled up the kitchen and the fridge, and went to talk to Marilyn about dinner.

However, Marilyn only wanted one shelf in the fridge and another in a kitchen cupboard. She had a boyfriend on a different course and spent time with him eating out. She told Audrey it was cheap to eat out. You could have a huge breakfast for only a dollar twenty, so what was the use of cooking for yourself.

Audrey, however, liked cooking, and resolved to mainly do her own meals.

The next day she went onto the Briefing course, which consisted of six different levels. Audrey was given a twin with whom to work. Her name was Shelia and she was from Melbourne. They were the only two Aussies on the Briefing course. Each level consisted of reading, understanding and then getting checked out on bulletins or books. There were many tapes to be listened to and also checked out to make sure that the data was known and could be applied. Modelling clay was to be used to demonstrate understanding and application of all that had been learned.

At the end of each level she had to find someone to audit on the processes for that level. She decided she needed to make friends so that she would have other people, other than her twin. She knew she needed to practise her auditing skills as much as possible.

At the end of the First level she earned a red ribbon with a medallion which she wore around her neck. It signified that she had completed a level without a pink slip and with all her auditing ending up with very happy people.

Just after she completed this level, she was turning a corner when she collided with a tall, bulky, rather handsome man. He was dark haired, brown eyed with a light olive skin. Audrey assumed he was probably of Italian ancestry. The folders they were carrying went everywhere. Papers skimmed over the floor, with both of them scrambling after them, Audrey leaned against the wall to sort out all she had rescued. The collision gentleman joined her with a smile. "Hi," he said, holding out a free hand. "John Rafanello, what's your name?'

When she told him and apologised for the collision he laughed and said, "Best bump I've had for ages. What a neat accent! Where are you from?"

Audrey filled him on her origins including being born and living her first fifteen years in England; especially after he queried what he thought must be an Australian accent. They talked about the course she was doing, and he informed her about the New Era Dianetics course he was doing. He said he had already completed the briefing course.

After a while they agreed to help each other by John auditing Audrey and Audrey auditing John on their different courses. Looking at John carefully, Audrey had some misgivings. However, he seemed very affable and constantly called her 'Neat 'and 'Cool'; so she decided to see if he could be 'neat and cool' also. Gazing at him she decided that a makeover would be very appropriate.

Audrey decided it would be applicable for John to do a program she wrote for him before she would be prepared to audit him. She told him she had certain conditions that had to be met; that she would write them out for him and give them to him tomorrow. Audrey also told him that he was under no obligation to do the program but that she felt the end result would 'make him smile'. He was intrigued and amused by this expression and said he would give it serious consideration.

That evening she wrote out the program:

1. *Wash and iron all your clothes or dry-clean if applicable.*

2. Wear clean underwear and socks and a clean shirt every day.
3. Shower and shave every day.
4. Polish your shoes.
5. Get a haircut.
6. Work out what you need to do to lose weight (I am willing to help you with this).
7. I would like to see where you live, please! If it needs attention or cleaning, I can help you by telling you the easiest way to do things or give you whatever education you desire if no-one has ever shown you how to make it clean and efficient. Remember, your environment is a reflection of you.

Audrey explained, "Being clean and looking good is 'super cool and super neat'. If you do the above you will end up with an image which is a correct reflection of the obvious gorgeous being that you have projected to me, and a credit to the unique John Rafanello that you are creating yourself to be. You see, you as a being makes me smile. Love and Light, Audrey."

She gave him the program at the end of a lunch break, leaving no time to chat. She was surprised and pleased when he said the next day at their agreed meeting, "I have started your program; what do you think?"

He stood before her with a big grin on his face. He was clean and his clothes were clean. The shoes still needed attention, but this was a wonderful start and Audrey told him so.

He simply said, "See you tomorrow at lunch break," as he left. The following day, only the haircut remained to be done. "That's for Sunday," he said, "our only day off course. Now I have to wash and iron again and clean my shoes again and then it's time to tackle the weight issue and my apartment."

He grinned at her. "Well, do I meet with your approval?" he said, bowing. She nodded, smiling at him. "Well done. 10 gold stars."

She stuck out her hand, but he lifted her with ease clean off the ground and gave her a loud smack on the lips. She was set down again before she had time to resist.

"I deserved that reward," he said, laughing

She made a time to come to his apartment, one week the following Sunday. This gave him a little time to start on that project. The courses ran from nine o'clock in the morning to ten o'clock at night for six days a week. Free time was not abundant on Scientology courses. Studies took priority.

She worked hard, though learning a subject that she thought was excellent made her devotion easy.

On the Sunday, she went to John's apartment after meeting him at a nearby restaurant for breakfast. She was amazed at the size of the helpings. Watching the plates come from the kitchen she began to understand how John's size had blossomed.

During breakfast John said, "I have some questions for you." Audrey smiled at him. "Fire away!"

"Are you by any chance the Australian Scientologist from Perth who audited a dead person and brought him back to life?"

She was amazed. "How did you hear about that? It was a long time ago."

John fixed his gaze on her, "Well, answer the question, was it you? Why are you looking so uncomfortable?"

Audrey sighed, "Because it wasn't the big deal that others think it was. On a free evening that I originally went too, I was told that processing was so powerful that it could probably revive the dead! I took it literally, so when my boss died at work I rang Stanley at the Org and asked him what process I should run on my boss. He took a while to respond, but he gave me *'Give me that hand; thank you'*. It worked, but it took a long time and afterwards I told Stanley that another one would have been better."

Audrey could see that John was amused and a little amazed. "What process did you recommend?" he asked, with a small smile on his face.

Audrey said, "Well, Ron says that the way you improve someone's ability is to find something they can do and get them to do it better. My boss was sitting in his office chair and couldn't give me his hand by himself, but he could *'sit his body in that chair'*, so I felt this might have worked faster and was obviously something he could do. I might have been wrong because I had never processed anyone before and had only done the five-night free course, so I guess it was a little presumptuous for me to suggest anything at all."

John laughed out loud. He scooped Audrey up in his arms and twirled her round and round. When he set her down again, he said, "I think you're amazing, absolutely amazing; don't ever change. I'm so glad that I'm about to experience you as an auditor. I can't wait."

One day after John finished auditing her, he asked her about wins and losses in life, saying "I feel you must have a unique way of dealing with them, particularly the losses."

She smiled and said well there is no such thing as a loss, it depends only on a viewpoint, a consideration, an evaluation of the rightness or wrongness of the event. John nodded, then said, "OK, suppose you were in charge of a destroyer, and a submarine that you had been playing cat and mouse with for some time sent a torpedo which almost cut your ship in half; you knew you were sinking, how would you view that?" Audrey was quiet for a moment, and then smiling she said. "I would break radio silence and send the commander of the submarine a message that said… *'It is my pleasure to inform you that we have just sunk your torpedo'*. After dropping the body, I would look forward to my next adventure…exploring the universe…picking daisies, or heading for the nearest hospital to pick up a body."

John roared with laughter. When he calmed down he asked, "Have you always turned liabilities into assets?"

Audrey smiled at him saying, "Well, I really don't know what else to do!"

John said, "I need to ask you if you can tell me in a nutshell your philosophy for living? Do you ask yourself questions for example when something crops up to be processed?"

"Not exactly! Questions that may be relevant in life, for me are *'For what purpose?'* and *'Does it make me smile?'*. That sometimes helps me to decide if I want to go along with a suggestion, whether it is positive or negative.

But my overall consideration is that **'everything is always perfect for my journey'** no matter how it looks to others or even to me in the first few minutes."

John smiled, asking, "And that's it, is it?"

When she nodded, he started laughing again. She laughed with him but said, "Let's get back to your program." And so they did.

CHAPTER 58

Disillusionment with the Org and Return to Australia

Audrey finished the six levels of the briefing course with her ribbon still intact, despite the odd rough patch along the way. She was beginning to question the application of administration, supervision and the ethics as practised in the teaching and learning environment.

Ron had brought out the Conditions formulas which were considered ethics for living. Audrey had no argument with the formula which she thought were applicable to the action or job that one was doing. However, the staff assigned to apply these conditions did not do so correctly; they applied and labelled the being and not the job or the action. This was an invalidation of the being and good indicators became very absent with collapsed esteem all over the place. When the being objected or did not wish to comply, even lower and more negative conditions were assigned. The whole tone and public empathy of the Scientology organizations began to collapse. Instead of this being investigated and rectified, even higher but not necessarily technical staff were brought in around the world. As these people were interested in ethics, policy and administration, they did not cognize that the philosophy and technology of Scientology was being severely violated and that this was the root of the trouble. The dysfunction and discrepancies were more and more instigated with horrifying results.

Audrey wrote a letter to Ron explaining and requesting that the formulas be clarified. According to Ron's Policy, *'All mail sent to me shall be received by me'*. This however did not eventuate. She did not receive a reply.

It was a relief for Audrey to meet up with Harry, a former twin from East Grinstead, during the Scientology convention held in Los Angeles. He invited her to San Francisco for a holiday to the home he shared with his wife Marga. "Perhaps," he had said, "you could give us some auditing in exchange." Audrey was happy to agree. When she explained that a Case supervisor was also required, she introduced John and found he was very acceptable as her accompaniment. They went to Belmont in San Francisco for a few weeks but ended up staying for eighteen months. Marga and Harry had many friends who wanted auditing. In turn, they recommended others who also wanted some of the wins they were experiencing. Audrey shared a room with John but with separate beds. However, this did not last long. John always seemed to be creeping into her bed, wanting to make love and handling her in such a way that she felt it would be churlish to refuse.

The San Francisco org decided the group around Audrey and John were clients who had been stolen from their organisation. It took quite a lot of handling by John and Audrey to quieten the hostility that was being shown.

For Audrey it was another source of disillusionment, evidenced by Scientologists in an organisation distrusting or being envious of results produced by another.

Her visa again came up for renewal. The original six months when they expired had been handled by Audrey talking to the immigration official, offering to buy him coffee and doughnuts at his cafeteria, and getting an extension. This had been handled two more times although he always insisted on paying. They talked of Australia, kangaroos, and koala bears, but he had said on her last visit that he could not extend her visa any more. Now she approached him with John at her side. John did not hesitate but simply pointed out that they were going to be married. An extension was granted but only for another six months.

Disillusionment with the Org and Return to Australia

Audrey had been aware for some time of John's interest in marriage, but trusted she had forestalled a proposal by telling him in the beginning of their relationship that she would never marry him. She had done this consistently with anyone who was exhibiting too much interest, because she felt it was honest and she was also getting tired of handling proposals. Somehow it did not work. Perhaps it was a challenge to be overcome by the interested party; perhaps she was too gentle in her statement. Some indicated that she was presumptuous; and maybe that was true in the beginning but sooner or later... When someone did propose, always she asked, "For what purpose?"

So far, the answers had always been a solution to a problem. Ranging from 'You complete me', to 'I need you', to 'I could be a success if only' or 'I could be anything with you by my side', and so forth. Audrey did not want to be anyone's solution or necessity or crutch, no matter the amount of love professed.

Now John was busy telling friends and clients that he was engaged to Audrey. When she objected, he pointed out that the immigration department had spies everywhere and one had to be careful.

They decided to leave San Francisco and return to Los Angeles to do the combined courses seven and eight. They twinned on this course. On the first day, the students were told that everything on the course was confidential and therefore no one, not a student or supervisor, was allowed in the room. They were told that the room had to be cleaned by the students and therefore the floor had to be cleaned by crawling around to pick up any offending article. Audrey promptly left the room and returned with a vacuum cleaner which she had seen on her way upstairs. The students were smiling at her return. The supervisor tried to give her a pink slip which Audrey refused to accept. She said, "You cannot flunk me for knowing and operating on a knowingness. Scientology means 'knowing how to know'. Accepting that pink slip is against my religion."

She was to find that that statement was to be used by her often as the course and auditing progressed.

A LIFE of Enlightenment

A few months later John and Audrey graduated as Class Eights: two of the most highly trained auditors on the planet. Audrey decided it was time to leave and go home to Perth Australia. They communicated this to Marga and Harry in San Francisco, who communicated it to many of the clients they had been auditing. Five people decided to accompany them and booked a passage on the same ship. They were quite a small but very friendly and happy group sailing to a new adventure.

On arrival, Audrey decided to stay at her parents' home. She assisted John and the others to find rental accommodation not far away.

Her mother was delighted to see her after two and a half years. She insisted that Audrey make an immediate phone call to a firm of country builders who had been calling for the last two weeks.

Audrey did not recognise the builder's name, nor did her mother know how they had got her name.

Puzzled, she rang the number only to be asked by the owner of the firm if she could have lunch and discuss a proposal the next day.

She agreed and was picked up by the owner and his father the next lunchtime. The father, Tom, had retired and as he smilingly said was there only to lend support. Maynard, the son was tall, good looking and seemed very amiable.

Audrey found over lunch that an Interior Designer Furniture manufacturer called Anton Jansen who had worked for some of her former clients from Keith Tennant Homes has been impressed by their praise of her designs. When the country builders with whom he was acquainted had asked him if he knew of a good house designer her name had naturally come to mind.

Audrey told Tom and Maynard that she had just returned from the USA and was seriously considering starting her own business as a building designer. However, they were persuasive and finally she agreed to work with them for one year.

There were three letters awaiting her at her mother's home; two from Brian in Swaziland and one from Gabriel. After their almost three-year

Disillusionment with the Org and Return to Australia

separation, Gabriel wrote that he had met a stewardess on an airflight some time ago and that they had decided to marry. Audrey had answered his infrequent correspondence over many months. However, his letter stated that he had confided his past love to his future wife. She was not happy with any type of ongoing relationship with Audrey and insisted that all photos and letters had to be destroyed and no further correspondence could ever be entered into. His letter asked Audrey to understand and begged her never to write to him again.

Audrey was shocked. She felt that Gabriel was not being very discerning if these were the conditions of his marriage. However, she also felt that it was not her place to interfere, only to comply.

She went to see John to tell him that she intended to go back to her old profession and that although she would always be available to help with his students after hours and on weekends, their close work proximity was no more. She had four days left to find an apartment, settle in, and be ready to start her new job on the Monday.

She divided the funds left from working with John, gave him half, and was able to find a one bedroom furnished apartment on the Esplanade South Perth overlooking the Swan river and only a stone's throw from the ferry. She spent some of the money leasing a small car and getting her driver's license up to date.

Audrey spent one day moving in and then a day with John and the students. They took a ferry ride to the City; visited KingsPark, a rare 100-acre area of natural beauty, on the edge of the City.

She went to sleep in her new apartment, loving her view, and looking forward to her new job, and driving her little Volkswagen.

CHAPTER 59

Audrey's New Job at Overmans

On Monday Audrey met the staff at Overmans New Homes. There were eight members in all. Three of them seemed to work outside. The Manager, Basil Dolan, was a former Bank manager; the accountant, a young man named Bryan Smyth; an estimator named Vince Walker, and two salesmen. They were not very welcoming and seemed very reticent when Audrey tried to draw them into conversation. She was given a desk in an office and soon arranged her drawing implements, notebooks and pencils. She was aware that her job was to design country homes for their clients. As these homes were mainly to be built on farms, individual design was appropriate according to the needs of the farmer and his family.

After a few days, she spent some time in the accountant's office asking how she would find the clients who needed something for her to design. She was shown a two-page advertisement which had been placed in the Sunday newspaper and for which the office expected a response. So far, not even a single phone call had eventuated. Audrey read the supplement and was appalled. There was a photo of each staff member and a written profile below each one. There was not really anything the country clients needed to know when they were looking for a builder. Audrey persuaded Bryan to come outside the office for lunch. After pinning him down, she found that the manager Basil had done the advertising for the last few months. None of the ads had produced any results. Brian pointed out that Basil considered that this was a family of well-established well-known country builders, and that was what people needed to know. The latest two-page supplement had cost a fortune and left the firm almost impoverished. Perhaps it was a bad time in the country, although the last harvest had been good... The firm had not had a new client for some months. Further investigation revealed that there was only sufficient funds in the last of the overdraft to pay two weeks' wages. She asked why she had been asked to join a company that was on the verge of bankruptcy. Bryan shook his head. He said the life of the firm was at the bottom as the bank would call up the overdraft and that would be the end. Audrey said, "When you keep doing the same sequence of events, you get the same result; even if it is a positive sequence. This advertising has been a negative one. I need to think about this. Advertising is something that I do know about, but doing anything is going to involve treading on toes." The staff were at sixes and sevens with each other. The manager was not popular, but as he had been also the best man at the owner's wedding...

Audrey gave the whole situation some thought; should she resign? Perhaps there was a reason she was there? She went to see Maynard and asked if she could place an advertisement promoting design in the top right-hand corner of page three of *The Countryman* and *The Farmer's Weekly*. It would only be about two columns wide and five inches deep. She got an OK for this but made the stipulation that all enquiries would be handled by her, as the firm's designer.

The ads appeared two days later. Within a week she had ten enquiries and eight appointments within the next few days. Some of the further enquiries were dealt with a lengthy phone call and then she sent the salesman to go to see them after careful briefing on what had already been said to each client. She saw each set of clients herself, got Bryan to take them to lunch and had a preliminary sketch available on their return.

Audrey's New Job at Overmans

Having listened carefully and in detail to what was needed and wanted, the clients were surprised and pleased with the results. Audrey handled them carefully but firmly, promoting them to a working drawing after getting a rough price from the estimator. Although the clients were there for the most part of a day, they left happy to pay an initial deposit. Within three weeks, Audrey felt the firm was moving out of danger and would soon be in a better place. which would stop the bank taking further action. She felt that the Manager Basil, as a former Bank manager, would relish this and be amiable to change.

The whole tone of the firm rose as work became available and there was good response to the advertisements. Audrey explained why the ads worked and suggested a policy for all future ads. All ads must be written from the viewpoint of the reader, not the writer. Tell your clients what *they* need to know that promotes dealing with your firm. Do not write ads that tell them what *you* think they should need to know.

The manager came to see her after she had handled the initial response. Audrey was coming up for air. She expected to be thanked. That was not to be. He was critical; he pointed out that he was in charge of managing and advertising, and seemed uninterested in anything she had to say. He obviously felt his position was usurped and very threatened. Audrey was not contrite. She explained that she understood but that the situation seemed to be urgent, as the firm was fairly obviously going bankrupt and something workable needed to be done. Audrey told him of her background and her success with Keith Tennant Homes, but to no avail.

The father and the owner came to her office. They congratulated her on the success and asked her if Basil could now take over the clients and the advertising, and if Audrey would only do design. Audrey pointed out that Basil was not willing to listen or learn and that his records over the last six months spoke for themselves. Basil had already told Maynard that what they'd been doing was very workable and that Audrey should design and have no authority for anything else.

Maynard was very uncomfortable through their talk. Audrey had the impression that he would like to get rid of Basil but did not know how to go about it. Audrey suggested he talk to the rest of the staff and listen to their viewpoints.

Two weeks later, with no goodbyes, Basil left the office.

Overmans continued to do well, with lots of work on hand and more in the offing. On the home front, Audrey had calls from Clyde and Tiffany who wanted to seek her advice. When they arrived, it was to say that their relationship was in trouble and could Audrey assist. She got them to separately write down their goals for the relationship and for themselves.

When this was done, the next step was to compare notes. For the relationship, it was appropriate to look at compromise for conflicting ideas. If these ideas or if the compromise could not be agreed, going separate pathways was indicated. Audrey left them to do this exercise at her kitchen table. When she returned, they told her that their individual goals were very different and their relationship goals also clashed. They had decided to go their separate ways. Audrey was not surprised but wished them well.

Audrey finally got the name again of the man who had recommended her to Overmans. His name was Anton Jensen. She called him, thanked him, and made an appointment to see him at his furniture place at Osborne Park. Apparently, his assessment of her was based on a few of Audrey's clients who had come to him for furniture once their home was built. Because he had also seen the finished homes, he had been impressed by the design and attention to detail, particularly in the cupboard line. He said that he had also formed an opinion of her in other ways.

Anton invited her to lunch. He was tall, very good looking, and very philosophical about life, particularly women. Audrey found him interesting and delighted in his company. He had a brilliant head of hair; thick and wavy; a mixture of pepper with some salt. She met his son who assisted him in the furniture store. His wife had gone back to Holland and he did not expect her to return. From his viewpoint, they had come to a parting of the ways some considerable time before.

They had an unusual and absorbing time over lunch. Audrey found him interesting, charming and exciting. He was Dutch, and she had been told that Dutch people were generally dour and rather stoic. There was no way that Anton would ever fit into this category.

Anton told Audrey he was intrigued by his vision of her and had wished to meet her for many months. He seemed overjoyed that she had contacted him and was not in the least reticent about his interest in getting to know her better. They had a leisurely lunch covering a wide range of subjects, but generally it had a base of being an unusual philosophical repartee. Always, Audrey was aware of his interest and his touch on her hand or her arm at the slightest excuse. He discussed relationships. Audrey joined in with her usual philosophical bent which seemed to delight him and promote further points of agreement. Altogether things seemed to be moving at a very fast pace.

Anton talked about women as opposed to men: "Women, apart from their breasts which are unbelievably beautiful, are all hidden. Their main delights are not on show even when they are naked. Men, however, have everything boldly on display so that even their desire cannot be hidden. However, when a man's heart is involved, this can create a little mystery, even when there is no mystery about their bodies. Women do not give themselves easily to men without flowing some affection or love. Some men do not require this, thinking only of the sensation of self-gratification."

Anton went on. "For me that is not enough. I think the mating act should be one of respect, affection towards the spirit of the person, and preferably love. When **WE** make love as we surely will, for me that will already be there. I feel I somehow know you and have loved you a little at a distance for some time, and this meeting has only served to confirm it."

Audrey was a little taken aback by this prophesy. "It would be a mistake to leave me out of this equation, Anton. I appreciate your attention and even perhaps your intention. I confess to having the most seductive lunch that I have ever experienced. I am giving you ten gold stars which is my highest reward. Tell me, do you find this approach is always a winner or do you find some reassessing necessary for individual prospects?"

He was silent. He rose and went to pay the cheque. She watched him walk back. She detected a hurt look on his face, or was that part of the plan? Audrey was not sure. She decided not to question it. They were silent walking towards her car. He opened the door, bent into the car to kiss the top of her head and said, "I will call you when the time is right." Audrey casually said, "Lovely, and thank you once again for…a breath-taking lunch." She waved as she drove away.

She did not hear from him again for 10 days. He invited her to dinner one Wednesday night. She wondered if the silence had been planned or whether she had offended him by naming the game. Or was this a planned campaign to keep up her interest and also confuse her. They had three more dinners, and two lunches, over a period of a month. Always they talked. Always he seemed to want to explain himself as though he was concerned that she only saw the surface of him; the part he presented to the world. The prospector. Here, Anton did not do her justice. Audrey almost always saw beneath the surface to the being that was orchestrating the dialogue; the event or the play in motion.

She decided to stay in present time and only handle things from that viewpoint. He always seemed delighted to see her. "I have been busy in the business; but I have missed you. I would have called you earlier had time permitted."

"What exactly did you miss?"

Anton studied her for a moment. "It isn't easy to define. I am aware of the friendly vivaciousness that you present to the world and the certainty that goes with the awareness of any event in which you are participating. Yet always there is a part of you, a very calm part that I feel I will never get a hold of. It is separate; perhaps it is sacred; sometimes it feels that way; like a 'do not disturb sign'. Yet I feel it could never be disturbed. Am I making sense?"

Audrey smiled. "Perfect sense. I have been aware of a part of me that watches everything that goes on. There is no judgement, no suggestions for handling a situation; only a part of me that is a spectator; that is interested and certain of my ability to handle. Perhaps this is what you sense. If so, ten gold stars. Being aware of that is unusual and does your own awareness much merit. Well done!"

They felt closer after this talk. When Anton suggested going to her apartment after their latest luncheon, she simply nodded her head. During all their time together, the sexual tension in the air was palpable. He would take her hand, turn it over; lightly run his finger over the inside of her wrist, just where her hand joined. Trickling tiny electrical vibrations would run up her arm. He had a whole box of seductive tricks. There was a spot behind her knee that he gently ran his fingers over and she would start to melt. Spotting them did not make them ineffective. Audrey, in defence, somewhat spoilt the game by telling him the exact effect he was producing. Anton felt that she should enjoy it rather than talk about it. Audrey smiled and said her usual lazy rejoinder, "yes well."

Now alone in her apartment, it was a relief to kiss him. He was the expert she expected. He did not rush her, but slowly slipped off her clothes until only her underwear was left. Picking her up he laid her gently on one side of the bed, turned back the blankets on the other side and tucked her in warmly between the sheets.

He removed his clothes. Audrey sat up in bed and watched him. When he was naked, she was reminded of their talk at their first lunch, when he said, 'men and their desire are not hidden'. Here was everything up front so to speak. She removed her bra and briefs, tossed them onto a nearby chair and lifting the cover she invited him in.

Every part of her body was given his gentle attention. She was lovingly and almost respectfully kissed all over. As he moved she could feel his erection rock hard as it bumped against a leg. She reached down feeling that more participation other than stroking his upper body and kissing him was required. He captured her hand, kissed all her fingertips, then her mouth and face, and whispered "Not now my love. It will be too much."

She resigned herself to total acceptance and approval of all she was experiencing. He gently tipped her over, lifted her to her knees and slowly but gently entered her from behind. She leaned forward enjoying the sensation. His thrusts were slow but thorough. She could feel him twirling around inside. She climaxed quickly. As she did, he said 'Oh my god!' and gripped her body very firmly.

It was quiet. Audrey had just got her breath back when Anton said, "May I turn you over?" She nodded. He entered her again immediately, but lay on top of her, kissing her breasts and running his hands down her body. He reached over and pulled a pillow and slid it under her hips. His twirling motion began again, slow and steady. This time his twirling was affecting her clitoris and she knew she was about to orgasm again. She tried to indicate this, but as she started to moan he said 'oh my god' again and then joined her with his own climax. It was breathtaking.

He lay next to her, one arm underneath her neck as he pulled her close to cuddle. He was silent for a while, bending his head to kiss the top of her head as she lay on his chest.

Suddenly he said, "That was absolutely devastating and completely unexpected!" She said obligingly "Yes. well" wondering what was coming next.

Anton stroked her hair and an arm, he continued. "When you climax you hold nothing back. It is like a complete surrender. You have quite loud, deep moans that come from your very core. My 'oh my gods' were very involuntary because your orgasm was incredible. If I was a cow I would have thought I had been thoroughly milked."

Audrey started to giggle. Between little laughs, she said, "Was this alright or would you like some changes?"

He joined in her laughter. "My love, I wouldn't change it for the world. No man would. You are an incredible lover and so unexpected. You are so dignified, almost regal sometimes, that the thought of you surrendering to love-making this way could hardly be comprehended. You are a very unique surprise. I should have expected this because you are a surprise in all you do and say. It is an education just chatting to you. You are wise beyond your years and you have a very exciting look at life and the world. Sometimes I have felt that you are not from this world but an older and wiser one; yet here you are, in bed with me and being loved like I hope no one has ever loved you before."

Audrey said, "Thank you for that. I'm glad you enjoyed it because I certainly did. You are a unique and exciting lover and I'm happy to have you as mine today."

Anton laughed. "Not just today, but all the days of my life would suit me fine. You talk as though this love is fleeting, why is this? Did I not please you? Do you dislike me as a person?"

"Yes, you did and No to the last question."

She sat up, then laying across his chest she kissed him gently and stroked his hair. Laying a hand to the side of his face and gazing into his eyes, she said, "Let us go with the flow, one day at a time. We will enjoy each other. You are a wonderful lover and I do enjoy you as a friend and companion."

Anton smiled, stroked her hair, kissed her gently and said "Ik hou van ye." Audrey said, "that must be Dutch. What does it mean?"

I will tell you one day but in the meantime I will say this every time I see you and soon you will learn at least this small part of my language and say it to me.

Audrey wanted to please him. She told him of the enjoyable effect his love-making created. He smiled and promised more. Audrey said, "Well, let us not waste time." So they didn't.

The rather intense and constant affair with Anton lasted for only two months. At the end of that time, he told her that his wife was returning from Holland and wanted him to consider saving their marriage.

Despite Anton's protest, Audrey immediately ended the affair and advocated not seeing him at all while the situation existed. He said he did not wish to save his marriage. Audrey told him it was his duty as a husband to always do his best to keep his vows. She was adamant and he was aware that this was not a force with which to argue. Reluctantly he left, promising not to call her as requested.

CHAPTER 60

Walter

Audrey threw her time into her job and also helping John as he trained and audited the clients who had accompanied them to Australia. Some of Overmans' staff had also become his clients, but she left these strictly to John.

John still wanted her to come to work with him full time. Despite the fact that Audrey felt that the technology of Scientology was excellent in many ways, the way in which the organization world-wide was being administered did not make her smile. She felt that she did not wish to participate in this new regime. Audrey had not been to the Perth organization since her return.

Overmans required a quick but fairly accurate price assessment of each house as she designed it. Audrey had never done pricing, but she telephoned Keith Tennant her old boss, and passed on his guidelines. Although his expertise related to City work, she felt that it could serve as a base with loadings added for transport and differing labour prices in the country.

The firm was expanding. Audrey agreed they needed a full-time receptionist and suggested Tiffany for the job, and also her own brother Charles for an in-house building consultant. She spent time with him showing him how to sketch and alter plans. Tiffany was easy to train and was naturally social in her outlook. Always Audrey stressed in training the purpose of things, as she felt that always made it easier to learn. Charles was bright and intelligent. He had worked in a builder's office, so he was fairly conversant with procedure. Tiffany was an instant hit. She flirted with all the male personnel. Audrey was aware that she would eventually seduce one of them, and felt Charles, her own brother, may be the most likely candidate. She sighed over this but let it go. It would be like trying to stop the sun coming up.

When Audrey had first arrived from Switzerland some years before, she had brought with her a cupboard that housed a folding bed. At the time, she had contacted a wholesale firm that specialized in beds. The Manager came to see her. He turned out to be Walter Dixon, an old friend who used to manage a section of a large Real Estate firm in the terrace opposite Keith Tennant Homes. Audrey often sent clients requiring a block of land to his office. Occasionally he would call at her office to thank her, have a coffee, and 'as always an interesting chat'.

While she was in the USA he had left Real Estate to manage this large company and now here he was, inspecting her bed. "Unfortunately," Walter said, "It is not the sort of thing we could or would manufacture. So sorry Audrey, it is a great concept but not for us."

She had not seen him since, but she remembered the lack of excitement he had for his present position. When a situation arose to negotiate with a transportable company for further work for Overmans, Audrey knew she had more than enough to handle, and needed someone else to negotiate. She called Walter Dixon and asked him if he would be interested in managing this aspect of the business.

He was, and soon he became another staff executive. He proved to be invaluable. Skilful at negotiating, always with the firm's best interest at heart.

He took her to lunch. There was something familiar about his energy, as though she had known it before. He complimented her on what she had done for Overmans. He said, "you have made them into a team with a common purpose; do you realise what skill it takes to take a bunch of people who were at cross purposes and barely talking to each other into the staff you now have; happy, willing to cooperate and working as a team? Apart from all this, I understand you pulled the company away from bankruptcy in a short time. Audrey said, "Where are you getting this information?"

"From the staff. I understand that all of them have also gone to someone called John Rafanello for some training and counselling. I should like to meet this gentleman. Could you arrange it?"

She said "of course" and arranged to take him after work that day.

Walter also did some work with John. She did not ask or find out why, as all the sessions were confidential; however, Walter did tell her that he was separated from his wife and that he had always wanted to be a politician, but never could be as his wife did not socialise well and refused to entertain. It was amazing the things that could be shared over lunch.

At one stage he pointed out that if Audrey had been his wife, everything would have been perfect. He came for dinner one evening to her apartment and discovered that she loved to cook. From his viewpoint, this sealed her fate.

She shared some of her past with him. The communication and shared confidences brought them closer. One evening, as he was about to leave he took her in his arms and lightly kissed her. Drawing back, he looked at her and said, "Was that alright?"

Audrey smiled. "Why not?"

He was quiet, gazing at her face. "I feel you are my friend and I do not want to jeopardise that for the world."

"Why would it?" She was puzzled.

He said, "Because I am not free... I'm a little overweight... and I'm aware that you could have anyone you choose."

"Choose," Audrey said, "that is the operative word. Now what happens if I choose you?"

He was silent, gazing into her eyes and she into his. This was a real connection. To Audrey this meant, "Yes I have known this before; a different body, a different relationship. I know this being from long ago."

Walter said, "What is happening? Something is happening that I cannot put my finger on…almost a sense of déjà vu. I'm aware of it whenever I am with you. You know what it is. I'm sure you do. What does it mean?"

Audrey wrapped her arms around him and said, "We have been together before. Long ago. But, if you wish, we can for a brief time be together again, any way you wish."

"Then I need your permission to love you, not just emotionally but physically too. Is this possible?"

Audrey took his hand and led him towards the bedroom. She felt that nurturing and loving were really the order of the day. Sex would be Walter's fulfilment but not necessarily hers; but then it could be a loving experience, why not. They undressed each other. They snuggled under the blankets. Audrey began to kiss him slowly but with gentle kisses over his face and neck. He was very virile. She had not expected this, but welcomed it. He was routine in his lovemaking. He caressed her breasts and sucked her nipples. After touching her sacred spot he felt she was ready and climbed on top. She guided him in, matched his rhythm, and found that with some manoeuvring they could climax together.

He was ecstatic. He was complimentary about her body, almost overwhelmed because she had loved him in this way. He felt he was the luckiest man alive. This was such a contrast to the confident managerial executive in the office, that Audrey was intrigued.

They talked. He told her that he had only known his wife in the biblical sense after they got married. She relented to his demands when he insisted but otherwise was not interested. They had two children, now away. One was a pilot, the other married and living overseas. He seldom saw them, although they communicated now and then. Audrey felt that he was a lonely man for all his acquaintances and the meetings he attended with his friendly political colleagues. Audrey decided to educate him. In her opinion there were no frigid women, only men who did not know or apply the "how to".

Audrey had a fleeting idea that setting up a sex school with Anton could be a raging success. Between them they could have sparks flying. If only she wasn't so busy and he wasn't sorting out his marriage. She had not heard directly from him, only his son had told a former client of Audrey's that his mother and father were holidaying in Holland.

Now here was a new affair. Walter and Audrey met at least twice a week. She talked to him about teaching him and he was very happy with the idea. He responded well and as his confidence grew he began to take charge, which was his natural bent. She taught him sensations that he did not know existed and he learned trigger points and erotic parts of the body that were new to him. He became a good and more than adequate lover, and they learned to please each other. There was something very friendly and cosy about this affair. It was not an affair of great passion like Gabriel and Anton had been. Almost as though friends had fallen into it and now were enjoying it in a satisfactory way.

CHAPTER 61

Brian's Visit to Australia

Audrey had been at Overmans for just over a year. She still wanted to leave and start her own company, but this was forestalled by a cassette tape arriving from Brian saying that he had long service leave and wanted to come to Perth. Would he be welcome? Audrey's immediate and excited "Yes" left even Audrey puzzled.

They had been communicating by letter and then cassette tapes since Audrey returned to Australia. In America, Brian had written at least once a month. They had swapped all sorts of ideas, asked tantalizing spiritual questions and generally shared their realties. Suddenly there had been a gap and then the next letter had stated that Audrey was not to answer the question he had asked in his last letter as it was silly and should not have occurred. As the letter had not arrived Audrey was unaware of the question.

Now he was arriving in early August, just before his birthday and would be leaving late September. Audrey decided to ask her mother to put him up in what used to be her bedroom, promising that he would be away most of the evening and that her parents would be at work during the day. Agreement was reluctant but given.

Audrey was so pleased to meet him at the airport. And he was so happy to see her. Driving to her parents' home, Audrey asked him about the question in the letter she never got to read or answer.

He laughed, "Like an idiot, I asked you to marry me. Here I was in Swaziland, you were doing your Course Eight in the US, and there couldn't have been a greater physical distance between us or a more inappropriate time. The universe obviously thought so, which is why that was the only letter I sent you that went astray. Rather frustrating in a way."

Audrey smiled. "So what did you do after that?"

Brian grinned at her. "Well, we had a visiting English girl at the Research station who turned out to be a nymphomaniac, so I spent a great deal of time with her."

"So, did you get it out of your system that way?"

"Not loving you, that has been going on for almost four years in the cleanest spiritual fashion that you can imagine. Mind you, I have had my fantasies about being with you in a physical sense, but I'm sure if that ever happens the fantasy will pale at the actuality."

She smiled and thought how good it was that each of them thought the other was so safe to talk to; that nothing would ever get in the way of the connection that had been there from the beginning.

She helped him unpack. She could tell that the arrangement with her parents was limiting and wouldn't work for long. She wondered if John could accommodate him and was it a good idea considering how John felt about her.

John could not. His spare rooms were taken up with auditing and training. Audrey left Brian with her parents for two nights then moved him into her apartment on the folding bed. She introduced him with some trepidation to John, and Brian decided to do one of his courses.

She asked Brian how things were going with John. He gave her a hug. "It's all OK. It took about five minutes to work out that he is in love with you. So I respect that and do not put my own feelings forward. Besides, I think he feels that I look too old for you anyway and that makes him feel safer. By the way, I met Walter from your office. We had a brief but friendly chat. Why do I get the feeling that he is in a similar situation to John?"

She said, "Yes…well…"

Brian smiled and gave her a hug. "Something you need to know, is that I expect everyone to love you. Male or female; in different ways of course; but that is who you are, and no one could really expect anything less to happen. You do not know how unique you are; how educational you are whenever you open your mouth to say what is perfectly ordinary to you but is an eye-opener to someone else. I used to watch you doing checkouts in the course at East Grinstead, asking questions that no one would have dreamed of, yet the recipient learned so much from finding the answer often with your guidance. I think I fell a little in love with you even then. You are so unaware of self, yet so aware of your awareness. I watch you, listen to you, and just adore you. You obviously have a mission here. Do you know exactly what it is? Do you know where you are from?"

Audrey stared at him for a moment, shaking her head. "I don't know, but then I'm not sure I'm supposed to know."

Brian said, "When you were little, did you ever feel that you did not fit in?"

Audrey shook her head. "It wasn't anything I ever noticed."

"Why would you even try to fit in, when in your unique way you were born to stand out," Brian continued.

Audrey laughingly said, "I don't really want to do that either. I would be perfectly happy to be invisible."

Brian was looking at her carefully. "I have a feeling that you would be more at home with angels or beings who did not have a physicality. My goodness, that really does make you smile... I'm not surprised, but I feel you may have just discovered something. Am I correct?"

She smiled and nodded. "How perceptive of you. I am beginning to think that you may know me better then I know myself!"

"Thank you, but that could never happen. I relish the glimpses. I am suddenly aware they indicate to me who you really are. You have no idea how lovable you are. I love all that you are, all that you intend to be and all that you have ever been. I would like to ask you to marry me. Is there ever going to be a correct time?"

She gave him a hug, adding "please ask me later but not now." He hugged her to him, kissing the top of her head. They were in her apartment and she pulled him over to the couch. Standing on it she gave him a hug now much closer to his height, and then gently kissed him on the mouth. They stayed in each other arms for quite a while enjoying the peaceful stillness that was their core.

He had arrived wearing safari suits. These seemed to be perfect for him but not really part of the Australian fashion scene. Audrey took him to town and together they bought a blue suit, three shirts, and two ties, together with socks and a pair of black shoes. In this gear he looked like a very intelligent professor. She was proud to walk beside him and hold his hand.

When Audrey introduced him to her parents, they were polite but cold. Her mother eventually took her aside, saying, "He is more our age group than yours, what are you doing with him?"

The next day Audrey moved him into her apartment.

Audrey was thoroughly enjoying Brian's visit. They talked for hours, finding more and more agreements spiritually mentally, and emotionally. There seemed to be nothing to ever disagree with. Communication on almost any subject seemed to be clarified or expanded to each other's delight.

Audrey was considering how to gently end the relationship with Walter. She felt it would be highly unethical to start even a non-sexual one with Brian. She was careful to avoid any physical contact with him that could be misconstrued. Having him sleep on the folding bed, even in the lounge room did not seem to place him far enough away. Audrey was very aware of his presence, only around the corner so to speak.

Brian's Visit to Australia

The Universe must have been watching or listening, because suddenly the correct event was manifested by Walter and his wife. Audrey had lunch at Garden City with a friend when she came across Walter and his wife at a nearby table. She rose and went to say hello. Walter introduced her to his wife who unsmilingly nodded her head. Audrey could see she had interrupted a close conversation and beat a hasty retreat.

Later that day at the office Walter told her that his wife had just found out she had cancer and that it was untreatable. She had asked him to return to their home until she died. He felt he had to oblige. He was apologetic to Audrey. She told him that she completely understood and that he must always do what made him smile and that doing his duty was the right thing for a man of his calibre.

Audrey knew that he would be miserable doing otherwise, despite any feelings he might have towards her.

Now she was free to concentrate on Brian. Audrey had been disappearing the odd night or two to see Walter, with no explanation and none requested by Brian. She felt he knew and understood, so now she shared the recent events with him and told him about her affair with Walter. He gathered her into his arms and said, "Why do I get the feeling that sometimes you are too kind?"

Audrey stared at him, "Did I give you that impression? It wasn't intended. This wasn't a pity affair. I did not intend that."

Brian smiled, "No, it was educational, and you saw a being who needed to be loved and nurtured and you stepped in. Have I got that right?"

She nodded, saying "How well you know me."

Brian said, "I respect your physical reticence, because I understand. I value and admire your thinking when it comes to ethics. I understood your restrictions on any physical activity with me while you were still involved with Walter. Now that is settled, here is someone who would love you to behave in any manner that makes you smile."

She started laughing and, standing on her couch, she wrapped her arms around him and kissed him lovingly and longingly. He so willingly reciprocated.

They went out to dinner. Brian talked between courses about his contract with the Research station. He was coming to the end of his long service leave, and his current contract ended next June. After June he did not wish to renew it. He wanted to go to East Grinstead and complete some of his upper Scientology levels. His discourse ended here. Audrey was aware that the next step depended on what she wanted. She felt that she would like to make love to him, but it almost seemed indecent after just ending with Walter. She gazed at him across the table. Brian smiling said, "You need some time to take a breath between lovers, don't you?"

Audrey grinned at him. "Thank you for understanding. I really appreciate how well you know what I am thinking. But hopping into bed with you right away seems indecent or at least inappropriate."

He reached for her hand, "I have been waiting almost four years for this. I still have a month left, so any time you are ready is good for me."

Audrey leaned across the table and kissed him.

"Maybe we can just concentrate on that for a while, he said, until you are ready to take it further."

She thanked him as she kissed him again.

The next morning, Brian was not to be seen. She thought perhaps he was doing something with John but felt it strange that he had not mentioned an appointment. She showered and dressed and then there he was, with a large bunch of flowers and a happy, loving look.

Audrey went to stand on the couch, thanked him, wrapped her arms around him and mischievously nibbled his ear. The effect was more than she intended; he scooped her up in his arms and carried her to the bedroom. He said 'alright?' and she nodded, aware that her doing had precipitated her undoing.

Brian's Visit to Australia

Audrey helped him remove her clothes and then his, and soon they were cuddled close between the sheets. For a very short while they both seemed content to be close and cuddly, then the kissing got more passionate and soon they were making love. They made love for hours. She was amazed at his stamina, his size, his gentleness and his passion.

At one stage Brian said, "You really should look in the mirror at your face. It is one huge glow! I have dreamed of this day for so long, yet the reality surpasses the dream. You are wonderful to love and a wonderful lover. I have made love or should I say had sex with many women, but I have never known anything like this; I drift up to the moon and back and feel as though you are with me all the way. I have never had such a spiritual journey as this; not even in any lifetime I remember; yet I know this is not the first time we have been together."

He turned to smile at her. "How come I missed out on this before?"

Audrey laughed, saying "I don't know, let me look at this... I think we were siblings before, at least that's what I get; does that idea make you smile?"

Brian nodded, and then holding her close, he told her in so many ways and in so many words how much he loved her.

He said, "Let me tell you something I get... I feel you will marry me before the end of this year! Does that idea make you smile?"

She laughed. "You haven't asked me yet."

Then let me amend that, "Audrey darling, I love you with all my heart and soul; I love you spiritually, physically, emotionally and mentally with a love that can only grow with time. I adore you. Audrey, will you please marry me?"

She was quiet. Did she really want to get married for the third time?

"I have a question that I ask for many things but particularly for this..."

"What is your question?"

"You want to marry me; the question is, for what purpose?" Brian was quiet for a moment. Then he said, "We have so many goals and purposes that are similar, it may be fun to achieve them together!"

Audrey could see instantly that she was *not* a solution to a problem. This in itself was a big change. She quickly looked it over. Perhaps she needed to consider that since Brian seemed to know her so well, he would be aware of the acceptable answer to her?

For once in her life she decided to be conservative. "I will seriously consider it. I do love you very much but contemplating marriage for a third time is a big decision. I am going to let you go back to Swaziland. We will send cassette tapes to each other and after a while I will let you know for sure. Marrying you makes me smile, but I really need to be sure before I say 'Yes'. Is this alright with you?"

Brian nodded. "Whatever my darling wants is fine with me. I will await your decision; not with bated breath because the Universe and I are sure of the outcome. We just await your acquiescence. I tell you this, because I know you will not consider my truth as pressure. You are too aware for that. Just know that, whatever your decision, I love you with all my heart. By the way, this has been the finest birthday gift that I have ever received. Today is the 26th August. I was born on that day in 1920, so you see my dear, I am fifteen years older than you."

Audrey took note but did not consider this data important. She smiled and moved into his arms again. They had been in bed for almost five hours. She had lost count of the number of times they had made love. Now here it was again. She gave up and surrendered.

Brian left for Swaziland towards the end of September. Audrey was disappointed to see him go. She had thoroughly enjoyed his company, their shared interests and communication, and the lovemaking that never seemed to stop. She began to wonder what it took to be a nymphomaniac.

There was a brief lunchtime discussion at Overmans on the subject of 'Love'. The final conclusion was it could not be defined. Audrey felt that it could. That night she set herself the task. She wrote:

Brian's Visit to Australia

LOVE…

Love is strong outgoing affinity. Affinity is basically a consideration of distance.

When you love someone, you wish to be close to them. To be them.

Being them is manifested by occupying the same space and seeing things from the others viewpoint. It is an ability and does not mean that one loses one's own identity.

Love is willingness for the other to be, do and have all that is desired and to be, do and have in whatever location they choose, despite the desire to be close to them.

Love is allowing another freedom of choice in all things, including the freedom to make mistakes.

Love is allowing another to be ethical and encouraging another to retain those ethics, despite all provocation to do other otherwise.

Love is flunking for goofs then giving help to stay on or get back on the right path.

Love is helping another to stay on their purpose and rekindling failed purposes when required.

Love is never sympathising when adversity strikes but validating the ability and courage that each being has to overcome that adversity.

Love is the willingness to allow the other to be cause and effect as chosen.

Love is granting another altitude and respect and allowing them the right to earn those qualities.

Love is validating another's abilities and helping them realise all the potential ability they have, and assisting them to bring this forth, so that it may be used to accomplish great things.

Love is allowing another to be free, to retain their individuality, self-sufficiency, and independence and achieve all their goals in life.

When the above is flowed and received and sincerely meant then it really is LOVE.

AUDREY, 4th October 1972
Perth, Western Australia

CHAPTER 62

An Unexpected Event

It was surprising to discover after a week of Brian's leaving she was pregnant. There was no doubt that the baby was Walter's; news that was not welcomed and most inappropriate at this time.

Audrey looked over each and every consequence. She did not want more children. A previous discussion with Brian revealed that he had no inkling for them either. Audrey knew that if she decided to keep it she would somehow cope, and without Walter's or anyone's help; simply because she always did.

Lying on her bed, she meditated and contacted the hovering being. She knew that cot deaths and miscarriages had much more than a physical cause. Somehow she knew that it was always a co-creation between the being and the mother, whether the mother was aware of it or not. Sometimes the being wanted only to experience a small amount of physicality rather than go the whole hog and create a full body. She contacted the hovering being and asked it if it needed a swim in the pool or just to experience a big toe dipped in. She felt that the being was happy and that a big toe dipped in was sufficient, but she was careful to check three times that this was correct.

A LIFE of Enlightenment

She found that a small termination clinic was available with hygiene, discretion and expertise. Audrey booked in; she spent a weekend there, and then reported back to work.

She made a cassette tape, revealing all to Brian and sent it to him with her love.

He telephoned her at the apartment, assuring her that he understood, that there was no judgement, and that his love was even stronger than ever. He would have liked to have been with her through this ordeal but recognised that she had handled it as well as she had processed all the past traumatic events in her life.

A cassette tape which arrived a few days later clarified and confirmed all that he had said, and Audrey was aware that Brian was a rare and very valued being that she really loved.

Overmans were very busy. Audrey spent more time with her family and with John, feeling that they had been neglected during Brian's visit. None of them questioned her about Brian, no doubt feeling that out of sight meant out of mind. Audrey had an amused awareness about this, but kept her considerations to herself.

Life went on. Time seemed to speed by as it does when you are very busy. Suddenly it was November and her birthday again. Her apartment was full of flowers, from Brian, Walter, John and a bouquet arriving with a card on which was written 'Remember the happy times darling', no signature. The florist when telephoned was only a forwarding agent and could not reveal any further data. Audrey thought it might be Gabriel but decided he had too much integrity to play these sorts of games.

A cassette from Brian asked, "How big is your aura?"

Audrey was puzzled: she knew what an aura was but did not know how to answer the question.

Brian went on saying, "I am picking up radio America on your tapes as well as taxi conversations and sometimes shipping information. I know you are on the fourth floor and overlooking water but why not get Tiffany or someone to talk on a tape and then you play it back. See if it is the same

An Unexpected Event

or just a normal sounding cassette. I have a strong feeling it is you, even though you may not know it."

Audrey did this, but the cassette tape from Tiffany revealed only a chatting Tiffany. Audrey parked the information on a shelf deciding that at this time it was interesting but unimportant.

In early December she sent Brian a tape saying that she loved him with all her heart, and that she was very happy to marry him and looked forward to being his wife.

His return cassette said that he had turned somersaults on his front lawn and that he was overjoyed. He couldn't get further leave at this time; would she come to Swaziland to marry him. She sent a telegram saying "Yes. When?"

Brian made arrangements for the wedding on the 23rd December and told her that she needed a flight to Durban and then to a place called Manzini, and that he would meet her there. They would then drive to Malkerns, the Research Station. He sent her a photo of his house and one of himself.

Audrey decided not to tell anyone she was getting married. She decided she did not want or need to handle any opposition or judgement from her parents or John. She asked Overmans for extra Christmas leave, which was granted. Telling her parents she was going overseas for a holiday but not revealing her destination, she left for South Africa on the 21st December 1972. She was 37 years old.

Tired after two flights and a drive with Brian, she was happy to arrive at his home. Ida, his cook and housekeeper, met her on the front steps and as Audrey alighted from the car she picked her up and hugged her. Ida was as wide as she was tall and only came up to Audrey's chin.

Audrey felt her ribs would break, but the hug did not go on too long. She smiled and said hello, looking at Brian with a question mark.

Later he explained that he had taught Ida many things from Scientology technology. African servants were taught never to look a white person in the eyes, always their look had to be downcast; never to express an opinion, just say 'no bwana' or 'yes bwana', and be completely subservient.

Brian said, "How can I expect someone who cannot confront me to be able to confront their job and never express an idea for betterment or so on?" He had taught Ida to confront him, ask questions about anything, and learn new things with her confidence.

The first day she had come to him along with two others to see if she could be his cook. He asked her to cook him breakfast. She was the only one who asked him for his preference. He ordered bacon and egg. Ida brought him a boiled egg with bacon wrapped around the base of the eggcup. This made him smile. He gave her the job and decided to train her. Now she visited other wives on the research station and asked them for copies of recipes, something unheard of before. Brian told Audrey that all the other wives had tried to steal her, but she was loyal and would never leave him. He also said that after Ida had picked Audrey up on the steps, she had said to him later, "She is lovely…no prickles!"

Brian had not wanted to use the African registry office. He had heard of a passing minister on his way to Mbabane and after contacting him, the Minister had agreed to perform the wedding ceremony in the garden as long as it was under a canopy. The Research wives and their cooks had organised a buffet for after the wedding.

Brian had arranged for his Research friend Peter to walk Audrey down the aisle, so to speak, and he along with his wife would act as witnesses.

He had written the ceremony from the article on Love she had sent him, and it was indeed lovely.

Audrey spent that evening and most of the next morning in bed, catching up on sleep. Ida brought her brunch in bed and then she climbed into a lovely bath feeling revived and ready for her next adventure. They went to a small jeweller in Mbabane and chose some wedding rings. Brian wanted to buy her an engagement ring, but she shook her head. She did not need

An Unexpected Event

it and wasn't fond of rings or bracelets, feeling they often got in the way. Instead, he bought her a very unusual and lovely pendant. The rest of the day and the eve of her wedding she spent with Brian, met a few of the resident men and wives on the Station. She checked her blue dress and white brimmed hat, refastening the blue ribbon and flowers that decorated the brim that had suffered in the travelling, and wandered about the house and grounds holding hands with Brian. She came to learn the names of some of the plants and trees, like the Monkey Puzzle tree, and exclaimed about the sunflowers that were as big as her head.

In the garden she found some pretty flowers and with the help of some of the ribbon from her hat and some cellophane paper, she made herself a little bouquet to carry. Brian was apologetic. Audrey was happy to contribute a little something to the ceremony.

She went to bed happy that on the next day she would become Audrey, loving and loved wife of Brian.

CHAPTER 63

Audrey's Wedding and Honeymoon in Africa

The wedding went off without a hitch. The Minister was happy to use the ceremony that Brian had written, and the visitors crowded round afterwards saying how beautiful and unusual the narration had been. The wives and cooks had done a lovely buffet. Everyone was friendly and welcoming to Audrey, and it was very pleasing to see how much Brian was admired and liked among his colleges. Brian had obviously done a wonderful job promoting Audrey, and had given his friends the very best data. This they shared with Audrey, who felt that she had much to live up to.

Eventually the guests left. Ida cleaned up the kitchen and retired to her own little house a few yards away.

Brian had no shower but a large bathtub. He invited Audrey to share a bath with him. She felt a little shy because it was weeks since he had seen her naked, and then not standing or all at once.

Brian climbed in and held out his arms but when she went to go to the opposite end he smiled shook his head and indicated that she should climb in front of him. Audrey lay against his chest. He kissed the top of her head and wrapped his arms around her. He began to whisper loving thoughts, kissing her shoulders and then her neck, and soon he was caressing her nipples. Eventually the idea of kissing him was too much to resist. She slithered around in the water and laying across him she kissed him again and again. She could feel his erection against her stomach. This time she could see it with nothing in the way. She was amazed and began to wonder how she had managed to accommodate this previously. Now wanting him more than ever, she knelt over him and mounted him. Locked together, they found it was difficult to proceed. The bathtub though long was not over wide and left no room to manoeuvre.

Brian suddenly said "Well, if I die in this position, I will feel privileged."

Audrey started laughing and the moment rescinded. She eased herself off and stood up reaching for a towel. "Come she said, let us go to bed and be comfortable."

It was dark by the time they lay side by side.

Their lovemaking was interrupted by something making loud tapping noises on the ceiling. Audrey sat up. "What was that?" Brian said "Don't worry it is just some bug banging its head on the ceiling. There goes another one. Just ignore it. They fly in through the window and eventually they will fly out again."

Audrey was aghast. "Don't you have any flywire?"

Brian laughed. "Yes. But I never bother with it. It is rolled up and when you roll it down you need to clip it both sides. Not really worth the bother."

Audrey put the bedside light on and stared at the fierce looking beetles sitting on the ceiling. Brian said, "They don't bite. Really, they won't hurt you."

Audrey said, "That's it! I did not invite these bugs to share my honeymoon."

She went to the two windows and began rolling down the blinds and clipping the sides.

Brian gave a small laugh "Darling, do you realise that you are trapping them inside? By the way, you look wonderful, I could watch you for hours, looking so lovely and naked."

Audrey came back to the bed asking, "Do you have any fly spray?"

He smiled, pointing at the dresser.

Audrey's Wedding and Honeymoon in Africa

Audrey picked up the fly spray and, standing on the bed, proceeded to give each bug a dose. They kept changing their ceiling position so that she ended up dancing around naked on top of the bed, trying to improve her aim She glanced at the label on the spray. It was called 'DOOM'.

She began to make up advertisements. *'Is your honeymoon doomed?',* and so on. Brian, sitting up against the head board, was wearing an expression between ecstasy and laughter. He said, "You have no idea how appealing you look dancing naked on my bed, Making up funny ads for 'Doom'. I could not love you more."

Audrey laughed and slid under the sheet, then pulled it over the top of her head and Brian's, saying, "Come under here with me. I don't want dead bugs dropping on us either." They cuddled under the sheet, Brian full of loving merriment, Audrey with a purpose firmly in mind.

Bugs on the honeymoon? Just not appropriate in the best circles. She shared her thoughts with Brian; telling him also that an un-fly-wired window would never be found in Perth.

They began to make up more advertisements for 'Doom', often collapsing with laughter.

Finally exhausted they fell asleep under the sheet in each other's arms, lovemaking temporarily forgotten.

The next morning they were awakened by Ida bringing them tea at seven o'clock, the time Brian usually arose for his workday.

They had a chat but agreed to get up and have an early breakfast and decide what to do for the day. Brian suggested they go somewhere for a honeymoon. Audrey agreed but only if it was important for Brian. She was happy to honeymoon right where she was. Brian was grateful knowing that he would need lots of funds for his Scientology courses, as prices seemed to be going up all the time.

A LIFE of Enlightenment

The Minister who had performed their wedding ceremony called in on his way to South Africa where he was to take up a post. He had brought them some African Grass table mats as a wedding present.

He talked to them about the ceremony and asked if Audrey and Brian would give him permission to use the wedding ceremony that Brian had written, in his own new Church. They were happy for him to use this and Brian said, "my wife wrote an article about Love. I am going to give you that also to use however you wish as she is the original author." It was gratifying that someone other than themselves placed a high value on love.

They wandered around the research station. Brian showed her the King's fields, of which he was solely in charge. Swaziland was ruled by King Sobuhza, a sole monarchy. Brian told Audrey that in 1968 Swaziland had obtained independence from the United Kingdom. A large celebration was called for, but the Swazis did not know what to do or what to organise. The King had appealed to Brian who had to orchestrate the whole event. Brian with irony did more than smile, but he did a really good job as the other research wives told Audrey.

On the fourth day Brian asked Audrey if she had ever read a book called 'Atlas Shrugged' by Ayn Rand. As she shook her head he handed her a copy and said, "you will love it; when you have finished it, I would like to share all the values with you and ascertain your favourite characters."

Audrey started to read it at eight o'clock that evening and found it difficult to put down. She read the eleven hundred and sixty-eight pages until five o'clock the next morning and finished it.

Brian seeing her so absorbed had left her alone; only bringing her a drink now and then and kissing the top of her head. He was amazed at her ability to read at such speed, so she explained and shared her trick with the black ribbon covering the margins.

They spent many happy hours during the next few days, discussing the book and the characters. It was gratifying to find again and again how much they were in accord with almost everything that was important, and even the unimportances in life; and yet there was always something that

Audrey's Wedding and Honeymoon in Africa

each one could add to clarify or expand what was being discussed.

Audrey had given her wedding hat to Ida who proudly wore it whenever she went shopping. It was admired and envied by her friends. Brian explained how Western garments were revered and admired by the natives. She understood this when she saw a lady walking down the street wearing a bra on the outside of her dress. After all, who would know she possessed one if it was worn inside.

Audrey shared the cooking with Ida and taught her many new dishes. This necessitated a trip to Manzini to get some herbs and spices. Ida was quick to learn and loved to experiment, although her initial sprinkling had to be curtailed.

There was a Picture theatre in Mbabane and also a small casino. The film was good but they skipped the Casino. Mostly they were content with each other's company and occasionally going to one of Brian's colleagues for drinks or a meal.

Time moved on, and it was time for Audrey to book her flight home. The airline was full. Five days later the next flight was cancelled, and then engine trouble made the next one a problem. Audrey was going to be very late getting back to work. Two days after the wedding, she had sent all her family, friends and Overman a telegram about her marriage. She decided that by the time she arrived they would have got used to the idea.

She packed, and Brian drove her to the airport. When she boarded the little six-seater plane for its short flight to Durban, she found there was a hole half the size of her vanity case in front of her feet. She decided that it felt ok. Audrey put her vanity over the hole and enjoyed the flight. Always, during the flight, you could see the ground and sometimes she would slide the vanity aside to watch the earth rollaway below. When she got to Durban, her flight was overbooked. Audrey wandered the Airport considering options. She ended up by cashing her ticket, getting a flight to

A LIFE of Enlightenment

London then a flight to Singapore and then one to Perth. It cost her even a little less, but of course with stops and changes it took quite a long time to get home.

She caught a taxi to her apartment and then slept for many hours before she felt ready to face the world again.

CHAPTER 64

Audrey's New Business

Audrey arrived back in Perth late Saturday. She slept most of Sunday, then washed and ironed her clothes, and reported to Overmans for work on the Monday. She apologised for the delay and was happy to find four of the executives having a meeting together. When Walter was refusing to meet her eyes, she felt for a moment that he was unhappy about her marriage with Brian; however, it soon became apparent that something else was afoot. Maynard seemed to be in charge, with the others looking sheepish and mainly staring at the floor.

Maynard said, "Are you aware how much the firm has been losing money-wise over the last few months?"

Audrey shook her head and said, "How?"

"Because of your pricing. You gave Vernon the pricing from Keith Tennant and it was all wrong!"

Audrey said, "That was pricing for building in the City. It was a rough guide of so much per square metre. You had to add on transport and all the associated costs for building in the country. Keith would not know that and I wouldn't have a clue, but Vernon would know that."

She appealed with a look to Vernon, the price estimator who was not meeting her gaze.

Maynard said, "you always behave as though you know everything. This time you have come a cropper, and that is all there is to say."

The recriminations from Maynard went on, and it seemed he had been building them up for some time. The others remained silent.

Audrey gazed at the group, so reluctant to meet her eyes. She suddenly realised that she was, in Scientology terms, being 'third partied', or in Aussie terms being 'white anted'. Audrey looked them over carefully.

She stood up and very firmly but quietly said, "Tell me, do you consider that I am of any further value to this company?" Maynard said "No" while the rest remained silent, still looking at the floor.

Audrey said, "Fine. I'm leaving." She picked up her bag and walked out of the office. The staff was quiet. Even Tiffany and her brother Charles said nothing, just watching her go.

She went home, changed into slacks and a top, and went for a walk along the esplanade. She sat on a bench in the Ferry dock and handled her knee-jerk reaction to the event. She remembered to respond rather than react, and then went on to play the glad game.

Suddenly the event made sense. She had promised herself that she would start her own business after one year, and here it was eighteen months later, and she was only just available now to do that.

She started smiling, amused at how the Universe worked to keep you on your journey, and, sent a silent thanks to it and to her friends at Overmans. She went home to prepare some lunch and pay her first visit to John after sending him the telegram.

John's main entrance was off a balcony that surrounded each floor of the flats. She knocked at his door, trusting that the timing was good and that he would not have clients or that they could stay inside.

John opened the door, stared at her for a moment, took a step towards her and then pushed her backwards so that her lower spine was resting against the balcony railing. She gasped and tried to straighten up, but his weight was holding her. Audrey gazed at him, wondering why he was behaving this way. His face was that of a very angry man. She realised that he had not recovered from her marrying Brian. She tried to push back, but not only did he resist, he increased the pressure and she knew that at any minute she would be over the balcony and down on the ground four floors below. Her back was bent and she was trying hard to keep her feet on the ground. Only Linda coming around the corner and shouting "John stop it! stop it!" made him pause. Audrey pushed him, and he let go, leaving Audrey balancing half over the railing.

Linda stood between him and Audrey. John went inside. Linda said, "Audrey are you alright?!"

Audrey nodded, pushing herself upright again.

"Audrey, go away…please let me handle him, he is so upset… He has been, since your telegram arrived."

Audrey said, "This is uncalled for. He has always known that I would never marry him!"

"Because of Gabriel?"

"No, because I would always have been John's crutch and he deserves better than that."

Audrey left, going home to her apartment to look over the current event. She was aware that given John's height and bulk that only the intervention of Linda had rescued her from what could possibly have been her death. She thought about the few times she had been told she would die, and how often she had said "that's alright." Now she looked at it again and knew she could give it the same response.

No-one ever died. They just dropped the body they were occupying and after a time, if so inclined, the being went on to choose another one with parents that they needed to complete their next journey. It was all so obvious to Audrey, she was at a loss to see why no-one else seemed to know this data. Instead, others believed that the body they currently manifested and controlled was highly precious and must be preserved at all costs. Even when their body was not capable of achieving their goals or giving them any physical quality of life, most beings hung on to it, living in God's waiting room for no good purpose that Audrey could define.

She eventually gave up fathoming this discourse that she was having with herself and mollified her thoughts by considering that 'it is their journey and that is that'.

Altogether, it had been a very interesting homecoming. She went to bed early and made Brian a cassette telling him of the day's events and all her thoughts on the matter. She posted it to him the next day, oblivious of all the different orchestrations that he said were on every tape.

The next day, she sat down planning her own business. By lunchtime she had a name: 'Creative Home Planners'. She telephoned Jack who was no longer available as a draftsman but suggested she contacted his daughter Joy, who had her own drafting business just north of the City.

Audrey put her own ad in *the Countryman, the Western Farmer,* and *Grazier* for the coming weekend; went to Jacksons Drawing Suppliers and outfitted herself, ready to start work. She bought a four-drawer metal filing cabinet, rearranged the furniture in the lounge and bedroom, started a business account at the bank, and by the weekend was ready to start work with an invoice book and a receipt book.

Audrey did not contact anyone at Overmans. She had always had the habit of ending a cycle on events as soon as she had handled any reaction and was at the stage where she could respond with ease. This usually occurred in a day or two. There was no emotion associated with any of the staff or the firm itself except to wish them fair weather and good sailing. Audrey was very much in present time and only interested in the "Now" of the new events as she created them.

Audrey's New Business

She went to visit Joy in her office and met David Pederson, a draftsman who would be assigned to look after her work.

They discussed standards and what was expected. He offered to call at her apartment to pick up and deliver work, relishing the idea of getting out of the office for a while.

Afterwards, she went to her parents for dinner and told them about her new business. Audrey told them nothing about Overmans, only that she had promised to stay for a year and had exceeded that time. Her father Fred, as usual gave her dire warnings about going it alone; but she parried these with interesting anecdotes about designing for past clients. Dorothy was, as always, encouraging and very happy to see her.

A telephone call the following Tuesday gave Audrey her first client. It was not to design a new home but to do extensive alterations to an existing farmhouse. This was a new field for Audrey, but she felt she could handle it. The farmer had no existing plans of the current house, so Audrey knew that a lot of measuring would be required, and also a camera. She mentally looked at doing alterations and additions to her parent's home and had a good picture of all the aspects that would be required. She would be driving to Williams about one hundred miles away. The distance and time made her aware that she required an answering machine.

Two days later she arrived at the Williams farmhouse. Like most country people, they were most welcoming. Audrey had designed a home for some neighbours, so she came with a recommendation.

The farmer helped her measure the whole house and all the verandas. Audrey took photos mainly outside because she had to judge the pitch and design of the roof, which she knew she had to blend into. She silently thanked Jack who had helped her so much with roof design.

Finding out what was needed and wanted in great detail saw her through lunch. This gave her an opportunity to meet the two children. As two of the bedroom additions were to accommodate them, it was good to chat and find out exactly the items that the space needed to accommodate. The parents were impressed as she explained that the way to design anything was to find out what was going to be placed in a space and then to add the windows and doors. This way, all the space was comfortably used, and no one would be shaking their heads later, saying the furniture does not fit or they need more space.

Audrey stayed for dinner, received a retainer fee, and was reminded by the clients to charge for travelling costs and time, which was kind of them after she had explained that this was her first work trip to the country. Altogether they were a lovely family and she was very happy to work with them.

Back in Perth she started on the plan the next day. Audrey called Jack after writing down two or three construction problems she felt could arrive. He was as always extremely helpful,

She bought an answering machine and eventually got it to work correctly. After three days she had a sketch ready for the draftsman, for a more professional sketch which she wanted to have the client's approval for before proceeding to a working drawing. David was happy to give her this after two days, and she rang the clients to visit them the following week. Audrey received two more calls in the first week, making further appointments.

She began to see that it would be a good idea to take a call and then call later for an exact appointment within a week. Otherwise she could see that she would be driving South one day, North the next, and then South again. This work needed to be more organised than she had originally thought. Nevertheless, she was very pleased with the response. Audrey was also aware talking to country clients at Overmans that if you did some approved act that was very acceptable, everyone within a sixty-mile radius would hear of it. If it heralded disapproval, then the radius spread to one hundred miles.

Audrey sent Brian a cassette tape sharing all her arrangements and her success. He sent a reply, saying that nothing else could ever be expected, which made her laugh. She felt that Brian would always give her his full support, not just because he had faith in her but because once committed to a relationship it would not occur to him to do otherwise.

Audrey's New Business

Audrey only repeated the ads one more time a month later. After that, the business was well away and taking all her waking time.

The red rose arrived each Saturday morning, always with a loving message from Brian. She occasionally saw her parents and had a meal with them, but mostly she worked, ate, slept and travelled. There was the odd phone call, but she really saw no-one. Linda called and said that John and all the Americans who had travelled with him had returned to California within two weeks of Audrey's last visit to John. Audrey was hoping that after about a month it would be safe to see John. Parting as friends, which they had always been, would have been preferable, but Audrey had heeded Linda's advice to leave John to come to terms with himself. Now it was too late. Audrey had also been made aware that the effect on another being under the guise of love could be so intense and hard for the being to handle. Altogether it had been an education.

CHAPTER 65

Only Time Gets In The Way

Time was speeding by. Business was the order of the day. Audrey occasionally went for a walk, read a book on the balcony, and sometimes walked down to the ferry and rode it to the City and back. She did most of her shopping in the Mends Street mall, getting to know most of the shop keepers. The record shop telephoned her when they had a new Robert Goulet, Matt Munro, Johnny Mathis, or Nat King Cole record arrive. The songs and soft gentle music she liked kept her company while she was busy with her drawings.

Audrey made her cassettes to Brian lying in bed, before she went to sleep. She never felt separate from him, as his energy seemed to be around, keeping her company. His cassettes and the single red rose that arrived with a message every Saturday were highlights of her days and sometimes he also wrote long, breezy, happy, very loving letters. She took these to bed and answered them from there. Her cassettes continued to have various accompaniments which Audrey was unaware of but which made Brian smile.

Brian left Swaziland and went to England to complete the Scientology training and auditing he wished to do. He called her with a date arriving the second week of August, almost an exact time of the year as before.

A LIFE of Enlightenment

She was overjoyed to meet him at the airport. They spent all the time waiting for his luggage, cuddling and smiling at each other. Once they were home it was a quick shower, a cup of coffee, and more cuddles. She sat on his knee and hugged him until he was sure he did not want to eat, but only to be close.

Eventually they went to bed, talked for a while and fell asleep in each other's arms. Making love got saved until the morning. Brian had arrived on a Friday and Audrey had kept the weekend and the Monday clear of all appointments.

They spent the most of Saturday loving and talking.

One Sunday morning, after breakfast, he gave her a verse he had written.

AUDREY

I love you!

With goodness and delight you fill my world.

Things of beauty are your thoughts. Strong and gentle are your flows.

Wide and deep, far and high you range your integrity. Your love and courage are inseparable;

I see these qualities in you and sing "Yes" in affirmation.

Your voyage of self is in full search of truth.

Your own adventure and decision. You are the compass of your quest,

As well as being Captain and the Crew together. My quest is the same as yours.

And as my love for you grows, Exultation shapes the future. Always you have refused to be The bait of self-entrapment.

You showed me that what I see in you, I will find within myself, Would I but look.

Only Time Gets In The Way

You love me in a way I have not known since long ago, Fully without stint, completely undemanding.

My love you accept with certainty and gladness.

I see a love for me and man, Open to the Universe.

No strings attached, no 'needs' to give or want. A static love that does not hold, or push or pull; But simply LOVES…

What I always knew existed is now found. All my dreams are true,

Only time got in the way.

BRIAN

Audrey wrapped her arms around him and thanked him with all her heart. He smiled and, holding her close, said, "You have no idea how beautiful you are, inside and out. I mean that, no idea. You go through life deciding to be the very best you can be at any given moment, with little or no analysis of you. You seem devoid of ego. Do you even know what it is, what that means?"

She hugged him, saying "I've heard of it, but I haven't gone into it… Is it really important?"

Brian just held her close, saying nothing. Eventually he held her away from him and with a warm smile, he said, "I could not love you more, but I'm sure I will in time!"

Audrey kissed him, thanked him and told him how much he meant to her. She said, "And, I will always love YOU more, given time."

She climbed on the couch, hugged him close and nibbled his ear.

She mischievously added, "Is it time now? Let's go back to bed."

The time they spent together over the three days was like a second honeymoon. Never had they experienced such closeness. Spiritually, mentally; emotionally they were like one entity. Physicality became a beautiful spiritual experience as well as a profound emotional expression.

A LIFE of Enlightenment

Audrey was extremely happy. Looking over her life to date, she felt blessed. All of her life events had brought her to where she was today. She was aware and grateful of how much she had been and was loved.

Now, she was wiser, more capable; more convinced that everything was really perfect, no matter how it may have looked on the day.

She reflected on a time when someone had begged for the formula she followed for being optimistic all the time. She recalled that she had given it much thought over two days. Although she probably could have dreamed up a probability formulae, she became aware that there was none she used. It was just that being pessimistic had never occurred to her. It was not a word that was in her vocabulary. Always there was something to be glad about if one did but look.

Now here was Brian, to build a life with, to love as he had never been loved before. To accept his love with joy and gladness. This was togetherness on a warm and cuddly scale. Audrey knew that acting almost as one, they looked forward to a life full of adventures, knowing that any adventure is better than no adventure, and as such had to be treasured.

End of Volume I

Appendix

WISDOM EXTRACTS

"You create and co-create your own reality. Nothing can happen to you without your presence. Your presence is always your choice."

"Suicide is a fear of living rather than a fear of dying."

"You only recognize in another that which you yourself hold."

"Jesus taught love, compassion, and understanding. The rules, rituals, doctrines, and judgement of most religions have nothing to do with compassion and understanding."

"Change is the evidence of life."

"Why marriage? Because we need a witness to our life to make it feel as though it was worth living."

"Why are you trying to fit in, when in your own unique way, you were born to stand out?"

"Abundance: the ability to do what you need to do when you need to do it. It isn't necessarily money, but it can be."

"When you surrender you also start to behave as though what you are manifesting is real."

A LIFE of Enlightenment

"What belief would I have to hold in order to experience the reality that I am experiencing?"

"Expansion is a product of inclusion, not exclusion."

"If you want to be enlightened then be willing to lighten up."

"Assigning positive meanings to everything that happens to you allows you to stay in touch and work with your higher self."

"All the tools that you use, whether they be cards, crystals, or mediums, serve as permission slips to assist you to be who you truly are."

"Circumstances do not dictate your state of being. Your state of being dictates circumstances."

"We are our own happiness."

"You are your own serenity."

"There is no balancing of merits. There is just acceptance when real love is there."

"Love is not blind. Love lets in the light and everything seems brighter."

"There is no life after death. There is only life after life."

"Responsibility does not mean blame, shame or regret. It means to respond with ability. Responsibility is the ability to respond."

"I only do things that make me smile."

"If I'm going to do something it will be done well. It is an attitude that makes me smile."

Appendix

"Bring in the awareness of a part of you that never gets involved but just looks on and is the spectator."

"Hearts don't really break. They just stretch with exercise."

"The only way to handle fears is to face them."

"I have to remember not to follow other people's ideas no matter how well meaning they may be."

If you are interested in further events and the attending

philosophy in Audrey's life,

Audrey can be contacted through her agent Natalie Brown at:

Email: agent@audreyo.com.au

Website: www.nataliejbrown.com

Or alternatively you may contact Audrey at:

Email: author@audreyo.com.au

Website: www.audreyo.com.au

www.ingramcontent.com/pod-product-compliance
Lightning Source LLC
Chambersburg PA
CBHW070246010526
44107CB00056B/2360